Oracle Essentials
Oracle Database 11g

Other Oracle resources from O'Reilly

Related titles
Mastering Oracle SQL

Optimizing Oracle
Performance

Oracle Application Server 10g
Essentials

Oracle DBA Pocket Guide

Oracle in a Nutshell

Oracle PL/SQL Programming

Oracle SQL*Plus: The Definitive Guide

Oracle Books Resource Center
oracle.oreilly.com is a complete catalog of O'Reilly's books on Oracle and related technologies, including sample chapters and code examples.

oreillynet.com is the essential portal for developers interested in open and emerging technologies, including new platforms, programming languages, and operating systems.

Conferences
O'Reilly brings diverse innovators together to nurture the ideas that spark revolutionary industries. We specialize in documenting the latest tools and systems, translating the innovator's knowledge into useful skills for those in the trenches. Visit *conferences.oreilly.com* for our upcoming events.

Safari Bookshelf (*safari.oreilly.com*) is the premier online reference library for programmers and IT professionals. Conduct searches across more than 1,000 books. Subscribers can zero in on answers to time-critical questions in a matter of seconds. Read the books on your Bookshelf from cover to cover or simply flip to the page you need. Try it today for free.

FOURTH EDITION

Oracle Essentials
Oracle Database 11g

Rick Greenwald, Robert Stackowiak, and
Jonathan Stern

Beijing · Cambridge · Farnham · Köln · Sebastopol · Tokyo

Oracle Essentials: Oracle Database 11g, Fourth Edition
by Rick Greenwald, Robert Stackowiak, and Jonathan Stern

Copyright © 2008 O'Reilly Media, Inc. All rights reserved.
Printed in the United States of America.

Published by O'Reilly Media, Inc., 1005 Gravenstein Highway North, Sebastopol, CA 95472.

O'Reilly books may be purchased for educational, business, or sales promotional use. Online editions are also available for most titles (*safari.oreilly.com*). For more information, contact our corporate/institutional sales department: (800) 998-9938 or *corporate@oreilly.com*.

Editors: Colleen Gorman and Deborah Russell	**Interior Designer:** David Futato
Production Editor: Sumita Mukherji	**Cover Designer:** Karen Montgomery
Production Services: Tolman Creek Design	**Illustrator:** Robert Romano

Printing History:

October 1999:	First Edition. Originally published under the title *Oracle Essentials: Oracle8 and Oracle8i*
June 2001:	Second Edition. Originally published under the title *Oracle Essentials: Oracle9i, Oracle8i and Oracle8*
February 2004:	Third Edition. Originally published under the title *Oracle Essentials: Oracle Database 10g*
November 2007:	Fourth Edition.

Nutshell Handbook, the Nutshell Handbook logo, and the O'Reilly logo are registered trademarks of O'Reilly Media, Inc. *Oracle Essentials: Oracle Database 11g*, the image of cicadas, and related trade dress are trademarks of O'Reilly Media, Inc.

Oracle® and all Oracle-based trademarks and logos are trademarks or registered trademarks of Oracle Corporation, Inc. in the United States and other countries. O'Reilly Media, Inc. is independent of Oracle Corporation. Java™ and all Java-based trademarks and logos are trademarks or registered trademarks of Sun Microsystems, Inc. in the United States and other countries. O'Reilly Media, Inc. is independent of Sun Microsystems. .NET is a registered trademark of Microsoft Corporation.

Many of the designations used by manufacturers and sellers to distinguish their products are claimed as trademarks. Where those designations appear in this book, and O'Reilly Media, Inc. was aware of a trademark claim, the designations have been printed in caps or initial caps.

While every precaution has been taken in the preparation of this book, the publisher and authors assume no responsibility for errors or omissions, or for damages resulting from the use of the information contained herein.

ISBN: 978-0-596-51454-9
[LSI]   [2011-01-20]

In memory of Jonathan

Table of Contents

Preface

We dedicate this book to the memory of one of our original coauthors, Jonathan Stern. Jonathan unexpectedly passed away in March of 2007. Yet his memory lives on for those of us who knew him and, in many ways, for those who will read this book. Let us explain.

The original outline for this book was first assembled at the ubiquitous coffee shop located in the Sears Tower in Chicago. It was 1998 and the authors had gathered there with a common goal. We were all Oracle employees working in technical sales roles and had visited many organizations and companies. We found that many IT managers, Oracle database administrators (DBAs), and Oracle developers were quite adept at reading Oracle's documentation, but seemed to be missing an understanding of the overall Oracle footprint and how to practically apply what they were reading. It was as if they had a recipe book, but were unclear on how to gather the right ingredients and mix them together successfully. This bothered all of us, but it particularly frustrated Jonathan.

Jonathan was the kind of person who sought to understand how things worked. Nothing delighted Jonathan more than gaining such an understanding, then spending hours thinking of ways to translate his understanding into something that would be more meaningful to others. He believed that a key role for himself while at Oracle was the transfer of such knowledge to others. He continued to perform similar roles later at other companies at which he worked.

Writing the first edition of *Oracle Essentials* was a lengthy process. Jonathan wrote several of the original chapters, and he also reviewed some of the other original work and was quick to identify where he thought something was wrong. For Jonathan, "wrong" meant that the text could be misinterpreted and that further clarity was needed to make sure the right conclusion was drawn. The first edition became much more useful through Jonathan's efforts. He was always quite proud of that effort. Even as the book changed with succeeding editions and Jonathan moved on to other companies, he continued to feel that this book remained an important accomplishment in his life.

Some explanations of how Oracle works are fundamental to the database and have not changed in subsequent editions of the book, so some of Jonathan's original work remains here, although much of the surrounding text is now considerably different. Of course, some entire sections describing the complex steps that were once needed to manage and deploy older releases of the database are no longer relevant and thus are no longer included. Jonathan would probably view Oracle's self-managing and self-tuning improvements as incredible achievements, but would also wonder whether it is a good thing that people can know even less today about how the database works but still deploy it.

So, we introduce you to the fourth edition of *Oracle Essentials*. We have made many changes in this edition. Some, of course, result from changes in features in Oracle Database 11g and the ways that you can now use and deploy the latest release of the database. But we have also made a considerable effort to go back and rewrite parts of the book that we did not believe possessed the clarity needed by our readers—clarity that Jonathan would want in such a book. So, he influences us still.

Goals of This Book

Our main goal is to give you a foundation for using the Oracle database effectively and efficiently. Therefore, we wrote with these principles in mind:

Focus
> We've tried to concentrate on the most important Oracle issues. Every topic provides a comprehensive but concise discussion of how Oracle handles an issue and the repercussions of that action.

Brevity
> One of the first decisions we made was to concentrate on principles rather than syntax. There simply isn't room for myriad syntax diagrams and examples in this book.

Uniqueness
> We've tried to make this an ideal first Oracle book for a wide spectrum of Oracle users—but not the last! You will very likely have to refer to Oracle documentation or other, more specific books for more details about using Oracle. However, we hope this book will act as an accelerator for you. Using the foundation you get from this book, you can take detailed information from other sources and put it to the best use.

This book is the result of more than 45 combined years of experience with Oracle and other databases. We hope you'll benefit from that experience.

Audience for This Book

We wrote this book for people possessing all levels of Oracle expertise. Our target audiences include DBAs who spend most of their workday managing Oracle, application developers who build their systems on the data available in an Oracle database, and system administrators who are concerned with how Oracle will affect their computing environments. Of course, IT managers and business users interact more peripherally with the actual Oracle product. On the one hand, anticipating the appropriate technical level of all our potential readers presented difficulties; on the other hand, we've tried to build a solid foundation from the ground up and believe that some introductory material benefits everyone. We've also tried to ensure that every reader receives all the fundamental information necessary to truly understand the topics presented.

If you're an experienced Oracle user, you may be tempted to skip over material in this book with which you are already familiar. But experience has shown that some of the most basic Oracle principles can be overlooked, even by experts. We've also seen how the same small "gotchas" trip up even the most experienced Oracle practitioners and cause immense damage if they go unnoticed. After all, an ounce of prevention, tempered by understanding, is worth a pound of cure, especially when you are trying to keep your systems running optimally. So we hope that even experienced Oracle users will find valuable information in every chapter of this book—information that will save hours in their busy professional lives.

Our guiding principle has been to present this information compactly without making it overly tutorial. We think that the most important ratio in a book like this is the amount of useful information you get balanced against the time it takes you to get it. We sincerely hope this volume provides a terrific bang for the buck.

About the Fourth Edition (Oracle Database 11g)

The first three editions of this book, covering the Oracle database up to the Oracle Database 10g version, have been well received, and we were pleased that O'Reilly Media agreed to publish this fourth edition. In this update to the book, we have added information describing the latest release of Oracle, Oracle Database 11g.

For the most part, the task of preparing this fourth edition was fairly clear-cut, because the Oracle Database 11g release is primarily incremental—the new features in the release extend existing features of the database. We've added the information about these extensions to each of the chapters, wherever this information was most relevant and appropriate. However, manageability has greatly changed over the release, and is reflected in many of the most significant changes to content.

Of course, this fourth edition cannot possibly cover everything that is new in Oracle Database 11g. In general, we have followed the same guidelines for this edition that we did for the first three editions. If a new feature does not seem to be broadly important, we have not necessarily delved into it. As with earlier editions we have not tried to produce a laundry list of every characteristic of the Oracle database. In addition, if a feature falls into an area outside the scope of the earlier editions, we have not attempted to cover it in this edition unless it has assumed new importance.

Structure of This Book

This book is divided into 15 chapters and 2 appendixes, as follows:

Chapter 1, *Introducing Oracle*, describes the range of Oracle products and features and provides a brief history of Oracle and relational databases.

Chapter 2, *Oracle Architecture*, describes the core concepts and structures (e.g., files, processes, and so on) that are the architectural basis of Oracle.

Chapter 3, *Installing and Running Oracle*, briefly describes how to install Oracle and how to configure, start up, and shut down the database and Oracle Net.

Chapter 4, *Oracle Data Structures*, summarizes the various datatypes supported by Oracle and introduces the Oracle objects (e.g., tables, views, indexes). This chapter also covers query optimization.

Chapter 5, *Managing Oracle*, provides an overview of managing an Oracle system, including the advisors available as part of Oracle Database 11g, using Oracle Enterprise Manager (EM), dealing with database fragmentation and reorganization using current database releases, information lifecycle management, and working with Oracle Support.

Chapter 6, *Oracle Security, Auditing, and Compliance*, provides an overview of basic Oracle security, Oracle's security options, basic auditing capabilities, and ways you can leverage the Oracle Database Vault Option and the Audit Vault Server to meet compliance needs.

Chapter 7, *Oracle Performance*, describes the main issues relevant to Oracle performance—especially the major performance characteristics of disk, memory, and CPU tuning. It describes how Oracle Enterprise Manager, the Automatic Workload Repository, and the Automatic Database Diagnostic Monitor are used for performance monitoring and management, as well as parallelism and memory management in Oracle.

Chapter 8, *Oracle Multiuser Concurrency*, describes the basic principles of multiuser concurrency (e.g., transactions, locks, integrity problems) and explains how Oracle handles concurrency.

Chapter 9, *Oracle and Transaction Processing*, describes online transaction processing (OLTP) in Oracle.

Chapter 10, *Oracle Data Warehousing and Business Intelligence*, describes the basic principles of data warehouses and business intelligence, Oracle database features used for such solutions, Oracle's business intelligence tools, relevant options such as OLAP and Data Mining, and best practices.

Chapter 11, *Oracle and High Availability*, discusses availability concepts, what happens when the Oracle database recovers, protecting against system failure, Oracle's backup and recovery facilities, and high availability and failover solutions.

Chapter 12, *Oracle and Hardware Architecture*, describes your choice of computer architectures, configuration considerations, and deployment strategies for Oracle, including grid computing.

Chapter 13, *Oracle Distributed Databases and Distributed Data*, briefly summarizes the Oracle facilities used in distributed processing including two-phase commits and Streams Advanced Queuing and replication.

Chapter 14, *Oracle Extended Datatypes*, describes Oracle's object-oriented features, Java's™ role, web services support, multimedia extensions to the Oracle datatypes, content management using the database, spatial capabilities, and the extensibility framework.

Chapter 15, *Beyond the Oracle Database*, describes Oracle Application Express, deploying to the Web using the Oracle Application Server and Fusion Middleware, and the overall use of Oracle in a Service-Oriented Architecture (SOA) environment.

Appendix A, *What's New in This Book for Oracle Database 11g*, lists the Oracle Database 11g changes described in this book.

Appendix B, *Additional Resources*, lists a variety of additional resources—both online and offline—so you can do more detailed reading.

Conventions Used in This Book

The following typographical conventions are used in this book:

Italic
> Used for file and directory names, emphasis, and the first occurrence of terms

`Constant width`
> Used for code examples and literals

`Constant width italic`
> In code examples, indicates an element (for example, a parameter) that you supply

UPPERCASE
> Generally indicates Oracle keywords

lowercase
> In code examples, generally indicates user-defined items such as variables

This icon indicates a tip, suggestion, or general note. For example, we'll tell you if you need to use a particular version of Oracle or if an operation requires certain privileges.

This icon indicates a warning or caution. For example, we'll tell you if Oracle doesn't behave as you'd expect or if a particular operation negatively impacts performance.

How to Contact Us

Please address comments and questions concerning this book to the publisher:

> O'Reilly Media, Inc.
> 1005 Gravenstein Highway North
> Sebastopol, CA 95472
> 800-998-9938 (in the United States or Canada)
> 707-829-0515 (international/local)
> 707-829-0104 (fax)

There is a web page for this book, which lists errata, the text of several helpful technical papers, and any additional information. You can access this page at:

> *http://www.oreilly.com/catalog/9780596514549*

To comment or ask technical questions about this book, send email to:

> *bookquestions@oreilly.com*

For more information about books, conferences, software, Resource Centers, and the O'Reilly Network, see the O'Reilly web site at:

> *http://www.oreilly.com*

Using Code Examples

This book is here to help you get your job done. In general, you may use the code in this book in your programs and documentation. You do not need to contact us for permission unless you're reproducing a significant portion of the code. For example, writing a program that uses several chunks of code from this book does not require permission. Selling or distributing a CD-ROM of examples from O'Reilly books *does* require permission. Answering a question by citing this book and quoting example code does not require permission. Incorporating a significant amount of example code from this book into your product's documentation *does* require permission.

We appreciate, but do not require, attribution. An attribution usually includes the title, author, publisher, and ISBN. For example: "*Oracle Essentials: Oracle Database 11g*, Fourth Edition, by Rick Greenwald, Robert Stackowiak, and Jonathan Stern. Copyright 2008 O'Reilly Media Inc., 978-0-596-51454-9."

If you feel your use of code examples falls outside fair use or the permission given above, feel free to contact us at *permissions@oreilly.com*.

Safari® Books Online

 When you see a Safari® Books Online icon on the cover of your favorite technology book, that means the book is available online through the O'Reilly Network Safari Bookshelf.

Safari offers a solution that's better than e-books. It's a virtual library that lets you easily search thousands of top tech books, cut and paste code samples, download chapters, and find quick answers when you need the most accurate, current information. Try it for free at *http://safari.oreilly.com*.

Acknowledgments

Each of the authors has arrived at this collaboration through a different path, but we would all like to thank the team at O'Reilly for making this book both possible and a joy to write. We'd like to thank our first editor for this edition, Colleen Gorman, and the rest of the O'Reilly crew, especially Sumita Mukherji, the production editor; Rob Romano, who developed the figures; and Shan Young, who wrote the index. Also, we'd like to thank our editor from the first three editions, Debby Russell, who was among the first to see the value in such a book and who stepped in to perform final editing on the fourth edition as well. It's incredible how all of these folks were able to strike the perfect balance—always there when we needed something, but leaving us alone when we didn't.

We're all grateful to each other. Giving birth to a book is a difficult process, but it can be harrowing when split three ways. Everyone hung in there and did their best throughout this process. We'd also like to give our sincere thanks to the technical reviewers for the fourth edition of this book: Darryl Hurley, Dwayne King, Arup Nanda, and Bert Scalzo. Thanks as well to reviewers of previous editions: Craig Shallahamer of OraPub, Domenick Ficarella, Jonathan Gennick, Jenny Gelhausen, and Dave Klein. This crucially important work really enhanced the value of the book you're reading. And thanks as well to Lance Ashdown for clarifying Oracle database writes.

Rick thanks the incredibly bright and gifted people who have shared their wealth of knowledge with him over the years, including Bruce Scott, Earl Stahl, Jerry Chang, and Jim Milbery. In particular, he thanks the two individuals who have been his technical mentors over the course of his entire career: Ed Hickland and Dave Klein, who have repeatedly spent time explaining to and discussing with him some of the broader and finer points of database technology.

For the later editions of this book, Rick would also like to thank all those colleagues at Oracle who helped him in his time of need, checking on those last-minute clarifications, including John Lang, Bruce Lowenthal, Alice Watson, Dave Leroy, Sushil Kumar, Mughees Minhas, Daniela Hansell, Penny Avril, Mark Townsend, and Mark Drake. And a special thank-you to Jenny Tsai-Smith, who always seemed to have the time and knowledge to clear up any Oracle database problem. And last, but certainly not least, his primary coauthor, Bob Stackowiak, who has become a good friend over the years of collaboration.

Bob acknowledges all his friends over the years around the world at Oracle Corporation, and from earlier stints at IBM, Harris Computer Systems, and the U.S. Army Corps of Engineers. Through personal relationships and email, they have shared a lot and provided him with incredible opportunities for learning. At Oracle, he especially thanks members of Andy Mendelsohn's team who have always been helpful in providing material ahead of releases, including Mark Townsend, Raymond Roccaforte, George Lumpkin, Hermann Baer, and many others. Bob also extends special thanks to his team in Oracle's Technology Business Unit that includes Louis Nagode, Jim Bienski, Gayl Czaplicki, Alan Manewitz, Joan Maiorana, Sandrine Ost, and Max Rivera. His management continues to recognize the value of such projects, including Mark Salser and Paul Cross. He'd also like to thank his customers, who have always had the most practical experience using the products and tools he has worked with and from whom he continues to learn. Finally, both Bob and Rick would like to thank Sheila Cepero for adding them to the Oracle Database 11g beta program, an important factor in enabling this book to appear so shortly after the initial release of the new database version.

In earlier editions, Jonathan thanked many of his professional contacts in previous editions, including Murray Golding, Sam Mele, and the Oracle Server Technologies members and their teams, including Juan Tellez, Ron Weiss, Juan Loaiza, and Carol Colrain for their help during his years at Oracle. And we thank him for all that he gave us in too short a life.

CHAPTER 1

Introducing Oracle

Where do we start? One of the problems in comprehending a massive product such as the Oracle database is getting a good sense of how the product works without getting lost in the details. This book aims to provide a thorough grounding in the concepts and technologies that form the foundation of Oracle's Database Server, currently known as Oracle Database 11g. The book is intended for a wide range of Oracle database administrators, developers, and users, from the novice to the experienced. It is our hope that once you have this basic understanding of the product, you'll be able to connect the dots when using Oracle's voluminous feature set, documentation, and the many other books and publications that describe the database.

Oracle also offers an Application Server and Fusion Middleware, business intelligence tools, and business applications (the E-Business Suite, PeopleSoft, JD Edwards, Siebel, Hyperion, and Project Fusion). Since this book is focused on the database, we will touch on these as they relate to specific Oracle database topics covered.

This first chapter lays the groundwork for the rest of the book. Of all the chapters, it covers the broadest range of topics. Most of these topics are discussed later in more depth, but some of the basics—for example, the brief history of Oracle and the contents of the different "flavors" of the Oracle database products—are unique to this chapter.

Over the past 30 years, Oracle grew from being one of many vendors that developed and sold a database product to being widely recognized as the database market leader. Although early products were typical of a startup company, the Oracle database quality and depth grew such that its technical capabilities are now often viewed as the most advanced in the industry. With each database release, Oracle has improved the scalability, functionality, and manageability of the database.

This book is now in its fourth edition. This edition, like the second and third editions, required many changes since the database has changed a great deal over this time. Highlights of Oracle releases include:

- Oracle8 (released in 1997) improved the performance and scalability of the database and added the ability to create and store objects in the database.
- Oracle8*i* (released in 1999) added a new twist to the Oracle database—a combination of enhancements that made the Oracle8*i* database a focal point in the world of Internet computing.
- Oracle9*i* (released in 2001) introduced Real Application Clusters as a replacement for Oracle Parallel Server and added many management and data warehousing features.
- Oracle Database 10*g* (released in 2003) enabled deployment of "grid" computing. A *grid* is simply a pool of computers and software resources providing resources for applications on an as-needed basis. To support this style of computing, Oracle added the ability to provision CPUs and data. Oracle Database 10*g* also further reduced the time, cost, and complexity of database management through the introduction of self-managing features such as the Automated Database Diagnostic Monitor, Automated Shared Memory Tuning, Automated Storage Management, and Automated Disk Based Backup and Recovery.
- Oracle Database 11*g* (released in 2007) is the current release. Many of the self-tuning and managing capabilities are further improved, especially Automatic Memory Management, partitioning, and security. The lifecycle of database change management is extended within Oracle's Enterprise Manager as Oracle now provides improved diagnosis capabilities and linkage to Oracle Support via a Support Workbench. This version also features improved online patching capabilities.

Before we dive into further details, let's step back and look at how databases evolved, how we arrived at the relational model, and Oracle's history. We'll then take an initial look at Oracle database packaging and key Oracle features today.

The Evolution of the Relational Database

The relational database concept was described first by Dr. Edgar F. Codd in an IBM research publication entitled "System R4 Relational" that was published in 1970. Initially, it was unclear whether any system based on this concept could achieve commercial success. Nevertheless, a company named Software Development Laboratories Relational Software came into being in 1977 and then released a product named Oracle V.2 as the world's first commercial relational database within a couple of years (also changing its name to Relational Software, Incorporated). By 1985, Oracle could claim more than 1,000 relational database customer sites. Curiously, IBM would not embrace relational technology in a commercial product until the Query Management Facility in 1983.

Why did relational database technology grow to become the de facto database technology? A look back at previous database technology may help to explain this phenomenon.

Database management systems were first defined in the 1960s to provide a common organizational framework for data formerly stored in independent files. In 1964, Charles Bachman of General Electric proposed a network model with data records linked together, forming intersecting sets of data, as shown on the left in Figure 1-1. This work formed the basis of the CODASYL Data Base Task Group. Meanwhile, the North American Aviation's Space Division and IBM developed a second approach based on a hierarchical model in 1965. In this model, data is represented as tree structures in a hierarchy of records, as shown on the right in Figure 1-1. IBM's product based on this model was brought to market in 1969 as the Information Management System (IMS). As recently as 1980, almost all database implementations used either the network or hierarchical approach. Although several competitors sold similar technologies around 1980, only IMS could still be found in many large organizations 20 years later.

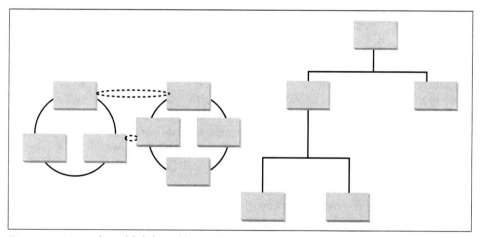

Figure 1-1. Network model (left) and hierarchical model (right)

Relational Basics

The relational database uses the concept of linked two-dimensional tables consisting of rows and columns, as shown in Figure 1-2. Unlike the hierarchical approach, no predetermined relationship exists between distinct tables. This means that data needed to link together the different areas of the network or hierarchical model need not be defined. Because relational users don't need to understand the representation of data in storage to retrieve it (and many such users create ad hoc queries), ease of use helped popularize the relational model.

DEPTNO	DEPTNAME	LOCATION
10	Accounting	San Francisco
20	Research	San Francisco
30	Sales	Chicago
40	Operations	Dallas

EMPNO	EMPNAME	TITLE	DEPTNO
71712	Johnson	Clerk	10
83321	Smith	Mgr	20
85332	Stern	SC Mgr	30
88888	Carter	Mgr	10

Figure 1-2. Relational model with two tables

Relational programming is nonprocedural and operates on a set of rows at a time. In a master-detail relationship between tables, there can be one or many detail rows for each individual master row, yet the statements used to access, insert, or modify the data simply describe the set of results. In many early relational databases, data access required the use of procedural languages that worked one record at a time. Because of this set orientation, programs access more than one record in a relational database more easily. Relational databases can be used more productively to extract value from large groups of data.

The contents of the rows in Figure 1-2 are sometimes referred to as *records*. A column within a row is referred to as a *field*. Tables are stored in a database *schema*, which is a logical organizational unit within the database. Other logical structures in the schema often include the following:

Views

Provide a single view of data derived from one or more tables or views. The view is an alternative interface to the data, which is stored in the underlying table(s) that make up the view.

Sequences
>   Provide unique numbers for column values.

Stored procedures
>   Contain logical modules that can be called from programs.

Synonyms
>   Provide alternative names for database objects.

Indexes
>   Provide faster access to table rows.

Database links
>   Provide links between distributed databases.

The relationships between columns in different tables are typically described through the use of *keys*, which are implemented through referential integrity constraints and their supporting indexes. For example, in Figure 1-2, you can establish a link between the DEPTNO column in the second table, which is called a *foreign key*, to the DEPTNO column in the first table, which is referred to as the *primary key* of that table.

Finally, even if you define many different indexes for a table, you don't have to understand them or manage the data they contain. Oracle includes a *query optimizer* (described in Chapter 4) that chooses whether to use indexes, and the best way to use those indexes, to access the data for any particular query.

The relational approach lent itself to the Structured Query Language (SQL). SQL was initially defined over a period of years by IBM Research, but it was Oracle Corporation that first introduced it to the market in 1979. SQL was noteworthy at the time for being the only language needed for relational databases since you could use SQL:

- For queries (using a SELECT statement)
- As a Data Manipulation Language or DML (using INSERT, UPDATE, and DELETE statements)
- As a Data Definition Language or DDL (using CREATE or DROP statements when adding or deleting tables)
- To set privileges for users or groups (using GRANT or REVOKE statements)

Today, SQL contains many extensions and follows ANSI/ISO standards that define its basic syntax.

How Oracle Grew

In 1983, Relational Software Incorporated was renamed Oracle Corporation to avoid confusion with a competitor named Relational Technologies Incorporated. At this time, the developers made a critical decision to create a portable version of Oracle written in C (version 3) that ran not only on Digital VAX/VMS systems, but also on Unix and other platforms. By 1985, Oracle claimed the ability to run on more than 30 platforms. Some of these platforms are historical curiosities today, but others remain in use. (In addition to VMS, early operating systems supported by Oracle included IBM MVS, HP/UX, IBM AIX, and Sun's Solaris version of Unix.) Oracle was able to leverage and accelerate the growth of minicomputers and Unix servers in the 1980s. Today, Oracle also leverages this portability to operating systems such as Microsoft Windows and Linux.

In addition to multiple platform support, other core Oracle messages from the mid-1980s still ring true today, including complementary software development and decision support (business intelligence) tools, ANSI standard SQL across platforms, and connectivity over standard networks. Since the mid-1980s, the database deployment model has evolved from dedicated database application servers to client/server to Internet computing implemented using browser-based clients accessing database applications.

Oracle introduced many innovative technical features to the database as computing and deployment models changed (from offering the first distributed database to supporting the first Java Virtual Machine in the core database engine to enabling grid computing). Oracle offered support for emerging standards such as XML, important in deploying a Service-Oriented Architecture (SOA). Table 1-1 presents a short list of Oracle's major product introductions.

Table 1-1. History of Oracle introductions

Year	Feature
1977	Software Development Laboratories founded by Larry Ellison, Bob Miner, Ed Oates
1979	Oracle version 2: first commercially available relational database to use SQL
1983	Oracle version 3: single code base for Oracle across multiple platforms
1984	Oracle version 4: with portable toolset, read consistency
1986	Oracle version 5 generally available: client/server Oracle relational database
1987	CASE and 4GL toolset
1988	Oracle Financial Applications built on relational database
1989	Oracle6 generally available: row-level locking and hot backups
1991	Oracle Parallel Server on massively parallel platforms
1993	Oracle7: with cost-based optimizer
1994	Oracle version 7.1 generally available: parallel operations including query, load, and create index
1996	Universal database with extended SQL via cartridges, thin client, and application server
1997	Oracle8 generally available: object-relational and Very Large Database (VLDB) features
1999	Oracle8*i* generally available: Java Virtual Machine (JVM) in the database
2000	Oracle9*i* Application Server generally available: Oracle tools integrated in middle tier
2001	Oracle9*i* Database Server generally available: Real Application Clusters, OLAP, and data mining in the database

Table 1-1. History of Oracle introductions (continued)

Year	Feature
2003	Oracle Database 10*g* and Oracle Application Server 10*g*: "grid" computing enabled; Oracle Database 10*g* automates key management tasks
2005	Oracle completes PeopleSoft acquisition and announces Siebel acquisition, thus growing ERP and CRM applications and business intelligence offerings
2007	Oracle Database 11*g*: extension of self-managing capabilities and end-to-end database change management; Hyperion acquisition adds database-independent OLAP and Financial Performance Management applications

The Oracle Database Family

Oracle Database 11g is the most recent version of the Oracle Relational Database Management System (RDBMS) family of products that share common source code. The family of database products includes:

Oracle Enterprise Edition

Flagship database product and main topic of this book, aimed at large-scale implementations that require Oracle's full suite of database features and options. For advanced security, only the Enterprise Edition features Virtual Private Database (VPD) support, Fine-Grained Auditing, and options including the Database Vault, Advanced Security, and Label Security. Data warehousing features only in Enterprise Edition include compression of repeating stored data values, cross-platform transportable tablespaces, Information Lifecycle Management (ILM), materialized views query rewrite, and the Partitioning, OLAP, and Data Mining Options. High-availability features unique to the Enterprise Edition include Data Guard and Flashback database, Flashback table, and Flashback transaction query. Added to Oracle Database 11g are an Advanced Compression Option for all workloads, including transaction processing, Large Object (LOB) storage, and backups; a database testing option called the Real Application Testing Option that includes Database Replay and SQL Performance Analyzer; and a Total Recall Option used to enable a Flashback Data Archive that retains data for historic queries (where a SQL construct specifies an "AS OF" date in the past).

Oracle Standard Edition

Oracle's database intended for small and medium-sized implementations. This database can be deployed onto server configurations containing up to 4 CPUs on a single system or on a cluster using Real Application Clusters (RAC).

Oracle Standard Edition One

Designed for small implementations. This database can support up to 2 CPUs and does not support RAC. The feature list is otherwise similar to Oracle Standard Edition.

Oracle Personal Edition

> Database used by single developers to develop code for implementation on Oracle multiuser databases. It requires a license, unlike Express Edition, but gives you the full Enterprise Edition set of functionality.

Oracle Express Edition

> Entry-level database from Oracle available at no charge for Windows and Linux. This database is limited to 1 GB of memory and 4 GB of disk. It provides a subset of the functionality in Standard Edition One, lacking features such as a Java Virtual Machine, server-managed backup and recovery, and Automatic Storage Management. Although this database is not manageable by Oracle Enterprise Manager, you can deploy it for and manage multiple users through the Oracle Application Express (formerly HTML-DB) administration interface.

Oracle generally releases new versions of the flagship database about every three to four years. New releases typically follow themes and introduce a significant number of new features. In recent releases, these themes are indicated in the product version naming. In 1998, Oracle announced Oracle8*i*, with the "*i*" added to denote new functionality supporting Internet deployment. Oracle9*i* continued using this theme. In 2003, Oracle released Oracle Database 10*g*, with the "*g*" denoting Oracle's focus on emerging grid computing deployment models. Oracle has continued that theme in the current database version highlighted in this book. In between major versions, Oracle issues point releases that also add features but are more typically focused on improvements to earlier capabilities.

The terms "Oracle," "Oracle8," "Oracle8*i*," "Oracle9*i*," "Oracle Database 10*g*," and "Oracle Database 11*g*" might appear to be used somewhat interchangeably in this book because Oracle Database 11*g* includes all the features of previous versions. When we describe a new feature that was first made available specifically in a certain release, we've tried to note that fact to avoid confusion, recognizing that many of you maintain older releases of Oracle. We typically use the simple term "Oracle" when describing features that are common to all these releases.

Oracle Development has developed releases using a single source code model for the core family of database products since 1983. While each database implementation includes some operating-system-specific source code at very low levels in order to better leverage specific platforms, the interfaces that users, developers, and administrators deal with for each version are consistent. Since feature behavior is consistent across platforms for implementations of these Oracle flavors, organizations can migrate Oracle applications and databases easily among various hardware platform vendors and operating systems. This development strategy also enables Oracle to focus on implementing new features only once across its product set.

Summary of Oracle Database Features

The Oracle database is a broad product. To give some initial perspective, we begin describing Oracle with a high-level overview of the basic areas of functionality. By the end of this portion of the chapter, you will have orientation points to guide you in exploring the topics in the rest of this book.

To give some structure to the broad spectrum of the Oracle database, we've organized our initial discussion of these features into the following sections:

- Database application development features
- Database connection features
- Distributed database features
- Data movement features
- Database performance features
- Database management features
- Database security features

In this chapter, we've included a lot of terminology and rather abbreviated descriptions of features. Oracle is a huge system. Our goal here is to quickly familiarize you with the full range of features in the system. Subsequent chapters will provide additional details. Obviously, though, whole books have been written about some of the feature areas summarized here.

Database Application Development Features

The Oracle database is typically used to store and retrieve data through applications. The features of the Oracle database and related products described in this section are used to create applications. We've divided the discussion in the following subsections into database programming and database extensibility options. Later in this chapter, we will describe Oracle's development tools and Oracle's other embedded database products that meet unique applications deployment needs.

Database Programming

All flavors of the Oracle database include languages and interfaces that enable programmers to access and manipulate the data in the database. Database programming features usually interest developers who are creating Oracle-based applications to be sold commercially or IT organizations building applications unique to their businesses. Data in Oracle can be accessed using SQL, ODBC, JDBC, SQLJ, OLE DB, ODP.NET, SQL/XML, XQuery, and WebDAV. Programs deployed within the database can be written in PL/SQL and Java.

SQL

The ANSI standard Structured Query Language (SQL) provides basic functions for data manipulation, transaction control, and record retrieval from the database. Most business users of the database interact with Oracle through applications or business intelligence tools that provide interfaces hiding the underlying SQL and its complexity.

PL/SQL

Oracle's PL/SQL, a procedural language extension to SQL, is commonly used to implement program logic modules for applications. PL/SQL can be used to build stored procedures and triggers, looping controls, conditional statements, and error handling. You can compile and store PL/SQL procedures in the database. You can also execute PL/SQL blocks via SQL*Plus, an interactive tool provided with all versions of Oracle. PL/SQL program units can be precompiled.

Java

Oracle8*i* introduced the use of Java as a procedural language and a Java Virtual Machine (JVM) in the database (originally called JServer). The JVM includes support for Java stored procedures, methods, triggers, Enterprise JavaBeans™ (EJBs), CORBA, IIOP, and HTTP.

The inclusion of Java within the Oracle database allows Java developers to leverage their skills as Oracle applications developers. Java applications can be deployed in the client, Application Server, or database, depending on what is most appropriate. Oracle Database 11*g* includes a just-in-time Java compiler that is enabled by default. We briefly discuss some aspects of Java development in Chapter 14.

Oracle and web services

As of Oracle Database 11*g*, the database can serve as a web services provider implemented through XML DB in the database. Web services enable SQL or XQuery to submit queries and receive results as XML, or invoke PL/SQL functions or package functions and to receive results. XQuery in Oracle Database 11*g* provides support for the emerging JSR-225 standard and includes a number of performance enhancements.

Large objects

Interest in the use of large objects (LOBs) is growing, particularly for the storage of nontraditional datatypes such as images. The Oracle database has been able to store large objects for some time. Oracle8 added the capability to store multiple LOB columns in each table. Oracle Database 10*g* essentially removed the space limitation on large objects. Oracle Database 11*g* greatly improved the performance of query and insert operations used with LOBs through the introduction of SecureFiles. Transparent data encryption is supported for SecureFiles LOB data.

Object-oriented programming

Support of object structures has existed since Oracle8*i* to provide support for an object-oriented approach to programming. For example, programmers can create user-defined datatypes, complete with their own methods and attributes. Oracle's object support includes a feature called Object Views through which object-oriented programs can make use of relational data already stored in the database. You can also store objects in the database as varying arrays (VARRAYs), nested tables, or index organized tables (IOTs). We discuss the object-oriented features of Oracle further in Chapter 14.

Third-generation languages (3GLs)

Programmers can interact with the Oracle database from C, C++, Java, or COBOL by embedding SQL in those applications. Prior to compiling the applications using a platform's native compilers, you must run the embedded SQL code through a precompiler. The precompiler replaces SQL statements with library calls the native compiler can accept. Oracle provides support for this capability through optional "programmer" precompilers for C and C++ using Pro*C and for COBOL using Pro*COBOL. In recent Oracle versions, Oracle features SQLJ, a precompiler for Java that replaces SQL statements embedded in Java with calls to a SQLJ runtime library, also written in Java.

Database drivers

All versions of Oracle include database drivers that allow applications to access Oracle via ODBC (the Open DataBase Connectivity standard) or JDBC (the Java DataBase Connectivity open standard). Also available are data providers for OLE-DB and for .NET.

The Oracle Call Interface

If you're an experienced programmer seeking optimum performance, you may choose to define SQL statements within host-language character strings and then explicitly parse the statements, bind variables for them, and execute them using the Oracle Call Interface (OCI). OCI is a much more detailed interface that requires more programmer time and effort to create and debug. Developing an application that uses OCI can be time-consuming, but the added functionality and incremental performance gains could make spending the extra time worthwhile. In certain programming scenarios, OCI improves application performance or adds functionality. For instance, in high-availability implementations in which multiple systems share disks using Real Application Clusters, you could write programs using OCI that allow users to reattach to a second server transparently if the first fails.

National Language Support

National Language Support (NLS) provides character sets and associated functionality, such as date and numeric formats, for a variety of languages. Oracle Database 11g features Unicode 5.0 support. All data may be stored as Unicode, or select columns may be incrementally stored as Unicode. UTF-8 encoding and UTF-16 encoding provide support for more than 57 languages and 200 character sets. Extensive localization is provided (for example, for data formats), and customized localization can be added through the Oracle Locale Builder. Oracle includes a Globalization Toolkit for creating applications that will be used in multiple languages.

Database Extensibility

The Internet and corporate intranets have created a growing demand for storage and manipulation of nontraditional datatypes within the database. There is a need for extensions to the standard functionality of a database for storing and manipulating image, audio, video, spatial, and time series information. These capabilities are enabled through extensions to standard SQL. For more details regarding these features of Oracle, see Chapter 14.

Oracle Multimedia

Oracle Multimedia (formerly *inter*Media) provides text manipulation and additional image, audio, video, and locator functions in the database. Oracle Multimedia offers the following major capabilities:

- The text portion of Multimedia (Oracle Text) can identify the gist of a document by searching for themes and key phrases within the document.

- The image portion of Multimedia can store and retrieve images of various formats; starting with Oracle Database 11g, these include DICOM medical images.

- The audio and video portions of Multimedia can store and retrieve audio and video clips, respectively.

- The locator portion of Multimedia can retrieve data that includes spatial coordinate information.

Oracle content management

Oracle's content management solutions include a Content Database Option used to store and manage documents in the database and Stellent's content management applications that were acquired by Oracle in 2007. The applications include Universal Content Management, Universal Records Management, and Information Rights Management.

Oracle search capabilities

The Oracle Database and Application Server include a search tool named Ultra Search. Ultra Search is typically used to search and gather location information for text data stored within an organization's network. Document retrieval is based on user access rights. In addition, Oracle offers an alternative Secure Enterprise Search offering that is more flexible in non-Oracle environments.

Oracle Spatial Option

The Spatial Option is available for Oracle Enterprise Edition. It can optimize the display and retrieval of data linked to coordinates and is used in the development of spatial information systems. Several vendors of Geographic Information Systems (GIS) products now bundle this option and leverage it as their search and retrieval engine.

XML DB

Oracle added native XML datatype support to the Oracle9i database and XML and SQL interchangeability for searching. The structured XML object is held natively in object relational storage meeting the W3C DOM specification. The XPath syntax for searching in SQL is based on the SQLX group specifications, and XQuery is also supported.

Database Connection Features

The connection between the client and the database server is a key component of the overall architecture. The database connection is responsible for supporting all communications between an application and the data it uses. Oracle includes a number of features that establish and tune your database connections, described in the following subsections. We've divided the discussion into two categories: database networking and Oracle Application Server.

Database Networking

Database users connect to the database by establishing a network connection. You can also link database servers via network connections. Oracle provides a number of features to establish connections between users and the database and/or between database servers, as described in the following subsections.

Oracle Net

Oracle's network interface, Oracle Net, was formerly known as Net8 when used in Oracle8, and SQL*Net when used with Oracle7 and previous versions of Oracle. You can use Oracle Net over a wide variety of network protocols, although TCP/IP is by far the most common protocol today. Features associated with Oracle Net, such as shared servers, are referred to as Oracle Net Services.

Oracle Internet Directory

The Oracle Internet Directory (OID) was introduced with Oracle8*i*. OID replaced Oracle Names used in prior database releases since it gives users a way to connect to an Oracle Server without having a client-side configuration file. OID is an LDAP (Lightweight Directory Access Protocol) directory and so it supports Oracle Net and other LDAP-enabled protocols.

Oracle Connection Manager

Each connection to the database takes up valuable network resources, which can impact the overall performance of a database application. Oracle's Connection Manager (CMAN), illustrated in Figure 1-3, reduces the number of Oracle Net client network connections to the database through the use of *concentrators*, which provide connection multiplexing to implement multiple connections over a single network connection. Connection multiplexing provides the greatest benefit when there are a large number of active users.

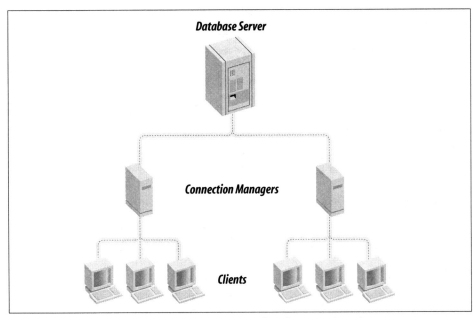

Figure 1-3. Concentrators with Connection Managers for a large number of users

You can also use the Connection Manager to provide multiprotocol connectivity if you still have some clients and servers not using TCP/IP. Oracle Database 10g introduced dynamic Connection Manager configuration, enabling the changing of CMAN parameters without shutting down the CMAN process.

Oracle Application Server

The popularity of Internet and intranet applications led to a change in deployment from client/server (with fat clients running a significant piece of the application) to a three-tier architecture (with a browser supplying everything needed for a thin client). Oracle Application Server enables deployment of the middle tier in a three-tier solution for web-based applications, component-based applications, and enterprise application integration. Oracle Application Server is a key part of Oracle's Fusion Middleware and can be scaled across multiple middle-tier servers.

This product includes a web listener based on the popular Apache listener, servlets and JavaServer Pages (JSPs), business logic, and/or data access components. Business logic often is deployed as Enterprise JavaBeans (EJBs). Data access components can include JDBC, SQLJ, and EJBs. TopLink provides a mapping tool that links Java objects to the database via JDBC such that the Java developer need not build SQL calls and or face broken Java applications resulting from database schema changes.

Oracle Application Server offers additional solutions in the cache, portal, business intelligence, and wireless areas:

Cache
    Oracle Application Server Web Cache introduced a middle tier for the caching of web pages or portions of pages. An earlier cache, Oracle Application Server Database Cache, was used for caching PL/SQL procedures and anonymous PL/SQL blocks but is no longer supported as of Oracle Application Server 10g.

Portal
    Oracle Application Server Portal is also a part of the Oracle Developer Suite (discussed later in this chapter) and is used for building easy-to-use enterprise dashboards. The developed portal is deployed to the Application Server.

Business Intelligence
    Application Server Business Intelligence components include the Portal as well as Oracle's original business intelligence tools:

    - Oracle Reports, which provides a scalable middle tier for the reporting of prebuilt query results
    - Oracle Discoverer, for ad hoc query and analysis
    - A deployment platform for JDeveloper custom-built OLAP and data mining applications

    These capabilities are discussed in Chapter 10.

Oracle Wireless

Oracle Wireless (formerly known as Oracle Portal-to-Go) includes:

- Content adapters for transforming content to XML
- Device transformers for transforming XML to device-specific markup languages
- Personalization portals for service personalization of alerts, alert addresses, location marks, and profiles; wireless personalization portal also used for the creation, servicing, testing, and publishing of URL service and for user management

Oracle Application Server is packaged in several editions: Enterprise Edition, Standard Edition, Standard Edition One, and Java Edition, which includes key components for Java developers. Portal, TopLink with the Application Development Framework, and the Web Cache are included in the Standard Edition and in Standard Edition One. The Enterprise Edition adds the following capabilities: Forms Services, Reports Services, Discoverer Viewer, Oracle Internet Directory, Oracle Application Interconnect, Wireless Option, and integration with Enterprise Service Bus (ESB). The Java Edition bundle includes an HTTP Server, OC4J, and TopLink with the Application Development Framework. We provide more details about Oracle Application Server in Chapter 15.

Oracle Application Server Enterprise Edition has several available options including:

BPEL Process Manager Option

Oracle's Business Process Execution Language (BPEL) tool is designed for Service-Oriented Architecture (SOA) environments and used for creating, managing, and deploying cross-application business processes. It supports standards such as BPEL, Web Services, XML, XSLT, XPATH, JMS, and JCA.

Business Activity Monitoring (BAM)

BAM is used for building real-time dashboards displaying key performance indicators (KPIs) populated with data from alerts monitored via the Web.

BI Publisher

A publishing and report layout tool used in generating high-fidelity reports from XML data.

Service Registry

The Oracle Service Registry enables publishing and advertising of services and provides a System of Record for SOA services.

SOA Suite for Oracle Middleware

The Suite bundles Oracle Fusion Middleware SOA offerings, including BPEL, BAM, business rules engine, Enterprise Service Bus (for messaging, routing, and transformations), Web Services Management (including a policy manager and monitoring dashboard), Web Services Registry, and applications and technology adapters.

Communication and Mobility Server

This bundle includes TimesTen, and also provides a SIP Servlet Container, enabler framework and enablers, voice access, and mobile access.

WebCenter

WebCenter is Oracle's latest portal framework used for deploying portlets and Ajax-based components, especially in Web 2.0 environments. It includes discussion forums, presence server, instant message client, Wiki, VOIP call setup and teardown, SIP Servlet Container, Java and Web Service APIs, Click-2-dial integration, and voice-enabled soft client.

Fusion Middleware Adapters

Adapters include Applications, Transaction Processing Monitors, EDI, and others.

The Fusion Middleware SOA Suite serves as the basis for Oracle's Application Integration Architecture (AIA). AIA also includes prepackaged business objects and business processes known as Process Integration Packs and provides key underpinnings used in integrating Oracle's current and future applications.

Distributed Database Features

The Oracle database is well known for its ability to handle extremely large volumes of data and users. Oracle not only scales through deployment on increasingly powerful single platforms, but also can be deployed in distributed configurations. Oracle deployed on multiple platforms can be combined to act as a single logical distributed database.

This section describes some of the basic ways that Oracle handles database interactions in a distributed database system.

Distributed Queries and Transactions

Data within an organization is often spread among multiple databases for reasons of both capacity and organizational responsibility. Users may want to query this distributed data or update it as if it existed within a single database.

Oracle first introduced distributed databases in response to the requirements for accessing data on multiple platforms in the early 1980s. *Distributed queries* can retrieve data from multiple databases. *Distributed transactions* can insert, update, or delete data on distributed databases. Oracle's two-phase commit mechanism, described in Chapter 13, guarantees that all the database servers that are part of a transaction will either commit or roll back the transaction. Background recovery processes can ensure database consistency in the event of system interruption during distributed transactions. Once the failed system comes back online, the same process will complete the distributed transactions.

Distributed transactions can also be implemented using popular transaction monitors (TPs) that interact with Oracle via XA, an industry-standard (X/Open) interface. Oracle8i added native transaction coordination with the Microsoft Transaction Server (MTS), so you can implement a distributed transaction initiated under the control of MTS through an Oracle database.

Heterogeneous Services

Heterogeneous Services allow non-Oracle data and services to be accessed from an Oracle database through generic connectivity via ODBC and OLE-DB included with the database.

Optional Transparent Gateways use agents specifically tailored for a variety of target systems. Transparent Gateways allow users to submit Oracle SQL statements to a non-Oracle distributed database source and have them automatically translated into the SQL dialect of the non-Oracle source system, which remains transparent to the user. In addition to providing underlying SQL services, Heterogeneous Services provide transaction services utilizing Oracle's two-phase commit with non-Oracle databases and procedural services that call third-generation language routines on non-Oracle systems. Users interact with the Oracle database as if all objects are stored in the Oracle database, and Heterogeneous Services handle the transparent interaction with the foreign database on the user's behalf.

Data Movement Features

Moving data from one Oracle database to another is often a requirement when using distributed databases, or when a user wants to implement multiple copies of the same database in multiple locations to reduce network traffic or increase data availability. You can export data and data dictionaries (metadata) from one database and import them into another. Oracle Database 10g introduced a high-speed data pump for the import and export.

Oracle also offers many other advanced features in this category, including transportable tablespaces, Advanced Queuing/Oracle Streams, and extraction, transformation and loading (ETL) solutions. We introduce these next.

Transportable Tablespaces

Transportable tablespaces first appeared in Oracle8i. Instead of using the export/import process, which dumps data and the structures that contain it into an intermediate file for loading, you can place a tablespace in read-only mode, move or copy it from one database to another, and then mount it. The same data dictionary (metadata) describing the tablespace must exist on the source and the target. This feature can save a lot of time since it simplifies the movement of large amounts of data.

Starting with Oracle Database 10g, you can move data with transportable tablespaces between heterogeneous platforms or operating systems.

Advanced Queuing and Oracle Streams

Advanced Queuing (AQ), first introduced in Oracle8, provides the means to asynchronously send messages from one Oracle database to another. Because messages are stored in a queue in the database and sent asynchronously when a connection is made, the amount of overhead and network traffic is much lower than it would be using traditional guaranteed delivery through the two-phase commit protocol between source and target. By storing the messages in the database, AQ provides a solution with greater recoverability than other queuing solutions that store messages in filesystems.

Oracle messaging adds the capability to develop and deploy a *content-based publish and subscribe solution* using a rules engine to determine relevant subscribing applications. As new content is published to a subscriber list, the rules on the list determine which subscribers should receive the content. This approach means that a single list can efficiently serve the needs of different subscriber communities. In the first release of Oracle9i, AQ added XML support and Oracle Internet Directory (OID) integration.

As of the second release of Oracle9i, AQ became part of Oracle Streams. Streams has three major components: log-based replication for data capture, queuing for data staging, and user-defined rules for data consumption. Since Oracle Database 10g, Streams also includes support for change data capture and file transfer solutions. Streams is managed through Oracle Enterprise Manager and described in more detail in Chapter 13.

Extraction, Transformation, and Loading

Oracle Warehouse Builder (OWB) is a tool used in the design of target databases, especially data warehouses, and provides a metadata repository. However, it is best known as a GUI-based tool used in building source-to-target maps and for generating extraction, transformation, and loading (ETL) scripts. OWB leverages key embedded ETL features in the Oracle database first made available in Oracle9i. OWB is included with the Oracle database as of Oracle Database 10g Release 2. We describe it further in Chapter 10.

Optionally, Oracle also offers a data integration tool, Oracle Data Integrator (ODI), that is not as Oracle database-centric as OWB (although the Oracle database can be a source and/or target). Oracle Data Integrator is based on a product and company that Oracle acquired named Sunopsis. In addition to providing ETL capabilities, ODI can generate code as web services for SOA deployment and is a key part of Oracle's SOA integration strategy.

Database Performance Features

Oracle includes several features specifically designed to boost performance in certain situations. We've divided the discussion in the following subsections into two categories: database parallelization and data warehousing.

Database Parallelization

Database tasks implemented in parallel speed up querying, tuning, and maintenance of the database. By breaking up a single task into smaller tasks and assigning each subtask to an independent process, you can dramatically improve the performance of certain types of database operations. Examples of query features implemented in parallel include:

- Table scans
- Nested loops
- Sort merge joins
- GROUP BYs
- NOT IN subqueries (anti-joins)
- User-defined functions
- Index scans
- Select distinct UNION and UNION ALL
- Hash joins
- ORDER BY and aggregation
- Bitmap star joins
- Partition-wise joins
- Stored procedures (PL/SQL, Java, external routines)

In addition to parallel query, many other Oracle features and capabilities are parallelized. Parallel operations are further identified and described in Chapter 7.

Data Warehousing and Business Intelligence

While parallel features improve the overall performance of the Oracle database, Oracle also has particular performance enhancements for business intelligence and data warehousing applications. We introduce many of them here, but see Chapter 10 for more detailed explanations of products and features specific to data warehousing and business intelligence.

Bitmap indexes

Oracle added support for stored bitmap indexes to Oracle 7.3 to provide a fast way of selecting and retrieving certain types of data. Bitmap indexes typically work best for columns that have few different values relative to the overall number of rows in a table.

Rather than storing the actual value, a bitmap index uses an individual bit for each potential value with the bit either "on" (set to 1) to indicate that the row contains the value or "off" (set to 0) to indicate that the row does not contain the value. Bitmap indexes are described in more detail in Chapter 4.

Star query optimization

Typical data warehousing queries occur against a large *fact table* with foreign keys to much smaller *dimension tables*. Oracle added an optimization for this type of *star query* in Oracle 7.3. Performance gains are realized through the use of Cartesian product joins of dimension tables with a single join back to the large fact table. Oracle8 introduced a further mechanism called a *parallel bitmap star join*, which uses bitmap indexes on the foreign keys to the dimension tables to speed star joins involving a large number of dimension tables.

Materialized views

Since Oracle8*i*, materialized views have provided another means of achieving a significant speedup of query performance. Summary-level information derived from a fact table and grouped along dimension values is stored as a materialized view. Queries that can use this view are directed to the view, transparently to the user and the SQL they submit. Oracle has continued to improve optimizer usage of materialized views with each new release of the database.

Analytic functions

A growing trend in Oracle and other databases is inclusion of SQL-accessible analytic and statistical functions in the database. Oracle first introduced such capabilities in Oracle8*i* with the CUBE and ROLLUP functions. Today, the functionality provided also includes ranking functions, windowing aggregate functions, lag and lead functions, reporting aggregate functions, statistical aggregates, linear regression, descriptive statistics, correlations, crosstabs, hypothesis testing, distribution fitting, and Pareto analysis.

OLAP Option

The OLAP Option physically stores dimensionally aware cubes in the Oracle relational database. These cubes are most frequently accessed using SQL, although a

Java API is also supported. As of Oracle Database 11g, Oracle's optimizer recognizes the levels within these cubes. As a result, any business intelligence tool that submits SQL to an Oracle database can transparently take advantage of the improved performance offered by deployment of this option. Refreshes of the values in these cubes are now maintained similar to refreshing materialized views.

Data Mining Option

Since Oracle9i, popular data-mining algorithms have been embedded in the database through the Data Mining Option and are exposed through a PL/SQL or Java data-mining API. Data-mining applications that use these algorithms are typically built using Oracle's DataMiner or using data-mining tools from Oracle partners such as InforSense and SPSS. Algorithms available in the Data Mining Option for Oracle Database 11g include Naïve Bayes, Associations, Adaptive Bayes Networks, Clustering, Support Vector Machines (SVM), Nonnegative Matrix Factorization (NMF), Decision Trees, and Generalized Linear Models.

Business intelligence tools

Oracle data warehouses are often accessed using business intelligence tools from other popular vendors. However, Oracle's own tools became more common for such deployment as Oracle grew its offerings through acquisitions. Oracle's initial offering included Oracle Discoverer and Reports, and these tools remain available in the Application Server or as a standalone Oracle Business Intelligence Standard Edition Suite.

Oracle's flagship product in this area is Oracle Business Intelligence Enterprise Edition Suite (OBI EE) originally consisting of former Siebel Analytics, including Oracle Answers, Dashboards, Delivers, BI Publisher, and Office Plug-ins. Oracle expanded this offering in OBI EE Plus adding Hyperion components that include Foundation Services, Interactive Reporting, SQR production reporting, Financial Reporting, SmartView for Office, and Web Analysis.

Essbase is available as an option for providing an OLAP cube and functionality independently of the data warehouse database. A subset OBI EE is included in Business Intelligence Standard Edition One, along with the Oracle Standard Edition One database and Oracle Warehouse Builder.

Oracle also offers business intelligence applications that include data models and reporting and analysis with prepopulated business metadata. Flagship applications include Oracle's Business Intelligence Applications (the former Siebel Business Analytics applications) and Hyperion Financial Performance Management applications.

Database Management Features

Oracle includes many features that make the database easier to manage. Ease in Oracle management fundamentally improved with the introduction of Oracle Database 10g, and has continued to evolve toward being more self-tuning and self-managing with the release of Oracle Database 11g. If you are still managing Oracle databases using techniques (such as scripts) from previous releases and are moving to one of the newer releases, now is the time to reevaluate your thinking on management.

Starting with Oracle Database 10g, statistics are automatically gathered to an Automatic Workload Repository (AWR) within the database. Oracle's Automatic Database Diagnostic Monitor (ADDM) evaluates the statistics on a regular basis and sends alerts of potential problem conditions to Oracle Enterprise Manager, where you can evaluate the condition in more detail and potentially take corrective actions. Some of the newer fully automated features, such as Automatic Memory Management, also leverage data gathered in the AWR.

Oracle has a near real-time view of current database conditions as it makes automated recommendations. Such recommendations will often be more accurate than would be possible with the manual processes you might have used in the past. In the following subsections we'll introduce the impact this has on Oracle Enterprise Manager and add-on packs, Information Lifecycle Management, backup and recovery, and database availability.

Oracle Enterprise Manager

Oracle includes Oracle Enterprise Manager (EM) with its most widely deployed database products. EM provides a database management tool framework and an HTML-based interface used to manage database users, instances, and features. EM can also manage Oracle Application Server, Oracle Applications, Oracle's Linux release, and software products from other vendors.

The database console in Oracle's current version provides information on database status, availability, schema, data movement configuration, and software maintenance. New with Oracle Database 11g is the Support Workbench and diagnosability infrastructure leveraged in reporting problems to Oracle Support. Multiple database administrators can access the EM repository at the same time.

EM can be deployed in several ways: as a central console for monitoring multiple databases leveraging agents, as a "product console" (installed by default with each individual database), or through remote access, also known as "studio mode." When deployed as a central console, Enterprise Manager is referred to as "Grid Control" and can be used for rapid installation of Oracle software, provisioning, and automated rolling patch updates.

A subset of Enterprise Manager functionality is accessible through Microsoft Pocket PC Internet Explorer on wireless PDAs using EM2Go. EM2Go can monitor the status of the Oracle database and Oracle Application Server.

Information Lifecycle Management and ILM Assistant

Introduced in 2006, Information Lifecycle Management (ILM) provides a means to define classes of data and storage tiers and move the data to the storage tiers that provide the right combination of performance and cost. The ILM Assistant interface for setting up and managing ILM can be downloaded from the Oracle Technology Network at *http://otn.oracle.com*. For more details, see Chapter 5.

Backup and Recovery

As every database administrator knows, backing up a database is a rather mundane but necessary task. An improper backup makes recovery difficult, if not impossible. Unfortunately, people often realize the extreme importance of this everyday task only after losing business-critical data resulting from a failure of a related system.

The following sections introduce some features used in performing database backup operations. We discuss backup and recovery strategies and options in much greater detail in Chapter 11.

Recovery Manager

Typical kinds of backups include complete database backups (the most common type), tablespace backups, datafile backups, control file backups, and archivelog backups. Oracle8 introduced the Recovery Manager (RMAN) for the server-managed backup and recovery of the database, leveraging a Recovery Catalog stored in the database. RMAN can automatically locate, back up, restore, and recover datafiles, control files, and archived redo logs. Since Oracle9*i*, RMAN can restart backups and restore and implement recovery window policies when backups expire. Oracle Enterprise Manager provides a GUI-based interface to RMAN. Oracle Enterprise Manager 10*g* introduced an improved job scheduler that can be used with RMAN for managing automatic backups to disk.

Incremental backup and recovery

RMAN can perform incremental backups of Enterprise Edition databases. Incremental backups will back up only the blocks modified since the last backup of a datafile, tablespace, or database; thus, they're smaller and faster than complete backups. RMAN can also perform point-in-time recovery, which allows the recovery of data until just prior to an undesirable event (such as the mistaken dropping of a table).

Oracle Secure Backup

Various media-management software vendors leverage Oracle's RMAN, but starting with Oracle Database 10g, the database also includes an entry-level tape storage management solution of its own known as Oracle Secure Backup XE. Optionally, Oracle offers an enterprise-class backup solution simply named Oracle Secure Backup.

Database Availability

Database availability depends upon the reliability and management of the database, the underlying operating system, and the specific hardware components of the system. Oracle has improved availability by reducing backup and recovery times by:

- Providing online and parallel backup and recovery
- Improving the management of online data through range partitioning
- Leveraging hardware capabilities for improved monitoring and failover

The relevant features are described in the following subsections.

Partitioning option

Oracle introduced partitioning as an option with Oracle8 to provide a higher degree of manageability and availability. You can take individual partitions offline for maintenance while other partitions remain available for user access. In data warehousing implementations, partitioning is sometimes used to implement rolling windows based on date ranges. Other partitioning types include hash partitioning (used to divide data into partitions using a hashing function and providing an even distribution of data) and list partitioning (enabling partitioning of data based on discrete values such as geography). Starting with Oracle Database 11g, interval partitioning can also be used to automatically create new fixed ranges as needed during data insertions.

Many of these partitioning types can be used in combination as "composite" partitions. Examples of composite partitions in Oracle Database 11g include range-range, range-hash, range-list, list-range, list-hash, and list-list.

Data Guard

Oracle first introduced a standby database feature in Oracle 7.3. The standby database provides a copy of the production database to be used if the primary database is lost—for example, in the event of primary site failure or during routine maintenance. Primary and standby databases may be geographically separated. The standby database is created from a copy of the production database and updated through the application of archived redo logs generated by the production database. Data Guard, first introduced in Oracle9i, fully automates this process; previously, you had to manually copy and apply the logs. Agents are deployed on both the production and standby database, and a Data Guard Broker coordinates commands. A single Data Guard command invokes the eight steps required for failover.

In addition to providing physical standby database support, Data Guard can create a logical standby database. In this scenario, Oracle archive logs are transformed into SQL transactions and applied to an open standby database.

Oracle Database 10g introduced several new features, including support for real-time application of redo data, integration with the Flashback database feature, and archivelog compression. Starting with Oracle Database 10g, rolling upgrades are supported. As of Oracle Database 11g, the Active Data Guard Opton enables the standby database to be used for queries, sorting, and reporting even as changes from the production system are being applied.

Fail Safe

The Fail Safe feature provides a higher level of reliability for an Oracle database. Failover is implemented through a second system or node that provides access to data residing on a shared disk when the first system or node fails. Oracle Fail Safe for Windows, in combination with Microsoft Cluster Services, provides a failover solution in the event of a system failure.

Fail Safe is primarily a disaster recovery tool, so some downtime does occur as part of a failover operation. The recommended solution for server availability, since Oracle9i, is Real Application Clusters.

Oracle Real Application Clusters

Real Application Clusters (RAC) replaced the Oracle Parallel Server (OPS) option beginning with Oracle9i. RAC can provide failover support as well as increased scalability on Unix, Linux, and Windows clusters. Key to improved scalability was the introduction of Cache Fusion that greatly minimizes the amount of writing to disk that was formerly used to control data locks. Oracle Database 10g introduced a new level of RAC portability and Oracle support by providing integrated "clusterware" for the supported RAC platforms.

With Real Application Clusters, you can deploy multiple Oracle instances on multiple nodes of a clustered solution or in a grid configuration. RAC coordinates traffic among the systems or nodes, allowing the instances to function as a single database. As a result, the database has proven to scale across dozens of nodes. Since the cluster provides a means by which multiple instances can access the same data, the failure of a single instance will not cause extensive delays while the system recovers. You can simply redirect users to another instance that's still operating. Applications can leverage the Oracle Call Interface (OCI) to provide failover to a second instance transparently to the user.

Data Guard and RAC

Data Guard and RAC in combination replaced Parallel Fail Safe beginning with Oracle9i. Data Guard provides automated failover with bounded recovery time in conjunction with Oracle Real Application Clusters. In addition, it provides client rerouting from the failed instance to the instance that is available with fast reconnect and automatically captures diagnostic data.

Automated Storage Management

Oracle Database 10g introduced Automated Storage Management (ASM), which provides optimum striping and mirroring of data for performance and availability. Because ASM is managed through Enterprise Manager, the database administrator now can perform this critical management task. The need to coordinate this activity with a system administrator is thus greatly reduced.

Real Application Testing Option

Oracle Database 11g introduced the capability to rerun production workloads and test system changes through the Real Application Testing Option. This database option includes a Database Replay facility and the SQL Performance Analyzer. Database Replay captures production workload information, including concurrency, dependencies, and timing. It transforms the workload capture files into replay files, provides a Replay Client for processing the replay files, and provides the means to report on performance statistics and any errors that might occur. The SQL Performance Analyzer captures a SQL workload to be analyzed, measures the performance before database changes and afterward, and identifies performance changes among SQL statements.

Database Security Features

Oracle includes basic security for managing user access through roles and privileges. These can be managed through Enterprise Manager on a local basis or on a global basis by leveraging Oracle's enterprise user security, a feature in the Advanced Security Option. We describe Oracle's database security features in Chapter 6.

Database security features allow you to implement a Virtual Private Database (VPD) using Oracle by creating and attaching policies to database tables, views, or synonyms. These policies are then enforced by placing a predicate WHERE clause on SELECT, INSERT, UPDATE, DELETE, and/or INDEX statements.

Many organizations face the need to meet more stringent compliance requirements for improved data protection, although database usage now can extend beyond organizational boundaries. Oracle has added several options to the database to enable secure deployment in such challenging environments. These options include the Advanced Security Option, Label Security Option, Database Vault, and Audit Vault.

Advanced Security Option

The Advanced Security Option was once known as the Advanced Networking Option (ANO). Key features for enabling a more secure Oracle Net include use of encryption services such as RSA Data Security's RC4, the U.S. Data Encryption Stanadard (DES), Triple DES, and the Advanced Encryption Standard (AES). Authentication can be through Kerberos, RADIUS, or the Distributed Computing Environment (DCE). Network data integrity checking uses MD5 or SHA-1. Oracle Database 11g added enhanced transparent data encryption and expanded Kerberos authentication leveraging of Oracle's encryption types.

Label Security Option

Oracle Label Security controls access to data by comparing labels assigned to rows of data with label authorizations granted to users through their privileges. Multiple authorization levels are possible within a single database. Label security authorizations are managed through a Policy Manager. Policies are enforced in the database instead of through views, thus greatly simplifying management of data accessibility and providing a more secure implementation.

Database Vault Option

Oracle Database Vault Option provides fine-grained access control to data for everyone with access to the database, including database administrators. The security administrator can set factors to define access to the database and audit specific dimensions of security. At a more granular level, realms can be defined for limiting access to specific schemas and roles.

Audit Vault Server

Oracle Audit Vault Server monitors database audit tables, redo logs, and operating system audit files for suspicious activities. It can then generate reports or send alerts showing where such unusual activity is occurring.

Oracle Development Tools

Many Oracle tools are available to developers to help them present data and build more sophisticated Oracle database applications. Although this book focuses on the Oracle database, this section briefly describes the main Oracle tools for application development: Oracle JDeveloper, Oracle SQL Developer, and Oracle Developer Suite. The Developer Suite, sometimes referred to as the Oracle Internet Developer Suite, consists of Oracle Forms Developer, Oracle Reports Developer, Oracle Designer, Oracle Discoverer Administrative Edition, and Oracle Portal.

Oracle JDeveloper

Oracle JDeveloper was introduced by Oracle in 1998 to enable the development of basic Java applications without the need to write code. JDeveloper is now available for free and can be downloaded from the Oracle Technology Network. It includes a Data Form wizard, a Beans Express wizard for creating JavaBeans and BeanInfo classes, and a Deployment wizard. JDeveloper includes database development features such as various Oracle drivers, a Connection Editor to hide the JDBC API complexity, database components to bind visual controls, and a SQLJ precompiler for embedding SQL in Java code that you can then use with Oracle. You can also deploy applications developed using JDeveloper to Oracle's Application Server. Although JDeveloper uses wizards to allow programmers to create Java objects without writing code, the end result is generated Java code.

Oracle SQL Developer

Oracle SQL Developer was introduced in 2006 and can be used to connect to any Oracle database dating back to Oracle9i Release 2. SQL Developer can create connections to Oracle databases, browse database objects, create and modify database objects, query and update data, export data and DDL, import data, process commands, and run and create reports. The product's tools support the editing, debugging, and running of PL/SQL scripts. In addition, SQL Developer can be pointed at non-Oracle databases to view their database objects and data, and it provides capabilities to begin a migration to an Oracle database.

SQL Developer is available at no charge and can be downloaded from the Oracle Technology Network. Versions are available for Windows, Linux, and Apple Mac OS X. Oracle also hosts a SQL Developer forum at the Oracle Technology Network site.

Oracle Forms Developer

Oracle Forms Developer is a tool for building forms-based applications and charts for deployment as traditional client/server applications or as three-tier browser-based applications via Oracle Application Server. Developer is a fourth-generation language (4GL). With a 4GL, you define applications by defining values for properties, rather than by writing procedural code. Developer supports a wide variety of clients, including traditional client/server and Java-based clients. The Forms Builder includes a built-in JVM for previewing web applications.

Oracle Reports Developer

Oracle Reports Developer provides a development and deployment environment for rapidly building and publishing web-based reports via Reports for Oracle Application

Server. Data can be formatted in tables, matrices, group reports, graphs, and combinations. High-quality presentation is possible using the HTML extension Cascading Style Sheets (CSS).

Oracle Designer

Oracle Designer provides a graphical interface for Rapid Application Development (RAD) for the entire database development process—from building the business model to schema design, generation, and deployment. Designs and changes are stored in a multiuser repository. The tool can reverse-engineer existing tables and database schemas for reuse and redesign from Oracle and non-Oracle relational databases.

Designer also includes generators for creating applications for Oracle Developer, HTML clients using Oracle Application Server, and C++. Designer can generate applications and reverse-engineer existing applications or applications that have been modified by developers. This capability enables a process called *round-trip engineering*, in which a developer uses Designer to generate an application, modifies the generated application, and reverse-engineers the changes back into the Designer repository.

Oracle Discoverer Administration Edition

Oracle Discoverer Administration Edition enables administrators to set up and maintain the Discoverer End User Layer (EUL) for Oracle's previous generation of business intelligence tools. The purpose of this layer is to shield business analysts using Discoverer as an ad hoc query and analysis tool from SQL complexity. Wizards guide the administrator through the process of building the EUL. In addition, administrators can place limits on resources available to analysts monitored by the Discoverer query governor.

Oracle Portal

Oracle Portal, introduced as WebDB in 1999, provides an HTML-based tool for developing web-enabled applications and content-driven web sites. Portal application systems are developed and deployed in a simple browser environment. Portal includes wizards for developing application components incorporating "servlets" and access to other HTTP web sites. Portals can be designed to be user-customizable and are deployed to the middle-tier Oracle Application Server.

Oracle Portal brought a key enhancement to WebDB, the ability to create and use *portlets*, which allow a single web page to be divided up into different areas that can independently display information and interact with the user. For example, Oracle Answers, Discoverer, and Reports can be accessed as portlets.

Oracle's next generation portal framework product, introduced in 2006, and initially made available as an Application Server option is WebCenter.

Embedded Databases

Although Oracle's database family can be deployed for embedded applications, the footprint and functionality might be more than what you need. Today, Oracle offers other embedded databases including TimesTen, Berkeley DB, and Oracle Database Lite. These database engines have unique code lines in order to provide small footprints and have different intended roles. For this reason, we will describe these briefly in the following subsections but will not explore their capabilities in great detail elsewhere in this book.

Oracle TimesTen

Oracle TimesTen is a relational database that is stored in physical memory and is typically used where very high-performance transaction-processing workloads are present. Access to the TimesTen database is available through SQL, JDBC, JMS, and ODBC. TimesTen databases can be deployed as exclusive or shared and can be created as permanent or temporary.

The database is refreshed by gathering data using TimesTen libraries deployed to applications or by using a Cache Connect option to an Oracle database. Because data is read and updated in memory, average update or read response times are typically measured in the millionths of seconds. The Cache Connect option supports both read and write caching of Oracle database data. Updates can be bidirectional between TimesTen and Oracle.

As is typical for embedded databases, TimesTen requires almost no ongoing administration. Replication is possible from one TimesTen database to another through an option and is, by default, asynchronous.

Oracle Berkeley DB

Oracle Berkeley DB is an extremely small-footprint embedded database engine providing record-level locking. It comes in Java and XML versions. It is designed to be deployed with and run in the same process as your applications. When Berkeley DB is deployed in this manner, no separate database administration is required. Footprints for the database can be as small as 400 KB.

The Java Edition of Berkeley DB supports the Java Transaction API (JTA), J2EE Connector Architecture (JCA), and Java Management Extensions (JMX). The database is a single JAR file that is 820 KB in size and runs in the same Java Virtual Machine (JVM) as the application. A Direct Persistence Layer (DPL) is supported for accessing Java objects.

The XML Edition of Berkeley DB is most commonly used in network-based applications where content is managed. XQuery and XPath are supported.

Both editions can be configured for high availability using replication. Automatic recovery is also supported. Deployment decisions such as these are made by the application designer at application design time.

Oracle Lite

Oracle Lite is a suite of products enabling mobile use of database-centric applications. Key components of Oracle Lite include the Oracle Lite Database, Mobile Development Kit, and Mobile Server (an extension of the Oracle Application Server).

The Oracle Lite Database engine requires a 50KB to 1 MB footprint depending on the platform. Applications written using Mobile SQL, C++, and Java can use the database. ODBC is also supported. Java support includes Java stored procedures and JDBC. The Oracle Lite Database is also designed to be self-tuning and self-administering and is supported on handheld devices running Windows CE, Symbian, Windows, and Linux.

In typical usage of Oracle Lite, the user will link her handheld or mobile device running the Oracle Lite Database to a large-footprint Oracle Database Server. Data is then automatically synchronized between the two systems. The user will then remove the link and work in disconnected mode. After she has performed her tasks, she will relink and resynchronize the data with the Oracle Database Server.

Oracle Lite supports a variety of synchronization capabilities, including the following:

- Bidirectional synchronization between the mobile device and Oracle's larger footprint databases
- Publish-and-subscribe based models
- Support for protocols such as TCP/IP, HTTP, CDPD, 802.1, and HotSync

You can define priority-based replication of subsets of data. Because data distributed to multiple locations can lead to conflicts—such as which location now has the "true" version of the data—automated conflict and resolution is provided. You can also customize the conflict resolution.

The Mobile Server provides a single platform for publishing, deploying, synchronizing, and managing mobile applications. The web-based control center can be used for controlling access to mobile applications. Oracle's former "Web-to-Go" product is also part of the Mobile Server and provides centralized wizard-based application development and deployment.

CHAPTER 2

Oracle Architecture

This chapter focuses on the concepts and structures at the core of the Oracle database. When you understand the architecture of the Oracle server, you'll have a context for understanding the rest of the features of Oracle described in this book.

An Oracle database consists of both physical and logical components. The first section of this chapter covers the difference between an Oracle database and an instance, and subsequent sections describe physical components, the instance, and the data dictionary.

Databases and Instances

Many Oracle practitioners use the terms *instance* and *database* interchangeably. In fact, an instance and a database are different (but related) entities. This distinction is important because it provides insight into Oracle's architecture.

In Oracle, the term *database* refers to the physical storage of information, and the term *instance* refers to the software executing on the server that provides access to the information in the database. The instance runs on the computer or server; the database is stored on the disks attached to the server. Figure 2-1 illustrates this relationship.

The database is *physical*: it consists of files stored on disks. The instance is *logical*: it consists of in-memory structures and processes on the server. For example, Oracle uses an area of shared memory called the System Global Area (SGA) and a private memory area for each process called the Program Global Area (PGA). An instance can be part of one and only one database, although multiple instances can be part of the same database. Instances are temporal, but databases, with proper maintenance, last forever.

Users do not directly access the information in an Oracle database. Instead, they pass requests for information to an Oracle instance.

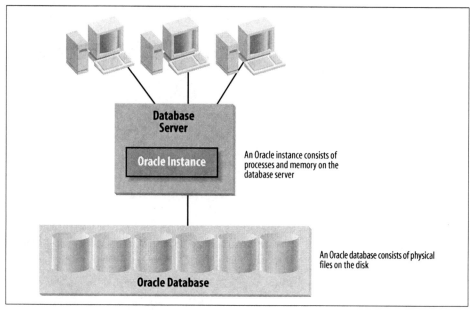

Figure 2-1. An instance and a database

The real world provides a useful analogy for instances and databases. An instance can be thought of as a bridge to the database, which can be thought of as an island. Traffic flows on and off the island via the bridge. If the bridge is closed, the island exists but no traffic flow is possible. In Oracle terms, if the instance is up, data can flow in and out of the database. The physical state of the database is changing. If the instance is down, users cannot access the database even though it still exists physically. The database is static: no changes can occur to it. When the instance comes back into service, the data will be there waiting for it.

Oracle Database Structure

Oracle's database structures include tablespaces, control files, redo log files, archived logs, block change tracking files, Flashback logs, and recovery backup (RMAN) files. This section introduces many of the structures and other components that make up a complete database.

Tablespaces

All of the data stored within an Oracle database must reside in a tablespace. A *tablespace* is a logical structure; you can't look at the operating system and see a tablespace. Each tablespace is composed of physical structures called *datafiles*; each tablespace must consist of one or more datafiles, and each datafile can belong to only one tablespace. When creating a table, you can specify the tablespace in which to create it. Oracle will then find space for it in one of the datafiles that make up the tablespace.

Figure 2-2 shows the relationship of tablespaces to datafiles for a database.

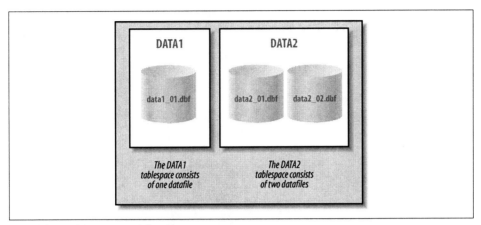

Figure 2-2. Tablespaces and datafiles

This figure shows two tablespaces within an Oracle database. When you create a new table in this Oracle database, you may place it in the DATA1 tablespace or the DATA2 tablespace. It will physically reside in one of the datafiles that make up the specified tablespace.

Oracle's default tablespaces for all types of tables are *locally managed tablespaces* as of Oracle Database 10*g* Release 2. Locally managed tablespaces enable creation of *bigfile tablespaces* that can leverage 64-bit systems and their ability to manage ultra-large files.

Oracle9*i* introduced the concept of Oracle Managed Files (OMFs), which enable your database to automatically create, name, and delete, where appropriate, all the files that make up your database. OMFs reduce the maintenance overhead of naming and tracking the filenames for your database, as well as avoiding the problems that can result from human errors in performing these tasks. Since Oracle Database 10*g*, OMFs and bigfile tablespaces combine to make datafiles appear completely transparent.

Oracle databases can be deployed on up to 64,000 datafiles. Because a bigfile tablespace can contain a file that is 1,024 times larger than a smallfile tablespace, and bigfile tablespaces have 32 KB block sizes on 64-bit operating systems, the Oracle database can grow to up to 8 exabytes in size (an exabyte is equivalent to a million terabytes).[*] The bigfile tablespace is designed for use with Oracle's Automatic Storage Management (ASM), other logical volume managers that support striping, and RAID.[†]

---

[*] The ultimate size of a bigfile depends on the limitations of the underlying operating system.

[†] RAID stands for "redundant array of inexpensive disks" and is described in Chapter 7.

Files of a database

There are actually three fundamental types of physical files that make up an Oracle database:

- Control files
- Datafiles
- Redo log files

These three fundamental types represent the physical database itself. Figure 2-3 illustrates the three types of files and their interrelationships.

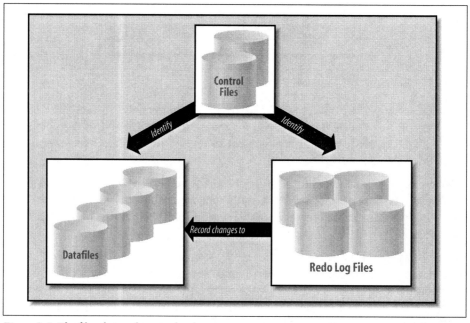

Figure 2-3. The files that make up a database

The control file contains locations for other physical files that form the database: the datafiles and redo log files. It also contains key information about the contents and state of the database, including:

- The name of the database
- When the database was created
- Names and locations of datafiles and redo log files
- Tablespace information
- Datafile offline ranges
- The log history and current log sequence information

- Archived log information
- Backup set, pieces, datafile, and redo log information
- Datafile copy information
- Checkpoint information

In addition to providing fundamental information at startup, control files are also useful when removing a database. Since Oracle Database 10*g*, the DROP DATABASE command can be used to delete the database files listed in the database control file as well as the control file itself.

Database Initialization

At Oracle database instance startup, initialization parameters are read to determine how the database will leverage physical infrastructure and for other key instance configuration information. Initialization parameters are stored in an instance initialization parameter file, often refered to as *INIT.ORA*, or, since Oracle9*i*, in a repository called the server parameter file (or *SPFILE*). The number of initialization parameters that must be specified has been greatly reduced with each Oracle database release. Oracle provides a sample initialization file that can be used at database startup, and the Database Configuraton Assistant (DCA) prompts you for values that must be provided on a custom basis (such as database name).

The set of initialization parameters that must be specified in Oracle Database 11*g* include:

CONTROL_FILES
> The control file locations

DB_NAME
> The local database name

DB_DOMAIN
> The database domain name (such as us.companyname.com)

LOG_ARCHIVE_DEST
> The log archive destination

LOG_ARCHIVE_DEST_STATE
> The parameter that enables log archiving

DB_RECOVERY_FILE_DEST
> The location of the database flash recovery area (directory, filesystem, or ASM disk group)

DB_RECOVERY_FILE_DEST_SIZE
> The database flash recovery area maximum size in total bytes

DB_BLOCK_SIZE
> The database block size in bytes (e.g., 4 KB = 4,096)

PROCESSES
The maximum number of concurrent database operating system processes

SESSIONS
The maximum number of database sessions

OPEN_CURSORS
The maximum number of database open cursors

SHARED_SERVERS
The minimum number of database shared servers

REMOTE_LISTENER
The remote listener name

COMPATIBLE
The database version you want for compatibility where features affect file format (e.g., 11.1.0, 10.0.0)

MEMORY_TARGET
The target memory size that is automatically allocated to SGA and instance PGA components

DDL_LOCK_TIMEOUT
For data definition language (DDL) statements, the time a DDL statement waits for an exclusive lock (in seconds) before failing

NLS_LANGUAGE
The National Language Support (NLS) language specified for the database

NLS_TERRITORY
The National Language Support territory specified for the database

As an example in the shift toward automation, in Oracle Database 11g, the UNDO_MANAGEMENT parameter default is now set to automatic undo management. Undo is used in the rollback of transactions, and for database recovery, read consistency, and flashback features. (Redo records, though, reside in the physical redo logs; they store changes to data segments and undo segment data blocks, and they hold a transaction table of the undo segments.) The undo retention period is now self-tuned by Oracle based on how the undo tablespace is configured.

For your database release, check the documentation regarding optional initialization parameters as these change from release to release. Some of them are described in the following sections.

Deploying Physical Components

This section is not a substitute for Oracle's installation procedures, but it should provide you with some practical guidance as you plan deployment of an Oracle database.

Control Files

A database should have at least two control files on different physical disks. Without a current copy of the control file, you run the risk of losing track of portions of your database. Losing control files is not necessarily fatal—there are ways to rebuild them. However, rebuilding control files can be difficult, introduces risk, and can be easily avoided.

The location of the control files is defined, as previously mentioned, by the CONTROL_FILES initialization parameter. You can specify multiple copies of control files by indicating multiple locations in the CONTROL_FILES parameter for the instance, as illustrated here:

```
control_files = (/u00/oradata/control.001.dbf,
        /u01/oradata/control.002.dbf,
        /u02/oradata/control.003.dbf)
```

This parameter tells the instance where to find the control files. Oracle will ensure that all copies of the control file are kept in sync so all updates to the control files will occur at the same time. If you do not specify this parameter, Oracle will create a control file using a default filename or by leveraging Oracle Managed Files (if enabled).

Many Oracle databases are deployed on some type of redundant disk solution such as RAID-1 or RAID-5 to avoid data loss when a disk fails. (RAID is covered in more detail in Chapter 7.) You might conclude that storing the control file on protected disk storage eliminates the need for maintaining multiple copies of control files and that losing a disk won't mean loss of the control file. But there are two reasons why this is not an appropriate conclusion:

1. If you lose more than one disk in a *striped array* or *mirror-pair*, you will lose the data on those disks. This type of event is statistically rare, but if it does occur, you could be faced with a damaged or lost control file. As you would have your hands full recovering from the multiple disk failures, you would likely prefer to avoid rebuilding control files during the recovery process. Multiplexing your control files, even when each copy is on redundant disk storage, provides an additional level of physical security.

2. Redundant disk storage does nothing to protect you from the perpetual threat of human error. Someone could inadvertently delete or rename a control file, copy another file over it, or move it. A mirrored disk will faithfully mirror these actions, and multiplexed control files will leave you with one or more surviving copies of the control file when one of the copies is damaged or lost.

You do not need to be concerned with additional performance impact when writing to multiple control files. Updates to the control files are insignificant compared to other disk I/O that occurs in an Oracle environment.

Datafiles

Datafiles contain the actual data stored in the database, the tables and indexes that store data, the data dictionary that maintains information about these data structures, and the rollback segments used to implement concurrency.

A datafile is composed of Oracle database blocks that, in turn, are composed of operating system blocks on a disk. Oracle block sizes range from 2 KB to 32 KB. Prior to Oracle9i, only a single block size could be present in the entire database. In versions of the database since the introduction of Oracle9i, you still set a default block size for the database, but you can also have up to five other block sizes in a database (though only a single block size for each tablespace). Figure 2-4 illustrates the relationship of Oracle blocks to operating system blocks.

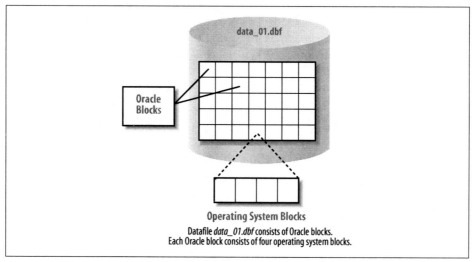

Figure 2-4. Oracle blocks and operating system blocks

Datafiles belong to only one database and to only one tablespace within that database. Data is read in units of Oracle blocks from the datafiles into memory as needed, based on the work users are doing. Blocks of data are written from memory to the datafiles stored on disk as needed to ensure that the database reliably records changes made by users.

Datafiles are the lowest level of granularity between an Oracle database and the operating system. When you lay a database out on the I/O subsystem, the smallest piece you place in any location is a datafile. Tuning the I/O subsystem to improve Oracle performance typically involves moving datafiles from one set of disks to another. Automatic Storage Management, included in Oracle databases since Oracle Database 10g, provides automatic striping and eliminates manual effort in this tuning task.

Setting the Database Block Size

Prior to Oracle9*i*, you set the database block size for an Oracle database at the time you created the database, and you couldn't change it without re-creating the database. Since Oracle9*i*, you have more flexibility, since you can have multiple block sizes in the same database. In all versions, the default block size for the database is set using the DB_BLOCK_SIZE instance initialization parameter.

How do you choose an appropriate block size for an Oracle database? Oracle defaults to a block size based on the operating system used, but understanding the implications of the block size can help you determine a more appropriate setting for your workload.

The block size is the minimum amount of data that can be read or written at one time. In online transaction processing (OLTP) systems, a transaction typically involves a relatively small, well-defined set of rows, such as the rows used for placing an order for a set of products for a specific customer. The access to rows in these types of operations tends to be through indexes, as opposed to through a scan of the entire table. Because of this, having smaller blocks (4 KB) might be appropriate. Oracle won't waste system resources by transferring larger blocks that contain additional data not required by the transaction.

Data warehouses workloads can include reading millions of rows and scans of all the data in a table. For this type of activity, using bigger database blocks enables each block read to deliver more data to the requesting user. To support these types of operations best, data warehouses usually have larger blocks, such as 8 KB or 16 KB. Each I/O operation might take a little longer due to the larger block size, but the reduced number of operations will end up improving overall performance.

Datafile structure

The first block of each datafile is called the *datafile header*. It contains critical information used to maintain the overall integrity of the database. One of the most critical pieces of information in this header is the *checkpoint structure*. This is a logical timestamp that indicates the last point at which changes were written to the datafile. This timestamp is critical during an Oracle recovery process as the timestamp in the header determines which redo logs to apply in bringing the datafile to the current point in time.

Extents and segments

From a physical point of view, a datafile is stored as operating system blocks. From a logical point of view, datafiles have three intermediate organizational levels: data blocks, extents, and segments. An *extent* is a set of data blocks that are contiguous within an Oracle datafile. A *segment* is an object that takes up space in an Oracle database, such as a table or an index that is composed of one or more extents.

When Oracle updates data, it first attempts to update the data in the same data block. If there is not enough room in the data block for the new information, Oracle will write the data to a new data block that could be in a different extent.

For more information on segments and extents and how they affect performance, refer to the section on "Fragmentation and Reorganization" in Chapter 5. This discussion is especially important if you are running an older release of Oracle. Oracle Database 10g added a Segment Advisor that greatly simplifies reclaiming unused space in current database versions.

Redo Log Files

Redo log files contain a "recording" of the changes made to the database as a result of transactions and internal Oracle activities. Since Oracle usually caches changed blocks in memory, when instance failure occurs, some changed blocks might not have been written out to the datafiles. The recording of the changes in the redo logs can be used to play back the changes lost when the failure occurred, thus protecting transactional consistency.

 These files are sometimes confused with rollback buffers supporting concurrency and described in Chapter 8. They are not the same!

In addition, redo log files are used for "undo" operations when a ROLLBACK statement is issued. Uncommitted changes to the database are rolled back to the database image at the last commit.

Suppressing Redo Logging

By default, Oracle logs all changes made to the database. The generation of redo logs adds a certain amount of overhead. You can suppress redo log generation to speed up specific operations, but doing so means the operation in question won't be logged in the redo logs and you will not be able to recover that operation in the event of a failure.

If you do decide to suppress redo logging for certain operations, you would include the NOLOGGING keyword in the SQL statement for the operation. (Note that prior to Oracle8, the keyword was UNRECOVERABLE.) If a failure occurred during the operation, you would need to repeat the operation. For example, you might build an index on a table without generating redo information. In the event that a database failure occurs and the database is recovered, the index will not be re-created because it wasn't logged. You'd simply execute the script originally intended to create the index again.

To simplify operations in the event of a failure, we recommend that you always take a backup after an unlogged operation if you cannot afford to lose the object created by the operation or you cannot repeat the operation for some reason. In addition to using the NOLOGGING keyword in certain commands, you can also mark a table or an entire tablespace with the NOLOGGING attribute. This will suppress redo information for all applicable operations on the table or for all tables in the tablespace.

Multiplexing redo log files

Oracle defines specific terminology to describe how it manages redo logs. Each Oracle instance uses a *thread* of redo to record the changes it makes to the database. A thread of redo is composed of redo log groups, which are composed of one or more redo log members.

Logically, you can think of a redo log group as a single redo log file. However, Oracle allows you to specify multiple copies of a redo log to protect the all-important integrity of the redo log. By creating multiple copies of each redo log file, you protect the redo log file from disk failure and other types of disasters.

Figure 2-5 illustrates a thread of redo with groups and members. The figure shows two members per group, with each redo log mirrored.

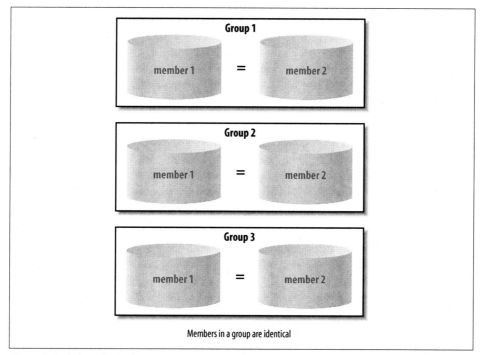

Figure 2-5. A thread of redo

When multiple members are in a redo log group, Oracle maintains multiple copies of the redo log files. The same arguments used for multiplexing of control files apply here. However, though you can rebuild the static part of a control file if you lose it, there is no way to reproduce a lost redo log file. So, be sure to have multiple copies of the redo file. Simple redundant disk protection is not sufficient for cases in which human error results in the corruption or deletion of a redo log file.

Oracle writes *synchronously* to all redo log members. Oracle will wait for confirmation that all copies of the redo log have been successfully updated on disk before the redo write is considered done. If you put one copy on a fast or lightly loaded disk, and one copy on a slower or busier disk, your performance will be constrained by the slower disk. Oracle has to guarantee that all copies of the redo log file have been successfully updated to avoid losing data.

Consider what could happen if Oracle were to write multiple redo logs asynchronously, writing to a primary log and then updating the copies later in the background. If a failure occurs that brings the system down and damages the primary log, Oracle might not have completed updating all the logs. At this point you have committed transactions that are lost—the primary log that recorded the changes made by the transactions is gone, and the copies of the log are not yet up to date with those changes. To prevent this from occurring, Oracle always waits until all copies of the redo log have been updated.

How Oracle uses the redo logs

Once Oracle fills one redo log file, it automatically begins to use the next log file. When the server cycles through all the available redo log files, it returns to the first one and reuses it. Oracle keeps track of the different redo logs by using a redo log sequence number. This sequence number is recorded inside the redo log files as they are used.

To understand the concepts of redo log filenames and redo log sequence numbers, consider three redo log files called *redolog1.log*, *redolog2.log*, and *redolog3.log*. The first time Oracle uses them the redo log sequence numbers for each will be 1, 2, and 3, respectively. When Oracle returns to the first redo log—*redolog1.log*—it will reuse it and assign it a sequence number of 4. When it moves to *redolog2.log*, it will initialize that file with a sequence number of 5.

Remember that the operating system uses the redo log file to identify the physical file, while Oracle uses the redo log file sequence number to determine the order in which the logs were filled and cycled. Because Oracle automatically reuses redo log files, the name of the redo log file is not necessarily indicative of its place in the redo log file sequence.

Figure 2-6 illustrates the filling and cycling of redo logs.

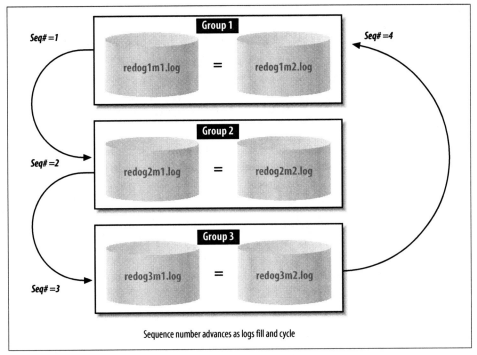

Figure 2-6. Cycling redo logs

Naming conventions for redo logs

The operating system names for the various files that make up a database are very important—at least to humans, who sometimes have to identify these files by their names. If you are not using Oracle Managed Files, you should use naming conventions that capture the purpose and some critical details about the nature of the file. Here's one possible convention for the names of the actual redo log files shown in Figure 2-6:

```
redog1m1.log, redog1m2.log, ...
```

The redo prefix and .log suffixes indicate that this is redo log information. The g1m1 and g1m2 character strings capture the group and member numbers. This convention is only an example; it's best to set conventions that you find meaningful and stick to them.

Archived redo logs

You may be wondering how to avoid losing the critical information in the redo log when Oracle cycles over a previously used redo log.

There are actually two ways to address this. The first is quite simple: you don't avoid losing the information and you suffer the consequences in the event of a failure. You will lose the history stored in the redo file when it is overwritten. If a failure occurs that damages the datafiles, you must restore the entire database to the point in time when the last backup occurred. Since no redo log history exists to reproduce the changes made since the last backup occurred, you will lose the effects of those changes. Very few Oracle shops make this choice, because the inability to recover to the point of failure is unacceptable—it results in lost work.

The second and more practical way to address the issue is to archive the redo logs as they fill. To understand archiving redo logs, you must first understand that there are actually two types of redo logs for Oracle:

Online redo logs
> The operating system files that Oracle cycles through to log the changes made to the database

Archived redo logs
> Copies of the filled online redo logs made to avoid losing redo data as the online redo logs are overwritten

An Oracle database can run in one of two modes with respect to archiving redo logs:

NOARCHIVELOG
> As the name implies, no redo logs are archived. As Oracle cycles through the logs, the filled logs are reinitialized and overwritten, which erases the history of the changes made to the database. This mode essentially has the disadvantage mentioned above, where a failure could lead to unrecoverable data.
>
> Choosing not to archive redo logs significantly reduces your options for database backups, as we'll discuss in Chapter 11, and is not advised by Oracle.

ARCHIVELOG
> When Oracle rolls over to a new redo log, it archives the previous redo log. To prevent gaps in the history, a given redo log cannot be reused until it is successfully archived. The archived redo logs, plus the online redo logs, provide a complete history of all changes made to the database. Together, they allow Oracle to recover all committed transactions up to the exact time a failure occurred. Operating in this mode enables tablespace and datafile backups.

The internal sequence numbers discussed earlier act as the guide for Oracle while it is using redo logs and archived redo logs to restore a database.

ARCHIVELOG mode and automatic archiving

Starting with Oracle Database 10g, automatic archiving for an Oracle database is enabled with the following SQL command:

```
ALTER DATABASE ARCHIVELOG
```

If the database is in ARCHIVELOG mode, Oracle marks the redo logs for archiving as it fills them. The full log files must be archived before they can be reused. The ALTER DATABASE ARCHIVELOG command will by default turn on automatic archiving and the archivers are started.

Prior to Oracle Database 10g, log files marked as ready for archiving did not mean they would be automatically archived. You also needed to set a parameter in the initialization file with the syntax:

```
LOG_ARCHIVE_START = TRUE
```

Setting this parameter started an Oracle process to copy a full redo log to the archive log destination.

The archive log destination and the format for the archived redo log names are specified using two additional parameters, LOG_ARCHIVE_DEST and LOG_ARCHIVE_FORMAT. A setting such as the following:

```
LOG_ARCHIVE_DEST = C:\ORANT\DATABASE\ARCHIVE
```

specifies the directory to which Oracle writes the archived redo log files, and:

```
LOG_ARCHIVE_FORMAT = ORCL%t_%s_%r.arc
```

defines the format Oracle will use for the archived redo log filenames. In this case, the filenames will begin with ORCL and will end with .arc. The parameters for the format wildcards are:

%t
> Include thread number as part of the filename

%s
> Include log sequence number as part of the filename

%r
> Include resetlogs ID as part of the filename

If you want the archived redo log filenames to include the thread number, log sequence number and resetlogs ID with the numbers zero-padded, capitalize the parameters and set:

```
LOG_ARCHIVE_FORMAT = "ORCL%T_%S_%R.arc"
```

Since the initialization file is read when an Oracle instance is started, changes to these parameters do not take effect until an instance is stopped and restarted. Remember, though, that turning on automatic archiving does not put the database in ARCHIVELOG mode. Similarly, placing the database in ARCHIVELOG mode does not enable the automatic archiving process.

You should also make sure that the archive log destination has enough room for the logs Oracle will automatically write to it. If the archive log file destination is full, Oracle will hang since it can't archive additional redo log files.

Figure 2-7 illustrates redo log use with archiving enabled.

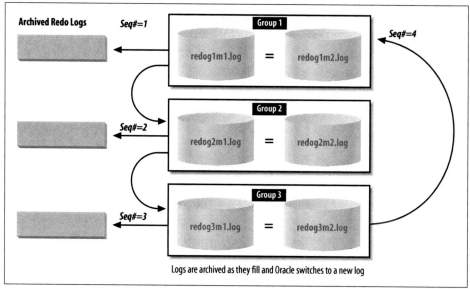

Figure 2-7. Cycling redo logs with archiving

The archived redo logs are critical for database recovery. Just as you can duplex the online redo logs, you can also specify multiple archive log destinations. Oracle will copy filled redo logs to specified destinations. You can also specify whether all copies must succeed or not. The initialization parameters for this functionality are as follows:

LOG_ARCHIVE_DUPLEX_DEST
> Specifies an additional location for redundant redo logs.

LOG_ARCHIVE_MIN_SUCCEED_DEST
> Indicates whether the redo log must be successfully written to one or all of the locations. Valid values are 1 through 10 if multiplexing and 1 or 2 if duplexing.

See your Oracle documentation for the additional parameters and views that enable and control this functionality.

Instance Memory and Processes

An Oracle instance can be defined as an area of shared memory and a collection of background processes. The area of shared memory for an instance is called the *System Global Area,* or SGA. The SGA is not really one large undifferentiated section of memory—it's made up of various components that we'll examine in the next section. All the processes of an instance—system processes and user processes—share the SGA.

Prior to Oracle9i, the size of the SGA was set when the Oracle instance was started. The only way to change the size of the SGA or any of its components was to change the initialization parameter and then stop and restart the instance. Since Oracle9i, you can also change the size of the SGA or its components while the Oracle instance is running. Oracle9i also introduced the concept of the *granule*, which is the smallest amount of memory that you can add to or subtract from the SGA.

Oracle Database 10g introduced Automatic Shared Memory Management, while Oracle Database 11g added Automatic Memory Management for the SGA and PGA instance components. Whenever the MEMORY_TARGET (new to Oracle Database 11g) or SGA_TARGET initialization parameter is set, the database automatically distributes the memory among various SGA components providing optimal memory management. The shared memory components automatically sized include the shared pool (manually set using SHARED_POOL_SIZE), the large pool (LARGE_POOL_SIZE), the Java pool (JAVA_POOL_SIZE), the buffer cache (DB_CACHE_SIZE), and the streams pool (STREAMS_POOL_SIZE). Automatic memory management initialization parameters can be set through Oracle Enterprise Manager.

The background processes interact with the operating system and each other to manage the memory structures for the instance. These processes also manage the actual database on disk and perform general housekeeping for the instance.

Figure 2-8 illustrates the memory structures and background processes discussed in the following section.

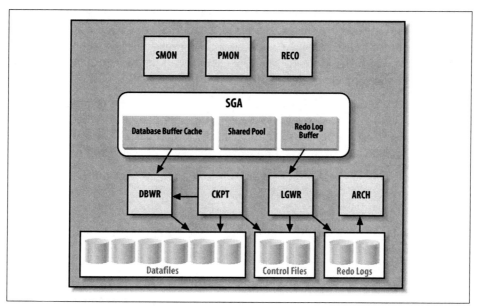

Figure 2-8. An Oracle instance

Additional background processes may exist when you use certain other features of the database: for example, shared servers (formerly the Multi-Threaded Server or MTS prior to Oracle9i), or job queues and replication.

Memory Structures for an Instance

As shown in Figure 2-8, the System Global Area is composed of multiple areas. These include a database buffer cache, a shared pool, and a redo log buffer as shown in the figure, and also possibly a Java pool, a large pool, and a Streams pool. The following sections describe these areas of the SGA. For a more detailed discussion of performance and the SGA, see "How Oracle Uses the System Global Area" in Chapter 7.

Database buffer cache

The database buffer cache holds blocks of data retrieved from the database. This buffer between the users' requests and the actual datafiles improves the performance of the Oracle database. If a piece of data can be found in the buffer cache (for example, as the result of a recent query), you can retrieve it from memory without the overhead of having to go to disk. Oracle manages the cache using a *least recently used* (LRU) algorithm. If a user requests data that has been recently used, the data is more likely to be in the database buffer cache; data in the cache can be delivered immediately without a disk-read operation being executed.

When a user wants to read a block that is not in the cache, the block must be read and loaded into the cache. When a user makes changes to a block, those changes are made to the block in the cache. At some later time, those changes will be written to the datafile in which the block resides. This avoids making users wait while Oracle writes their changed blocks to disk.

This notion of waiting to perform I/O until absolutely necessary is common throughout Oracle. Disks are the slowest component of a computer system, so the less I/O performed, the faster the system runs. By deferring noncritical I/O operations instead of performing them immediately, an Oracle database can deliver better performance.

Since Oracle8, the database buffer cache can be configured with buffer pools of the following types:

DEFAULT
    The standard Oracle database buffer cache. All objects use this cache unless otherwise indicated.

KEEP
    For frequently used objects you wish to cache.

RECYCLE
    For objects you're less likely to access again.

Both the KEEP and RECYCLE buffer pools remove their objects from consideration by the LRU algorithm.

You can mark a table or index for caching in a specific buffer pool. This helps to keep more desirable objects in the cache and avoids the "churn" of all objects fighting for space in one central cache. Of course, to use these features properly you must be aware of the access patterns for the various objects used by your application.

Oracle Database 10g simplifed management of buffer cache size by introducing a new dynamic parameter, DB_CACHE_SIZE. This parameter can be used to specify cache memory size and replaced the DB_BLOCK_BUFFERS parameter present in previous Oracle releases. DB_CACHE_SIZE is automatically sized if MEMORY_TARGET or SGA_TARGET is set. Other initialization parameters include DB_KEEP_CACHE_SIZE and DB_RECYCLE_CACHE_SIZE and these must be manually sized if used.

Shared pool

The shared pool caches various constructs that can be shared among users. For example, SQL queries and query fragments issued by users and results are cached so they can be reused if the same statement is submitted again. PL/SQL functions are also loaded into the shared pool for execution and the functions and results are cached, again using an LRU algorithm. As of Oracle Database 11g, a PL/SQL function can be marked in such a way that its result will be cached to allow lookup rather than recalculation when it is called again using the same parameters. The shared pool is also used for caching information from the Oracle data dictionary, which is the metadata that describes the structure and content of the database itself.

You can specify a SHARED_POOL_SIZE initialization parameter, or it will be automatically sized if MEMORY_TARGET or SGA_TARGET is specified. Note that prior to Oracle Database 10g, "out of memory" errors were possible if the shared pool was undersized, but current Oracle database releases now can leverage automatic shared memory tuning.

Redo log buffer

The redo log buffer caches redo information until it is written to the physical redo log files stored on a disk. This buffer also improves performance. Oracle caches the redo until it can be written to a disk at a more optimal time, which avoids the overhead of constantly writing the redo logs to disk.

Other pools in the SGA

The SGA includes several other pools:

Large pool
> Provides memory allocation for various I/O server processes, backup, and recovery, and provides session memory where shared servers and Oracle XA for transaction processing are used.

Java pool
> Provides memory allocation for Java objects and Java execution, including data in the Java Virtual Machine in the database.

Streams pool
> Provides memory allocation used to buffer Oracle Streams queued messages in the SGA instead of in database tables and provides memory for capture and apply.

Dynamic initialization parameters available for these pools include LARGE_POOL_SIZE, JAVA_POOL_SIZE, and STREAMS_POOL_SIZE. These are automatically set if MEMORY_TARGET or SGA_TARGET is specified.

Automatic PGA management

Oracle automatically manages the memory allocated to an instance Program Global Area (PGA). The PGA consists of session memory and a private SQL area. The memory amount can be controlled by setting the PGA_AGGREGATE_TARGET initialization parameter. Automatic PGA management, available since Oracle Database 10g, greatly simplified management of SQL work areas and eliminated the need to set several different initialization parameters that previously existed. As of Oracle Database 11g, PGA memory allocation is automatically tuned along with the SGA memory allocations by setting MEMORY_TARGET.

Background Processes for an Instance

The most common background processes are shown in Figure 2-8 and vary from Oracle release to release. Among the background processes in Oracle Database 11g are the following:

Database Writer (DBWn)
> Writes database blocks from the database buffer cache in the SGA to the datafiles on disk. An Oracle instance can have up to 20 DBW processes to handle the I/O load to multiple datafiles—hence the notation DBWn. Most instances run one DBW. DBW writes blocks out of the cache for two main reasons:
>
> - If Oracle needs to perform a checkpoint (i.e., to update the blocks of the datafiles so that they "catch up" to the redo logs). Oracle writes the redo for a transaction when it's committed, and later writes the actual blocks. Periodically, Oracle performs a checkpoint to bring the datafile contents in line with the redo that was written out for the committed transactions.
>
> - If Oracle needs to read blocks requested by users into the cache and there is no free space in the buffer cache. The blocks written out are the least recently used blocks. Writing blocks in this order minimizes the performance impact of losing them from the buffer cache.

Log Writer (LGWR)

Writes the redo information from the log buffer in the SGA to all copies of the current redo log file on disk. As transactions proceed, the associated redo information is stored in the redo log buffer in the SGA. When a transaction is committed, Oracle makes the redo information permanent by invoking the Log Writer to write it to disk.

System Monitor (SMON)

Maintains overall health and safety for an Oracle instance. SMON performs crash recovery when the instance is started after a failure and coordinates and performs recovery for a failed instance when you have more than one instance accessing the same database, as with Real Application Clusters. SMON also cleans up adjacent pieces of free space in the datafiles by merging them into one piece and gets rid of space used for sorting rows when that space is no longer needed.

Process Monitor (PMON)

Watches over the user processes that access the database. If a user process terminates abnormally, PMON is responsible for cleaning up any of the resources left behind (such as memory) and for releasing any locks held by the failed process.

Archiver (ARCn)

Reads the redo log files once Oracle has filled them and writes a copy of the used redo log files to the specified archive log destination(s).

Up to 10 Archiver processes are possible—hence the notation ARCn. LGWR will start additional Archivers as needed, based on the load, up to a limit specified by the initialization parameter LOG_ARCHIVE_MAX_PROCESSES. By default, this initialization parameter has a default value of 2 and is rarely changed.

Checkpoint (CKPT)

Updates datafile headers whenever a checkpoint is performed.

Recover (RECO)

Automatically cleans up failed or suspended distributed transactions.

Dispatcher

Optional background processes used when shared server configurations are deployed.

Global Cache Service (LMS)

Manages resources for Real Application Clusters and interinstance resource control.

Job Queue

Provides a scheduler service used to schedule user PL/SQL statements or procedures in batch.

Queue Monitor (QMNn)
> Monitors Oracle Streams message queues with up to 10 monitoring processes supported.

Automatic Storage Management (ASM) processes
> RBAL coordinates rebalancing of activities for disk groups. ORB*n* performs the actual rebalancing. ASMB provides communication between the database and the ASM instance.

Processes or Threads?

With all this talk about processes, you may be wondering whether Oracle actually uses threads or processes in the underlying operating system to implement these services.

For simplicity, throughout this book we use the term *process* generically to indicate a function that Oracle performs, such as DBW or LGWR. For Oracle on Windows, each "Oracle process" is a *thread* within a process. For Oracle on Unix, the "processes" are more commonly actual operating system processes, not threads. Thus, on Unix DBW and LGWR are specific operating system processes, while on Windows they are threads within a single process.

There are some exceptions, however, and how the database is implemented at this level of detail can be both database version and operating system dependent. In the final analysis, Oracle makes this issue largely unimportant to users and administrators, as database management using Enterprise Manager is consistent regardless of platform.

The Data Dictionary

Each Oracle database includes a set of *metadata* that describes the data structure including table definitions and integrity constraints. The tables and views that hold this metadata are referred to as the Oracle *data dictionary*. All of the components discussed in this chapter have corresponding system tables and views in the data dictionary that fully describe the characteristics of the component. You can query these tables and views using standard SQL statements. Table 2-1 shows where you can find some of the information available about each of the components in the data dictionary.

The SYSTEM tablespace always contains the data dictionary tables. Data dictionary tables that are preceded by the V$ or GV$ prefixes are dynamic tables, which are continually updated to reflect the current state of the Oracle database. Static data dictionary tables can have a prefix such as DBA_, ALL_, or USER_ to indicate the scope of the objects listed in the view.

Table 2-1. Partial list of database components and their related data dictionary views

Component	Data dictionary tables and views
Database	V$DATABASE, V$VERSION, V$INSTANCE
Shared server	V$QUEUE, V$DISPATCHER, V$SHARED_SERVER
Connection pooling	DBA_CPOOL_INFO, V$CPOOL_STAT, V$CPOOL_CC_STATS
Tablespaces	USER_FREE_SPACE, DBA_FREE_SPACE, V$TEMPFILE, DBA_USERS, DBA_TS_QUOTAS
Control files	V$CONTROLFILE, V$PARAMETER, V$CONTROLFILE_RECORD_SECTION
Datafiles	V$DATAFILE, V$DATAFILE_HEADER, DBA_DATA_FILES, DBA_EXTENTS, USER_EXTENTS
Segments	DBA_SEGMENTS, USER_SEGMENTS
Extents	DBA_EXTENTS, USER_EXTENTS
Redo logs	V$THREAD, V$LOG, V$LOGFILE, V$LOG_HISTORY
Undo	V$UNDOSTAT, V$ROLLSTAT, V$TRANSACTION
Archiving status	V$DATABASE, V$LOG, V$ARCHIVED_LOG, V$ARCHIVE_DEST
Database instance	V$INSTANCE, V$PARAMETER, V$SYSTEM_PARAMETER
Memory structure	VSGA, VSGASTAT, V$SGAINFO, V$SGA_DYNAMIC_COMPONENTS, V$SGA_DYNAMIC_FREE_MEMORY, VSGA_RESIZE_OPS, VSGA_RESIZE_CURRENT_OPS, V$MEMORY_TARGET_ADVICE, V$SGA_TARGET_ADVICE, V$PGA_TARGET_ADVICE
Work area memory	V$PGASTAT, V$SYSSTAT
Processes	V$PROCESS, V$BGPROCESS, V$SESSION
Alerting	DBA_THRESHOLDS, DBA_OUTSTANDING_ALERTS, DBA_ALERT_HISTORY, V$ALERT_TYPES, V$METRIC
Performance monitoring	V$LOCK, DBA_LOCK, V$SESSION_WAIT, V$SQLAREA, V$LATCH
RMAN recovery	V$RECOVER_FILE
User passwords	V$PWFILE_USERS
Tables	DBA_TABLES, ALL_TABLES, USER_TABLES
Indexes	DBA_INDEXES, ALL_INDEXES, USER_INDEXES
Data dictionary	DBA_OBJECTS, ALL_OBJECTS, USER_OBJECTS

CHAPTER 3
Installing and Running Oracle

If you've been reading this book sequentially, you should understand the basics of the Oracle database architecture by now. This chapter begins with a description of how to install a database and get it up and running. (If you've already installed your Oracle database software, you can skim through this first section.) We'll describe how to create an actual database and how to configure the network software needed to run Oracle. Finally, we'll discuss how users access databases and begin a discussion of how to manage databases—a topic that will be continued in subsequent chapters.

Installing Oracle

Prior to Oracle8*i*, the Oracle installer came in both character and GUI versions for Unix. The Unix GUI ran in Motif using the X Windows system. Windows NT came with a GUI version only. Since Oracle8*i*, the installer has been Java-based.

The Oracle installer is one of the first places in which you can see the benefits of the portability of Java; the installer looks and functions the same way across all operating systems. For some time now, installing Oracle has been quite simple, requiring only a few mouse clicks and answers to some questions about options and features.

Oracle made great strides in further simplifying installation with Oracle Database 10*g*. Both that install and the installation of Oracle Database 11*g* can be accomplished in less than 20 minutes. Figure 3-1 shows a version of the launch screen of the installer for Oracle Database 10*g*.

The current version of the Oracle Universal Installer begins the process by checking the target environment to make sure there are enough resources for the Oracle database. If the target is a bit light, you will be informed with a warning and given the option to continue.

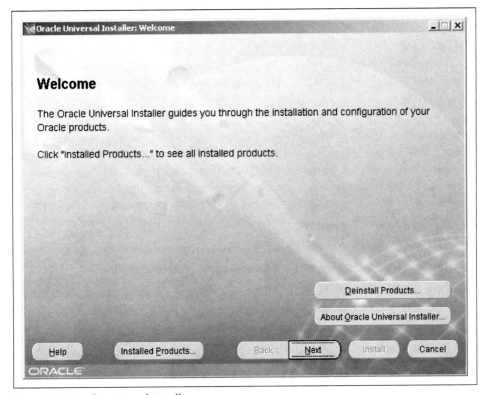

Figure 3-1. Oracle Universal Installer

As part of the installation process, the Installer also runs the Net Configuration Assistant and the Database Configuration Assistant so that you will end up with a working Oracle instance when the process is complete.

If, for some reason, the installation fails, the commands that did not succeed are listed in a log file, which helps you understand where the problem may lie and gives you a handy set of commands you can run yourself once the problem is fixed.

Although the installation process is now the same for all platforms, there are still particulars about the installation of Oracle that relate to specific platforms. Each release of the Oracle Database Server software is shipped with its own set of documentation. Included in each release are an installation guide, release notes (which include installation information added after the installation guide was published), and a "getting started" book. You should read all of these documents prior to starting the installation process, since each of them contains invaluable information about the specifics of the installation. You will need to consider details such as where to establish the Oracle Home directory and where database files will reside. These issues are covered in detail in the documentation. In addition to the hardcopy documentation, online documentation is shipped on the database server media, and this provides additional information regarding the database and related products.

You'll typically find the installation guide in the server software CD case. The installation guide includes system requirements (memory and disk), preinstallation tasks, directions for running the installation, and notes regarding migration of earlier Oracle databases to the current release. You should remember that complete installation of the software includes not only loading the software, but also configuring and starting key services.

One of the more important decisions you needed to make before actually installing Oracle in older releases concerned the directory structure and naming conventions you would follow for the files that make up a database. Clear, consistent, and well-planned conventions were crucial for minimizing human errors in system and database administration. Today, this naming is largely automated during the installation process. Some of the more important database naming that takes place includes the following:

- Disk or mount point names
- Directory structures for Oracle software and database files
- Database filenames: control files, database files, and redo log files

The Optimal Flexible Architecture (OFA), described in the next section, became the basis for naming conventions for all of these files.

Optimal Flexible Architecture

Oracle consultants working at large Oracle sites created (out of necessity) a comprehensive set of standards for database directory structures and filenames prior to Oracle's introduction of more automated installation procedures. This set of standards is called *An Optimal Flexible Architecture for a Growing Oracle Database* or, as it is lovingly known in the Oracle community, the OFA. For example, the OFA provides a clear set of standards for handling multiple databases and multiple versions of Oracle if deployed on the same machine. It includes recommendations for mount points, directory structures, filenames, and scripting techniques. Anyone who knows the OFA can navigate an Oracle environment to quickly find the software and files used for the database and the instance. This standardization increased productivity and avoided errors.

Since Oracle7 releases, the OFA standards are embedded in the Oracle installer. System administrators and database administrators working with Oracle will find understanding the OFA worthwhile, even if your Oracle system is already installed. OFA documentation is included in the Oracle installation guide.

Supporting Multiple Oracle Versions on a Machine

You can install and run multiple versions of Oracle on a single-server machine. All Oracle products use a directory referred to by the environment or system variable ORACLE_HOME to find the base directory for the software they will use. Because of this, you can run multiple versions of Oracle software on the same server, each with a different ORACLE_HOME variable defined. Whenever a piece of software accesses a particular version of Oracle, the software simply uses the proper setting for the ORACLE_HOME environment variable.

Oracle supports multiple ORACLE_HOME variables on Unix and Windows systems by using different directories. The OFA provides clear and excellent standards for this type of implementation.

Upgrading an Oracle Database

Oracle Database 10g added two additional features that apply to upgrading an existing Oracle database: the Database Upgrade Assistant and support for rolling upgrades.

If you want to upgrade a single instance, you can use the Database Upgrade Assistant, which can be started from the Oracle Universal Installer. As of Oracle Database 11g, you can upgrade from the free version of Oracle, Oracle XE, to a single instance with the Database Upgrade Assistant.

One of the longstanding problems with upgrades has been the requirement to bring down the database, upgrade the database software, and then restart the database. This necessary downtime can impinge on your operational requirements. If you are using a Real Application Clusters implementation since Oracle Database 10g, you can perform a *rolling upgrade*. A rolling upgrade allows you to bring down some of the nodes of the cluster, upgrade their software, and then bring them back online as part of the cluster. You can then repeat this procedure with the other nodes. The end result is that you can achieve a complete upgrade of your Oracle database software without having to bring down the database.

Creating a Database

As we noted in Chapter 2, Oracle might be installed for a variety of workloads. You should take a two-step approach for any new databases you create. First, understand the purpose of the database, and then create the database with the appropriate parameters.

Planning the Database

As with installing the Oracle software, you should spend some time learning the purpose of an Oracle database before you create the database itself. Consider what the database will be used for and how much data it will contain. You should understand the underlying hardware that you'll use—the number and type of CPUs, the amount of memory, the number of disks, the controllers for the disks, and so on. Because the database is stored on the disks, many tuning problems can be avoided with proper capacity and I/O subsystem planning.

Planning your database and the supporting hardware requires insights into the scale or size of the workload and the type of work the system will perform. Some of the considerations that will affect your database design and hardware configuration include the following:

How many users will the database have?
> How many users will connect simultaneously and how many will concurrently perform transactions or execute queries?

Is the database supporting OLTP applications or data warehousing?
> This distinction leads to different types and volumes of activity on the database server. For example, online transaction processing (OLTP) systems usually have a larger number of users performing smaller transactions, while data warehouses usually have a smaller number of users performing larger queries.

What are the expected size and number of database objects?
> How large will these objects be initially and what growth rates do you expect?

What are the access patterns for the various database objects?
> Some objects will be more popular than others. Understanding the volume and type of activity in the database is critical to planning and tuning your database. Some people employ a so-called *CRUD matrix* that contains Create, Read, Update, and Delete indicators, or even estimates for how many operations will be performed for each key object used by a business transaction. These estimates may be per minute, per hour, per day, or for whatever time period makes sense in the context of your system. For example, the CRUD matrix for a simple employee update transaction might be as shown in Table 3-1, with the checkmarks indicating that each transaction performs the operation against the object shown.

Table 3-1. Access patterns for database objects

Object	Create	Read	Update	Delete
EMP	✓	✓		
DEPT		✓		
SALARY		✓	✓	

How much hardware do I have now, and how much will I add as the database grows?
> Disk drives tend to get cheaper and cheaper. Suppose you're planning a database of 100 GB that you expect to grow to 300 GB over the next two years. You may have all the disk space available to plan for the 300 GB target, but it's more likely that you'll buy a smaller amount to get started and add disks as the database grows. It's important that you plan the initial layout with the expected growth in mind.
>
> Prior to Oracle9*i*, running out of tablespace in the middle of a batch operation meant that the entire operation had to be rolled back. Oracle9*i* introduced the

concept of *resumable space allocation*. When an operation encounters an out-of-space condition, if the resumable statement option has been enabled for the session, the operation is suspended for a specific length of time, which allows the operator to correct the out-of-space condition. You even have the option to create an AFTER SUSPEND trigger to fire when an operation has been suspended.

With Automatic Storage Management (ASM), introduced in Oracle Database 10g, you can add additional disk space or take away disks without interrupting database service. Although you should still carefully estimate storage requirements, the penalty for an incorrect judgment, in terms of database downtime, is significantly reduced with ASM.

What are the availability requirements?

What elements of redundancy, such as additional disk drives, do you need to provide the required availability? ASM also provides automatic mirroring for data, which can help to provide data resiliency.

What are my performance requirements?

What response times do your users expect, and how much of that time can you give them? Will you measure performance in terms of average response time, maximum response time, response time at peak load, total throughput, or average load?

What are my security requirements?

Will the application, the operating system, or the Oracle database (or some combination of these) enforce security?

The Value of Estimating

Even if you are unsure of things such as sizing and usage details, take your best guess as to initial values and growth rates and document these estimates. As the database evolves, you can compare your initial estimates with emerging information to react and plan more effectively. For example, suppose you estimate that a certain table will be 5 GB in size initially and will grow at 3 GB per year, but when you are up and running you discover that the table is actually 3 GB, and six months into production you discover that it has grown to 8 GB. You can now revise your plans to reflect the higher growth rate and thereby avoid space problems. Comparing production measures of database size, growth, and usage patterns with your initial estimates will provide valuable insights to help you avoid problems as you move forward. In this way, documented guesses at an early stage are useful later on.

The same is true for key requirements such as availability and performance. If the exact requirements are not clear, make some assumptions and document them. These core requirements will heavily influence the decisions you make regarding redundancy and capacity. As the system evolves and these requirements become clearer, the history of these key decision criteria will be crucial in understanding the choices that you made and will make in the future.

The Automatic Workload Repository (AWR), first available in Oracle Database 10g, maintains a history of workload and performance measurements, which are used by the Automatic Database Diagnostic Monitor (ADDM) to spot performance anomalies. You can also use AWR to track ongoing changes in workload.

Tools for Creating Databases

There are two basic ways to create an Oracle database:

- Use the GUI Oracle Database Configuration Assistant.
- Run character-mode scripts.

Oracle ships with a GUI utility called the Oracle Database Configuration Assistant, which can be run standalone or from the Oracle Installer. It is written in Java and therefore provides the same look and feel across platforms. The Assistant is a quick and easy way to create, modify, or delete a database. It allows you to create a typical preconfigured database (with minimal input required) or a custom database (which involves making some choices and answering additional questions). The Database Configuration Assistant is typically initially accessed as part of a standard installer session. The Assistant is shown in Figure 3-2.

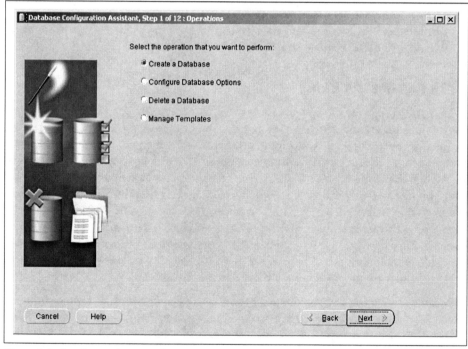

Figure 3-2. Oracle Database Configuration Assistant

If you choose to create a database, you can then select the type of database you want to create, as shown in Figure 3-3 for Oracle Database 11g. The different types of databases will be created with different default configuration values.

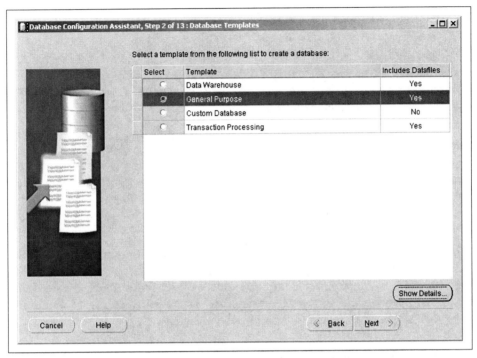

Figure 3-3. *Selecting a database to create*

The alternative method for creating a database is to create or edit an existing SQL script that executes the various required commands. Most Oracle DBAs have a preferred script that they edit as needed. In Oracle7 and Oracle8, you executed the script using a character-mode utility called Server Manager; since Oracle8i, you could use SQL*Plus. The Oracle software CD-ROM also includes a sample script called *BUILD_DB.SQL*, described in the Oracle documentation. Today, most users choose to create the database with the standard installer interface.

Configuring Oracle Net

Oracle Net (known as Net8 for Oracle8 and Oracle8i and SQL*Net prior to Oracle8) is a layer of software that allows different physical machines to communicate for the purpose of accessing an Oracle database.

The name Net8 was changed to Oracle Net in Oracle9*i*, and we will generally use "Oracle Net" in this chapter as a neutral term to apply to all versions of Oracle networking. The term "Oracle Net Services" in Oracle refers to all the components of Oracle Net, including dispatchers, listeners, and shared servers; these are explained later in this chapter.

A version of Oracle Net runs on the client machine and on the database server, and allows clients and servers to communicate over a network using virtually any popular network protocol. Oracle Net can also perform network protocol interchanges. For example, it allows clients that are speaking LU 6.2 to interact with database servers that are speaking TCP/IP.

Oracle Net also provides *location transparency*—that is, the client application does not need to know the server's physical location. The Oracle Net layer handles the communications, which means that you can move the database to another machine and simply update the Oracle Net configuration details accordingly. The client applications will still be able to reach the database, and no application changes will be required.

Oracle Net supports the notion of *service names*, or *aliases*. Clients provide a service name or Oracle Net alias to specify which database they want to reach without having to identify the actual machine or instance for the database. Oracle Net looks up the actual machine and the Oracle instance, using the provided service name, and transparently routes the client to the appropriate database.

Resolving Oracle Net Service Names

The following Oracle Net configuration options resolve the service name the client specifies into the host and instance names needed to reach an Oracle database:

Local name resolution
> For local name resolution, you install a file called *TNSNAMES.ORA* on each client machine that contains entries that provide the host and Oracle instance for each Oracle Net alias. You must maintain this file on the client machines if any changes are made to the underlying database locations. Your network topology is almost certain to change over time, so use of this option can lead to an increased maintenance load. If you are using Oracle Internet Directory, described later in this section, you do not need a *TNSNAMES.ORA* file.

Oracle Names service
> Oracle Names was supported in earlier Oracle releases, providing a way to eliminate the need for a *TNSNAMES.ORA* file on each client. That was the good part. The bad part was that Oracle Names was a proprietary solution. Since Oracle Internet Directory is based on standards and provides this functionality, Oracle declared Oracle Names obsolete after the Oracle9*i* release.

Oracle Internet Directory

The need for a centralized naming service extends far beyond the Oracle environment. In fact, there is a well-defined standard for accessing this type of information, the Lightweight Directory Access Protocol (LDAP). As of the Oracle Database 11g release, Oracle Internet Directory (OID) is a part of Fusion Middleware, which is described in Chapter 15. OID is an LDAP-enabled directory that can fulfill the same role as the previously available Oracle Names service. The OID is also used for a variety of other purposes, such as enabling single sign-on for the Oracle Application Server Portal product, also described in Chapter 15. Since Oracle Database 10g, you can export directory entries to create a local *TNSNAMES.ORA* file; this file may be used for clients not using the directory or if the directory is unavailable.

Host naming

Clients can simply use the name of the host on which the instance runs. This is valid for TCP/IP networks with a mechanism in place for resolving the hostname into an IP address. For example, the Domain Name Service (DNS) translates a hostname into an IP address, much as Oracle Names translates service names. Since Oracle Database 10g, you can use this method with either a host name, domain-qualified if appropriate, or a TCP/IP address, but the connection will not support advanced services such as connection pooling.

Third-party naming services

Oracle Net can interface with external or third-party naming and authentication services such as Kerberos or Radius. Use of such services may require Oracle Advanced Security (known as the Advanced Networking Option prior to Oracle8i).

These name resolution options are not mutually exclusive. For example, you can use Oracle Internet Directory and local name resolution (*TNSNAMES.ORA* files) together. In this case, you specify the order Oracle should use in resolving names in the *SQLNET.ORA* file (for example, check OID first, and if the service name isn't resolved, check the local *TNSNAMES.ORA* file). This is useful for cases in which there are corporate database services specific to certain clients. You would use OID for the standard corporate database services, such as email, and then use *TNSNAMES.ORA* entries for the client-specific database services, such as a particular development database.

You also have the option to connect directly to an Oracle database with what Oracle refers to as the *easy connect naming method*. This method uses the host name or TCP/IP identifier for the Oracle server machine and the name of the Oracle database instance. The method is limited to use with TCP/IP networks, and is recommended only for fairly small installations where the host identifier is rarely changed.

Oracle Net Manager

In Oracle8, Oracle provided a GUI utility called the Net8 Assistant used to create the various configuration files required for Net8; this utility was renamed the Oracle Net Manager with the Oracle9i release.

Like the Database Configuration Assistant, the Oracle Net Manager is written in Java, provides the same look and feel across platforms, and is typically first accessed from the installer. The Oracle Net configuration files have a very specific syntax with multiple levels of nested brackets. Using the Oracle Net Manager allows you to avoid the errors that are common to hand-coded files. This utility, which automates the configuration of various Oracle Net components, is shown in Figure 3-4 as it appears in Oracle Database 11g.

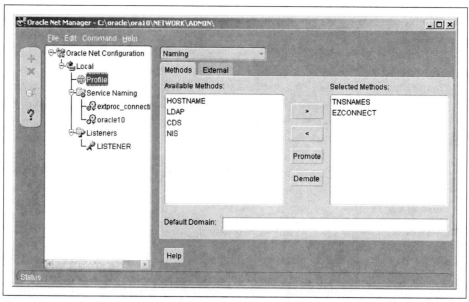

Figure 3-4. Oracle Net Manager

Debugging Network Problems

If you're having a problem with your network, one of the first steps toward debugging the problem is to check that the Oracle Net files were generated, not hand-coded. If you're in doubt, back up the current configuration files and use the Oracle Net Manager to regenerate them. In fact, when Oracle Support assists customers with Oracle Net problems, one of the first questions they ask is whether or not the files were handcoded.

Auto-Discovery and Agents

Beginning with Oracle 7.3, Oracle provided auto-discovery features that allowed it to find new databases automatically. Support for auto-discovery increased and improved with each Oracle release since then. Since Oracle8i, the Universal Installer and Oracle Net Manager work together smoothly to automatically configure your Oracle Net network.

A key piece of the Oracle network that enables auto-discovery is the Oracle Intelligent Agent. The agent is a piece of software that runs on the machine with your Oracle database(s). It acts as an agent for other functions that need to find and work with the database on the machine. For example, the agent knows about the various Oracle instances on the machine and handles critical management functions, such as monitoring the database for certain events and executing jobs. The agent provides a central point for auto-discovery: Oracle Net discovers instances and databases by interrogating the agent. We'll examine the general use of agents and their role in managing Oracle in Chapter 5.

Oracle Net Configuration Files

Oracle Net requires several configuration files. The default location for the files used to configure an Oracle Net network are as follows:

- On Windows, *ORACLE_HOME\net80\admin* for Oracle8 and *ORACLE_HOME\network\ admin* for Oracle8i and more current releases
- On Unix, *ORACLE_HOME/network/admin*

You can place these files in another location, in which case you must set an environment or system variable called TNS_ADMIN to the nondefault location. Oracle then uses TNS_ADMIN to locate the files. The vast majority of systems are configured using the default location.

The files that form a simple Oracle Net configuration are as follows:

LISTENER.ORA

Contains details for configuring the Oracle Net Listener, such as which instances or services the Listener is servicing. As the name implies, the Listener "listens" for incoming connection requests from clients that want to access the Oracle database over the network. For details about the mechanics of the Listener's function, see the later section "Oracle Net and Establishing Network Connections."

TNSNAMES.ORA

Decodes a service name into a specific machine address and Oracle instance for the connection request. (If you're using Oracle Names or OID, as described earlier, you don't need to use the *TNSNAMES.ORA* file as part of your configuration.) This file is key to Oracle Net's location transparency. If you move a database from one machine to another, you can simply update the *TNSNAMES.*

ORA files on the various clients to reflect the new machine address for the existing service name. For example, suppose that clients reach the database using a service name of SALES. The *TNSNAMES.ORA* file has an entry for the service name SALES that decodes to a machine named HOST1 and an Oracle instance called PROD. If the Oracle database used for the SALES application is moved to a machine called HOST2, the *TNSNAMES.ORA* entry is updated to use the machine name HOST2. Once the *TNSNAMES.ORA* files are updated, client connection requests will be routed transparently to the new machine with no application changes required.

SQLNET.ORA
Provides important defaults and miscellaneous configuration details. For example, *SQLNET.ORA* contains the default domain name for your network.

LDAP.ORA
For Oracle8*i* and later releases, the *LDAP.ORA* file contains the configuration information needed to use an LDAP directory, such as the Oracle Internet Directory. This information includes the location of the LDAP directory server and the default administrative context for the server. This is no longer required for an LDAP server that is registered with the Domain Name Server (DNS) since Oracle Database 10*g*.

As mentioned in Chapter 2, Oracle9*i* added a server parameter file, named *SPFILE*, which provides storage for system parameters you have changed while your Oracle9*i* instance is running, using the ALTER SYSTEM command. With the *SPFILE*, these new parameter values are preserved and used the next time you restart your Oracle instance. You can indicate whether a particular change to a system parameter is intended to be persistent (in which case it will be stored in the *SPFILE*) or temporary.

The *SPFILE* is a binary file that is kept on the server machine. By default, an Oracle9*i* or later instance will look for the *SPFILE* at startup and then for an instance of the *INIT.ORA* file.

The *SPFILE* can also be kept on a shared disk, so that it can be used to initialize multiple instances in an Oracle Real Application Clusters configuration.

Starting Up the Database

Starting a database is quite simple—on Windows you simply start the Oracle services (or specify that the services are started when the machine boots), and on Unix and Linux you issue the STARTUP command from SQL*Plus, or through Enterprise Manager. While starting a database appears to be a single action, it involves an instance and a database and occurs in several distinct phases. When you start a database, the following actions are automatically executed:

1. *Starting the instance*. Oracle reads the instance initialization parameters from the *SPFILE* or *INIT.ORA* file on the server. Oracle then allocates memory for the System Global Area and starts the background processes of the instance. At this point, none of the physical files in the database have been opened, and the instance is in the NOMOUNT state. (Note that the number of parameters that must be defined in the *SPFILE* in Oracle Database 10g and Oracle Database 11g as part of the initial installation setup have been greatly reduced. We described the initialization parameters required in Oracle Database 11g in Chapter 2.)

   There are problems that can prevent an instance from starting. For example, there may be errors in the initialization file, or the operating system may not be able to allocate the requested amount of shared memory for the SGA. You also need the special privilege SYSOPER or SYSDBA, granted through either the operating system or a password file, to start an instance.

2. *Mounting the database*. The instance opens the database's control files. The initialization parameter CONTROL_FILES tells the instance where to find these control files. At this point, only the control files are open. This is called the MOUNT state, and the database is accessible only to the database administrator. In this state, the DBA can perform only certain types of database administration. For example, the DBA may have moved or renamed one of the database files. The datafiles are listed in the control file but aren't open in the MOUNT state. The DBA can issue a command (ALTER DATABASE) to rename a datafile. This command will update the control file with the new datafile name.

3. *Opening the database*. The instance opens the redo log files and datafiles using the information in the control file. At this point, the database is fully open and available for user access.

Shutting Down the Database

Logically enough, the process of shutting down a database or making it inaccessible involves steps that reverse those discussed in the previous section:

1. *Closing the database*. Oracle flushes any modified database blocks that haven't yet been written to the disk from the SGA cache to the datafiles. Oracle also writes out any relevant redo information remaining in the redo log buffer. Oracle then checkpoints the datafiles, marking the datafile headers as "current" as of the time the database was closed, and closes the datafiles and redo log files. At this point, users can no longer access the database.

2. *Dismounting the database*. The Oracle instance dismounts the database. Oracle updates the relevant entries in the control files to record a clean shutdown and then closes them. At this point, the entire database is closed; only the instance remains.

3. *Shutting down the instance*. The Oracle software stops the background processes of the instance and frees, or deallocates, the shared memory used for the SGA.

In some cases (e.g., if there is a machine failure or the DBA aborts the instance), the database may not be closed cleanly. If this happens, Oracle doesn't have a chance to write the modified database blocks from the SGA to the datafiles. When Oracle is started again, the instance will detect that a crash occurred and will use the redo logs to automatically perform what is called *crash recovery*. Crash recovery guarantees that the changes for all committed transactions are done and that all uncommitted or in-flight transactions will be cleaned up. The uncommitted transactions are determined after the redo log is applied and automatically rolled back.

Accessing a Database

The previous sections described the process of starting up and shutting down a database. But the database is only part of a complete system—you also need a client process to access the database, even if that process is on the same physical machine as the database.

Server Processes and Clients

To access a database, a user connects to the instance that provides access to the desired database. A program that accesses a database is really composed of two distinct pieces—a client program and a server process—that connect to the Oracle instance. For example, running the Oracle character-mode utility SQL*Plus involves two processes:

- The SQL*Plus process itself, acting as the client
- The Oracle server process, sometimes referred to as a *shadow process*, that provides the connection to the Oracle instance

Server process

The Oracle server process always runs on the computer on which the instance is running. The server process attaches to the shared memory used for the SGA and can read from it and write to it.

As the name implies, the server process works for the client process—it reads and passes back the requested data, accepts and makes changes on behalf of the client, and so on. For example, when a client wants to read a row of data stored in a particular database block, the server process identifies the desired block and either retrieves it from the database buffer cache or reads it from the correct datafile and loads it into the database buffer cache. Then, if the user requests changes, the server process modifies the block in the cache and generates and stores the necessary redo information in the redo log buffer in the SGA. The server process, however, does not write the redo information from the log buffer to the redo log files, and it does not write the modified database block from the buffer cache to the datafile. These actions are performed by the Log Writer (LGWR) and Database Writer (DBWR) processes, respectively.

Client process

The client process can run on the same machine as the instance or on a separate computer. A network connects the two computers and provides a way for the two processes to talk to each other. In either case, the concept is essentially the same—two processes are involved in the interaction between a client and the database. When both processes are on the same machine, Oracle uses local communications via Inter Process Communication (IPC); when the client is on one machine and the database server is on another, Oracle uses Oracle Net over the network to communicate between the two machines.

Application Servers and Web Servers As Clients

Although the discussion in the previous section used the terms *client* and *server* extensively, please don't assume that Oracle is strictly a client/server database. Oracle was one of the early pioneers of client/server computing based on the notion of two tasks: a client and a server. But when you consider multitier computing involving web and application servers, the notion of a client changes somewhat. The "client" process becomes the middle tier, or application server.

You can logically consider any process that connects to an Oracle instance a client in the sense that it is served by the database. Don't confuse this usage of the term *client* with the actual client in a multitier configuration. The eventual client in a multitier model is some type of program providing a user interface—for example, a browser running Java.

The Oracle Application Server, which is part of the overall Oracle platform, is designed to act as this middle tier. Application Server works seamlessly with the Oracle database and shares some of the same technology. Application Server is described in more detail in Chapter 15.

Figure 3-5 illustrates users connecting to an Oracle instance to access a database in both two-tier and three-tier configurations, involving local and network communication. This figure highlights the server process connection models as opposed to the interaction of the background processes. There is a traditional two-tier client/server connection on the left side, a three-tier connection with an application server on the right side, and a local client connection in the middle of the figure. The two-tier and three-tier connections use a network to communicate with the database, while the local client uses local IPC.

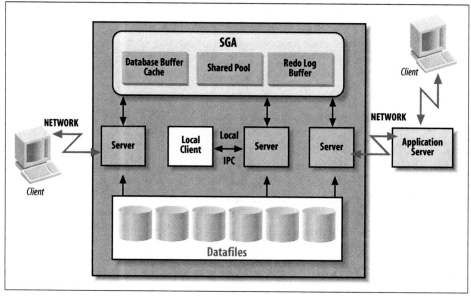

Figure 3-5. Accessing a database

Oracle Net and Establishing Network Connections

The server processes shown in Figure 3-5 are connected to the client processes using some kind of network. How do client processes get hooked up with Oracle server processes to begin working?

The matchmaker that arranges marriages between Oracle clients and server processes is called the Oracle Net Listener. The Listener "listens" for incoming connection requests for one or more instances. The Listener is not part of the Oracle instance—it directs connection requests to the instance. The Listener is started and stopped independently of the instance. If the Listener is down and the instance is up, clients accessing the database over a network cannot find the instance because there is no Listener to guide them. If the Listener is up and the instance is down, there is nowhere to send clients.

The Listener's function is relatively simple:

1. The client contacts the Listener over the network.

2. The Listener detects an incoming request and introduces the requesting client to an Oracle server process.

3. The Listener introduces the server to the client by letting each know the other's network address.

4. The Listener steps out of the way and lets the client and server communicate directly.

Once the client and the server know how to find each other, they communicate directly. The Listener is no longer required.

Figure 3-6 illustrates the steps outlined above for establishing a networked connection. Network traffic appears as dotted lines.

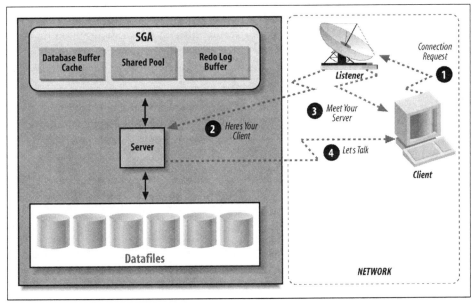

Figure 3-6. Connecting with the Oracle Net Listener

The Shared Server/Multi-Threaded Server

The server processes shown in the diagram are *dedicated*; they serve only one client process. So, if an application has 1,000 clients, the Oracle instance will have 1,000 corresponding server processes. Each server process uses system resources such as the memory and the CPU. Scaling to large user populations can consume a lot of system resources. To support the ever-increasing demand for scalability, Oracle introduced the Multi-Threaded Server (MTS) in Oracle7, known as the *shared server* since Oracle9*i*.

Shared servers allow the Oracle instance to share a set of server processes across a larger group of users. Instead of each client connecting to and using a dedicated server, the clients use shared servers, which can significantly reduce the overall resource requirements for serving large numbers of users.

In many systems there are times when the clients aren't actively using their server process, such as when users are reading and absorbing data retrieved from the database. When a client is not using its server process in the *dedicated model*, that server process still has a hold on system resources even though it isn't doing any useful work. In the *shared server model*, the shared server can use the resources of an inactive client to do work for another client process.

You don't have to make a mutually exclusive choice between shared server processes and dedicated server processes for an Oracle instance. Oracle can mix and match dedicated and shared servers, and clients can connect to one or the other. The choice is based on your Oracle Net configuration files. In the configuration files there will be one service name that leads the client to a dedicated server, and another for connecting via shared servers. The Oracle Net manuals provide the specific syntax for this configuration.

The type of server process a client is using is transparent to the client. From a client perspective, the multithreading or sharing of server processes happens "under the covers," on the database server. The same Listener handles dedicated and multithreaded connection requests.

The steps the Listener takes in establishing a shared server connection are a little different and involve some additional background processes for the instance dispatchers and the shared servers themselves:

Dispatchers

> In the previous description of the Listener, you saw how it forms the connection between a client and server process and then steps out of the way. The client must now be able to depend on a server process that is always available to complete the connection. Because a shared server process may be servicing another client, the client connects to a dispatcher, which is always ready to receive any client request. There are separate dispatchers for each network protocol being used (e.g., dispatchers for TCP/IP, etc.). The dispatchers serve as surrogate dedicated servers for the clients. Clients directly connect to their dispatchers instead of to a server. The dispatchers accept requests from clients and place them in a request queue, which is a memory structure in the SGA. There is one request queue for each instance.

Shared servers

> The shared server processes read from the request queue, process the requests, and place the results in the response queue for the appropriate dispatcher. There is one response queue for each dispatcher. The dispatcher then reads the results from the response queue and sends the information back to the client process.

There is a pool of dispatchers and a pool of shared servers. Oracle starts a certain number of each based on the initialization parameter SHARED_SERVERS that specifies the minimum number of shared servers. Oracle can start additional shared servers up to the value of an optionally specified initialization parameter MAX_SHARED_SERVERS. If Oracle starts additional processes to handle a heavier request load and the load dies down again, Oracle gradually reduces the number of processes to the floor specified by SHARED_SERVERS.

The following steps show how establishing a connection and using shared server processes differ from using a dedicated server process:

1. The client contacts the Listener over the network.

2. The Listener detects an incoming request and, based on the Oracle Net configuration, determines that it is for a multithreaded server. Instead of handing the client off to a dedicated server, the Listener hands the client off to a dispatcher for the network protocol the client is using.

3. The Listener introduces the client and the dispatcher by letting each know the other's network address.

4. Once the client and the dispatcher know where to find each other, they communicate directly. The Listener is no longer required. The client sends each work request directly to the dispatcher.

5. The dispatcher places the client's request in the request queue in the SGA.

6. The next available shared server process reads the request from the request queue and does the work.

7. The shared server places the results for the client's request in the response queue for the dispatcher that originally submitted the request.

8. The dispatcher reads the results from its queue.

9. The dispatcher sends the results to the client.

Figure 3-7 illustrates the steps for using the shared servers. Network traffic appears as dotted lines.

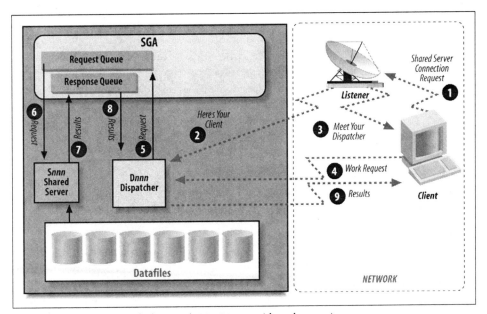

Figure 3-7. Connecting with the Oracle Net Listener (shared servers)

Session memory for shared server processes versus dedicated server processes

There is a concept in Oracle known as *session memory* or *state*. State information is basically data that describes the current status of a session in Oracle. For example, state information contains information about the SQL statements executed by the session. When you use a dedicated server, this state is stored in the private memory used by the dedicated server. This works out well because the dedicated server works with only one client. The term for this private memory is the Program Global Area (PGA).

If you're using the shared servers, however, any server can work on behalf of a specific client. The session state cannot be stored in the PGA of the shared server process. All servers must be able to access the session state because the session can migrate between different shared servers. For this reason, Oracle places this state information in the System Global Area (SGA).

All servers can read from the SGA. Putting the state information in the SGA allows a session and its state to move from one shared server to another for processing different requests. The server that picks up the request from the request queue simply reads the session state from the SGA, updates the state as needed for processing, and puts it back in the SGA when processing has finished.

The request and response queues, as well as the session state, require additional memory in the SGA, so in older Oracle releases, you would allocate more memory manually if you were using shared servers. By default, the memory for the shared server session state comes from the shared pool. Alternatively, you could also configure something called the *large pool* as a separate area of memory for shared servers. (We introduced the large pool in Chapter 2 in the "Memory Structures for an Instance" section.) Using the large pool memory avoided the overhead of coordinating memory usage with the shared SQL, dictionary caching, and other functions of the shared pool. This allowed memory management from the large pool and avoided competing with other subsystems for space in and access to the shared pool. Since Oracle Database 10g, shared memory is automatically managed by default. Oracle Database 11g introduced automated memory management of the SGA and PGA size by default when you set the MEMORY_TARGET initialization parameter.

Data dictionary information about the shared server

The data dictionary, which we introduced in Chapter 2, also contains information about the operation of the MTS in the following views:

V$SHARED_SERVER_MONITOR
> This view contains dynamic information about the shared servers, such as high-water marks for connections and how many shared servers have been started and stopped in response to load variations.

V$DISPATCHER

This view contains details of the dispatcher processes used by the shared server. It can determine how busy the dispatchers are.

V$SHARED_SERVER

This view contains details of the shared server processes used by the shared server. It can determine how busy the servers are, to help set the floor and ceiling values appropriately.

V$CIRCUIT

You can think of the route from a client to its dispatcher and from the dispatcher to the shared server (using the queues) as a virtual circuit. This view details these virtual circuits for user connections.

Oracle at Work

To help you truly understand how all the disparate pieces of the Oracle database work together, this section walks through an example of the steps taken by the Oracle database to respond to a user request. This example examines the work of a user who is adding new information to the database—in other words, executing a transaction.

Oracle and Transactions

A *transaction* is a work request from a client to insert, update, or delete data. The statements that change data are a subset of the SQL language called Data Manipulation Language (DML). Transactions must be handled in a way that guarantees their integrity. Although Chapter 8 delves into transactions more deeply, we must visit a few basic concepts relating to transactions now in order to understand the example in this section:

Transactions are logical and complete

In database terms, a transaction is a logical unit of work composed of one or more data changes. A transaction may consist of multiple INSERT, UPDATE, and/or DELETE statements affecting data in multiple tables. The entire set of changes must succeed or fail as a complete unit of work. A transaction starts with the first DML statement and ends with either a commit or a rollback.

 Oracle also supports autonomous transactions, transactions whose work is committed or rolled back, but that exist within the context of a larger transaction. Autonomous transactions are important because they can commit work without destroying the context of the larger transaction.

Commit or rollback

Once a user enters the data for his transaction, he can either *commit* the transaction to make the changes permanent or *roll back* the transaction to undo the changes.

System Change Number (SCN)

A key factor in preserving database integrity is an awareness of which transaction came first. For example, if Oracle is to prevent a later transaction from unwittingly overwriting an earlier transaction's changes, it must know which transaction began first. The mechanism Oracle uses is the System Change Number, a logical timestamp used to track the order in which events occurred. Oracle also uses the SCN to implement multiversion read consistency, which is described in detail in Chapter 8.

Rollback segments

Rollback segments are structures in the Oracle database used to store "undo" information for transactions, in case of rollback. This undo information restores database blocks to the state they were in before the transaction in question started. When a transaction starts changing some data in a block, it first writes the old image of the data to a rollback segment. The information stored in a rollback segment is used for two main purposes: to provide the information necessary to roll back a transaction and to support multiversion read consistency.

A rollback segment is not the same as a redo log. The redo log is used to log all transactions to the database and to recover the database in the event of a system failure, while the rollback segment provides rollback for transactions and read consistency.

Blocks of rollback segments are cached in the SGA just like blocks of tables and indexes. If rollback segment blocks are unused for a period of time, they may be aged out of the cache and written to the disk.

 Chapter 8 discusses Oracle's method for concurrency management, multiversion read consistency. This method uses rollback segments to retrieve earlier versions of changed rows. If the required blocks are no longer available, Oracle delivers a "snapshot too old" error.

Oracle9*i* introduced automatic management of rollback segments. In previous versions of the Oracle database, DBAs had to explicitly create and manage rollback segments. In Oracle9*i*, you had the option of specifying automatic management of all rollback segments through the use of an undo tablespace. With automatic undo management, you can also specify the length of time that you want to keep undo information; this feature is very helpful if you plan on using flashback queries, discussed in the following section. Oracle Database 10*g* added an undo management retention time advisor.

Fast commits

Because redo logs are written whenever a user commits an Oracle transaction, they can be used to speed up database operations. When a user commits a transaction, Oracle can do one of two things to get the changes into the database on the disk:

- Write all the database blocks the transaction changed to their respective datafiles.

- Write only the redo information, which typically involves much less I/O than writing the database blocks. This recording of the changes can be replayed to reproduce all the transaction's changes later, if they are needed due to a failure.

To provide maximum performance without risking transactional integrity, Oracle writes out only the redo information. When a user commits a transaction, Oracle guarantees that the redo for those changes writes to the redo logs on disk. The actual changed database blocks will be written out to the datafiles later. If a failure occurs before the changed blocks are flushed from the cache to the datafiles, the redo logs will reproduce the changes in their entirety. Because the slowest part of a computer system is the physical disk, Oracle's fast-commit approach minimizes the cost of committing a transaction and provides maximum risk-free performance.

Flashback

In Oracle9*i*, rollback segments were also used to implement a feature called *Flashback Query*. Remember that rollback segments are used to provide a consistent image of the data in your Oracle database at a previous point in time. With Flashback Query, you can direct Oracle to return the results for a SQL query at a specific point in time. For instance, you could ask for a set of results from the database as of two hours ago. Flashback provided extra functionality by leveraging the rollback feature that was already a core part of the Oracle architecture.

Since Flashback uses rollback segments, you can only flash back as far as the information in the current rollback segment. This requirement typically limits the span of flashback to a relatively short period of time—you normally would not be able to roll back days, since your Oracle database doesn't keep that much rollback information around. Despite this limitation, there are scenarios in which you might be able to use a Flashback Query effectively, such as going back to a point in time before a user made an error that resulted in a loss of data.

The use of Flashback has increased as Oracle has added more flashback capabilities to the database. Oracle Database 10*g* greatly expanded the flashback capabilities available to include:

- Flashback Database, to roll back the entire database to a consistent state
- Flashback Table, to roll back a specific table

- Flashback Drop to roll back a DROP operation
- Flashback Versions Query, to retrieve changes to one or more rows

Oracle Database 11g continues this expansion with the Flashback Transaction feature, which can be used to reverse the effect of a transaction and any other transactions that are dependent on it.

A Transaction, Step by Step

This simple example illustrates the complete process of a transaction. The example uses the EMP table of employee data, which is part of the traditional test schema shipped with Oracle databases. In this example, an HR clerk wants to update the name of an employee. The clerk retrieves the employee's data from the database, updates the name, and commits the transaction.

The example assumes that only one user is trying to update the information for a row in the database. Because of this assumption, it won't include the steps normally taken by Oracle to protect the transaction from changes by other users, which are detailed in Chapter 8.

The HR clerk already has the employee record on-screen and so the database block containing the row for that employee is already in the database buffer cache. The steps from this point would be:

1. The user modifies the employee name on-screen and the client application sends a SQL UPDATE statement over the network to the server process.

2. The server process looks for an identical statement in the shared SQL area of the shared pool. If it finds one, it reuses it. Otherwise, it checks the statement for syntax and evaluates it to determine the best way to execute it. This processing of the SQL statement is called *parsing and optimizing*. (The optimizer is described in more detail in Chapter 4.) Once the processing is done, the statement is cached in the shared SQL area.

3. The server process copies the old image of the employee data about to be changed to a rollback segment and to a redo seqment. The rollback segment changes are part of the redo. This may seem a bit odd, but remember that redo is generated for *all* changes resulting from the transaction. The contents of the rollback segment have changed because the old employee data was written to the rollback segment for undo purposes. This change to the contents of the rollback segment is part of the transaction and therefore part of the redo for that transaction.

4. Once the server process has completed this work, the process modifies the database block to change the employee name. The database block is stored in the database cache at this time.

5. The HR clerk commits the transaction.

6. The Log Writer (LGWR) process writes the redo information for the entire transaction from the redo log buffer to the current redo log file on disk. When the operating system confirms that the write to the redo log file has successfully completed, the transaction is considered committed.

7. The server process sends a message to the client confirming the commit.

The user could have canceled or rolled back the transaction instead of committing it, in which case the server process would have used the old image of the employee data in the rollback segment to undo the change to the database block.

Figure 3-8 shows the steps described here. Network traffic appears as dotted lines.

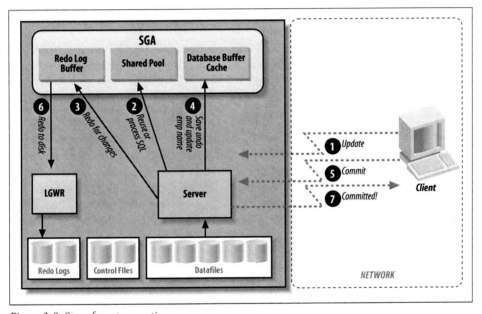

Figure 3-8. Steps for a transaction

CHAPTER 4

Oracle Data Structures

In the previous chapters, we examined some distinctions between the different components that make up an Oracle database. For example, we pointed out that the Oracle instance differs from the files that make up the physical storage of the data in tablespaces, that you cannot access the data in a tablespace except through an Oracle instance, and that the instance itself isn't very valuable without the data stored in those files.

The instance is the logical entity used by applications and users, separate from the physical storage of data. In a similar way, the actual tables and columns are logical entities within the physical database. The user who makes a request for data from an Oracle database probably doesn't know anything about instances and tablespaces, but does know about the structure of her data, as implemented with tables and columns. To fully leverage the power of Oracle, you must understand how the Oracle database server implements and uses these logical data structures, the topic of this chapter.

Datatypes

The *datatype* is one of the attributes for a *column* or a variable in a stored procedure. A datatype describes and limits the type of information stored in a column, and can limit the operations that you can perform on columns.

You can divide Oracle datatype support into three basic varieties: character datatypes, numeric datatypes, and datatypes that represent other kinds of data. You can use any of these datatypes when you create columns in a table, as with this SQL statement:

```
CREATE SAMPLE_TABLE(
    char_field CHAR(10),
    varchar_field VARCHAR2(10),
    todays_date DATE)
```

You also use these datatypes when you define variables as part of a PL/SQL procedure.

Character Datatypes

Character datatypes can store any string value, including the string representations of numeric values. Assigning a value larger than the length specified or allowed for a character datatype results in a runtime error. You can use string functions, such as UPPER, LOWER, SUBSTR, and SOUNDEX, on standard (not large) character value types.

There are several different character datatypes:

CHAR

> The CHAR datatype stores character values with a fixed length. A CHAR datatype can have between 1 and 2,000 characters. If you don't explicitly specify a length for a CHAR, it assumes the default length of 1. If you assign a value that's shorter than the length specified for the CHAR datatype, Oracle will automatically pad the value with blanks. Some examples of CHAR values are:
>
> ```
> CHAR(10) = "Rick      ", "Jon       ", "Stackowiak"
> ```

VARCHAR2

> The VARCHAR2 datatype stores variable-length character strings. Although you must assign a length to a VARCHAR2 datatype, this length is the maximum length for a value rather than the required length. Values assigned to a VARCHAR2 datatype aren't padded with blanks. The VARCHAR2 datatype can have up to 4,000 characters. Because of this, a VARCHAR2 datatype can require less storage space than a CHAR datatype, because the VARCHAR2 datatype stores only the characters assigned to the column.
>
> At this time, the VARCHAR and VARCHAR2 datatypes are synonymous in Oracle8 and later versions, but Oracle recommends the use of VARCHAR2 because future changes may cause VARCHAR and VARCHAR2 to diverge. The values shown earlier for the CHAR values, if entered as VARCHAR2 values, are:
>
> ```
> VARCHAR2(10) = "Rick", "Jon", "Stackowiak"
> ```

NCHAR and NVARCHAR2

> The NCHAR and NVARCHAR2 datatypes store fixed-length or variable-length character data, respectively, using a different character set from the one used by the rest of the database. When you create a database, you specify the character set that will be used for encoding the various characters stored in the database. You can optionally specify a secondary character set as well (which is known as the *National Language Set*, or NLS). The secondary character set will be used for NCHAR and NVARCHAR2 columns. For example, you may have a description field in which you want to store Japanese characters while the rest of the database uses English encoding. You would specify a secondary character set that supports Japanese characters when you create the database, and then use the NCHAR or NVARCHAR2 datatype for the columns in question.

Starting with Oracle9*i*, you can specify the length of NCHAR and NVARCHAR2 columns in characters, rather than in bytes. For example, you can indicate that a column with one of these datatypes is 7 characters. The Oracle9*i* database will automatically make the conversion to 14 bytes of storage if the character set requires double-byte storage.

 Oracle Database 10*g* introduced the Globalization Development Kit (GDK), which is designed to aid in the creation of Internet applications that will be used with different languages. The key feature of this kit is a framework that implements best practices for globalization for Java and PL/SQL developers.

Oracle Database 10*g* also added support for case- and accent-insensitive queries and sorts. You can use this feature if you want to use only base letters or base letters and accents in a query or sort.

LONG

The LONG datatype can hold up to 2 GB of character data. It is regarded as a legacy datatype from earlier versions of Oracle. If you want to store large amounts of character data, Oracle now recommends that you use the CLOB and NCLOB datatypes. There are many restrictions on the use of LONG datatypes in a table and within SQL statements, such as the fact that you cannot use LONGs in WHERE, GROUP BY, ORDER BY, or CONNECT BY clauses or in SQL statements with the DISTINCT qualifier. You also cannot create an index on a LONG column.

CLOB and NCLOB

The CLOB and NCLOB datatypes can store up to 4 GB of character data prior to Oracle Database 10*g*. Starting with Oracle Database 10*g*, the limit has been increased to 128 TBs, depending on the block size of the database. The NCLOB datatype stores the NLS data. Oracle Database 10*g* and later releases implicitly perform conversions between CLOBs and NCLOBs. For more information on CLOBs and NCLOBs, please refer to the discussion about large objects (LOBs) in the section "Other Datatypes" later in this chapter.

Numeric Datatype

Oracle uses a standard, variable-length internal format for storing numbers. This internal format can maintain a precision of up to 38 digits.

The numeric datatype for Oracle is NUMBER. Declaring a column or variable as NUMBER will automatically provide a precision of 38 digits. The NUMBER datatype can also accept two qualifiers, as in:

```
column NUMBER( precision, scale )
```

The *precision* of the datatype is the total number of significant digits in the number. You can designate a precision for a number as any number of digits up to 38. If no value is declared for *precision*, Oracle will use a precision of 38. The *scale* represents the number of digits to the right of the decimal point. If no scale is specified, Oracle will use a scale of 0.

If you assign a negative number to the *scale*, Oracle will round the number up to the designated place to the *left* of the decimal point. For example, the following code snippet:

```
column_round NUMBER(10,-2)
column_round = 1,234,567
```

will give column_round a value of 1,234,600.

The NUMBER datatype is the only datatype that stores numeric values in Oracle. The ANSI datatypes of DECIMAL, NUMBER, INTEGER, INT, SMALLINT, FLOAT, DOUBLE PRECISION, and REAL are all stored in the NUMBER datatype. The language or product you're using to access Oracle data may support these datatypes, but they're all stored in a NUMBER datatype column.

With Oracle Database 10g, Oracle added support for the precision defined in the IEEE 754-1985 standard with the number datatypes of BINARY_FLOAT and BINARY_DOUBLE. Oracle Database 11g added support for the number datatype SIMPLE_INTEGER.

Date Datatype

As with the NUMERIC datatype, Oracle stores all dates and times in a standard internal format. The standard Oracle date format for input takes the form of DD-MON-YY HH:MI:SS, where DD represents up to two digits for the day of the month, MON is a three-character abbreviation for the month, YY is a two-digit representation of the year, and HH, MI, and SS are two-digit representations of hours, minutes, and seconds, respectively. If you don't specify any time values, their default values are all zeros in the internal storage.

You can change the format you use for inserting dates for an instance by changing the NLS_DATE_FORMAT parameter for the instance. You can do this for a session by using the ALTER SESSION SQL statement or for a specific value by using parameters with the TO_DATE expression in your SQL statement.

Oracle SQL supports date arithmetic in which integers represent days and fractions represent the fractional component represented by hours, minutes, and seconds. For example, adding .5 to a date value results in a date and time combination 12 hours later than the initial value. Some examples of date arithmetic are:

```
12-DEC-07 + 10 = 22-DEC-07
31-DEC-2007:23:59:59 + .25 = 1-JAN-2008:5:59:59
```

As of Oracle9*i* Release 2, Oracle also supports two INTERVAL datatypes, INTERVAL YEAR TO MONTH and INTERVAL DAY TO SECOND, which are used for storing a specific amount of time. This data can be used for date arithmetic.

Other Datatypes

Aside from the basic character, number, and date datatypes, Oracle supports a number of specialized datatypes:

RAW and LONG RAW

Normally, your Oracle database not only stores data but also interprets it. When data is requested or exported from the database, the Oracle database sometimes massages the requested data. For instance, when you dump the values from a NUMBER column, the values written to the dump file are the representations of the numbers, not the internally stored numbers.

The RAW and LONG RAW datatypes circumvent any interpretation on the part of the Oracle database. When you specify one of these datatypes, Oracle will store the data as the exact series of bits presented to it. The RAW datatypes typically store objects with their own internal format, such as bitmaps. A RAW datatype can hold 2 KB, while a LONG RAW datatype can hold 2 GB.

ROWID

The ROWID is a special type of column known as a *pseudocolumn*. The ROWID pseudocolumn can be accessed just like a column in a SQL SELECT statement. There is a ROWID pseudocolumn for every row in an Oracle database. The ROWID represents the specific address of a particular row. The ROWID pseudocolumn is defined with a ROWID datatype.

The ROWID relates to a specific location on a disk drive. Because of this, the ROWID is the fastest way to retrieve an individual row. However, the ROWID for a row can change as the result of dumping and reloading the database. For this reason, we don't recommend using the value for the ROWID pseudocolumn across transaction lines. For example, there is no reason to store a reference to the ROWID of a row once you've finished using the row in your current application.

You cannot set the value of the standard ROWID pseudocolumn with any SQL statement.

The format of the ROWID pseudocolumn changed with Oracle8. Beginning with Oracle8, the ROWID includes an identifier that points to the database object number in addition to the identifiers that point to the datafile, block, and row. You can parse the value returned from the ROWID pseudocolumn to understand the physical storage of rows in your Oracle database.

You can define a column or variable with a ROWID datatype, but Oracle doesn't guarantee that any value placed in this column or variable is a valid ROWID.

ORA_ROWSCN

Oracle Database 10g and later releases support a pseudocolumn ORA_ROWSCN, which holds the System Change Number (SCN) of the last transaction that modified the row. You can use this pseudocolumn to check easily for changes in the row since a transaction started. For more information on SCNs, see the discussion of concurrency in Chapter 8.

LOB

A LOB, or large object datatype, can store up to 4 GB of information. LOBs come in three varieties:

- CLOB, which can store only character data

- NCLOB, which stores National Language character set data

- BLOB, which stores data as binary information

You can designate that a LOB should store its data within the Oracle database or that it should point to an external file that contains the data.

LOBs can participate in transactions. Selecting a LOB datatype from Oracle will return a pointer to the LOB. You must use either the DBMS_LOB PL/SQL built-in package or the OCI interface to actually manipulate the data in a LOB.

To facilitate the conversion of LONG datatypes to LOBs, Oracle9i included support for LOBs in most functions that support LONGs, as well as an option to the ALTER TABLE statement that allows the automatic migration of LONG datatypes to LOBs.

BFILE

The BFILE datatype acts as a pointer to a file stored outside of the Oracle database. Because of this fact, columns or variables with BFILE datatypes don't participate in transactions, and the data stored in these columns is available only for reading. The file size limitations of the underlying operating system limit the amount of data in a BFILE.

XMLType

As part of its support for XML, Oracle9i introduced a datatype called XMLType. A column defined as this type of data will store an XML document in a character LOB column. There are built-in functions that allow you to extract individual nodes from the document, and you can also build indexes on any particular node in the XMLType document.

User-defined data

Oracle8 and later versions allow users to define their own complex datatypes, which are created as combinations of the basic Oracle datatypes previously discussed. These versions of Oracle also allow users to create objects composed of both basic datatypes and user-defined datatypes. For more information about objects within Oracle, see Chapter 14.

AnyType, AnyData, AnyDataSet

Oracle9*i* and newer releases include three datatypes that can be used to explicitly define data structures that exist outside the realm of existing datatypes. Each of these datatypes must be defined with program units that let Oracle know how to process any specific implementation of these types.

Type Conversion

Oracle automatically converts some datatypes to other datatypes, depending on the SQL syntax in which the value occurs.

When you assign a character value to a numeric datatype, Oracle performs an implicit conversion of the ASCII value represented by the character string into a number. For instance, assigning a character value such as 10 to a NUMBER column results in an automatic data conversion.

If you attempt to assign an alphabetic value to a numeric datatype, you will end up with an unexpected (and invalid) numeric value, so you should make sure that you're assigning values appropriately.

You can also perform explicit conversions on data, using a variety of conversion functions available with Oracle. Explicit data conversions are better to use if a conversion is anticipated, because they document the conversion and avoid the possibility of going unnoticed, as implicit conversions sometimes do.

Concatenation and Comparisons

The concatenation operator for Oracle SQL on most platforms is two vertical lines (||). Concatenation is performed with two character values. Oracle's automatic type conversion allows you to seemingly concatenate two numeric values. If NUM1 is a numeric column with a value of 1, NUM2 is a numeric column with a value of 2, and NUM3 is a numeric column with a value of 3, the following expressions are TRUE:

```
NUM1 || NUM2 || NUM3 = "123"
NUM1 || NUM2 + NUM3 = "15" (12 + 3)
NUM1 + NUM2 || NUM3 = "33" (1+ 2 || 3)
```

The result for each of these expressions is a character string, but that character string can be automatically converted back to a numeric column for further calculations.

Comparisons between values of the same datatype work as you would expect. For example, a date that occurs later in time is larger than an earlier date, and 0 or any positive number is larger than any negative number. You can use relational operators to compare numeric values or date values. For character values, comparisons of single characters are based on the underlying code pages for the characters. For multicharacter strings, comparisons are made until the first character that differs between the two strings appears.

If two character strings of different lengths are compared, Oracle uses two different types of comparison semantics: *blank-padded comparisons* and *nonpadded comparisons*. For a blank-padded comparison, the shorter string is padded with blanks and the comparison operates as previously described. For nonpadded comparisons, if both strings are identical for the length of the shorter string, the shorter string is identified as smaller. For example, in a blank-padded comparison the string "A " (a capital A followed by a blank) and the string "A" (a capital A by itself) would be seen as equal, because the second value would be padded with a blank. In a nonpadded comparison, the second string would be identified as smaller because it is shorter than the first string. Nonpadded comparisons are used for comparisons in which one or both of the values are VARCHAR2 or NVARCHAR2 datatypes, while blank-padded comparisons are used when neither of the values is one of these datatypes.

Oracle Database 10g and later releases include a feature called the Expression Filter, which allows you to store a complex comparison expression as part of a row. You can use the EVALUATE function to limit queries based on the evaluation of the expression. The Expression Filter uses regular expressions, which are described later in this chapter.

NULLs

The NULL value is one of the key features of the relational database. The NULL, in fact, doesn't represent any value at all—it represents the lack of a value. When you create a column for a table that must have a value, you specify it as NOT NULL, meaning that it cannot contain a NULL value. If you try to write a row to a database table that doesn't assign a value to a NOT NULL column, Oracle will return an error.

You can assign NULL as a value for any datatype. The NULL value introduces what is called *three-state logic* to your SQL operators. A normal comparison has only two states: TRUE or FALSE. If you're making a comparison that involves a NULL value, there are three logical states: TRUE, FALSE, and neither.

None of the following conditions are true for Column A if the column contains a NULL value:

    A > 0
    A < 0
    A = 0
    A != 0

The existence of three-state logic can be confusing for end users, but your data may frequently require you to allow for NULL values for columns or variables.

You have to test for the presence of a NULL value with the relational operator IS NULL, since a NULL value is not equal to 0 or any other value. Even the expression:

```
NULL = NULL
```

will always evaluate to FALSE, since a NULL value doesn't equal any other value.

Should You Use NULLs?

The idea of three-state logic may seem somewhat confusing, especially when you imagine your poor end users executing ad hoc queries and trying to account for a value that's neither TRUE nor FALSE. This prospect may concern you, so you may decide not to use NULL values at all.

We believe that NULLs have an appropriate use. The NULL value covers a very specific situation: a time when a column has not had a value assigned. The alternative to using a NULL is using a value with another meaning—such as 0 for numbers—and then trying to somehow determine whether that value has actually been assigned or simply exists as a replacement for NULL.

If you choose not to use NULL values, you're forcing a value to be assigned to a column for every row. You are, in effect, eliminating the possibility of having a column that doesn't require a value, as well as potentially assigning misleading values for certain columns. This situation can be misleading for end users and can lead to inaccurate results for summary actions such as AVG (average).

Avoiding NULL values simply replaces one problem—educating users or providing them with an interface that implicitly understands NULL values—with another set of problems, which can lead to a loss of data integrity.

Basic Data Structures

This section describes the three basic Oracle data structures: tables, views, and indexes. This section also discusses partitioning, which affects the way that data in tables and indexes is stored.

Tables

The *table* is the basic data structure used in a relational database. A table is a collection of rows. Each *row* in a table contains one or more *columns*. If you're unfamiliar with relational databases, you can map a table to the concept of a file or database in a nonrelational database, just as you can map a row to the concept of a record in a nonrelational database.

As of Oracle9*i*, you can define *external tables*. As the name implies, the data for an external table is stored outside the database, typically in a flat file. The external table is read-only; you cannot update the data it contains. The external table is good for loading and unloading data to files from a database, among other purposes.

Oracle Database 11g introduces the ability to create virtual columns for a table. These columns are defined by an expression and, although the results of the expression are not stored, the columns can be accessed by applications at runtime.

Views

A *view* is an Oracle data structure defined through a SQL statement. The SQL statement is stored in the database. When you use a view in a query, the stored query is executed and the base table data is returned to the user. Views do not contain data, but represent ways to look at the base table data in the way the query specifies.

You can use a view for several purposes:

- To simplify access to data stored in multiple tables.
- To implement specific security for the data in a table (e.g., by creating a view that includes a WHERE clause that limits the data you can access through the view). Starting with Oracle9i, you can use *fine-grained access control* to accomplish the same purpose. Fine-grained access control gives you the ability to automatically limit data access based on the value of data in a row.
- To isolate an application from the specific structure of the underlying tables.

A view is built on a collection of *base tables*, which can be either actual tables in an Oracle database or other views. If you modify any of the base tables for a view so that they no longer can be used for a view, that view itself can no longer be used.

In general, you can write to the columns of only one underlying base table of a view in a single SQL statement. There are additional restrictions for INSERT, UPDATE, and DELETE operations, and there are certain SQL clauses that prevent you from updating any of the data in a view.

You can write to a nonupdateable view by using an INSTEAD OF trigger, which is described later in this chapter.

Oracle8i introduced *materialized views*. These are not really views as defined in this section, but are physical tables that hold presummarized data providing significant performance improvements in a data warehouse. Materialized views are described in more detail in Chapter 10.

Indexes

An *index* is a data structure that speeds up access to particular rows in a database. An index is associated with a particular table and contains the data from one or more columns in the table.

The basic SQL syntax for creating an index is shown in this example:

```
CREATE INDEX emp_idx1 ON emp (ename, job);
```

in which emp_idx1 is the name of the index, emp is the table on which the index is created, and ename and job are the column values that make up the index.

The Oracle database server automatically modifies the values in the index when the values in the corresponding columns are modified. Because the index contains less data than the complete row in the table and because indexes are stored in a special structure that makes them faster to read, it takes fewer I/O operations to retrieve the data in them. Selecting rows based on an index value can be faster than selecting rows based on values in the table rows. In addition, most indexes are stored in sorted order (either ascending or descending, depending on the declaration made when you created the index). Because of this storage scheme, selecting rows based on a range of values or returning rows in sorted order is much faster when the range or sort order is contained in the presorted indexes.

In addition to the data for an index, an index entry stores the ROWID for its associated row. The ROWID is the fastest way to retrieve any row in a database, so the subsequent retrieval of a database row is performed in the most optimal way.

An index can be either unique (which means that no two rows in the table or view can have the same index value) or nonunique. If the column or columns on which an index is based contain NULL values, the row isn't included in an index.

An index in Oracle refers to the physical structure used within the database. A *key* is a term for a logical entity, typically the value stored within the index. In most places in the Oracle documentation, the two terms are used interchangeably, with the notable exception of the foreign key constraint, which is discussed later in this chapter.

Four different types of index structures, which are described in the following sections, are used in Oracle: standard B*-tree indexes; reverse key indexes; bitmap indexes; and function-based indexes, which were introduced in Oracle8*i*. Oracle Database 11*g* delivers the ability to use invisible indexes, which are described below. Oracle also gives you the ability to cluster the data in the tables, which can improve performance. This is described later, in the section "Clusters."

B*-tree indexes

The *B*-tree index* is the default index used in Oracle. It gets its name from its resemblance to an inverted tree, as shown in Figure 4-1.

The B*-tree index is composed of one or more levels of branch blocks and a single level of leaf blocks. The branch blocks contain information about the range of values contained in the next level of branch blocks. The number of branch levels between the root and leaf blocks is called the *depth* of the index. The leaf blocks contain the actual index values and the ROWID for the associated row.

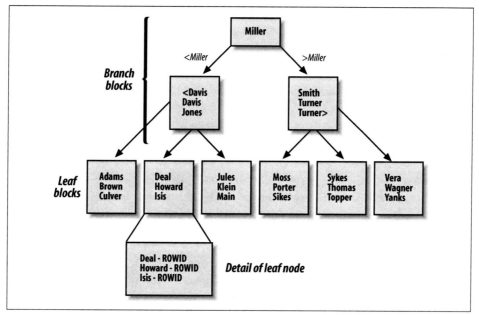

Figure 4-1. A B*-tree index

The B*-tree index structure doesn't contain many blocks at the higher levels of branch blocks, so it takes relatively few I/O operations to read quite far down the B*-tree index structure. All leaf blocks are at the same depth in the index, so all retrievals require essentially the same amount of I/O to get to the index entry, which evens out the performance of the index.

Oracle allows you to create *index organized tables* (IOTs), in which the leaf blocks store the entire row of data rather than only the ROWID that points to the associated row. Index organized tables reduce the total amount of space needed to store an index and a table by eliminating the need to store the ROWID in the leaf page. But index organized tables cannot use a UNIQUE constraint or be stored in a cluster. In addition, index organized tables don't support distribution, replication, and partitioning (covered in greater detail in other chapters), although IOTs can be used with Oracle Streams for capturing and applying changes with Oracle Database 10*g* and later releases.

There were a number of enhancements to index organized tables as of Oracle9*i*, including a lifting of the restriction against the use of bitmap indexes as secondary indexes for an IOT and the ability to create, rebuild, or coalesce secondary indexes on an IOT. Oracle Database 10*g* continued this trend by allowing replication and all types of partitioning for index organized tables, as well as providing other enhancements.

Reverse key indexes

Reverse key indexes, as their name implies, automatically reverse the order of the bytes in the key value stored in the index. If the value in a row is "ABCD", the value for the reverse key index for that row is "DCBA".

To understand the need for a reverse key index, you have to review some basic facts about the standard B*-tree index. First and foremost, the depth of the B*-tree is determined by the number of entries in the leaf nodes. The greater the depth of the B*-tree, the more levels of branch nodes there are and the more I/O is required to locate and access the appropriate leaf node.

The index illustrated in Figure 4-1 is a nice, well-behaved, alphabetic-based index. It's balanced, with an even distribution of entries across the width of the leaf pages. But some values commonly used for an index are not so well behaved. Incremental values, such as ascending sequence numbers or increasingly later date values, are always added to the right side of the index, which is the home of higher and higher values. In addition, any deletions from the index have a tendency to be skewed toward the left side as older rows are deleted. The net effect of these practices is that over time the index turns into an unbalanced B*-tree, where the left side of the index is more sparsely populated than the leaf nodes on the right side. This unbalanced growth has the overall effect of having an unnecessarily deep B*-tree structure, with the left side of the tree more sparsely populated than the right side, where the new, larger values are stored. The effects described here also apply to the values that are automatically decremented, except that the left side of the B*-tree will end up holding more entries.

You can solve this problem by periodically dropping and re-creating the index. However, you can also solve it by using the reverse value index, which reverses the order of the value of the index. This reversal causes the index entries to be more evenly distributed over the width of the leaf nodes. For example, rather than having the values 234, 235, and 236 be added to the maximum side of the index, they are translated to the values 432, 532, and 632 for storage and then translated back when the values are retrieved. These values are more evenly spread throughout the leaf nodes.

The overall result of the reverse index is to correct the imbalance caused by continually adding increasing values to a standard B*-tree index. For more information about reverse key indexes and where to use them, refer to your Oracle documentation.

Bitmap indexes

In a standard B*-tree index, the ROWIDs are stored in the leaf blocks of the index. In a *bitmap index,* each bit in the index represents a ROWID. If a particular row contains a particular value, the bit for that row is "turned on" in the bitmap for that value. A mapping function converts the bit into its corresponding ROWID. Unlike other index types, bitmap indexes include entries for NULL values.

You can store a bitmap index in much less space than a standard B*-tree index if there aren't many values in the index. Figure 4-2 shows an illustration of how a bitmap index is stored. Figure 10-3 in Chapter 10 shows how a bitmap index is used in a selection condition.

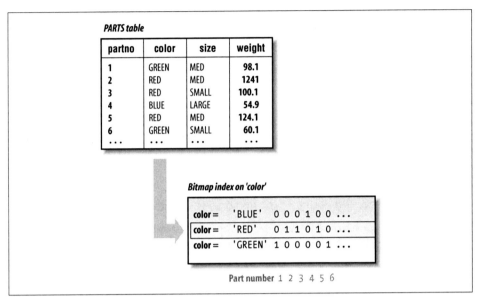

Figure 4-2. Bitmap index

The functionality provided by bitmap indexes is especially important in data warehousing applications in which each dimension of the warehouse contains many repeating values, and queries typically require the interaction of several different dimensions. For more about data warehousing, see Chapter 10.

Function-based indexes

Function-based indexes were introduced in Oracle8*i*. A function-based index is just like a standard B*-tree or bitmap index, except that you can base the index on the result of a SQL function, rather than just on the value of a column or columns.

Prior to Oracle8*i*, if you wanted to select on the result of a function, Oracle retrieved every row in the database, executed the function, and then accepted or rejected each row. With function-based indexes you can simply use the index for selection, without having to execute the function on every row, every time.

For example, without a function-based index, if you wanted to perform a case-insensitive selection of data you would have to use the UPPER function in the WHERE clause, which would retrieve every candidate row and execute the function. With a function-based index based on the UPPER function, you can select directly from the index.

As of Oracle Database 10g, you can perform case- or accent-insensitive queries; these queries provide another way to solve this problem.

This capability becomes even more valuable when you consider that you can create your own functions in an Oracle database. You can create a very sophisticated function and then create an index based on the function, which can dramatically affect the performance of queries that require the function.

Invisible indexes

Oracle Database 11g introduces a new option for all of the index types we've discussed in previous sections—the *invisible index*. Normally, all indexes are used by the optimizer, which is described later in this chapter. You can eliminate an index from optimizer consideration by taking the index offline or by deleting the index. But with both of these methods you will have to take some actions to bring the index up to date when you bring it back into the database environment.

But what if you want to just remove the index from optimizer consideration for a limited time, such as when you are testing performance? With the invisible option, an index is not considered as a possible step in an access path, but updates and deletes to the underlying data are still applied to the index.

Partitioning

With the Enterprise Editions of Oracle8 and beyond, you can purchase the Partitioning Option. As the name implies, this option allows you to partition tables and indexes. Partitioning a data structure means that you can divide the information in the structure among multiple physical storage areas. A partitioned data structure is divided based on column values in the table. You can partition tables based on the range of column values in the table (often date ranges), or as the result of a hash function (which returns a value based on a calculation performed on the values in one or more columns). As of Oracle9i you can also use a list of values to define a partition, which can be particularly useful in a data warehouse environment. Oracle Database 11g adds *interval partitioning*, providing the ability to automatically generate a new partition of a fixed interval or range when data to be inserted does not fit into existing partition ranges.

You can also have two levels of partitions, called *composite partitions*, using a combination of partition methods. Prior to Oracle Database 11g, you could partition using a composite of range and hash partitioning. Oracle Database 11g adds the ability to combine list partitioning with list, range, or hash partitioning, or range partitioning with a different range partitioning scheme.

Oracle is smart enough to take advantage of partitions to improve performance in two ways:

- Oracle won't bother to access partitions that won't contain any data to satisfy the query.
- If all the data in a partition satisfies a part of the WHERE clause for the query, Oracle simply selects all the rows for the partition without bothering to evaluate the clause for each row.

Partitioned tables are especially useful in a data warehouse, in which data can be partitioned based on the time period it spans.

Equally important is the fact that partitioning substantially reduces the scope of maintenance operations and increases the availability of your data. You can perform all maintenance operations, such as backup, recovery, and loading, on a single partition. This flexibility makes it possible to handle extremely large data structures while still performing those maintenance operations in a reasonable amount of time. In addition, if you must recover one partition in a table for some reason, the other partitions in the table can remain online during the recovery operation.

If you have been working with other databases that don't offer the same type of partitioning, you may have tried to implement a similar functionality by dividing a table into several separate tables and then using a UNION SQL command to view the data in several tables at once. Partitioned tables give you all the advantages of having several identical tables joined by a UNION command without the complexity that implementation requires.

To maximize the benefits of partitioning, it sometimes makes sense to partition a table and an index identically so that both the table partition and the index partition map to the same set of rows. You can automatically implement this type of partitioning, which is called *equipartitioning*, by specifying an index for a partitioned table as a LOCAL index. Local indexes simplify maintenance, since standard operations, such as dropping a partition, will work transparently with both the index partition and the table partition.

Oracle has continued to increase the functionality of partitioning features. Since Oracle Database 10g Release 2, you can reorganize individual partitions online, the maximum number of partitions increased from 64 KB − 1 to 128 KB − 1, and query optimization using partition pruning improved.

Oracle Database 11g further improves partition pruning, enables applications to control partitioning, and adds a Partition Advisor that can help you to understand when partitioning might improve the performance of your Oracle database.

For more details about the structure and limitations associated with partitioned tables, refer to your Oracle documentation.

Additional Data Structures

There are several other data structures available in your Oracle database that can be useful in some circumstances.

Sequences

One of the big problems that occurs in a multiuser database is the difficulty of supplying unique numbers for use as keys or identifiers. For this situation, Oracle allows you to create an object called a *sequence*. The sequence object is fairly simple. Whenever anyone requests a value from it, it returns a value and increments its internal value, avoiding contention and time-consuming interaction with the requesting application. Oracle can cache a range of numbers for the sequence so that access to the next number doesn't have to involve disk I/O—the requests can be satisfied from the range in the SGA.

Sequence numbers are defined with a name, an incremental value, and some additional information about the sequence. Sequences exist independently of any particular table, so more than one table can use the same sequence number.

Consider what might happen if you didn't use Oracle sequences. You might store the last sequence number used in a column in a table. A user who wanted to get the next sequence number would read the last number, increment it by a fixed value, and write the new value back to the column. But if many users tried to get a sequence number at the same time, they might all read the "last" sequence number before the new "last" sequence number had been written back. You could lock the row in the table with the column containing the sequence number, but this would cause delays as other users waited on locks. What's the solution? Create a sequence.

Oracle Database 11g allows the use of sequences within PL/SQL expressions.

Synonyms

All data structures within an Oracle database are stored within a specific *schema*. A schema is associated with a particular username, and all objects are referenced with the name of the schema followed by the name of the object.

For instance, if there were a table named EMP in a schema named DEMO, the table would be referenced with the complete name of DEMO.EMP. If you don't supply a specific schema name, Oracle assumes that the structure is in the schema for your current username.

Schemas are a nice feature because object names have to be unique only within their own schemas, but the qualified names for objects can get confusing, especially for end users. To make names simpler and more readable, you can create a *synonym* for any table, view, snapshot, or sequence, or for any PL/SQL procedure, function, or package.

Synonyms can be either *public*, which means that all users of a database can use them, or *private*, which means that only the user whose schema contains the synonym can use it.

For example, if the user DEMO creates a public synonym called EMP for the table EMP in his schema, all other users can simply use EMP to refer to the EMP table in DEMO's schema. Suppose that DEMO didn't create a public synonym and a user called SCOTT wanted to use the name EMP to refer to the EMP table in DEMO's schema. The user SCOTT would create a private synonym in his schema. Of course, SCOTT must have access to DEMO's EMP table for this to work.

Synonyms simplify user access to a data structure. You can also use synonyms to hide the location of a particular data structure, making the data more transportable and increasing the security of the associated table by hiding the name of the schema owner.

Prior to Oracle Database 10g, if you changed the location referenced by a synonym, you would have to recompile any PL/SQL procedures that accessed the synonym.

Clusters

A *cluster* is a data structure that improves retrieval performance. A cluster, like an index, does not affect the logical view of the table.

A cluster is a way of storing related data values together on disk. Oracle reads data a block at a time, so storing related values together reduces the number of I/O operations needed to retrieve related values, since a single data block will contain only related rows.

A cluster is composed of one or more tables. The cluster includes a cluster index, which stores all the values for the corresponding cluster key. Each value in the cluster index points to a data block that contains only rows with the same value for the cluster key.

If a cluster contains multiple tables, the tables should be joined together and the cluster index should contain the values that form the basis of the join. Because the value of the cluster key controls the placement of the rows that relate to the key, changing a value in that key can cause Oracle to change the location of rows associated with that key value.

Clusters may not be appropriate for tables that regularly require full table scans, in which a query requires the Oracle database to iterate through all the rows of the table. Because you access a cluster table through the cluster index, which then points to a data block, full table scans on clustered tables can actually require more I/O operations, lowering overall performance.

Hash Clusters

A *hash cluster* is like a cluster with one significant difference that makes it even faster. Each request for data in a clustered table involves at least two I/O operations, one for the cluster index and one for the data. A hash cluster stores related data rows together, but groups the rows according to a *hash value* for the cluster key. The hash value is calculated with a hash function, which means that each retrieval operation starts with a calculation of the hash value and then goes directly to the data block that contains the relevant rows.

By eliminating the need to go to a cluster index, a hash clustered table can be even faster for retrieving data than a clustered table. You can control the number of possible hash values for a hash cluster with the HASHKEYS parameter when you create the cluster.

Because the hash cluster directly points to the location of a row in the table, you must allocate all the space required for all the possible values in a hash cluster when you create the cluster.

Hash clusters work best when there is an even distribution of rows among the various values for the hash key. You may have a situation in which there is already a unique value for the hash key column, such as a unique ID. In such situations, you can assign the value for the hash key as the value for the hash function on the unique value, which eliminates the need to execute the hash function as part of the retrieval process. In addition, you can specify your own hash function as part of the definition of a hash cluster.

Oracle Database 10g introduced sorted hash clusters, where data is not only stored in a cluster based on a hash value, but is also stored in the order in which it was inserted. This data structure improves performance for applications that access data in the order in which it was added to the database.

Extended Logic for Data

There are a several features that have been added to the Oracle database that are not unique data structures, but rather shape the way you can use the data in the database: the Rules Manager and the Expression Filter.

Rules Manager

The database has been continually extending the functionality it can provide, from mere data storage, which still enforced some logical attributes on data, to stored procedures. The Rules Manager, introduced with Oracle Database 10g Release 2, takes this extension a step further.

The concept behind the Rules Manager is simple. A *rule* is stored in the database and is called and evaluated by applications. If business conditions or requirements change, the rule covering those scenarios can be changed without having to touch the application code. Rules can be shared across multiple application systems, bringing standardization along with reduced maintenance across the set of applications. You can also create granular rules that can be used in different combinations to implement a variety of conditions.

Rules are invoked by events. The *event* causes the rule to be evaluated and results in a rule action being performed, either immediately or at some later time.

The Rules Manager follows the event-condition action structure and helps users to define five elements required for a Rules Manager application:

- Define an event structure, which is an object in your Oracle database. Different events have different values for the attributes of the event object.
- Create rules, which include conditions and their subsequent actions.
- Create rule classes to store and group rules with similar structures.
- Create PL/SQL procedures to implement rules.
- Define a results view to configure the rules for external use when the PL/SQL actions cannot be called, such as an application that runs on multiple tiers and has rule actions that are invoked from the application server tier.

You can define conflict resolution routines to handle situations where more than one rule is matched by an event. The Rules Manager also can aggregate different events into composite events and maintain state information until all events are received.

Using rules can be a very powerful tool for implementing complex logic, but the use of rules can affect your application design. For more information on the Rules Manager, please refer to the Oracle documentation.

The Expression Filter

The Expression Filter, available since Oracle Database 10g, uses the Rules Manager to work with expressions. An *expression* is another object type that contains attributes evaluated by the Expression Filter. You add a VARCHAR2 column to a table that stores the values for the attributes of an expression, use a PL/SQL built-in package to add the expression to the column, and use standard SQL to set the values for the expression. To compare values to an expression, you use the EVALUATE operator in the WHERE clause of your SQL statement.

Expressions can be used to define complex qualities for rows, since an expression can have many attributes. You can also use expressions to implement many-to-many relationships without an intermediary table by using expressions from two tables to join the tables.

With the Enterprise Edition of Oracle, you can add an index to an expression, which can provide the same performance benefits of an index to the qualities defined as an expression.

Data Design

Tables and columns present a logical view of the data in a relational database. The flexibility of a relational database gives you many options for grouping the individual pieces of data, represented by the columns, into a set of tables. To use Oracle most effectively, you should understand and follow some firmly established principles of database design.

The topic of database design is vast and deep: we won't even pretend to offer more than a cursory overview. For more information, we recommend the book *Oracle Design* by Dave Ensor and Ian Stevenson (O'Reilly; see Appendix B for details).

When E. F. Codd created the concept of a relational database in the 1960s, he also began work on the concept of *normalized* data design. The theory behind normalized data design is pretty straightforward: a table should contain only the information that is directly related to the key value of the table. The process of assembling these logical units of information is called *normalization* of the database design.

Normalized Forms

In fact, there is more than one type of normalization. Each step in the normalization process ends with a specific result called a *normalized form*. There are five standard normalized forms, which are referred to as first normal form (1NF), second normal form (2NF), and so on. The normalization process that we describe briefly in this section results in third normal form (3NF), the most common type of normalization.

Explaining the complete concepts that lie behind the different normal forms is beyond the scope of this chapter and book.

The concept of normalized table design was tailored to the capabilities of the relational database. Because you could join data from different tables together in a query, there was no need to keep all the information associated with a particular object together in a single record. You could decompose the information into associated units and simply join the appropriate units together when you needed information that crossed table boundaries.

There are many different methodologies for normalizing data. The following is one example:

1. Identify the objects your application needs to know (the *entities*). Examples of entities, as shown in Figure 4-3, include employees, locations, and jobs.

2. Identify the individual pieces of data, referred to by data modelers as *attributes*, for these entities. In Figure 4-3, employee name and salary are attributes. Typically, entities correspond to tables and attributes correspond to columns.

3. As a potential last step in the process, identify *relationships* between the entities based on your business. These relationships are implemented in the database schema through the use of a combination known as a *foreign key*. For example, the primary key of the DEPARTMENT NUMBER table would be a foreign key column in the EMPLOYEE NAME table used to identify the DEPARTMENT NUMBER in which an employee works. A foreign key is a type of constraint; constraints are discussed later in this chapter.

Normalization provides benefits by avoiding storage of redundant data. Storing the department in every employee record not only would waste space but also would lead to a data maintenance issue. If the department name changed, you would have to update every employee record, even though no employees had actually changed departments. By normalizing the department data into a table and simply pointing to the appropriate row from the employee rows, you avoid both duplication of data and this type of problem.

Normalization also reduces the amount of data that any one row in a table contains. The less data in a row, the less I/O is needed to retrieve it, which helps to avoid this performance bottleneck. In addition, the smaller the size of a row, the more rows are retrieved per data block, which increases the likelihood that more than one desired row will be retrieved in a single I/O operation. And the smaller the row, the more rows will be kept in Oracle's system buffers, which also increases the likelihood that a row will be available in memory when it's needed, thereby avoiding the need for any disk I/O at all.

Finally, the process of normalization includes the creation of foreign key relationships and other data constraints. These relationships build a level of data integrity directly into your database design.

Figure 4-3 shows a simple list of attributes grouped into entities and linked by a foreign key relationship.

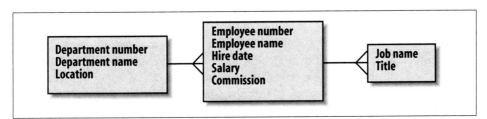

Figure 4-3. The normalization process

However, there is an even more important reason to go through the process of designing a normalized database. You can benefit from normalization because of the planning process that normalizing a data design entails. By really thinking about the way the intended applications use data, you get a much clearer picture of the needs the system is designed to serve. This understanding leads to a much more focused database and application.

Gaining a deep understanding of the way your data will be used also helps with your other design tasks. For instance, once you've completed an optimal logical database design, you must go back and consider what indexes you should add to improve the anticipated performance of the database and whether you should designate any tables as part of a cluster or hash cluster.

Since adding these types of performance-enhancing data structures doesn't affect the logical representation of the database, you can always make these types of modifications later when you see the way an application uses the database in test mode or in production.

Constraints

A *constraint* enforces certain aspects of data integrity within a database. When you add a constraint to a particular column, Oracle automatically ensures that data violating that constraint is never accepted. If a user attempts to write data that violates a constraint, Oracle returns an error for the offending SQL statement.

Constraints may be associated with columns when you create or add the table containing the column (via a number of keywords) or after the table has been created with the SQL command ALTER TABLE. Since Oracle8, the following constraint types are supported:

NOT NULL
> You can designate any column as NOT NULL. If any SQL operation leaves a NULL value in a column with a NOT NULL constraint, Oracle returns an error for the statement.

Unique
> When you designate a column or set of columns as unique, users cannot add values that already exist in another row in the table for those columns, or modify existing values to match other values in the column.
>
> The unique constraint is implemented by the creation of an index, which requires a unique value. If you include more than one column as part of a unique key, you will create a single index that will include all the columns in the unique key. If an index already exists for this purpose, Oracle will automatically use that index.

Should You Normalize Your Data?

Whenever possible, we recommend that you go through the process of designing a normalized structure for your database.

Data normalization has been proven, both theoretically and in decades of practice, to provide concrete benefits. In addition, the process of creating a normalized data design is intimately intertwined with the process of understanding the data requirements for your application system. You can improve even the simplest database by the discoveries made during the process of normalization.

However, there may be times when you feel that the benefits of a fully normalized design will counteract the performance penalty that a design imposes on your production systems. For example, you may have one, two, or three contact names to be placed in their own table, with a foreign key linking back to the main row for the organization. But because you want to see all the contact names every time you request contact information, you might decide to save the overhead and added development effort of the join and simply include the three contact names in your organization table. This technique is common in decision-support/data warehousing applications.

Of course, this violation of the rules of normalization limits the flexibility of your application systems—for example, if you later decide that you need four contact names, some modification of every application and report that uses the contact names will be necessary. Normalization leads to a more flexible design, which is a good thing in the constantly changing world we live in.

For this reason, we suggest that you always implement a fully normalized database design and then, if necessary, go back and denormalize certain tables as needed. With this approach, you will at least have to make a conscious decision to "break" the normalization, which involves an active consideration of the price of denormalization.

If a column is unique but allows NULL values, any number of rows can have a NULL value, because the NULL indicates the absence of a value. To require a truly unique value for a column in every row, the column should be both unique and NOT NULL.

Primary key

Each table can have, at most, a single primary key constraint. The primary key may consist of more than one column in a table.

The primary key constraint forces each primary key to have a unique value. It enforces both the unique constraint and the NOT NULL constraint. A primary key constraint will create a unique index, if one doesn't already exist for the specified column(s).

Foreign key

The foreign key constraint is defined for a table (known as the *child*) that has a relationship with another table in the database (known as the *parent*). The value entered in a foreign key must be present in a unique or primary key of another specific table. For example, the column for a department ID in an employee table might be a foreign key for the department ID primary key in the department table.

A foreign key can have one or more columns, but the referenced key must have an equal number of columns. You can have a foreign key relate to the primary key of its own table, such as when the employee ID of a manager is a foreign key referencing the ID column in the same table.

A foreign key can contain a NULL value if it's not forbidden through another constraint.

By requiring that the value for a foreign key exist in another table, the foreign key constraint enforces referential integrity in the database. Foreign keys not only provide a way to join related tables but also ensure that the relationship between the two tables will have the required data integrity.

Normally, you cannot delete a row in a parent table if it causes a row in the child table to violate a foreign key constraint. However, you can specify that a foreign key constraint causes a *cascade delete*, which means that deleting a referenced row in the parent table automatically deletes all rows in the child table that reference the primary key value in the deleted row in the parent table.

Check

A check constraint is a more general-purpose constraint. A check constraint is a Boolean expression that evaluates to either TRUE or FALSE. If the check constraint evaluates to FALSE, the SQL statement that caused the result returns an error. For example, a check constraint might require the minimum balance in a bank account to be over $100. If a user tries to update data for that account in a way that causes the balance to drop below this required amount, the constraint will return an error.

Some constraints require the creation of indexes to support them. For instance, the unique constraint creates an implicit index used to guarantee uniqueness. You can also specify a particular index that will enforce a constraint when you define that constraint.

All constraints can be either immediate or deferred. An *immediate constraint* is enforced as soon as a write operation affects a constrained column in the table. A *deferred constraint* is enforced when the SQL statement that caused the change in the constrained column completes. Because a single SQL statement can affect several rows, the choice between using a deferred constraint or an immediate constraint can significantly affect how the integrity dictated by the constraint operates. You can specify that an individual constraint is immediate or deferred, or you can set the timing for all constraints in a single transaction.

Finally, you can temporarily suspend the enforcement of constraints for a particular table. When you enable the operation of the constraint, you can instruct Oracle to validate all the data for the constraint or simply start applying the constraint to the new data. When you add a constraint to an existing table, you can also specify whether you want to check all the existing rows in the table.

Triggers

You use constraints to automatically enforce data integrity rules whenever a user tries to write or modify a row in a table. There are times when you want to use the same kind of timing for your own application-specific logic. Oracle includes *triggers* to give you this capability.

 Although you can write triggers to perform the work of a constraint, Oracle has optimized the operation of constraints, so it's best to always use a constraint instead of a trigger if possible.

A trigger is a block of code that is fired whenever a particular type of database event occurs to a table. There are three types of events that can cause a trigger to fire:

- A database UPDATE
- A database INSERT
- A database DELETE

You can, for instance, define a trigger to write a customized audit record whenever a user changes a row.

Triggers are defined at the row level. You can specify that a trigger be fired for each row or for the SQL statement that fires the trigger event. As with the previous discussion of constraints, a single SQL statement can affect many rows, so the specification of the trigger can have a significant effect on the operation of the trigger and the performance of the database.

There are three times when a trigger can fire:

- Before the execution of the triggering event
- After the execution of the triggering event
- Instead of the triggering event

Combining the first two timing options with the row and statement versions of a trigger gives you four possible trigger implementations: before a statement, before a row, after a statement, and after a row.

Oracle Database 11g introduced the concept of compound triggers; with this enhancement, a single trigger can have a section for the different timing implementations. Compound triggers help to improve performance, since the trigger has to be loaded only once for multiple timing options.

INSTEAD OF triggers were introduced with Oracle8. The INSTEAD OF trigger has a specific purpose: to implement data-manipulation operations on views that don't normally permit them, such as a view that references columns in more than one base table for updates. You should be careful when using INSTEAD OF triggers because of the many potential problems associated with modifying the data in the underlying base tables of a view. There are many restrictions on when you can use INSTEAD OF triggers. Refer to your Oracle documentation for a detailed description of the forbidden scenarios.

You can specify a *trigger restriction* for any trigger. A trigger restriction is a Boolean expression that circumvents the execution of the trigger if it evaluates to FALSE.

Triggers are defined and stored separately from the tables that use them. Since they contain logic, they must be written in a language with capabilities beyond those of SQL, which is designed to access data. Oracle8 and later versions allow you to write triggers in PL/SQL, the procedural language that has been a part of Oracle since Version 6. Oracle8i and beyond also support Java as a procedural language, so you can create Java triggers with those versions.

You can write a trigger directly in PL/SQL or Java, or a trigger can call an existing stored procedure written in either language.

Triggers are fired as a result of a SQL statement that affects a row in a particular table. It's possible for the actions of the trigger to modify the data in the table or to cause changes in other tables that fire their own triggers. The end result of this may be data that ends up being changed in a way that Oracle thinks is logically illegal. These situations can cause Oracle to return runtime errors referring to *mutating tables*, which are tables modified by other triggers, or *constraining tables*, which are tables modified by other constraints. Oracle8i eliminated some of the errors caused by activating constraints with triggers.

Oracle8i also introduced a very useful set of system event triggers (sometimes called *database-level event triggers*), and user event triggers (sometimes called *schema-level event triggers*). For example, you can place a trigger on system events such as database startup and shutdown and on user events such as logging on and logging off.

Query Optimization

All of the data structures discussed so far in this chapter are server entities. Users request data from an Oracle server through database queries. Oracle's query optimizer must then determine the best way to access the data requested by each query.

One of the great virtues of a relational database is its ability to access data without predefining the access paths to the data. When a SQL query is submitted to an Oracle database, Oracle must decide how to access the data. The process of making this decision is called *query optimization*, because Oracle looks for the optimal way to retrieve the data. This retrieval is known as the *execution path*. The trick behind query optimization is to choose the most efficient way to get the data, since there may be many different options available.

For instance, even with a query that involves only a single table, Oracle can take either of these approaches:

- Use an index to find the ROWIDs of the requested rows and then retrieve those rows from the table.
- Scan the table to find and retrieve the rows; this is referred to as a *full table scan.*

Although it's usually much faster to retrieve data using an index, the process of getting the values from the index involves an additional I/O step in processing the query. Query optimization may be as simple as determining whether the query involves selection conditions that can be imposed on values in the index. Using the index values to select the desired rows involves less I/O and is therefore more efficient than retrieving all the data from the table and then imposing the selection conditions.

Another factor in determining the optimal query execution plan is whether there is an ORDER BY condition in the query that can be automatically implemented by the presorted index. Alternatively, if the table is small enough, the optimizer may decide to simply read all the blocks of the table and bypass the index since it estimates the cost of the index I/O plus the table I/O to be higher than just the table I/O.

The query optimizer has to make some key decisions even with a query on a single table. When a more involved query is submitted, such as one involving many tables that must be joined together efficiently or one that has complex selection criteria and multiple levels of sorting, the query optimizer has a much more complex task.

Prior to Oracle Database 10g, you could choose between two different Oracle query optimizers, a *rule-based optimizer* and a *cost-based optimizer*; these are described in the following sections. With Oracle Database 10g, the rule-based optimizer is desupported. The references to syntax and operations for the rule-based optimizer in the following sections are provided for reference and are applicable only if you are running an older release of Oracle.

Rule-Based Optimization

Oracle has always had a query optimizer, but until Oracle7 the optimizer was only rule-based. The rule-based optimizer, as the name implies, uses a set of predefined rules as the main determinant of query optimization decisions. Since the rule-based optimizer has been desupported as of Oracle Database 10g, your interest in this topic is likely be limited to supporting old Oracle databases where this choice may have been made.

Rule-based optimization sometimes provided better performance than the early versions of Oracle's cost-based optimizer for specific situations. The rule-based optimizer had several weaknesses, including offering only a simplistic set of rules. The Oracle rule-based optimizer had about 20 rules and assigned a weight to each one of them. In a complex database, a query can easily involve several tables, each with several indexes and complex selection conditions and ordering. This complexity means that there were a lot of options, and the simple set of rules used by the rule-based optimizer might not differentiate the choices well enough to make the best choice.

The rule-based optimizer assigned an optimization score to each potential execution path and then took the path with the best optimization score. Another weakness in the rule-based optimizer was resolution of optimization choices made in the event of a "tie" score. When two paths presented the same optimization score, the rule-based optimizer looked to the syntax of the SQL statement to resolve the tie. The winning execution path was based on the order in which the tables occur in the SQL statement.

You can understand the potential impact of this type of tie-breaker by looking at a simple situation in which a small table with 10 rows, SMALLTAB, is joined to a large table with 10,000 rows, LARGETAB, as shown in Figure 4-4. If the optimizer chose to read SMALLTAB first, the Oracle database will read the 10 rows and then read LARGETAB to find the matching rows for each of the 10 rows. If the optimizer chose to read LARGETAB first, the database read 10,000 rows from LARGETAB and then read SMALLTAB 10,000 times to find the matching rows. Of course, the rows in SMALLTAB would probably be cached, reducing the impact of each probe, but you could see a dramatic difference in performance.

Differences like this could occur with the rule-based optimizer as a result of the ordering of the table names in the query. In the previous situation the rule-based optimizer returned the same results for the query, but it used widely varying amounts of resources to retrieve those results.

Cost-Based Optimization

To improve the optimization of SQL statements, Oracle introduced the *cost-based optimizer* in Oracle7. As the name implies, the cost-based optimizer does more than simply look at a set of optimization rules; instead, it selects the execution path that requires the least number of logical I/O operations. This approach avoids the error

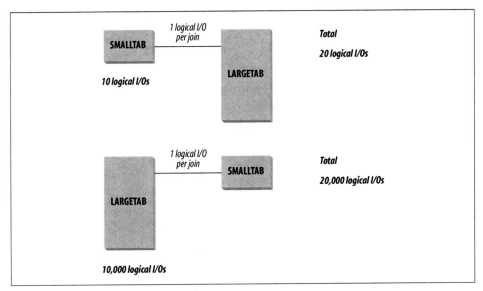

Figure 4-4. The effect of optimization choices

discussed in the previous section. After all, the cost-based optimizer would know which table was bigger and would select the right table to begin the query, regardless of the syntax of the SQL statement.

Oracle8 and later versions, by default, use the cost-based optimizer to identify the optimal execution plan. And, since Oracle Database 10g, the cost-based optimizer is the only supported optimizer. To properly evaluate the cost of any particular execution plan, the cost-based optimizer uses statistics about the composition of the relevant data structures. These statistics are automatically gathered by default since the Oracle Database 10g release into the Automatic Workload Repository (AWR). Among the statistics gathered in the AWR are database segment access and usage statistics, time model statistics, system and session statistics, SQL statements that produce the greatest loads, and Active Session History (ASH) statistics.

How statistics are used

The cost-based optimizer finds the optimal execution plan by assigning an optimization score for each of the potential execution plans using its own internal rules and logic along with statistics that reflect the state of the data structures in the database. These statistics relate to the tables, columns, and indexes involved in the execution plan. The statistics for each type of data structure are listed in Table 4-1.

Table 4-1. Database statistics

Data structure	Type of statistics
Table	Number of rows
	Number of blocks
	Number of unused blocks
	Average available free space per block
	Number of chained rows
	Average row length
Column	Number of distinct values per column
	Second-lowest column value
	Second-highest column value
	Column density factor
Index	Depth of index B*-tree structure
	Number of leaf blocks
	Number of distinct values
	Average number of leaf blocks per key
	Average number of data blocks per key
	Clustering factor

Oracle Database 10g and more current database releases also collect overall system statistics, including I/O and CPU performance and utilization. These statistics are stored in the data dictionary, described in this chapter's final section, "Data Dictionary Tables."

You can see that these statistics can be used individually and in combination to determine the overall cost of the I/O required by an execution plan. The statistics reflect both the size of a table and the amount of unused space within the blocks; this space can, in turn, affect how many I/O operations are needed to retrieve rows. The index statistics reflect not only the depth and breadth of the index tree, but also the uniqueness of the values in the tree, which can affect the ease with which values can be selected using the index.

The accuracy of the cost-based optimizer depends on the accuracy of the statistics it uses, so updating statistics has always been a must. Formerly, you would have used the SQL statement ANALYZE to compute or estimate these statistics. When managing an older release, many database administrators also used a built-in PL/SQL package, DBMS_STATS, that contains a number of procedures that helped automate the process of collecting statistics.

Stale statistics can lead to database performance problems, which is why database statistics gathering has been automated by Oracle. This statistics gathering can be quite granular. For example, as of Oracle Database 10g, you can enable automatic statistics collection for a table, which can be based on whether a table is either stale (which means that more than 10 percent of the objects in the table have changed) or empty.

The use of statistics makes it possible for the cost-based optimizer to make a much more well-informed choice of the optimal execution plan. For instance, the optimizer could be trying to decide between two indexes to use in an execution plan that involves a selection based on a value in either index. The rule-based optimizer might very well rate both indexes equally and resort to the order in which they appear in the WHERE clause to choose an execution plan. The cost-based optimizer, however, knows that one index contains 1,000 entries while the other contains 10,000 entries. It even knows that the index that contains 1,000 values contains only 20 unique values, while the index that contains 10,000 values has 5,000 unique values. The selectivity offered by the larger index is much greater, so that index will be assigned a better optimization score and used for the query.

Testing the Effect of New Statistics

There may be times when you don't want to update your statistics, such as when the distribution of data in your database has reached a steady state or when your queries are already performing optimally (or at least deliver adequate, consistent performance). Oracle gives you a way you can try out a new set of statistics to see if they might make things better while still maintaining the option of returning to the old set: you can save your statistics in a separate table and then collect new ones. If, after testing your application with these new statistics, you decide you preferred the way the old statistics worked, you can simply reload the saved statistics.

In Oracle9i, you have the option of allowing the cost-based optimizer to use CPU speed as one of the factors in determining the optimal execution plan. An initialization parameter turns this feature on and off. As of Oracle Database 10g, the default cost basis is calculated on the CPU cost plus the I/O cost for a plan.

Even with all the information available to it, the cost-based optimizer did have some noticeable initial flaws. Aside from the fact that it (like all software) occasionally had bugs, the cost-based optimizer used statistics that didn't provide a complete picture of the data structures. In the previous example, the only thing the statistics tell the optimizer about the indexes is the number of distinct values in each index. They don't reveal anything about the distribution of those values. For instance, the larger index can contain 5,000 unique values, but these values can each represent two rows in the associated table, or one index value can represent 5,001 rows while the rest of the index values represent a single row. The selectivity of the index can vary wildly, depending on the value used in the selection criteria of the SQL statement. Fortunately, Oracle 7.3 introduced support for collecting histogram statistics for indexes to address this exact problem. You could create histograms using syntax within the ANALYZE INDEX command when you gathered statistics yourself in Oracle versions prior to Oracle Database 10g. This syntax is described in your Oracle SQL reference documentation.

Influencing the cost-based optimizer

There are two ways you can influence the way the cost-based optimizer selects an execution plan. The first way is by setting the OPTIMIZER_MODE initialization parameter. ALL_ROWS is the default setting for OPTIMIZER_MODE enabling optimization with the goal of best throughput. FIRST_ROWS optimizes plans for returning the first set of rows from a SQL statement. You can specify the number of rows using this parameter. The optimizer mode tilts the evaluation of optimization scores slightly and, in some cases, may result in a different execution plan.

Oracle also gives you a way to influence the decisions of the optimizer with a technique called *hints*. A hint is nothing more than a comment with a specific format inside a SQL statement. Hints can be categorized as follows:

- Optimizer SQL hints for changing the query optimizer goal
- Full table scan hints
- Index unique scan hints
- Index range scan descending hints
- Fast full index scan hints
- Join hints, including index joins, nested loop joins, hash joins, sort merge joins, Cartesian joins, and join order
- Other optimizer hints, including access paths, query transformations, and parallel execution

Hints come with their own set of problems. A hint looks just like a comment, as shown in this extremely simple SQL statement. Here, the hint forces the optimizer to use the EMP_IDX index for the EMP table:

```
SELECT /*+ INDEX(EMP_IDX) */ LASTNAME, FIRSTNAME, PHONE FROM EMP
```

If a hint isn't in the right place in the SQL statement, if the hint keyword is misspelled, or if you change the name of a data structure so that the hint no longer refers to an existing structure, the hint will simply be ignored, just as a comment would be. Because hints are embedded into SQL statements, repairing them can be quite frustrating and time-consuming if they aren't working properly. In addition, if you add a hint to a SQL statement to address a problem caused by a bug in the cost-based optimizer and the cost-based optimizer is subsequently fixed, the SQL statement will still not use the corrected (and potentially improved) optimizer.

However, hints do have a place—for example, when a developer has a user-defined datatype that suggests a particular type of access. The optimizer cannot anticipate the effect of user-defined datatypes, but a hint can properly enable the appropriate retrieval path.

For more details about when hints might be considered, see the sidebar "Accepting the Verdict of the Optimizer" later in this chapter.

Specifying an Optimizer Mode

In the previous section we mentioned two optimizer modes: ALL_ROWS and FIRST_ROWS. Two other optimizer modes for Oracle versions prior to Oracle Database 10g were:

RULE
> Forces the use of the rule-based optimizer

CHOOSE
> Allowed Oracle to choose whether to use the cost-based optimizer or the rule-based optimizer

With an optimizer mode of CHOOSE, which previously was the default setting, Oracle would use the cost-based optimizer if any of the tables in the SQL statement have statistics associated with them. The cost-based optimizer would make a statistical estimate for the tables that lacked statistics. If you are running an older Oracle release using rules, you probably wonder if moving to a newer release with only cost-based optimizer support is a good idea. Let's have a closer look at the advantages of the cost-based optimizer.

Newer database releases and the cost-based optimizer

The cost-based optimizer makes decisions with a wider range of knowledge about the data structures in the database. Although the cost-based optimizer isn't flawless in its decision-making process, it does make more accurate decisions based on its wider base of information, especially because it has matured since its introduction in Oracle7 and has improved with each new release.

The cost-based optimizer also takes into account improvements and new features in the Oracle database as they are released. For instance, the cost-based optimizer understands the impact that partitioned tables have on the selection of an execution plan, while the rule-based optimizer did not. The cost-based optimizer optimizes execution plans for star schema queries, heavily used in data warehousing, while the rule-based optimizer has not been enhanced to deal effectively with these types of queries or leverage many other such business intelligence query features.

Oracle Corporation was quite frank about its intention to make the cost-based optimizer *the* optimizer for the Oracle database through a period of years when both optimizer types were supported. In fact, since Oracle Database 10g, the rule-based optimizer is no longer supported.

We will remind you of one fact of database design at this point. As good as the cost-based optimizer is today, it is not a magic potion that remedies problems brought on by a poor database and application design or a badly selected hardware and storage platform. When performance problems occur today, they are most often due to bad design and deployment choices.

Accepting the Verdict of the Optimizer

Some of you may doubt the effectiveness of Oracle query optimization if you are on an old Oracle database release, especially prior to Oracle Database 10g where tuning often required running scripts. You may have seen cases in which the query optimizer chose an incorrect execution path that resulted in poor performance. You may feel that you have a better understanding of the structure and use of the database than the query optimizer. For these reasons, you might look to hints to force the acceptance of the execution path you feel is correct.

We recommend using the query optimizer for all of your queries rather than using hints. Although the Oracle developers who wrote the query optimizer had no knowledge of your particular database, they did depend on a lot of customer feedback, experience, and knowledge of how Oracle processes queries during the creation of the query optimizer. They designed the cost-based optimizer to efficiently execute all types of queries that may be submitted to the Oracle database.

In addition, there are three advantages that the query optimizer has over your discretion in all cases:

- The optimizer sees the structure of the entire database. Many Oracle databases support a variety of applications and users and it's quite possible that your system shares data with other systems, making the overall structure and composition of the data somewhat out of your control. In addition, you probably designed and tested your systems in a limited environment, so your idea of the optimal execution path may not match the reality of the production environment, especially as it evolves.

- The optimizer has a dynamically changing view of the database and its data. The statistics used by the cost-based optimizer can change with each automated collection. In addition to the changing statistical conditions, the internal workings of the optimizer are occasionally changed to accommodate changes in the way the Oracle database operates. Since Oracle9i, the cost-based optimizer takes into account the speed of the CPU, and since Oracle Database 10g leverages statistics on I/O. If you force the selection of a particular query plan with a hint, you might not benefit from changes in Oracle.

- A bad choice by the optimizer may be a sign that something is amiss in your database. For the most part, the query optimizer selects the optimal execution path. What may be seen as a mistake by the query optimizer can, in reality, be traced to a misconception about the database and its design or to an improper implementation. A mistake is always an opportunity to learn, and you should always take advantage of any opportunity to increase your overall understanding of how Oracle and its optimizer work.

—continued—

We recommend that you consider using hints only when you have determined them to be absolutely necessary by thoroughly investigating the causes for an optimization problem. The hint syntax was included in Oracle syntax as a way to handle exceptional situations, rather than to allow you to circumvent the query optimizer. If you've found a performance anomaly and further investigation has led to the discovery that the query optimizer is choosing an incorrect execution path, then and only then should you assign a hint to a query.

Even in this situation, we recommend that you keep an eye on the hinted query in a production environment to make sure that the forced execution path is still working optimally.

Saving the Optimization

There may be times when you want to prevent the optimizer from calculating a new plan whenever a SQL statement is submitted. For example, you might do this if you've finally reached a point at which you feel the SQL is running optimally, and you don't want the plan to change regardless of future changes to the optimizer or the database.

Starting with Oracle8i, you could create a *stored outline* that stored the attributes used by the optimizer to create an execution plan. Once you had a stored outline, the optimizer simply used the stored attributes to create an execution plan. As of Oracle9i, you could also edit the hints that were in the stored outline.

With the release of Oracle Database 11g, Oracle suggests that you move your stored outlines to *SQL plan baselines*. Now, in addition to manually loading plans, Oracle can be set to automatically capture plan histories into these SQL plan baselines. Included in this gathered history is the SQL text, outline, bind variables, and compilation environment. When a SQL statement is compiled, Oracle will first use the cost-based optimizer to generate a plan and will evaluate any matching SQL plan baselines for relative cost, choosing the plan with the lowest cost.

Comparing Optimizations

Oracle makes changes to the optimizer in every release. These changes are meant to improve the overall quality of the decisions the optimizer makes, but a generally improved optimizer could still create an execution plan for any particular SQL statement that could result in a decrease in performance.

The SQL*Analyzer tool is designed to give you the ability to recognize potential problems caused by optimizer upgrades. This tool compares the execution plans for the SQL statements in your application, flagging the ones in which the plans differ.

Once these statements are identified, SQL*Analyzer executes the SQL in each environment and provides feedback on the performance and resource utilization for each. Although SQL*Analyzer cannot avoid potential problems brought on by optimizer upgrades, the tool can definitely simplify an otherwise complex testing task.

Oracle Database 11g also includes a feature called Database Replay. This feature captures workloads from production systems and allows them to be run on test systems. With this capability, you can test actual production scenarios against new configurations or versions of the database, and Database Replay will spot areas of potential performance problems on the changed platform.

Performance and Optimization

The purpose of the optimizer is to select the best execution plan for your queries. But there is a lot more to optimizing the overall performance of your database. Oracle performance is the subject of Chapter 7 of this book.

Understanding the Execution Plan

Oracle's query optimizer automatically selects an execution plan for each query submitted. By and large, although the optimizer does a good job of selecting the execution plan, there may be times when the performance of the database suggests that it is using a less-than-optimal execution plan.

The only way you can really tell what path is being selected by the optimizer is to see the layout of the execution plan. You can use two Oracle character-mode utilities to examine the execution plan chosen by the Oracle optimizer. These tools allow you to see the successive steps used by Oracle to collect, select, and return the data to the user.

The first utility is the SQL EXPLAIN PLAN statement. When you use EXPLAIN PLAN, followed by the keyword FOR and the SQL statement whose execution plan you want to view, the Oracle cost-based optimizer returns a description of the execution plan it will use for the SQL statement and inserts this description into a database table. You can subsequently run a query on that table to get the execution plan, as shown in SQL*Plus in Figure 4-5.

The execution plan is presented as a series of rows in the table, one for each step taken by Oracle in the process of executing the SQL statement. The optimizer also includes some of the information related to its decisions, such as the overall cost of each step and some of the statistics that it used to make its decisions.

The optimizer writes all of this information to a table in the database. By default, the optimizer uses a table called PLAN_TABLE; make sure the table exists before you use EXPLAIN PLAN. (The *utlxplan.sql* script included with your Oracle database

```
SQL> EXPLAIN PLAN FOR
  2   SELECT DNAME, ENAME FROM EMP, DEPT
  3   WHERE EMP.DEPTNO = DEPT.DEPTNO
  4   ORDER BY DNAME;

Explained.

SQL> SELECT OBJECT_NAME, OPERATION, OPTIONS FROM PLAN_TABLE ORDER BY ID;

OBJECT_NAME                 OPERATION                   OPTIONS
--------------------------- --------------------------- -------------------------
                            SELECT STATEMENT
                            SORT                        ORDER BY
                            NESTED LOOPS
EMP                         TABLE ACCESS                FULL
DEPT                        TABLE ACCESS                BY INDEX ROWID
SYS_C004911                 INDEX                       UNIQUE SCAN

6 rows selected.
```

Figure 4-5. Results of a simple EXPLAIN PLAN statement in SQL*Plus

creates the default PLAN_TABLE table.) You can specify that EXPLAIN PLAN uses a table other than PLAN_TABLE in the syntax of the statement. For more information about the use of EXPLAIN PLAN, please refer to your Oracle documentation.

There are times when you want to examine the execution plan for a single statement. In such cases, the EXPLAIN PLAN syntax is appropriate. There are other times when you want to look at the plans for a group of SQL statements. For these situations, you can set up a trace for the statements you want to examine and then use the second utility, TKPROF, to give you the results of the trace in a more readable format in a separate file. At other times, you might also use Oracle's SQL Trace facility to generate a file containing the SQL generated when using TKPROF in tuning applications.

You must use the EXPLAIN keyword when you start TKPROF, as this will instruct the utility to execute an EXPLAIN PLAN statement for each SQL statement in the trace file. You can also specify how the results delivered by TKPROF are sorted. For instance, you can have the SQL statements sorted on the basis of the physical I/Os they used; the elapsed time spent on parsing, executing, or fetching the rows; or the total number of rows affected.

The TKPROF utility uses a trace file as its raw material. Trace files are created for individual sessions. You can start collecting a trace file either by running the target application with a switch (if it's written with an Oracle product such as Developer) or by explicitly turning it on with an EXEC SQL call or an ALTER SESSION SQL statement in an application written with a 3GL. The trace process, as you can probably guess, can significantly affect the performance of an application, so you should turn it on only when you have some specific diagnostic work to do.

You can also view the execution plan through Enterprise Manager for the SQL statements that use the most resources. Tuning your SQL statements isn't a trivial task, but with the EXPLAIN PLAN and TKPROF utilities you can get to the bottom of the decisions made by the cost-based optimizer. It takes a bit of work to understand exactly how to read an execution plan, but it's better to have access to this type of information than not. In large-scale system-development projects, it's quite common for developers to submit EXPLAIN PLANs for the SQL they're writing to a DBA as a formal step toward completing a form or report. While time-consuming, this is the best way to ensure that your SQL is tuned before going into production.

SQL Advisors

Oracle Database 10g added a tool called the SQL Tuning Advisor. This tool performs advanced optimization analysis on selected SQL statements, using workloads that have been automatically collected into the Automatic Workload Repository or that you have specified yourself. Once the optimization is done, the SQL Tuning Advisor makes recommendations, which could include updating statistics, adding indexes, or creating a *SQL profile*. This profile is stored in the database and is used as the optimization plan for future executions of the statement, which allows you to "fix" errant SQL plans without having to touch the underlying SQL.

The tool is often used along with the SQL Access Advisor since that tool provides advice on materialized views and indexes. Oracle Database 11g introduces a SQL Advisor tool that combines functions of the SQL Tuning Advisor and the SQL Access Advisor (and now includes a new Partition Advisor). The Partition Advisor component advises on how to partition tables, materialized views, and indexes in order to improve SQL performance.

Data Dictionary Tables

The main purpose of the Oracle data dictionary is to store data that describes the structure of the objects in the Oracle database. Because of this purpose, there are many views in the Oracle data dictionary that provide information about the attributes and composition of the data structures within the database.

All of the views listed in this section actually have three varieties, which are identified by their prefixes:

DBA_
> Includes all the objects in the database. A user must have DBA privileges to use this view.

USER_
> Includes only the objects in the user's own database schema.

*ALL_*

> Includes all the objects in the database to which a particular user has access. If a user has been granted rights to objects in another user's schema, these objects will appear in this view.

This means that, for instance, there are three views that relate to tables: DBA_TABLES, USER_TABLES, and ALL_TABLES.

Some of the more common views that directly relate to the data structures are described in Table 4-2.

Table 4-2. Data dictionary views about data structures

Data dictionary view	Type of information
ALL_TABLES	Information about the object and relational tables
TABLES	Information about the relational tables
TAB_COMMENTS	Comments about the table structures
TAB_HISTOGRAMS	Statistics about the use of tables
TAB_PARTITIONS	Information about the partitions in a partitioned table
TAB_PRIVS*	Different views detailing all the privileges on a table, the privileges granted by the user, and the privileges granted to the user
TAB_COLUMNS	Information about the columns in tables and views
COL_COMMENTS	Comments about individual columns
COL_PRIVS*	Different views detailing all the privileges on a column, the privileges granted by the user, and the privileges granted to the user
LOBS	Information about large object (LOB) datatype columns
VIEWS	Information about views
INDEXES	Information about the indexes on tables
IND_COLUMNS	Information about the columns in each index
IND_PARTITIONS	Information about each partition in a partitioned index
PART_*	Different views detailing the composition and usage patterns for partitioned tables and indexes
CONS_COLUMNS	Information about the columns in each constraint
CONSTRAINTS	Information about constraints on tables
SEQUENCES	Information about sequence objects
SYNONYMS	Information about synonyms
TAB_COL_STATISTICS	Statistics used by the cost-based analyzer
TRIGGERS	Information about the triggers on tables
TRIGGER_COLS	Information about the columns in triggers

CHAPTER 5

Managing Oracle

Many Oracle users and developers are not actively aware of the system and database management activities that go on around them. But effective management is vital to providing a reliable, available, and secure platform that delivers optimal performance. This chapter focuses on how you can manage Oracle to ensure these virtues for your environment.

Much of the management responsibility usually falls upon the database administrator. Users and developers of Oracle also need to be aware of some of the techniques described here. The DBA is typically responsible for the following management tasks:

- Installing and upgrading the database and options
- Creating tables and indexes
- Creating and managing tablespaces
- Managing control files, online redo logs, archived redo logs, job queues, and server processes
- Creating, monitoring, and tuning data-loading procedures
- Adding users and groups and implementing security procedures
- Implementing backup, recovery, information lifecycle management, and high availability plans
- Monitoring database performance and exceptions
- Reorganizing and tuning the database
- Troubleshooting database problems
- Coordinating with Oracle Worldwide Customer Support Services

Particularly in smaller companies, DBAs are also often called upon to take part in database schema design and security planning. DBAs in large enterprises may also help set up replication strategies, disaster and high-availability strategies, hierarchical storage management procedures, and the linking of database event monitoring (e.g., specific database tasks and status) into enterprise network monitors.

Oracle's feature list has grown with each database release. Yet managing Oracle can be much less labor-intensive today than it was in the past. While database releases highlighted in early editions of this book described the novelty of an easier-to-use management interface, producing better versions of Oracle Enterprise Manager (EM) was only part of the effort to simplify management underway within Oracle Server Development. The database itself has now become more self-tuning and self-managing.

Initially, this effort was focused mostly on better management of single instances of the Oracle database. Oracle Database 10g expanded its capabilities with a focus on *grid computing*. Grid computing highlighted the need for effective management of scores of computers and database instances.

Manageability of a grid must take into account disk virtualization, resource pooling, provisioning of computer resources, dynamic workload management, and dynamic control of changing grid components. Oracle's grid initiative resulted in many significant changes in managing the database geared toward significantly reducing this complexity. While targeted at simplifying grid management, most of these improvements also provide great impact in simplifying management of more traditional Oracle database implementations.

 As a consequence of the grid initiative and self-tuning and self-managing initiatives, readers of early editions of this book will find a large number of management changes in this chapter and in others throughout this book.

All of the tasks we've just described come under the heading of managing the database. Many of the provisioning duties, including installation, initial configuration, and cloning, are discussed in Chapter 3. Security issues are discussed in Chapter 6. This chapter explores the following aspects of managing Oracle:

- Using Oracle Enterprise Manager, which provides an easy-to-use interface and underlying framework for many database-management tasks, including new database capabilities
- Managing database fragmentation, which can affect database performance
- Performing backup and recovery operations and information lifecycle management, which are the foundation of database integrity protection
- Working with Oracle Support

In subsequent chapters, we'll cover other related topics in more depth, including security, performance, and high availability. You will need an understanding of all of these areas as you plan and implement effective management strategies for your Oracle database environment.

Manageability Features

Oracle Database 10g and its "Intelligent Infrastructure" was a huge step forward in simplifying management of the Oracle database. Many manual steps needed to manage database releases previous to Oracle Database 10g were eliminated. Oracle Database 11g introduced still more self-tuning and self-management features. Key maintenance tasks are automated, including optimizer statistics gathering, the Segment Advisor, and the SQL Tuning Advisor. Management of the entire infrastructure is accomplished through self-managing capabilities within the database and through Oracle Enterprise Manager.

Statistics containing active session history are now gathered and populate the Automatic Workload Repository (AWR). The Automatic Database Diagnostic Monitor (ADDM) automatically tracks changes in database performance leveraging the data in the AWR. Server-generated alerts occur "just-in-time" and appear in Enterprise Manager. Resolving system utilization problems can be as simple as reviewing the alerts and accepting the recommendations. This is in sharp contrast to steps typically taken prior to Oracle Database 10g that included actively watching for events, exploring V$ tables, identifying related SQL, and then figuring out the needed steps to resolve the problem.

Database Advisors

ADDM is one of several advisors present in Oracle and accessible using Enterprise Manager today. Other performance related advisors include:

SQL Advisor
> Oracle Database 11g includes the SQL Tuning Advisor, SQL Access Advisor, and Partition Advisor. The SQL Tuning Advisor analyzes SQL statements and makes SQL improvement recommendations. The SQL Access Advisor and Partitioning Advisor recommend when to create indexes, materialized views, or partitioned tables.

SQL Performance Impact Advisor
> Introduced in Oracle Database 11g, this advisor enables you to forecast how a system change will impact SQL performance.

Memory Advisors
> The Memory Advisor is an expert system that provides automatic memory management and eliminates manual adjustment of the SGA and PGA when enabled (and recommended in Oracle Database 11g). If just automatic shared memory is enabled instead, you will have access to the Shared Pool (SGA) Advisor and PGA Advisor. Finally, if you are manually managing shared memory, you will have access to the Shared Pool (SGA) Advisor, Buffer Cache Advisor, and PGA Advisor.

Segment Advisor

Use of the Segment Advisor eliminates the need to identify fragmented objects and reorganize the objects using scripts. The Segment Advisor advises which objects to shrink and allows you to simply accept the recommendations. You might also use this information in capacity planning.

Undo Advisor

The Undo Advisor helps size the undo tablespace and can be used to set the low threshold of undo retention for Flashback. Oracle Database 11g features automatic undo management.

MTTR Advisor

The Mean Time to Recovery (MTTR) Advisor provides guidance regarding the impact of MTTR settings and physical writes. The mean time for recovery from a system failure is specified based on business needs by the database administrator using Enterprise Manager, and then needed reconfiguration of Oracle components automatically takes place.

Streams Tuning Advisor

The Streams Tuning Advisor reports on throughput and latency for a Streams topology among Oracle databases and can identify bottlenecks.

Another class of advisors introduced in Oracle Database 11g can be used to resolve database issues. When critical errors are detected, the fault diagnosability infrastructure for Oracle Database 11g can perform a deeper analysis called a *health check* using a Health Monitor. The advisors leverage diagnostic data including database traces, the alert log, Health Monitor reports, and other diagnostic information stored in the Automatic Diagnostic Repository (ADR). The infrastructure also includes a SQL Test Case Builder used for reproducing the problem and transmitting the information to Oracle Support. The advisors in this infrastructure include:

SQL Repair Advisor

If a SQL statement fails with a critical error, the SQL Repair Advisor will analyze the statement and recommend a patch to repair it.

Data Recovery Advisor

The Data Recovery Advisor is used in recovering from corrupted blocks, corrupted or missing files, and other data failures and is integrated with database health checks and RMAN.

Automatic Storage Management

Oracle Database 10g introduced Automatic Storage Management (ASM). ASM provides a file system and volume manager in the database, enabling automated striping of files and automating mirroring of database extents. DBAs simply define a pool of storage or disk group and manage the disk group through EM. Disk groups are created with normal redundancy as the default (2-way mirroring). You can also create disk groups with high redundancy (3-way mirroring) or external redundancy (no mirroring). Failure groups are ASM disks that share a common failure point, so mirroring will automatically occur to a different failure group to provide high availability.

Oracle manages the files that are stored in ASM disk groups. ASM can manage Oracle datafiles, logfiles, control files, archive logs, and RMAN/backup sets. Workloads can be dynamically rebalanced as storage is reconfigured such that when storage is added or removed from the pool, data can be redistributed in the background.

Oracle Enterprise Manager

Oracle Enterprise Manager was first distributed with Oracle7 and was designed for simplifying database management. Early EM versions required Windows-based workstations as client machines. A Java applet browser-based EM console appeared with the Oracle8i database release. The HTML-based console was introduced with Oracle9i products, including the Oracle Application Server, and is now the basis for Enterprise Manager included with the database. As of Oracle Database 11g, the Java applet console is no longer available.

Today, EM is far more than just a database management interface. EM has many optional packs that extend its ability to manage not only Oracle databases but also other infrastructure components commonly present. These packs include:

Database Management Packs
Diagnostics, Tuning, Change Management, Configuration Management, Provisioning

Standalone Management Packs
Provisioning, Service Level Management

Application Management Packs
E-Business Suite, PeopleSoft Enterprise, Siebel

Middleware (Oracle Application Server) Management Packs
Diagnostics, Configuration Management, Identity Management, Provisioning, SOA Management

Management Connectors
Microsoft Operations Manager, Remedy Helpdesk

Operating System Management Packs
Oracle Linux

System Monitoring Plug-ins
EMC Celerra, EMC Symmetrix DMX, NetApp Filer, BEA WebLogic, JBoss Application Server, IBM WebSphere, IBM WebSphere MQ, IBM DB2, Microsoft IIS Server, Microsoft Active Directory, Microsoft BizTalk Server, Microsoft

Commerce Server, Microsoft ISA Server, Microsoft .NET framework, Microsoft SQL Server, Check Point Firewall, Juniper Netscreeen Firewall, F5 BigIP Local Traffic Manager, Linux Hosts, Unix Hosts, Windows Hosts

Since our primary focus in this book is on the Oracle's database, we'll focus on EM's role in such management. Taking a closer look at the Database Management Packs, the functionality provided by each is as follows:

Database Diagnostics Pack
> Provides automatic performance diagnostics by leveraging ADDM, the AWR, monitoring templates, and advanced event notification and alerting

Database Tuning Pack
> Provides the statistics, SQL profiling, access path, and SQL structure analysis leveraged by the SQL Tuning Advisor and includes the SQL Access Advisor and Object Reorganization Wizard

Database Change Management Pack
> Provides capture and version baselines, database object and data copying, and object definition updates

Database Configuration Management Pack
> Provides system inventory collection and reporting, configuration comparisons and history, policy manager, and critical patch advisor

Database Provisioning Pack
> Provides automated patching, cloning, provisioning, and single instance to RAC conversion

Enterprise Manager Architecture

Enterprise Manager can be used for management tasks locally, remotely, and/or through firewalls. Individual consoles can manage single databases or multiple databases. Where EM is managing Oracle deployed on a cluster of computers, it is sometimes referenced as *Grid Control*.

The home page for Grid Control lists the software being managed and provides a high-level view of the status of Grid components. You can drill from Grid Control into the consoles for individual databases, application servers, and other targets. Figure 5-1 illustrates a typical Grid Control home page.

The Enterprise Manager architecture includes the following components:

Oracle Management Agents
> These agents monitor targets for health, status, and performance. Agents automatically discover all Oracle components and also report back other relevant hardware and software configuration information to EM via HTTP/HTTPS. Each monitored Oracle instance has its own agent.

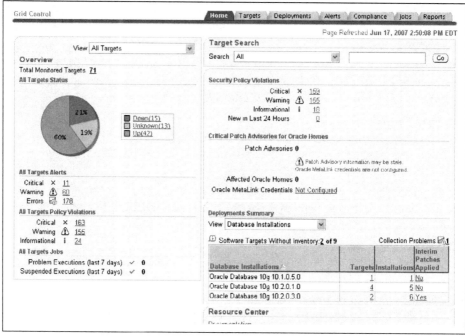

Figure 5-1. Typical Grid Control home page

Enterprise Manager Console

The console allows you to view the status of all monitored components and provides management and diagnostic tools.

Oracle Management Service (OMS)

Receives information from Oracle Management Agents and stores it in the Oracle Management Repository. A local version of OMS services Management Repositories on each local database. The OMS is a J2EE Web application that also renders the Grid Control console user interface at the central location.

Oracle Management Repository

Enterprise Manager accesses this repository of health, status, and performance data. A repository is automatically installed on each local database to service each local Enterprise Manager Database Control console. Oracle Grid Control accesses a central Oracle Management Repository serviced by a central OMS and central Oracle Management Agent.

The EM architecture is shown in Figure 5-2.

Management Agents are available for the wide variety of operating systems on which the Oracle database is available and are responsible for automatic service discovery, event monitoring, and job (predefined task) execution. Management Agents can also send Simple Network Management Protocol (SNMP) traps to database performance monitors in other system monitoring tools.

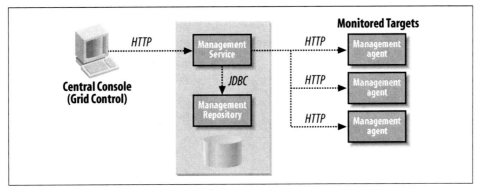

Figure 5-2. Oracle Enterprise Manager architecture

Oracle Enterprise Manager Consoles

EM's popularity grew as deployment of the Oracle database expanded within companies to multiple operating systems and as additional Oracle software components were added to the mix. EM provides a common interface to managing all of these environments, something that DBA scripts were not always designed for. Further, the Enterprise Manager interface and framework provide simple access to new database self-monitoring features, responding to alerts, and managing jobs, reports, roles, and privileges. An EM console and the underlying "Intelligent Infrastructure" are installed as part of the normal Oracle database installation process. EM automatically discovers target databases as soon as it is installed.

Simple EM management interfaces can also be deployed through the Oracle Application Server Portal. Management portlets are prepackaged for use with the Portal providing displays of target summaries, outstanding alerts (notifications where thresholds are reached or exceeded), metric details, availability timelines, and executive summary information.

Logging into Enterprise Manager after a typical installation brings you to the home page database management console. Tabs are shown to enable quick navigation of EM and can vary based on the Enterprise Manager version deployed. Oracle has continued to modify the interface over the years to make finding management capabilities through the interface more intuitive. The version shipping with early versions of Enterprise Manager for Oracle Database 11g includes tabs for Home, Performance, Availability, Server, Schema, Data Movement, and Software and Support pages. Prior to Oracle Database 11g, the Enterprise Manager version included tabs for Home, Administration, Maintenance, and Performance pages (see Figure 5-3). At the top of the console page in each of these versions are links to setup (for setting up and managing additional administrators, notification methods, etc.), preferences (for example, notification schedules), help, and logout.

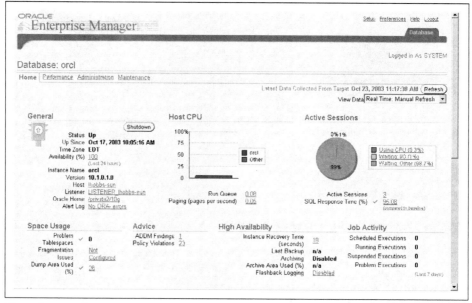

Figure 5-3. Oracle Enterprise Manager Database home page

In the Oracle Database 11g version, some of the key manageability functionality in each of the tabs includes:

Home page

> Provides a quick view of database status including whether the database is up, the database version, the hostname, and listener. Key metrics describing status of the host CPU, active sessions, and SQL response time are typically displayed in graphical form. Summaries of diagnostics, space utilized, and high availability status, alerts, and policy violations are also typically displayed. Related links are provided from this page to Advisor Central (a page for quick access to the advisors) and other key metrics such as the alert log content.

Performance page

> Includes a summary of important performance statistics such as CPU utilization, average active sessions, disk I/O, and instance throughput.

Availability page

> Here you can manage backup and recovery using tools such as RMAN and LogMiner.

Server page

> Includes links to automated maintenance features, such as Automatic Memory Management, the AWR, and scheduling.

Schema page

Here you can manage users and privileges, Oracle tables, indexes, views, synonyms, sequences, and database links, and can initiate related management functions such as Flashback.

Data Movement page

Manages data movement features such as Streams and transportable tablespaces.

Software and Support page

Provides access to the Support Workbench for reporting problems to Oracle Support that you observe in the AWR.

The sophistication of Enterprise Manager continues to grow, as illustrated by the Real Applications Testing Option's database workload capture and replay capability introduced in Oracle Database 11g. You can now use Enterprise Manager to re-create your production environment in a test environment and test your changes in the test environment before propagating those changes back into production.

You will find this new capability under the Software and Support tab. Here you can define and start or schedule the capture of the production workload (e.g., the load and concurrency in the production system). You can also view other previous captured workloads, manage replays, and stop an active capture or replay. You then move the captured workload, in replay format, to the test system. You can then replay the production workload against the changes you make to the test system while checking for errors, data divergence, and performance changes.

EM2Go

EM2Go is a mobile version of Enterprise Manager introduced with Oracle Database 10g. It can be used for remote wireless management of Oracle database instances and Oracle Application Servers. Providing a subset of the functionality in Enterprise Manager, EM2Go leverages the previously described OMS, associated Management Repository, and Oracle Agents in the EM architecture. The Enterprise Manager Console is accessed through a Microsoft Pocket PC Internet Explorer browser on a PDA device. Communication between the console and OMS and between OMS and the Agents is via HTTP.

The administrator begins by logging into Enterprise Manager from the EM2Go Home page by entering the appropriate EM username and password. Upon logging in, administrators are presented with a summary of alerts and targets. Each is a link that you can drill to for more detail.

You can set up EM2Go to forward alert notifications by way of email directly to your PDA. It supports ad-hoc SQL and operating system commands. Performance monitoring includes metrics history graphing of warnings and alerts from the Oracle database and Oracle Application Server and access to the database home page.

Fragmentation and Reorganization

Fragmentation is a problem that can negatively impact performance—and one that many DBAs have struggled to manage in the past. Fragmentation can be an unwanted phenomenon if it results in small parts of noncontiguous "free space" that cannot be reused.

In Oracle, a collection of contiguous blocks is referred to as an *extent*. A collection of extents is referred to as a *segment*. Segments can contain anything that takes up space—for example, a table, an index, or a rollback segment. Segments typically consist of multiple extents. As one extent fills up, a segment begins to use another extent. As fragmentation occurs, by database activity that leaves "holes" in the contiguous space represented by extents, segments acquire additional extents. As fragmentation grows, increased I/O activity results in reduced performance.

Resolving Fragmentation

As of Oracle Database 10*g*, resolving fragmentation issues became fairly trivial. You can perform an online segment shrink using the Segment Advisor interface accessible through EM. ADDM recommends segments to shrink, and you simply choose to accept the recommendations.

For Oracle9*i* databases, a common means of reducing fragmentation was through an online reorganization accomplished through a CREATE TABLE...AS SELECT online operation—that is, the copying of the contents of one table to another while the original table is updated. Changes to the original table were tracked and applied to the new table. Physical and logical attributes of the table could be changed during this online operation, thus allowing an online reorganization.

Prior to Oracle9*i*, reducing fragmentation was more difficult. The general recommendation was to avoid fragmentation through careful planning. But the usual way to solve fragmentation was to reorganize a table by exporting the table, dropping it, and importing it. The data was unavailable while the table was in the process of being reorganized. Many DBAs claimed that they saw improved performance after reorganizing segments into a single extent. Over time, a decrease in performance reoccurred as the number of extents the table occupied increased.

Oracle performance increased as a result of these reorganization operations, but this improvement was *not* due to a decrease in the number of extents. When a table is dropped and re-created, several things happened that increased performance:

- Each block was loaded as full of rows as possible.
- As a consequence, the high-water mark of the table (the highest block that has ever had data in it) was set to its lowest point.

- All indexes on the table were rebuilt, which meant that the index blocks were as full as possible. The depth of the index, which determined the number of I/Os it takes to get to the leaf blocks or the index, was sometimes minimized.

By eliminating fragments and shrinking segments in a much more automated and online fashion, database releases since Oracle Database 10g greatly simplify solving fragmentation problems; the result is that optimal conditions exist for performance.

Backup and Recovery

Even if you've taken adequate precautions, critical database records can sometimes be destroyed as a result of human error or hardware or software failure. The only way to prepare for this type of potentially disastrous situation is to perform regular backup operations.

Two basic types of potential failures can affect an Oracle database: *instance failure*, in which the Oracle instance terminates without going through the shutdown process; and *media failure*, in which the disks that store the information in an Oracle database are corrupted or damaged.

After an instance failure, Oracle will automatically perform crash recovery. For example, you can use Real Application Clusters to automatically perform instance recovery when one of its instances crashes. However, DBAs must initiate recovery from media failure. The ability to recover successfully from this type of failure is the result of careful planning. The recovery process includes restoring older copies of the damaged datafile(s) and rolling forward by applying archived and online redo logs.

To ensure successful recovery, the DBA should have prepared for this eventuality by performing the following actions:

- Multiplexing online redo logs by having multiple log members per group on different disks and controllers
- Running the database in ARCHIVELOG mode so that redo log files are archived before they are reused
- Archiving redo logs to multiple locations
- Maintaining multiple copies of the control file(s)
- Backing up physical datafiles frequently—ideally, storing multiple copies in multiple locations

Running the database in ARCHIVELOG mode ensures that you can recover the database up to the time of the media failure; in this mode, the DBA can perform online datafile backups while the database is available for use. In addition, archived redo logs can be sent to a standby database (explained in Chapter 10) to which they may be applied.

Recovery Manager, also known as RMAN, first introduced in Oracle8 and greatly enhanced since, provides an easy-to-use frontend to manage this process. RMAN is accessible today through Enterprise Manager.

Types of Backup and Recovery Options

There are two major categories of backup:

Full backup
> Includes backups of datafiles, datafile copies, tablespaces, control files (current or backup), or the entire database (including all datafiles and the current control file). Reads entire files and copies all blocks into the backup set, skipping only datafile blocks that have never been used (with the exception of control files and redo logs where no blocks are skipped).

Incremental backup
> Includes backups of datafiles, tablespaces, or the whole database. Reads entire files and backs up only those data blocks that have changed since a previous backup.

You can begin backups through the Recovery Manager or the Oracle Enterprise Manager interface to RMAN, which uses the database export facility, or you can initiate backups via standard operating system backup utilities.

In general, RMAN supports most database backup features, including open or online backups, closed database backups, incremental backups at the Oracle block level, corrupt block detection, automatic backups, backup catalogs, and backups to sequential media. RMAN added capabilities in Oracle9*i* for one-time backup configuration, recovery windows to determine and manage expiration dates of backups, and restartable backups and restores. Also added was support for testing of restores and recovery.

Since Oracle Database 10*g*, RMAN can perform image copy backups of the database, tablespaces, or datafiles. RMAN can be used to apply incremental backups to datafile image backups. The speed of incremental backups is increased through a change-tracking feature by reading and backing up only changed blocks.

Recovery options include the following:

* Complete database recovery to the point of failure
* Tablespace point-in-time recovery (recovery of a tablespace to a time different from the rest of the database)
* Time-based or point-in-time database recovery (recovery of the entire database to a time before the most current time)
* Recovery until the CANCEL command is issued
* Change-based or log sequence recovery (to a specified System Change Number, or SCN)

You can recover through RMAN, using either the recovery catalog or control file or via SQL or SQL*Plus.

RMAN in Oracle Database 10g improved the reliability of backups and restores through a number of added features. This version added backup and restore of standby control files. RMAN now can automatically retry a failed backup or restore operation. During recovery, RMAN can automatically create and recover datafiles not in the most recent backup. Where backups are missing or corrupt during the restore process, RMAN automatically uses an older backup.

To speed backups and restore operations, Oracle Database 10g introduced the Flash Recovery Area, thus organizing recovery files to a specific area on disk. These files include a copy of the control file, archived log files, flashback database logs, datafile copies, and RMAN backups. You can set a RETENTION AREA parameter to retain needed recovery files for specific time windows. As backup files and archivelogs age beyond the time window, they are automatically deleted. ASM (described earlier in this chapter) can configure the Flash Recovery Area. If availability of disk space is an issue, you can also take advantage of RMAN's ability to compress backup sets.

Making Sure the Backup Works

The key to providing an adequate backup and recovery strategy is to simulate recovery from failure using the backups from your test system before using the backups to restore a live production database. Many times, backup media that were thought to be reliable prove not to be, or backup frequencies that were thought to be adequate prove to be too infrequent to allow for timely recoveries. It's far better to discover that recovery is slow or impossible in test situations than after your business has been impacted by the failure of a production system.

This section provided only a very brief overview of standard backup and recovery. For more information on providing high availability, refer to Chapter 11.

Oracle Secure Backup

Oracle began bundling its own Secure Backup solution with Oracle Database 10g. Called Oracle Secure Backup Express (XE), it replaced Legato's Single Server Version (LSSV) tape storage management. Since Enterprise Manager 10g Release 2, Secure Backup is integrated into the Enterprise Manager interface. Secure Backup XE leverages RMAN's reading the database block layout directly and provides tape data protection for one server attached to one tape drive. Where an enterprise solution is needed, Oracle offers an optional Secure Backup version that can support multiple drives for any number of servers.

Oracle Secure Backup provides support for more than 200 different kinds of tape drives. Secure Backup also provides Netwrok Data Management Protocol (NDMP) support for network attached storage (NAS), Virtual Tape Library (VTL) support, policy-based management, storage classification, dynamic drive sharing, certificate-based authentication, and the ability to create encrypted backups.

Of course, there remain a wide variety of alternative solutions available providing Oracle backup solutions. Oracle continues to maintain the Oracle Backup Solutions Program (BSP) such that partners can certify their products to perform backup and recovery for tape storage devices using RMAN. A current list of these solutions is posted on the Oracle Technology Network web site.

Information Lifecycle Management

Information Lifecycle Management (ILM) provides a means to define classes of data, create storage tiers for the data classes, create data access and data movement policies, and implement data compliance policies. ILM is most frequently used to move data among various devices that are most appropriate for hosting that data, such as different classifications of disk. The reason for doing this is that most administrators would like to have their most frequently accessed data on the fastest but most expensive disk, and the least frequently accessed data on the on the slowest but cheapest disk.

Oracle first began supporting ILM in 2006 for database releases dating back to Oracle9i and introduced a tool, the ILM Assistant, that can be downloaded from the Oracle Technology Network. In addition to the ILM Assistant, you will need to have Oracle Application Express (formerly HTML DB) installed in the database where the data is managed.

The ILM Assistant presents a graphical user interface used in creating lifecycle definitions and policies for database tables. It can advise when it is time to move, archive, or delete data and also illustrate cost savings and storage required. The ILM Assistant can also guide you in creating partitioning to match your ILM needs. Once you have defined a strategy, it generates the scripts for moving the data.

The first time you start the ILM Assistant, you should select the Lifecycle Setup tab. On this tab you define logical storage tiers, create lifecycle definitions, and select the tables to be managed (see Figure 5-4). The ILM Assistant can then provide advice on data placement. Optionally, you can also view partition simulation, a lifecycle summary, and storage costs, and can define policy notes.

In subsequent restarts of the ILM Assistant, you will see a Lifecycle Events Calendar that will display a list of all outstanding events. The calendar, and also the events and history of event scans, might be viewed subsequently by selecting the Lifecycle Management tab.

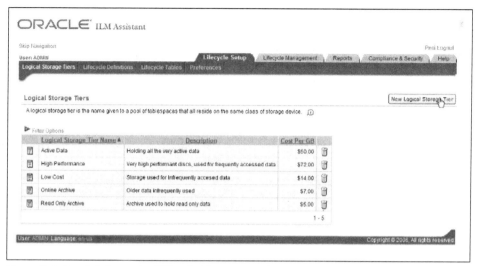

Figure 5-4. Oracle Information Lifecycle Management Assistant

A number of reports are provided under the Reports tab, including multitier storage costs by lifecycle or table, logical storage tier summary, partitions by table or storage tier, lifecycle retention summary, and data protection summary. Under the Compliance and Security tab, you can view the status of virtual private database (VPD) policies and when digital signatures were generated; create digitally signed result sets for tracking immutability; view a summary of privacy and security definitions, policies, views, and access privileges; manage and view fine-grained audit (FGA) policies; and view and provide policy notes.

Working with Oracle Support

Regardless of the extent of your training, there are bound to be some issues that you can't resolve without help from Oracle Corporation. Part of the job of the DBA is to help resolve any issues with the Oracle database. Oracle offers several levels of support including basic product support, advanced support, and incident support. Each of these support options costs extra, but regardless of your support level, you can get the most from Oracle by understanding how to best work with them.

Resolving problems with the assistance of Oracle Worldwide Customer Support Services can initially be frustrating to novice DBAs and others who may report problems. Oracle responds to database problems reported as Service Requests (SRs), sometimes referred to by their old name as Technical Assistance Requests (TARs). The response is based on the priority or severity level at which those problems are reported. If the problem is impacting your ability to complete a project or do business, the problem should be reported as "priority level 2" in order to assure a timely response. If the problem is initially assigned a lower level and the response hasn't been adequate, you should escalate the problem-resolution priority.

If business is halted because of the problem, the priority level assigned should be "priority level 1." However, if a problem is reported at level 1, the caller must be available for a callback (even if after hours). Otherwise, Oracle will assume that the problem wasn't as severe as initially reported and may lower the priority level for resolution.

Reporting Problems

You can report problems via phone, email, or the web browser-based MetaLink interface. MetaLink support, included with basic product support, has grown extremely popular as answers to similar problems can be rapidly found by you directly, which may result in eliminating time required for a physical response. MetaLink provides proactive notifications, customized home pages, technical libraries and forums, product lifecycle information, a bug database, and the ability to log SRs.

When contacting technical support, you will need your Customer Support Identification (CSI) number. Oracle Sales Consultants can also provide advice regarding how to report problems. Additionally, Oracle Worldwide Customer Support Services offers training for DBAs regarding effective use of Support services.

As we noted earlier, Oracle Database 11g provides a Support Workbench in Enterprise Manager that you can use to report problems. This release also offers a SQL Test Case Builder that can help Oracle Support re-create the problem and resolve it sooner. You typically would first see problems as critical error alerts on the Enterprise Manager Database home page, then would view problem details, gather additional information, create a SR, package and upload the diagnostic data to Oracle Support, then track the SR and close it when resolved.

Automated Patching

Oracle Support issues MetaLink Notes whenever software bugs or vulnerabilities are discovered and issues appropriate patches. Automated patching and notification provided since Oracle Database 10g can reduce the time delay between Oracle's discovery of such problems and your reaction to them. Alerts can now be issued to your Enterprise Manager console alerting you to the newly discovered bugs or vulnerabilities. Through the Enterprise Configuration Management capabilities in Enterprise Manager, you'll see a link to the patch and the target where the patch should be applied.

In RAC and grid environments, "rolling" patch updates can be applied across your nodes without taking the cluster or grid down. (We described the process of applying rolling patch updates in Chapter 3.) Further, you can roll back a patch (e.g., uninstall it) on an instance if you observe unusual behavior and want to remove the patch.

CHAPTER 6

Oracle Security, Auditing, and Compliance

The primary purpose of Oracle database software is to manage the valuable data that lies at the core of virtually every operation in your organization. Part of the value of that data is that the data is *yours*—the data that can be used to give your company unique advantages. For this reason, you need to protect your data from others who should not have access to it. This protection is the subject of this chapter. Here we focus on three different aspects of the overall task of protecting your data:

- *Security* covers the tools that you use to allow access only to those people you designate.
- *Auditing* allows you to discover who did what with your data. Auditing is the process of creating a history of access that can be used to understand database operations as well as spot access violations and attempts. When you are configuring Oracle Database 11g, you will be asked if you want to keep the default security settings. If you do, auditing will be enabled and a new default password profile option will be in place. A number of other database initialization parameters will be reset at this time.
- *Compliance* is the ability to prove that your data is secure and reliable—a proof that is now legally required in many cases. Although compliance may strike many technical folks as overkill, the simple fact is that a lack of compliance alone may result in significant penalties to your company. Compliance is thus a topic of great interest to management.

Security

One of the most important aspects of managing the Oracle database effectively in a multiuser environment is the creation of a security scheme to control access to and modification of the database. In an Oracle database you grant security clearance to individual users or database roles, as we describe in the following sections.

Security management is typically performed at three different levels:

- Database level
- Operating system level
- Network level

At the operating system level, DBAs should have the ability to create and delete files related to the database, whereas typical database users do not need these privileges. Oracle includes operating-system-specific security information as part of its standard documentation set. In many large organizations, DBAs or database security administrators work closely with computer system administrators to coordinate security specifications and practices.

Database security specifications control user database access and place limits on user capabilities through the use of username/password pairs. Such specifications may limit the allocation of resources (disk and CPU) to users and mandate the auditing of users. Database security at the database level also provides control of the access to and use of specific schema objects in the database.

Usernames, Privileges, Groups, and Roles

The DBA or database security administrator creates *usernames* that can be used to connect to the database. Two user accounts are automatically created as part of the installation process and are assigned the DBA role: SYS and SYSTEM. (The DBA role is described in a later section.)

Each database username has a password associated with it that prevents unauthorized access. A new or changed password should:

- Contain at least eight characters
- Contain at least one number and one character
- Not be the username reversed
- Differ from the username or use name with 1 through 100 appended
- Not match any word on an internal list of simple words
- Differ from the previous password (if there is one) by at least three characters

Oracle can check for these characteristics each time a password is created or modified as part of enforced security policies.

Once a user has successfully logged into the database, that user's access is restricted based on *privileges*, which are the rights to execute certain SQL commands. Some privileges may be granted systemwide (such as the ability to delete rows anywhere in the database), while others may apply only to a specific schema object in the database (such as the ability to delete rows in a specific table).

Roles are named groups of privileges and may be created, altered, or dropped. In most implementations, the DBA or security administrator creates usernames for users and assigns roles to specific users, thereby granting them a set of privileges. This is most commonly done today through the Oracle Enterprise Manager (EM) console, described in Chapter 5. For example, you might grant a role to provide access to a specific set of applications, such as "Human Resources," or you might define multiple roles so that users assigned a certain role can update hourly pay in the Human Resources applications, while users assigned other roles cannot.

Every database has a pseudorole named PUBLIC that includes every user. All users can use privileges granted to PUBLIC. For example, if database links are created using the keyword PUBLIC, they will be visible to all users who have privileges to the underlying objects for those links and synonyms. As we describe in the "Auditing" section of this chapter, the privilege CREATE PUBLIC DB LINK is now audited. As database vulnerability is an increasing concern, you may want to consider limited privileges for the PUBLIC role.

Identity Management

No amount of security can overcome the handicap of poor security administration. The more complex the administration tasks that are being performed, the more likely it is that errors will occur, leaving security holes in your system. In situations where you want to centrally control access to a number of databases, Oracle Identity Management can provide a solution by storing user information and their authorization in a LDAP directory such as the Oracle Internet Directory (OID). For example, you might use OID to authorize SYSDBA and SYSOPER connections.

Security Privileges

Four basic types of database operations can be limited by security privileges in an Oracle database:

- SELECT to perform queries
- INSERT to put rows into tables or views
- UPDATE to update rows in tables or views
- DELETE to remove rows from tables, table partitions, or views

In addition to these data-specific privileges, several other privileges apply to the objects within a database schema:

- CREATE to create a table in a schema
- DROP to remove a table in a schema
- ALTER to alter tables or views

All of these privileges can be handled with two simple SQL commands. The GRANT command gives a particular privilege to a user or role, while the REVOKE command takes away a specific privilege. You can use GRANT and REVOKE to modify the privileges for an individual or a role. You can also grant the ability to regrant privileges to others. You can use either of these commands with the keyword PUBLIC to issue or revoke a privilege for all database users.

Another security privilege, EXECUTE, allows users to run a PL/SQL procedure or function. By default, the PL/SQL routine runs with the security privileges of the user who compiled the routine. Alternately, you can specify that a PL/SQL routine run with what is termed *invoker's rights*, which means that the routine is run with the security privileges of the user who is invoking the routine.

Special Roles: DBA, SYSDBA, and SYSOPER

Your Oracle database comes with three special roles defined. The DBA role is one of the most important default roles in Oracle. The DBA role includes most system privileges. By default, it is granted to the users SYS and SYSTEM, both created at database creation time. Base tables and data dictionary views are stored in the SYS schema. SYSTEM schema tables are used for administrative information and by various Oracle tools and options. A number of other administrative users also exist, as consistent with the specific Oracle features deployed.

The DBA role does not include basic database administrative tasks included in the SYSDBA or SYSOPER system privileges. Therefore, SYSDBA or SYSOPER should be specifically granted to administrators. They will "CONNECT AS" either SYSDBA or SYSOPER to the database and will have access to a database even when it is not open. SYSDBA privileges can be granted to users by SYS or by other administrators with SYSDBA privileges. When granted, the SYSDBA privileges allow a user to perform the following database actions from the command line of SQL*Plus or by logging into Oracle Enterprise Manager's point-and-click interface:

STARTUP
Start up a database instance.

SHUTDOWN
Shut down a database instance.

ALTER DATABASE OPEN
Open a mounted but closed database.

ALTER DATABASE MOUNT
Mount a database using a previously started instance.

ALTER DATABASE BACKUP CONTROLFILE
Start a backup of the control file. However, backups are more frequently done through RMAN today, as described in the "Backup and Recovery" section in Chapter 5.

ALTER DATABASE ARCHIVELOG

Specify that the contents of a redo log file group must be archived before the redo log file group can be reused.

ALTER DATABASE RECOVER

Apply logs individually or start automatic application of the redo logs.

CREATE DATABASE

Create and name a database, specify datafiles and their sizes, specify logfiles and their sizes, and set parameter limits.

DROP DATABASE

Delete a database and all of the files included in the control file.

CREATE SPFILE

Create a server parameter file from a text initialization (*INIT.ORA*) file.

RESTRICTED SESSION privilege

Allow connections to databases started in Restricted mode. Restricted mode is designed for activities such as troubleshooting and some types of maintenance, similar to what SYS can do.

Administrators connected as SYSOPER can perform a more limited set of commands: STARTUP and SHUTDOWN, CREATE SPFILE, ALTER DATABASE OPEN or MOUNT or BACKUP, ALTER DATABASE ARCHIVELOG, ALTER DATABASE RECOVER, as well as the RESTRICTED SESSION privilege.

Database administrators are authenticated using either operating system authentication or a password file. The CONNECT INTERNAL syntax supported in earlier releases of Oracle is no longer available. When operating system authentication is used, administrative users must be named in the OSDBA or OSOPER defined groups. For password file authentication, the file is created with the ORAPWD utility. Users are added by SYS or by those having SYSDBA privileges.

With each release of Oracle, fewer default users and passwords are automatically created during database installation and creation. Regardless, it is generally recommended practice to reset all default passwords that are documented in Oracle.

Policies

A *policy* is a way to extend your security framework. You can specify additional requirements in a policy that are checked whenever a user attempts to activate a role. Policies are written in PL/SQL and can be used, for example, to limit access to a particular IP address or to particular hours of the day.

Since the release of Oracle Database 10g Oracle Enterprise Manager has featured a visual interface to a policy framework in the EM repository that aids management of database security. Security policies or rules are built and stored in a policy library.

Violations of rules are reported as critical, warning, or informational through the EM interface. Out of the box, security violations are checked on a daily basis. Policies may be adjusted according to business demands, and violations can be overridden when they are reported.

Restricting Data Access

There are situations in which a user will have access to a table, but not all of the data in the table should be viewed. For example, you might have competing suppliers looking at the same tables. You may want them to be able to see the products they supply and the total of all products from suppliers, but not detailed information about their competitors. There are a number of ways to do this, as we'll describe in the following sections, using other examples from Human Resources (HR).

View-based security

You can think of *views* as virtual tables defined by queries that extract or derive data from physical *base tables*. You can use views to present only the rows or columns that a certain group of users should be able to access.

For example, in an HR application, users from the HR department may have full access to the employee base table, which contains basic information such as employee names, work addresses, and work phone numbers, as well as more restricted information such as Social Security numbers, home addresses, and home telephone numbers. For other users in the company, you'll want to hide more personal information by providing a view that shows only the basic information.

Creating a virtual private database or leveraging the Label Security Option, described in subsequent sections of this chapter provide a more secure means of restricting access to certain data.

Fine-grained access control

Implementing security is a critical but time-consuming process, especially if you want to base security on an attribute with a wide range of values. A good example of this type of situation in the HR scenario previously described would be the need to limit the data an HR representative can see to only the rows relating to employees that he supports. Here you're faced with a situation in which you might have to define a view for every HR representative, which might mean many, many different views, views that would have to change every time an HR representative left or joined the company. And if you want to grant write access for a representative's own employees and read access for other employees, the situation gets even more complex. The smaller the scope, or *grain*, of the access control you desire, the more work is involved in creating and maintaining the security privileges.

Oracle offers a type of security that you can use to grant this type of *fine-grained access control* (FGAC). *Security policies* implemented as PL/SQL functions can be associated with tables or views enabling creation of a virtual private database (VPD). A security policy returns a condition that's dynamically associated with a particular SQL statement, which transparently limits the data that's returned. In the HR example, suppose that each representative supports employees with a last name in a particular alphabetic range, such as A through G.

The security policy would return a WHERE clause, based on a particular representative's responsibilities, that limits the rows returned. You can keep the range for each representative in a separate table that is dynamically queried as part of the security policy function. This simplifies management of allowable access if roles and responsibilities change frequently.

You can associate a security policy with a particular view or table by using the built-in PL/SQL package DBMS_RLS, which also allows you to refresh, enable, or disable a security policy.

Oracle Database 10g and newer database releases feature a VPD that is even more fine-grained, enabling enforced rewrites when a query references a specific column. Performance of queries in VPD implementations is also improved in Oracle Database 10g through the support of parallel query. Fine-grained security can also be based on the type of SQL statement issued. The security policy previously described could be used to limit UPDATE, INSERT, and DELETE operations to one set of data, but allow SELECT operations on a different group of data. For a good description of FGAC through PL/SQL, please refer to *Oracle PL/SQL Programming* by Steven Feuerstein and Bill Pribyl and *Oracle PL/SQL for DBAs* by Arup Nanda and Steven Feuerstein (O'Reilly; see Appendix B for details).

Label Security Option

The Oracle Label Security Option eliminates the need to write VPD PL/SQL programs to enforce row-level label security where sensitivity labels are desired. The collections of labels, label authorizations, and security enforcement options can be applied to entire schemas or to specific tables.

Sensitivity labels are defined based on a user's need to see and/or update data. They consist of a level denoting the data sensitivity, a category or compartment that further segregates the data, and a group used to record ownership (which may be hierarchical in nature) and access.

Standard group definitions given to users provide them access to data containing those group labels. Inverse groups in the data can be used to define what labels a user must have in his profile in order to access it.

Policies are created and applied, sensitivity labels are defined, and user labels are set and authorized through a policy manager tool accessible through EM. You can also add SQL predicates and label functions and manage trusted program units, Oracle VPD fine-grained access control policies, and VPD application contexts. Label Security policy management is possible in Oracle Database 10g and later versions when the Oracle Internet Directory is also used.

Security and Application Roles and Privileges

Applications can involve data and logic in many different schemas with many different privileges. To simplify the issues raised by this complexity, roles are frequently used in applications. Application roles have all the privileges necessary to run the applications, and users of the applications are granted the roles necessary to execute them.

Application roles may contain privileges that should be granted to users only while they're running the application. Application developers can place a SET ROLE command at the beginning of an application to enable the appropriate role and disable others only while the application is running. Similarly, you can invoke a DBMS_SESSION.SET_ROLE procedure from PL/SQL.

Another way application security is sometimes accomplished is by encapsulating privileges in stored procedures. Instead of granting direct access to the various tables for an application, you can create stored procedures that provide access to the tables and grant access to the stored procedures instead of the tables. For example, instead of granting INSERT privileges for the EMPLOYEE table, you might create and grant access to a stored procedure called HIRE_EMPLOYEE that accepts as parameters all the data for a new employee.

When you run a stored procedure normally, the procedure has the access rights that were granted to the owner of the procedure; that owner is the schema in which the procedure resides. If a particular schema has access to a particular database object, all stored procedures that reside in that schema have the same rights as the schema. When any user calls one of those stored procedures, that user has the same access rights to the underlying data objects that the procedure does.

For example, suppose there is a schema called HR_REP. This schema has write access to the EMP table. Any stored procedure in the HR_REP schema also has write access to the EMP table. Consequently, if you grant a user access to a stored procedure in the HR_REP schema, that user will also have write access to the EMP table regardless of her personal level of security privilege. However, she will have access only through the stored procedures in the schema.

 One small but vitally important caveat applies to access through stored procedures: the security privilege must be *directly* granted to the schema, not granted by means of a role.

If you attach the keyword AUTHID CURRENT_USER to a stored procedure when it is compiled, security restrictions will be enforced based on the username of the user invoking the procedure, rather than the schema that owns the stored procedure (the definer of the procedure). If a user has access to a particular database object with a particular privilege, that user will have the same access through stored procedures compiled with the AUTHID CURRENT_USER.

Distributed Database and Multitier Security

All the security features available for standard Oracle databases are also available for the distributed database environment, which is covered in Chapter 13. However, the distributed database environment introduces additional security considerations. For example, user accounts needed to support server connections must exist in all of the distributed databases forming the system. As database links (which define connections between distributed database instances) are created, you will need to allow the user accounts and roles needed at each site.

Distributed security management

For large implementations, you may want to configure global authentication across these distributed databases for users and roles. Global authentication allows you to maintain a single authentication list for multiple distributed databases. Where this type of external authentication is required, Oracle's Advanced Security Option, discussed in the next section, provides a solution.

Enterprise Manager is commonly used to configure valid application users to Oracle's LDAP-compliant OID server. A user who accesses an application for which he is not authenticated is redirected to a login server. There, he is prompted for a username and password that are checked against the OID server. A cookie is returned and the user is redirected from the login server to the application.

Oracle Identity Management, described earlier in this chapter, can be used to manage security across multiple platforms and security systems.

Multitier security

In typical three-tier implementations, the Oracle Application Server runs some of the application logic, serves as an interface between the clients and database servers, and provides much of the Oracle Identity Management (OIM) infrastructure. The Oracle Internet Directory provides directory services running as applications on an Oracle database. The directory synchronization service, provisioning integrated service, and delegated administrative service are part of OID. Security in middle-tier applications is controlled by applications' privileges and the preservation of client identities through all three tiers.

Using multiple tiers, as with large applications or web-based applications, can also call for proxy authentication. The application connects to code in the middle tier, which accesses the database through a proxy, frequently through shared connections. Some databases associate security with a session, which means that sessions must be reestablished when the user identity changes. This limitation makes the multitier approach harder.

Oracle separates authentication from sessions, so the use of a proxy in the middle tier is feasible. A single session can support different users with different identities. Prior to Oracle 10g Release 2, the only way to take advantage of this capability was by using the OCI interface, which was code-intensive. With Release 2, this limitation was lifted, so standard SQL and SQL tools, such as SQL*Plus, could use proxy authentication.

Advanced Security Option

The Oracle Advanced Security Option (ASO), formerly known as the Advanced Networking Option (ANO), is used in distributed environments linked via Oracle Net in which there are concerns regarding secure access and transmission of data. This option specifically provides data encryption during transmission to protect data from unauthorized viewing over Oracle Net, as well as Net/SSL, IIOP/SSL, and between thin JDBC clients and the database. Encryption algorithms supported include RC4_40, RC4_56, RC4_128, RC4_256, DES, DES_40, 3DES112, 3DES168, AES128, AES192, and AES256. Communications packets are protected against data modification, transaction replay, and removal through use of MD5 and SHA-1 algorithms.

Transparent Data Encryption (described in the next section) is included as part of the Advanced Security Option beginning with Oracle Database 10g Release 2. Transparent Data Encryption provides an easy way to encrypt data in the database, and the network data encryption option of ASO protects the data during transmission to the client.

ASO also provides support for a variety of identity authentication methods to ensure that user identities are accurately known. Third-party authentication services supported include Kerberos, RADIUS, and DCE. RADIUS enables support of third-party authentication devices, including smart cards and token cards. Public Key Infrastructure (PKI) authentication, popular for securing Internet-based e-commerce applications, uses X.509 v3 digital certificates and can leverage Entrust Profiles stored in Oracle Wallets. Oracle Database 10g added authentication capabilities for users who have Kerberos credentials, and enables Kerberos-based authentication across database links.

In a typical scenario, the Oracle Enterprise Security Manager configures valid application users to the LDAP-compliant OID server. An X.509 certificate authority creates private key pairs and publishes them in Oracle wallets (through Oracle Wallet

Manager) to the LDAP directory. A user who wants to log in to a database server will need a certificate and a private key, which can be retrieved from that user's password-protected wallet, which resides in the LDAP directory. When the user's key on the client device is sent to the database server, it is matched with the paired key retrieved by the server via SSL from the LDAP directory and the user is authenticated to use the database.

Encryption

The previous sections of this chapter all deal with the need to protect access to data in the Oracle database. There may be times when you want to take the extra step of protecting the actual data values from unauthorized viewing by encrypting the data.

Oracle has provided data encryption for several releases, but Oracle Database 10g Release 2 included a significant new feature called Transparent Data Encryption. Prior to the introduction of this feature, encrypted data stored in the Oracle database had to be decrypted by an application before it could be used. This scenario caused a number of limitations, the most prominent being that decryption of data was done by applications. If you wanted to start encrypting a particular piece of data, you would have to change all data access routines in every application that used the data. This limitation alone made it difficult to consider adding encryption to existing data.

With Transparent Data Encryption, the database does the work of encrypting and decrypting data automatically. Data sent to the database is encrypted by Oracle, and data requested from the database is decrypted. No additional code is required in an application, which means that you can encrypt existing data without changing any of your SQL access statements.

Oracle Database 11g allows you to encrypt entire tablespaces (described in Chapter 4) with Transparent Data Encryption, and this feature should reduce management overhead for this feature.

Secure Backup

The security features described in previous sections give you the tools you need to keep the data in your Oracle database secure. But what about when the data leaves your Oracle database—for example, when you perform the necessary maintenance step of backing up the data?

Recent events have shown that lost backup tapes are a reality, and backup tapes can be stolen. Secure Backup, released between Oracle Database 10g Release 2 and Oracle Database 11g, automatically encrypts your backup data. The data can be decrypted only by the source database, so even if a backup tape is lost or stolen, the recipient will not be able to see your data.

Auditing

The Oracle database gives you the ability to restrict unauthorized access to your valuable data. However, your security is only as good as your implementation, and people do make mistakes. In addition, you may want to understand what type of activities—legitimate or not—are taking place with your data. The ability to audit database activity can address both of these issues.

Oracle's audit capabilities let you track actions at the statement level, privilege level, or schema object level for the entire database or particular users. Auditing can also gather data about database activities for planning and tuning purposes. Auditing of connections with administrative privileges to an instance and audit records recording database startup and shutdown occur by default.

You can also audit sessions at the user level, which captures some basic but extremely useful statistics such as the number of logical I/Os, the number of physical I/Os, and the total time logged on. As noted in the previous chapter, gathering performance statistics is low in terms of overhead, and Oracle Database 10g and later releases automatically gather statistics in populating the Automatic Workload Repository (AWR).

Audit records always contain the following information:

- Username
- Session identifier
- Terminal identifier
- Name of schema object accessed
- Operation performed or attempted
- Completion code of the operation
- Date and timestamp

The records may be stored in a data dictionary table (AUD$ in the SYS schema), which is also called the database audit trail, or in an operating system audit trail.

Oracle9i added fine-grained auditing, which enabled selective audits of SELECT statements with bind variables based on access of specified columns. Oracle Database 10g added extended SQL support for fine-grained auditing. You can now perform granular auditing of queries, UPDATE, INSERT, and DELETE operations through SQL.

In Oracle Database 11g, auditing is turned on by default, and the AUDIT_TRAIL initialization parameter is set to DB. Privileges audited by default include:

- ALTER ANY PROCEDURE
- ALTER ANY TABLE
- ALTER DATABASE

- ALTER PROFILE
- ALTER SYSTEM, ALTER USER
- AUDIT SYSTEM
- CREATE ANY JOB, CREATE ANY LIBRARY, CREATE ANY PROCEDURE, CREATE ANY TABLE, CREATE EXTERNAL JOB, CREATE PUBLIC DB LINK, CREATE SESSION, CREATE USER
- DROP ANY PROCEDURE, DROP ANY TABLE, DROP PROFILE, DROP USER
- EXEMPT ACCESS POLICY
- GRANT ANY OBJECT PRIVILEGE, GRANT ANY PRIVILEGE, and GRANT ANY ROLE

Compliance

The slogan "trust, but verify" could apply to the functions of security and auditing. Compliance extends that slogan to "trust, verify, and prove it" and describes the tools necessary to provide proof that your data has been used properly.

Compliance is based on the security and audit features described in previous sections. For the most part, compliance is the result of a new element introduced into the corporate landscape—government requirements. In the United States and elsewhere, compliance is being increasingly required by government regulation, so the ability of the Oracle database to make compliance easy is becoming correspondingly important. Compliance is crucial for many organizations, and the people responsible for guaranteeing compliance are not necessarily in the IT department. Consequently, the implementation of security and audit schemes has had to be simplified and coordinated to address compliance needs.

Oracle has two options specifically designed to address compliance challenges—Oracle Data Vault and Oracle Audit Vault; these are described in the following sections. The related Flashback Data Archive capability, also mentioned below, is described in greater detail in Chapter 3.

Oracle Database Vault Option

The Oracle Database Vault Option was introduced in 2006 and restricts DBAs and other highly privileged users from accessing application data to which they should not have access. It can also be set up so that applications' DBAs are not allowed to manipulate the database or access other applications. A security administrator can use the Oracle Database Vault Option to describe the security scheme that the organization wants to implement, and this option automatically implements the schemes using the features described earlier in this chapter.

Key parameters defined in the Oracle Database Vault Option are called *factors*. A factor is essentially a descriptive dimension that will affect security across the entire database. Factors include things such as specific application programs, locations, or times of day. This option comes with more than 40 factors defined, and users can create their own factors.

Factors are used to define access and audit particular security dimensions. You can create rules that limit types of access to a particular factor and rule sets that combine multiple factor rules together. Once you have defined rule sets, you can create application roles based on these sets, as well as command rules that control whether database commands can be executed, based on the outcome of rule evaluation. For example, you could prevent anyone from dropping a particular table unless the command came from a particular location defined by a factor, or specify that new users can be defined only by the combined actions of two administrators.

Rules can also be used to define database *realms*, which consist of a subset of the schemas and roles that an administrator can administer. This ability is essential if an organization uses its Oracle database to service multiple communities. You can define a realm and give an administrator privileges on that realm without compromising data in other schemas. The overall effect of realms is to allow secure delegation of administrative responsibilities.

All of the rule enforcement is audited as part of the the Oracle Database Vault Option, which provides the type of documentation required for complete compliance. Figure 6-1 illustrates the various components of the Oracle Database Vault Option solution.

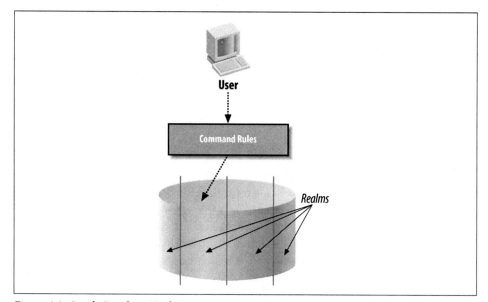

Figure 6-1. Oracle Database Vault Option components

Oracle Audit Vault Server

The Oracle Audit Vault Server was introduced in 2007 and collects data from audit files in Oracle and in the underlying operating system. It consolidates this data in a secure repository and provides out-of-the-box compliance reporting. Among the reports provided are privileged user accesses, account management, data access, and failed login attempts. Stored in an Oracle data warehouse schema, the data is easily accessible by business intelligence tools such as Oracle's BI Publisher.

Because the Oracle Audit Vault Server monitors all incoming audit data, it can generate alerts based on IT policies. For example, policies can be defined to trigger alerts for privileged users' changes and sensitive data access. Oracle databases dating back to Oracle 9*i* Release 2 can be monitored. A software development kit (SDK) is available for building custom audit collectors.

Flashback Data Archive

Flashback technology was introduced in Chapter 3, because this capability is based on rollback segments. Although Flashback was initially introduced with Oracle9*i*, Oracle Database 11*g* enables a particular use of Flashback that can help address compliance issues.

Flashback Data Archive gives you the ability to see all of the changes that occur to a record throughout its lifetime. This type of history tracking can provide the key information required to demonstrate compliance, as well as to track the source of errors in compliance or usage.

CHAPTER 7
Oracle Performance

As this book illustrates, the Oracle database has a wide range of features. As you gain experience with Oracle, you'll reap more of the benefits it has to offer. One area on which you will eventually focus is performance tuning, since you will inevitably be forced to wring additional performance from your Oracle database in the face of increasing demands. This chapter gives you the basics you'll need to understand as you address performance.

Oracle database performance tuning has been extensively documented in the Oracle community. There are numerous books that provide detailed and excellent information; many of these are listed in Appendix B. This book is focused more on the concepts of the Oracle database, so we won't delve too deeply into specific tuning recommendations. Instead, we'll touch on the importance of tuning and discuss some basic notions of how Oracle uses resources. Here, we're simply laying a foundation for understanding Oracle performance. This understanding will help you implement the tuning procedures most suited for your own particular implementation. Where appropriate, we'll provide some basic guidance on how the latest Oracle features help you manage performance.

Certainly, Oracle provides more and better automated tuning options in the current release than it did when we wrote earlier editions of this book. However, getting optimal performance is about more than tuning. There is no substitute for getting your hardware platform properly configured with appropriate CPUs, memory, and especially storage. Good database design is also critical for achieving optimal performance, based on how your lines of business use the system.

Performance Tuning Basics

Performance is one of the trickiest aspects in the operation of your database since so many factors can be involved. There is the database, to be sure. But there are also platform deployment strategies to consider. Today, the infrastructure likely resides across multiple platforms, including database servers and applications servers. There is network and interconnect bandwidth to consider and varying complexity in use among your users.

One of the curious aspects of performance is that "good performance" is defined by its absence rather than by its presence. You can recognize bad performance easily, but good performance is usually defined as simply the absence of bad performance. Performance is simultaneously a very simple topic—any novice user can implicitly understand it—and an extremely complex topic that can strain the ingenuity of the most proficient database administrator.

Before getting into a specific discussion of Oracle performance, it makes sense to define a basic methodology for investigating performance problems.

There are three basic steps to understanding how to address performance issues with your Oracle database:

1. Define performance and performance problems.
2. Check the performance of the Oracle server software.
3. Check the overall performance of the server machine.

Defining Performance and Performance Problems

The first step in performance tuning is to determine if there actually *is* a performance problem. In the previous section, we mentioned the concept of poor performance and how users often are the first to recognize it. But what exactly is poor performance?

Poor performance is inevitably the result of disappointment—a user feels that the system is not performing as expected. Consequently, you must first evaluate how real these expectations are in the first place.

If expectations are realistic—for example, a scenario where performance has degraded from a previous level and the business is impacted—you then need to identify which of the system's components are causing the problems. You must refine a general statement like "the system is too slow" to identify which types of operations are too slow, what constitutes "too slow," and when these operations are slowing down. For example, the problem may occur only on specific transactions and at specific times, or all transactions and reports may be performing below the users' expectations.

Once you've defined the performance expected from your system, you can begin to try to determine where your performance problem lies. Performance problems occur when there is a greater demand for a particular resource than the resources available to service that demand, and the system slows down while applications wait to share the resource.

Oracle Server Performance

The first place you'll likely begin looking for resource bottlenecks is in the Oracle database software using Oracle Enterprise Manager (introduced in Chapter 5) to identify less than optimal use of Oracle's internal resources. Bottlenecks within your database result in sessions waiting unnecessarily, and performance tuning is aimed at removing these bottlenecks.

Oracle's dynamic performance views provide insight into bottlenecks within your Oracle database. Prior to the introduction of Oracle's Automatic Workload Repository (AWR), the Automatic Database Diagnostics Monitor (ADDM), and Oracle Enterprise Manager Grid Control in Oracle Database 10g, querying the performance views often was the first step database administrators performed in determining bottlenecks. All of these performance views have names that begin with V$, and, from Oracle9i on, there are also global views (for all nodes in a Real Application Clusters or RAC database) that begin with GV$. Two views, in particular, identify the sources of these waits; these are invaluable for guiding your analysis:

V$SYSTEM_EVENT
> Provides aggregated, systemwide information about the resources for which the whole instance is waiting

V$SESSION_EVENT
> Provides cumulative list of events waited for in each session

V$SESSION_WAIT
> Provides detailed, session-specific information about the resources for which individual sessions are currently waiting or last waited for

V$SESSION
> Provides session information for each current session including event currently or last waited for

You can use these views to pinpoint the resources that are causing the most waits. Focusing on the resources causing the most waiting can provide large performance improvements.

 Oracle Database 10g and newer releases provide an enhanced wait model that makes it easier to determine exactly who is waiting for what resource at what time.

You may find that your problem has a simple source, such as a lower-than-expected database buffer cache hit ratio. Since the cache is not working at its optimal level, you could simply increase the initialization parameter DB_BLOCK_BUFFERS to increase the size of the cache and possibly improve the hit ratio. You can monitor the performance of the buffer cache hit ratio in V$METRICNAME.

Other situations may not be quite so clear cut, using the approach of investigating parameters exposed by views. For example, you could find that it takes a relatively long time to fetch database rows from the disk. This situation may be caused by contention on the database server's disks and could be caused by less than optimal placement of Oracle files on disk or by other applications on the server.

AWR, ADDM, and Enterprise Manager

A much better approach today is to use Enterprise Manager (also known as Grid Control for RAC implementations) as the starting point for performance monitoring and management. The Automatic Workload Repository (AWR) captures and stores information about resource utilization by Oracle workloads. By default, statistics are captured every 30 minutes and are stored for 7 days. These statistics are accessible through views, but Enterprise Manager provides a much simpler-to-use interface.

The AWR helps the Oracle database identify potential performance issues by comparing workloads over time. It also acts as the foundation for many of the manageability features introduced since Oracle Database 10g, such as the Automatic Database Diagnostic Monitor (ADDM).

Oracle's ADDM automatically identifies and reports on resource bottlenecks, such as CPU contention, locking issues, or poor performance from specific SQL statements. In Oracle Database 11g, ADDM can perform analysis on clusters. Alerts sent by ADDM to the Enterprise Manager dashboard can point to causes of contention as they occur. Enterprise Manager provides both high-level and detailed views of resource utilization for Oracle servers, and these can give a quick indication of the cause of performance problems. Thresholds can be set such that the dashboard informs you when a particular resource is nearing a critical usage level. Enterprise Manager includes a set of advisors, which can be run to give you suggestions on how to tune your applications or optimize performance in the Oracle database.

For tuning your applications, you'll likely look to the SQL Advisor. Introduced in Oracle Database 11g, it combines the functionality of the SQL Tuning Advisor, the SQL Access Advisor, and the new Partition Advisor. The SQL Advisor leverages information on CPU and I/O consumption captured in the AWR and identifies high-impact SQL statements indicated by the ADDM to make recommendations. The advisor checks to make sure statistics are not stale, identifies optimal paths through SQL profiling, determines if the addition of indexes, materialized views, or other database structures would be beneficial, and indicates whether changes to the high-impact SQL statements would improve efficiency.

Key database tuning advisors include:

Memory Advisor
> For optimal setting of MEMORY_TARGET for automatic memory management in Oracle Database 11g (described later in this chapter) and optimal setting of SGA_TARGET for shared memory management

Segment Advisor
For storage management and space allocation

Undo Advisor
For managing transactions

Other advisors, such as the Mean Time to Recovery (MTTR) Advisor, optimize the setup of Oracle, including log files. (See the "Database Advisors" section in Chapter 5 for more information on the various Oracle advisor tools.)

Machine Resource Usage

You can also run into performance issues if inadequate resources are available to the database server. If your Oracle database is not properly deployed, adding machine resources might help initially reduce performance bottlenecks, but can be an expensive way to solve the problem. Further, the problem will likely resurface as additional resources are consumed. But if your Oracle database is properly designed and configured and you find such resource shortages, adding machine resources can be in order.

The performance of your Oracle database is based on how it uses the machine resources that are available. These machine resources include processing power or CPU, memory, disk I/O, and network bandwidth. You can trace the bulk of database performance problems back to a bottleneck on one or more of these resources.

Network bandwidth between the server and a client is less of a problem today because of the better bandwidth available in most locations. In a RAC deployment, you should also pay attention to the interconnect bandwidth as excessively heavy traffic can slow performance. But such interconnects continue to increase in speed as well, and network bandwidth in general is much less of an issue today if proper design choices are made.

Because of this trend, we will next focus on how Oracle uses the three key machine resources: CPU, memory, and disk I/O. The slowest access is to disk and, as a result, the most common database performance issues are I/O related. The majority of this chapter therefore focuses on performance as it relates to physical disk I/O.

 Network bandwidth can become a concern when using your Oracle database to retrieve very large data sets over the network. Although you can't typically surmount this type of problem simply by improving the performance of your Oracle database; you can monitor network and application server bottlenecks with Enterprise Manager, as of Oracle Database 10g.

The database server machine may encounter bottlenecks caused by contention for multiple resources. In fact, computer environments are designed so that one resource can try to compensate for the lack of another resource, sometimes leading to a deficit in the compensating resource as well. If you run out of physical memory, the operating system will swap areas of memory out to the disk and can cause I/O bottlenecks.

You can identify your machine resource usage using Oracle Enterprise Manager and tools provided by the machine vendor or operating system utilities. Since the introduction of Enterprise Manager 10g, a performance analyzer called Automatic Performance Monitoring (APM) has been included. APM gives you the ability to set up *beacons*, which are client processes that periodically execute transactions and report the response time. APM goes beyond the Oracle environment to help you understand performance from an end user's point of view, and this, in turn, can help you to spot other sources of performance problems, such as network transmission slowdowns.

When All Else Fails

Your performance problems could be caused by your applications in situations where performance tuning falls short in delivering desired results. For example, to solve slow I/O, you might try restriping or adding throughput to the disk subsystem. However, this situation could be caused by poorly tuned SQL and would thus be better fixed by rewriting the SQL.

At this point, you should analyze the interaction of individual modules and SQL statements in your application system and the database server. You could find that a handful of SQL statements are causing your performance problem. However, it's more likely that you will have to reconsider the design of your application system.

Enterprise Manager and the Automatic Database Diagnostic Monitor (ADDM) can automatically identify SQL statements that are using the most resources or are less than optimal—the SQL Tuning Advisor component can even suggest solutions for the identified performance problems. (These tools are described later in this chapter.)

Needless to say, more complex application redesign is far beyond the scope of this book, so the rest of this chapter will concentrate on helping you to understand Oracle machine resources. For more details about the vast topic of Oracle performance, refer to the tuning books mentioned in Appendix B.

A Final Note on Performance Basics

Performance has real-world business implications. Whenever you attempt to address performance problems, you must make sure to carefully monitor the areas that you are attempting to improve, both before and after your changes. Important baseline data gathered by the AWR includes application, database, operating system, disk I/O, and network statistics.

You should use a systematic approach to both discovering the source of a performance problem and implementing the appropriate solution. This approach calls for establishing baselines for resource usage and response time before making any changes, and only making a small group of changes before reexamining the performance in the changed environment. It might be tempting to simply try to fix a problem without taking a measured approach, but this tactic will usually lead to additional problems down the road.

In Oracle Database 11g, such performance comparisons are made much easier. You can preserve AWR baselines that contain performance data from specific time periods. Baselines can be established for fixed times or moving windows, or they can serve as a template.

Oracle and Disk I/O Resources

From the perspective of machine resources, an input/output operation, or I/O, can be defined as the operating system of the computer reading or writing some bytes from or to the underlying disk subsystem of the database server. I/Os can be small, such as 4 KB of data, or large, such as 64 KB or 128 KB of data. The lower and upper limits on the size of an I/O operation vary according to the operating system. Your Oracle database also has a block size that you can define, called the *database block size*.

An Oracle database issues I/O requests in two basic sizes:

Single database block I/Os
> For example, one 8 KB datablock at a time. This type of request reads or writes a specific block. For example, after looking up a row in an index, Oracle uses a single block I/O to retrieve the desired database block.

Multiblock I/Os
> For example, 32 database blocks, each consisting of 8 KB, for a total I/O size of 256 KB. Multiblock I/O is used for large-scale operations, such as full table scans. The number of blocks in one multiblock I/O is determined by the initialization parameter DB_FILE_MULTIBLOCK_READ_COUNT.

The Oracle database can read larger amounts of data with multiblock I/Os, so there are times when a full table scan might actually retrieve data faster than an index-based retrieval (e.g., if the selectivity of the index is low). Oracle can perform multiblock operations faster than the corresponding collection of single-block operations.

I/O Planning Principles for an Oracle Database

When you're planning the disk layout and subsequent placement of the various files that make up your database, you need to consider the different reasons Oracle performs I/O and the potential performance impacts.

The main destinations of the I/O operations Oracle performs are the following:

- Redo logs
- Data contained in tables
- Indexes on the tables
- The data dictionary, which goes in the SYSTEM tablespace
- Sort activity, which goes in the TEMP tablespace of the user performing the sort
- Rollback information, which is spread across the datafiles of the tablespace containing the database's rollback segments
- Archived redo logs, which go to the archived log destination (assuming the database is in ARCHIVELOG mode)

The following simple principles for managing these types of I/O can optimize Oracle's use of the database server's disk subsystem:

Use disk-striping technologies to spread I/O evenly across multiple spindles
These technologies are covered in detail in the next section, "Using RAID Disk Array Technology." Oracle has simplified striping in Oracle Database 10g and newer releases by enabling striping through Enterprise Manager leveraging ASM.

Use tablespaces to clearly segregate and target different types of I/O
Separate table I/O from index I/O by placing these structures in different tablespaces. You can then place the datafiles for these tablespaces on various disks to provide better performance for concurrent access.

Using tablespaces to segregate objects also simplifies tuning later on. Oracle implements I/O activity at the level of the datafile, or the physical object the operating system sees as a file, and each file is a part of only one tablespace, as described in Chapter 4. Placing specific objects in specific tablespaces allows you to accurately measure and direct the I/O for those objects by tracking and moving the underlying datafiles as needed.

For example, consider a database with several large, busy tables. Placing multiple large tables in a single tablespace makes it difficult to determine which table is causing the I/O to the underlying datafiles. Segregating the objects allows you to directly monitor the I/O associated with each object. Your Oracle documentation details the other factors to consider in mapping objects to tablespaces.

Place redo logs and redo log mirrors on the two least-busy devices
This placement maximizes throughput for transactional systems. Oracle writes to all copies of the redo log file, and this I/O is not completed until all copies have been successfully written to. If you have two copies of the redo log file, one on a slow device and the other on a fast device, your redo log I/O performance will be constrained by the slower device.

As described in Chapter 8, Oracle Database 10g Release 2 gives you the option of delaying write operations to the redo log for transactions. This capability can improve performance in very high transactional environments, but carries with it the possibility of losing committed data if your database crashes.

Distribute "system overhead" evenly over the available drives
System overhead consists of I/O to the SYSTEM tablespace for the data dictionary, the TEMP tablespace for sorting, and the tablespaces that contain rollback segments for undo information. You should consider the system profile in spreading the system overhead over multiple drives. For example, if the application generates a lot of data changes versus data reads, the I/O to the rollback segments may increase due to higher writes for changes and higher reads for consistent read functionality.

Sort activity can also affect disk I/O. Prior to Oracle Database 10g, you would get the majority of sorts to occur in memory through tuning the SORT_AREA_SIZE parameter in the initialization file. Oracle constantly queries and updates the data dictionary stored in the SYSTEM tablespace, and this information is cached in the shared pool section of the SGA, so sizing your shared pool properly is a key to overall performance. As of Oracle Database 10g, Oracle can automatically and dynamically size the different pools in the SGA.

Use a different device for archiving and redo log files
To avoid archiving performance issues due to I/O contention, make sure that the archive log destination uses different devices from those used for the redo logs and redo log mirrors.

Some other file placement issues to consider from the perspective of database availability include the following:

If you are directing database backups to disk, store the backups on devices that don't contain any database components
This protects the system from the potential loss of the database and the needed backups from the failure of an I/O device.

Make sure the device used for the archive log destination doesn't contain any database components or database backups
If the failure of a single device results in the loss of both database components and archived redo logs, or backup components and archived redo logs, recovery will be endangered.

Fault-tolerant disk arrays don't eliminate the need for a sound backup and recovery strategy. Fault-tolerant storage merely reduces the likelihood of undergoing database recovery due to the failure of a single drive. For full coverage of Oracle databases and high availability, see Chapter 11.

Using RAID Disk Array Technology

One of the most powerful ways to reduce performance bottlenecks due to disk I/O is the use of RAID disk arrays. RAID stands for Redundant Array of Inexpensive (or Independent) Disks and is used to group disks into arrays for two reasons: redundancy and performance. The use of RAID for redundancy is detailed in Chapter 11. Our focus in this chapter is on the performance aspects of RAID technology.

RAID Basics

RAID disk arrays provide a hardware solution for both reliability and performance. There are different levels of RAID hardware; the following are most relevant to performance:

RAID-0
> Where availability isn't a concern, the disks can be configured as RAID-0, which is nonredundant disk striping.

RAID-1
> Provides the simplest form of redundancy, full duplication of data, which is referred to as *mirroring*.

RAID-0+1
> Combines the one-to-one mirroring of RAID-1 with the striping of RAID-0.

RAID-3
> Provides redundancy by storing parity information on a single disk in the array. This parity information can help to recover the data on other disks, should they fail. RAID-3 saves on disk storage compared to RAID-1, but isn't often used because the parity disk can be a bottleneck.

RAID-5
> Uses parity data for redundancy in a way that is similar to RAID-3, but stripes the parity data across all of the disks, like the way in which the actual data is striped. This alleviates the bottleneck on the parity disk.

There are additional levels of RAID, including RAID-6, which adds dual parity data, and RAID-7 and RAID-8, which add performance enhancements to the characteristics of RAID-5.

RAID groups disk drives into arrays to automatically spread I/O operations across multiple spindles, reducing contention on individual drives. For example, suppose you place a datafile containing an index on a single drive. If multiple processes use the index simultaneously, they will all issue I/O requests to the one disk drive, resulting in contention for the use of that drive.

Instead, suppose you placed the same datafile on a "disk" that was actually an array of five physical disks. Each physical disk in the array can perform I/O operations independently on different data blocks of the index, automatically increasing the amount of I/O Oracle can perform without causing contention.

Simply using disk arrays won't, by itself, give you optimal I/O performance. As discussed earlier, you also need to logically place the different types of Oracle files across the available drives, even if the drives are grouped into arrays. As of Oracle Database 10g, striping considerations are made simpler through Automatic Storage Management. ASM provides automatic striping and rebalancing of stripe sets. By default, ASM also provides automated mirroring.

Volume managers

With host-based striping, logical volume-management software runs on the database server. Examples of this type of software often used under older Oracle database releases include Hewlett Packard's Logical Volume Manager (LVM) and Veritas Software's Volume Manager. The LVM acts as an interface between the operating system that requests I/O and the underlying physical disks. Volume-management software groups disks into arrays, which are then seen by the operating system as single "disks." The actual disks are usually individual devices attached to controllers or disks contained in a prepackaged array containing multiple disks and controllers. This striping is handled by the volume-management software and is completely transparent to Oracle. Figure 7-1 illustrates host-based volume management.

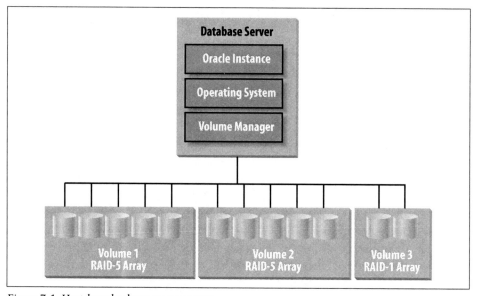

Figure 7-1. Host-based volume management

Oracle began providing its own volume manager software for Linux and Windows in Oracle9*i* Release 2. Since Oracle Database 10*g*, database releases for all supported operating systems include a cluster file system and volume manager in the database that is leveraged by ASM. When using ASM, it is recommended that you not try to leverage an operating system volume manager.

Dedicated storage subsystems

Dedicated storage systems, often referred to as *disk farms*, contain disks, controllers, CPUs, and (usually) memory used as an I/O cache. Vendors include EMC, Network Appliance, Hewlett-Packard, IBM, and Sun. These subsystems offload the task of managing the disk arrays from the database server. The I/O subsystem is attached to the server using controllers. These dedicated storage devices are sometimes grouped into *storage area networks* (SANs) to denote their logical organization as a separate set of networked devices. The disk arrays are defined and managed within the dedicated I/O subsystem, and the resulting logical "disks" are seen by the operating system as physical disks.

This type of disk-volume management is completely transparent to the database server and offers many benefits:

- The database server does not spend CPU resources managing the disk arrays.
- The I/O subsystem uses memory for an I/O cache, so the performance of Oracle I/O can improve significantly (for example, from an average I/O time of 10–12 milliseconds to 3–5 milliseconds).
- Write I/O is completed as soon as the data has been written to the subsystem's cache.
- The I/O subsystem will destage the data from cache to actual disk later.
- Read I/O can be satisfied from the cache. The subsystem can employ some type of algorithm to sense I/O patterns and preload the cache in anticipation of pending read activity.

Note that you must back up the cache with some type of battery so a power failure doesn't result in the loss of data that was written to the cache, but hasn't yet been destaged to the physical disk. Otherwise, data that Oracle assumes made it to disk may be lost, thereby potentially corrupting the database. Figure 7-2 illustrates a database server with a dedicated I/O subsystem.

Combined host-based and I/O subsystem volume management

In this configuration, disks are grouped into arrays within the I/O subsystem and grouped again into coarser arrays using operating system volume management. On EMC systems, for example, the physical disks are grouped into either RAID-1 mirrored disk pairs or into a RAID-S striped configuration using four disks per stripe set.

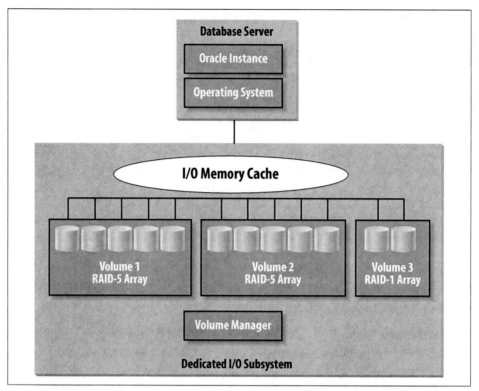

Figure 7-2. Dedicated I/O subsystems

(RAID-S is the term EMC [*http://www.emc.com*] uses for its specialized striping hardware and software.)

Using EMC technology as an example, the operating system sees horizontal sections of disk space across each RAID-1 disk or RAID-S array as single "disks." You can use the operating system volume management to group these "disks" into arrays. With RAID-1 disks, this configuration delivers the benefits of using a dedicated I/O subsystem with its own cache and processing power while leveraging striping for simplicity. With RAID-S arrays you get the benefit of the dedicated I/O subsystem and further simplify disk management by a striping multiplier effect. An array of five "disks" at the operating system level could map back to five arrays of four disks each in the I/O subsystem. This configuration maps a logical disk seen by Oracle to 20 physical disks in the underlying I/O subsystem. Figure 7-3 illustrates a logical drive on the database server mapping to horizontal sections across multiple RAID-S arrays.

Flexibility, Manageability, and Disk Arrays

Many systems today use some type of RAID technology that groups multiple individual disk drives, also referred to as *spindles*, into arrays. Each disk array is then treated

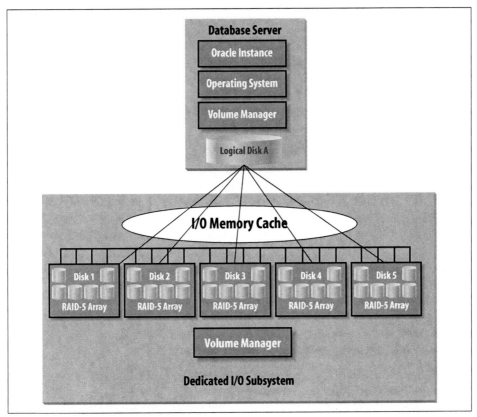

Figure 7-3. Combining host-based striping and an EMC I/O subsystem

as a single logical disk for the purpose of planning I/O. Striping allows you to simply spread I/O across multiple disks, without incurring the planning and administrative overhead of dealing with many individual disk drives.

The decision about how many disks should be in each array is often the topic of intense debate. At one extreme, using multiple disks without grouping any of them into arrays provides the most control and flexibility because every disk is visible and can be targeted in isolation by placing certain files on each disk. However, this approach requires more planning and can result in more ongoing administration, because you will have to deal with every individual disk drive. As databases become larger and larger, this approach can become unmanageable.

At the other extreme, you can group all disks into one single array, seen by the operating system and Oracle as a single "disk." This makes for extremely simple planning and administration; no effort is required to analyze where you should place the various files, as there is only one "disk." However, this approach sacrifices flexibility and leads to brute-force solutions to I/O bottlenecks. If I/O performance across the array is unsatisfactory, the solution is to add more controllers and disks. The entire set of disks becomes a black box that either works or doesn't work as a unit.

The most useful configuration is one that balances manageability with flexibility. For example, consider a system with 1,000 disks. Neither a single array of 1,000 disks nor a set of 1,000 individual disks is likely to be appropriate. Perhaps 50 arrays of 20 disks each would provide the needed I/O performance without any undue administrative burden. If less flexibility is needed, 20 arrays of 50 disks are more suitable. On the other hand, grouping all the disks into one array may be the simplest way to manage a system with only five disks. For the "right" answer, you must assess your needs to determine the appropriate balance.

Oracle Database 10g simplified this by automating the striping and stripe set rebalancing process. ASM divides files into 1 MB extents and spreads the extents evenly across each disk group. Pointers are used to track placement of each extent (instead of using a mathematical function such as a hashing algorithm to stripe the data). So when the disk group configuration changes, individual extents can be moved. In comparison to traditional algorithm-based striping techniques, the need to rerun that algorithm and reallocate all of the data is eliminated. Extent maps are updated when rebalancing the load after a change in disk configuration, opening a new database file, or extending a database file by enlarging a tablespace. By default, each 1 MB extent is also mirrored, so management of redundancy is also simplified. Mirroring can be extended to triple mirroring or can be turned off. Although you still have to consider how many disk groups to use, implementation of these groups with striping and redundancy is automated with ASM.

Shortly after the initial release of Oracle Database 11g, Oracle exposed additional storage management capabilities in the database. These features are especially useful in configuring storage for Oracles's Information Appliances, described in Chapter 8.

How Oracle I/O and Striped Arrays Interact

In almost all large databases, disk striping increases disk I/O rates without adding too heavy an administrative burden for managing a large number of datafiles across many individual disks. The disks may be organized into RAID arrays using a volume manager on the database server, a dedicated I/O subsystem, or a combination of both.

If you are using an Oracle release without ASM, when you set up striped disk arrays, you can set the *chunk size* used to stripe across the disks. The chunk size is the amount of data written to one disk before moving to the next disk in the array. Understanding the interaction between different stripe chunk sizes and the two sizes of Oracle I/O is critical in maximizing your I/O performance.

Consider an Oracle database with an 8 KB data block size and the DB_FILE_MULTIBLOCK_READ_COUNT initialization parameter set to 32. There will be two sizes of I/O by Oracle: a single 8 KB data block and a 256 KB multiblock read (32 times 8 KB). Suppose you configure a four-disk array for use by Oracle with a chunk size of 64 KB so that the 256 KB of data will be spread across the four drives, with 64 KB on each.

Each 8 KB I/O will hit one spindle, as the 8 KB will lie within one 64 KB chunk.* Striping can increase performance for small I/Os by maximizing concurrency: each disk can service a different I/O. The multiblock I/Os of 256 KB may hit all four disks. If the chunk size were 256 KB instead of 64 KB, on average each 256 KB I/O call would hit one disk. In this case, the multiblock I/O will require fewer I/O calls with a larger chunk size on the disks. In either case, a single disk will clearly satisfy single-data-block I/O calls. Striping can increase I/O rates for large reads by driving multiple disks with a single I/O call, as illustrated with a 64 KB chunk size and a 256 KB multiblock I/O.

Figure 7-4 illustrates the interaction of different-sized Oracle I/Os with arrays striped using different chunk sizes.

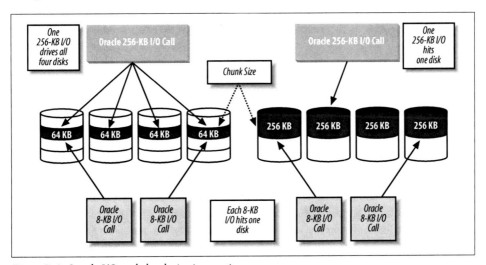

Figure 7-4. Oracle I/O and chunk size interaction

Oracle and Parallelism

The ability to parallelize operations is one of the most important features of the Very Large Database (VLDB). Database servers with multiple CPUs, which are called *symmetric multiprocessing* (SMP) machines, are the norm today for most database servers, and the ability to perform operations in parallel also works well with multi-core CPU chips. As performance demands increase and data volumes continue to grow, you will increasingly need to use multiple processors, cores and disks to reduce

---

* It's difficult to say exactly what will occur due to the alignment of the stripe-chunk boundaries with Oracle data blocks, but to illustrate the single versus multiple disk point, let's assume the simple case—they line up! For a more detailed discussion of striping issues, see the document "Configuring Oracle Server for VLDB," by Cary Millsap, formerly of Oracle Corporation and now with Hotsos (see Appendix B). Anyone who is tempted is welcome to perform detailed testing for all the permutations of stripe chunk size and Oracle I/O. If you happen to perform this extensive testing, please tell all the rest of us what you find!

the time needed to complete a given task. Oracle supports parallelism within a single SMP server and parallelism across multiple nodes, using Oracle Real Application Clusters. Executing a SQL statement in parallel will consume more of the machine resources—CPU, memory, and disk I/O—but complete the overall task faster.

Parallelism affects the amount of memory and CPU resources used to execute a given task in a fairly linear fashion—the more parallel processes used, the more resources consumed for the composite task. Each parallel execution process has a Program Global Area (PGA) that consumes memory and performs work. Each parallel execution process takes its own slice of CPU, but more parallel processes can reduce the total amount of time spent on disk I/O, which is the place in which bottlenecks can most readily appear.

Two types of parallelism are possible within an Oracle database:

Block-range parallelism
    Driven by ranges of database blocks

Partition-based parallelism
    Driven by the number of partitions or subpartitions involved in the operation

The following sections describe these types of parallelism.

Block-Range Parallelism

In 1994, Oracle 7.1 introduced the ability to dynamically parallelize table scans and a variety of scan-based functions. This parallelism was based on the notion of *block ranges*, in which the Oracle server would understand that each table contained a set of data blocks that spanned a defined range of data. Oracle7 implemented block-range parallelism by dynamically breaking a table into pieces, each of which was a range of blocks, and then used multiple processes to work on these pieces in parallel. Oracle's implementation of block-range parallelism was unique in that it didn't require physically partitioned tables, described in Chapter 4, to achieve parallelism.

With block-range parallelism, the client session that issued the SQL statement transparently becomes the parallel execution coordinator, dynamically determining block ranges and assigning them to a set of parallel execution (PE) processes. Once a PE process has completed an assigned block range, it returns to the coordinator for more work. Not all I/O occurs at the same rate, so some PE processes may process more blocks than others. This notion of "stealing work" allows all processes to participate fully in the task, providing maximum leverage of the machine resources.

Block-range parallelism scales linearly based on the number of PE processes, provided you have adequate hardware resources. The key to achieving scalability with parallelism lies in hardware basics. Each PE process runs on a CPU and requests I/O to a device. If you have enough CPUs reading enough disks, parallelism will scale. If the system encounters a bottleneck on one of these resources, scalability will suffer.

For example, four CPUs reading two disks will not scale much beyond the two-way scalability of the disks and may even sink below this level if the additional CPUs cause contention for the disks. Similarly, 2 CPUs reading 20 disks will not scale to a 20-fold performance improvement. The system hardware must be balanced for parallelism to scale.

Most large systems have far more disks than CPUs. In these systems, parallelism results in a randomization of I/O across the I/O subsystem. This is useful for concurrent access to data as PE processes for different users read from different disks at different times, resulting in I/O that is distributed across the available disks.

A useful analogy for dynamic parallelism is eating a pie. The pie is the set of blocks to be read for the operation, and the goal is to eat the pie as quickly as possible using a certain number of people. Oracle serves the pie in helpings, and when a person finishes his first helping, he can come back for more. Not everyone eats at the same rate, so some people will consume more pie than others. While this approach in the real world is somewhat unfair, it's a good model for parallelism because if everyone is eating all the time, the pie will be consumed more quickly. The alternative is to give each person an equal serving and wait for the slower eaters to finish.

Figure 7-5 illustrates the splitting of a set of blocks into ranges.

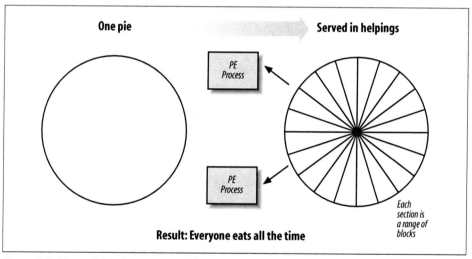

Figure 7-5. Dynamic block-range parallelism

Parallelism for Tables and Partitions of Tables

With *partitioned tables*, introduced in Oracle8, an operation may involve one, some, or all of the partitions of a partitioned table. There is essentially no difference in how block-range parallelism dynamically splits the set of blocks to be read for a regular table as opposed to a partitioned table. Once the optimizer has determined which partitions should be accessed for the operation, all the blocks of all partitions involved are treated as a pool to be broken into ranges.

This assumption by the optimizer leads to a key consideration for using parallelism and partitioned tables. The degree of parallelism (i.e., the number of parallel execution processes used for the table as a whole) is applied to the set of partitions that will be used for an operation. The optimizer will eliminate the use of partitions that do not contain data an operation will use. For instance, if one of the partitions for a table contains ID numbers below 1,000, and if a query requests ID numbers between 1,100 and 5,000, the optimizer understands that this query will not access this partition.

Since Oracle9i, you can also partition tables based on a list of specific values, although this type of partitioning is typically used to partition tables for maintenance operations. As explained in Chapter 4, Oracle has continued to add more choices in ways to implement partitioning.

If you expect that your queries will use partition elimination or pruning and you plan on using parallelism, you should stripe each partition over a sufficient number of drives to scale effectively. This will ensure scalability regardless of the number of partitions accessed. This striping can be achieved manually through the use of multiple datafiles on multiple disks, through the use of striped arrays, or through a combination of both approaches.

What Can Be Parallelized?

Oracle can parallelize far more than simple queries. The list of operations that can be parallelized using block-range parallelism includes the following:

- Tablespace creation
- Index creation and rebuilds
- Online index reorganizations and rebuilds
- Index-organized table reorganizations and movements
- Table creation, such as summary creation using CREATE TABLE…AS SELECT
- Partition-maintenance operations, such as moving and splitting partitions
- Data loading
- Integrity constraints imposing
- Statistics gathering (automatically gathered since Oracle Database 10g)
- Backups and restores (including very large files in Oracle Database 11g)
- DML operations (INSERT, UPDATE, DELETE)
- Query processing operations
- OLAP aggregate (as of Oracle Database 10g)

Oracle can also provide the benefits of parallelism to individual processing steps for queries. The specific features of query processing that may be parallelized include:

- Table scans
- Nested loops
- Sort merge joins
- Hash joins
- Bitmap star joins
- Index scans
- Partition-wise joins
- Anti-joins (NOT IN)
- SELECT DISTINCT
- UNION and UNION ALL
- ORDER BY
- GROUP BY
- Aggregations
- Import
- User-defined functions

Degree of parallelism

An Oracle instance has a pool of parallel execution (PE) processes that are available to the database users. Controlling the number of active PE processes was an important task in older Oracle database releases; too many PE processes would overload the machine, leading to resource bottlenecks and performance degradation. A high degree of parallelism will also force full-table scans and this may or may not be appropriate. Figure 7-6 illustrates transparent parallelism within and between sets of PE processes.

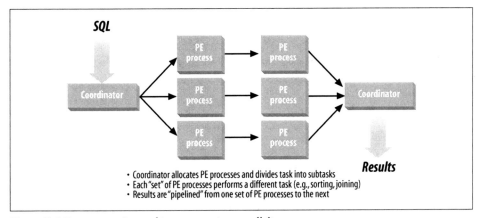

Figure 7-6. Intra-operation and inter-operation parallelism

Determining the optimal degree of parallelism in the presence of multiple users and varying workloads proved challenging. For example, a degree of 8 for a query would provide excellent performance for 1 or 2 users, but what if 20 users queried the same table? This scenario called for 160 PE processes (8 PEs for each of the 20 users), which could overload the machine.

Setting the degree to a lowest common denominator value (for example, 2) provided effective parallelism for higher user counts, but did not leverage resources fully when fewer users are active.

Self-tuning adaptive parallelism

Oracle8*i* introduced the notion of *self-tuning adaptive parallelism*. This feature automatically scales down parallelism as the system load increases and scales it back up as the load decreases. When an operation requests a degree of parallelism, Oracle will check the system load and lower the actual degree the operation uses to avoid overloading the system. As more users request parallel operations, the degree they receive will become lower and lower until operations are executing serially. If activity decreases, subsequent operations will be granted increasing degrees of parallelism. This adaptability frees the DBA from the difficult task of trying to determine the optimal degree of parallelism in the face of constant changes in workload.

Adaptive parallelism takes two factors into account in determining the degree of parallelism granted to an operation:

- System load.
- Parallelism resource limitations of the user's consumer group if the Database Resource Manager is active. (The Database Resource Manager is explained in Chapter 9 and also later in this chapter.) This is important, because it means that adaptive parallelism respects resource plans if they're in place.

Partition-Based Parallelism

A small subset of Oracle's parallel functionality is based on the number of partitions or subpartitions accessed by the statement to be parallelized. For block-range parallelism, the piece of data each PE process works on is a range of blocks. For partition-based parallelism, the pieces of data that drive parallelism are partitions or subpartitions of a table. The operations in which parallelism is based on the number of partitions or subpartitions include the following:

- Updates and deletes
- Index scans
- Index creation and rebuilds on partitioned tables

Parallelism for partitions and subpartitions of a table

Oracle8 introduced support for parallel Data Manipulation Language (DML), or the ability to execute INSERT, UPDATE, and DELETE statements in parallel. This type of parallelism improves the performance of large bulk operations (for example, an update to all the rows of a very large table).

In Oracle8 the degree of parallelism for updates and deletes is tied to the number of partitions involved, while in Oracle8*i* and beyond the degree of parallelism for updates and deletes is tied to the number of partitions or subpartitions involved. A table with 12 partitions (for example, one partition for each month of the year) can have a maximum number of 12 PEs for an update or delete. An update to only one month of data would have no parallelism because it involves only one partition. If the table were created using Oracle's composite partitioning (for example, with 4 hash subpartitions by PRODUCT_ID within each month), the maximum degree of parallelism for the entire table would be 48, or 12 partitions with 4 subpartitions each. An update to one month of data could have a degree of 4 because each month contains 4 hash subpartitions. If the table is not partitioned, Oracle cannot perform updates or deletes in parallel.

Oracle8 and later versions can execute index creation, index rebuilds, and index scans for partitioned indexes in parallel using the same semantics as parallel DML: one PE process per partition or subpartition of the index.

Fast full index scans for nonpartitioned tables

People often assume that the Oracle database can parallelize index scans only if the target index is partitioned. Oracle 7.3 introduced the ability to perform parallel index scans on nonpartitioned indexes for a certain case. If the index scan operation were "unbounded," meaning that the entire index was going to be accessed to satisfy the query, then Oracle 7.3 and higher would use block-range parallelism to access the entire index in parallel. While Oracle can perform index scans for nonpartitioned indexes, this feature applies to a narrow set of queries. Partition-based index scans apply to a much broader range of queries.

Parallel insert for nonpartitioned and partitioned tables

Oracle can execute an INSERT statement of the form INSERT INTO *tableX* SELECT...FROM *tableY* in parallel for nonpartitioned and partitioned tables. Oracle uses a set of PE processes executing block-range parallelism for the SELECT portion of the INSERT statement. These PE processes pass the rows to a second set of PE processes, which insert the rows into the target table. The target table can be a nonpartitioned or partitioned table. Parallelism for an insert is not exactly block-range or partition-based.

Oracle and Memory Resources

Accessing information in memory is much faster than accessing information on a disk. An Oracle instance uses the database server's memory resources to cache the information accessed to improve performance. Oracle utilizes an area of shared memory called the System Global Area (SGA) and a private memory area for each server process called the Program Global Area (PGA).

Prior to Oracle9i, you could only specify the size for the SGA or any of its components—database buffer cache, shared pool, or large pool—in the initialization file, and the size of these memory allocations could not be changed without shutting down and restarting the instance. Oracle9i enabled dynamic resizing of these pools based on a minimum memory allocation called a *granule*. Oracle Database 10g and later releases can automatically manage shared memory. Oracle Database 11g adds automatic memory management of the SGA and PGA.

Exhausting a database server's supply of memory will cause poor performance. If you are running an older release of Oracle, you should gauge the size of the various memory areas Oracle uses or add more memory to the machine to prevent a memory deficit from occurring. What constitutes the right size for the various areas is a function of your application behavior, the data it uses, and your performance requirements.

How Oracle Uses the System Global Area

Oracle uses the SGA for the following operations:

- Caching of database blocks containing table and index data in the database buffer cache
- Caching of parsed and optimized SQL statements, stored procedures, and data dictionary information in the shared pool
- Buffering of redo log entries in the redo log buffer before they're written to disk

In versions prior to Oracle 9i, the amount of memory allocated to each of these areas within the SGA was determined at instance startup using initialization parameters and could not be altered without restarting the instance.

The majority of tuning efforts focused on the database buffer cache and the shared pool.

Automatic sizing for the SGA

Oracle Database 10g eliminated manual tuning of SGA pools with automatic sizing for the SGA. Using automatic shared memory management, the database automatically allocates memory for the following SGA pools: database buffer cache, shared pool, large pool, Java pool, and Streams pool. You have to specify only the total amount of memory required by setting the SGA_TARGET initialization parameter.

Since Oracle Database 10g, the database proactively monitors the memory requirements for each pool and dynamically reallocates memory when appropriate. You can also specify the minimum amount of memory for any of the SGA pools while using automatic SGA sizing using the following initialization parameters: DB_CACHE_SIZE, SHARED_POOL_SIZE, LARGE_POOL_SIZE, JAVA_POOL_SIZE, and STREAMS_POOL_SIZE. A few SGA pools, specified using such parameters as LOG_BUFFER, DB_KEEP_CACHE_SIZE, and DB_RECYCLE_CACHE_SIZE, are still manually sized.

The database buffer cache

If you decide to disable SGA_TARGET by setting it to 0, you will need to manually set initialization parameters for the memory pools (unless you want to use previous sizes). For the database buffer cache, you would assess the percentage of the database blocks requested by users read from the cache versus from the disk. This percentage is termed the *hit ratio*. If response times are too high and this ratio is lower than 90% (as a rule of thumb), increasing the value of the initialization parameter DB_CACHE_SIZE can increase performance.

 You can use Oracle Enterprise Manager to get information about the cache hit ratio.

It's tempting to assume that continually increasing the size of the database buffer cache will translate into better performance. However, this is true only if the database blocks in the cache are actually being reused. Most OLTP systems have a relatively small set of core tables that are heavily used (for example, lookup tables for things such as valid codes). The rest of the I/O tends to be random, accessing a row or two in various database blocks in the course of the transaction. Because of this, having a larger buffer cache may not contribute to performance since there isn't much reuse of data blocks occurring.

In addition, not all operations read from the database buffer cache. For example, large full-table scans are limited to a small number of buffers to avoid adversely impacting other users by dominating the cache. If your application performs a lot of table scans, increasing the buffer cache may not help performance because the cache will not contain the needed data blocks. Parallel table scans completely bypass the buffer cache and pass rows directly to the requesting user process. As with most performance issues, your understanding of how your application is actually using your data is the key that will help guide your database buffer-cache tuning.

The shared pool

The shared pool is used at several points during the execution of every operation that occurs in an Oracle database. For example, the shared pool is accessed to cache the

SQL sent to the database and for the data dictionary information required to execute the SQL. Because of its central role in database operations, a shared pool that is too small may have a greater impact on performance than a database buffer cache that is too small. If the requested database block isn't in the database buffer cache, Oracle will perform an I/O to retrieve it, resulting in a one-time performance hit.

A shared pool that is too small will cause poor performance for a variety of reasons, affecting all users. These reasons include the following:

- Not enough data dictionary information can be cached, resulting in frequent disk access to query and update the data dictionary.

- Not enough SQL can be cached, leading to memory "churn," or the flushing of useful statements to make room for incoming statements. A well-designed application issues the same statements repeatedly. If there isn't enough room to cache all the SQL the application uses, the same statements get parsed, cached, and flushed over and over, wasting valuable CPU resources and adding overhead to every transaction.

- Not enough stored procedures can be cached, leading to similar memory churn and performance issues for the program logic stored and executed in the database.

If you are manually managing the shared pool and you've diagnosed which of these problems is occurring, the solution is fairly simple: increase the size of the shared pool using the SHARED_POOL_SIZE initialization parameter. Shared pool sizes in the 150–250 MB range are not uncommon for large, active databases. For more information about examining shared pool activity to identify problems, see the appropriate *Oracle Performance Tuning Guide*, as well as the third-party books listed in Appendix B.

The redo log buffer

While the redo log buffer consumes a very small amount of memory in the SGA relative to the database buffer cache and the shared pool, it's critical for performance. Transactions performing changes to the data in the database write their redo information to the redo log buffer in memory. The redo log buffer is flushed to the redo logs on disk when a transaction is committed (normally) or when the redo log buffer is one-third full. Oracle "fences" off the portion of the redo log buffer that's being flushed to disk to make sure that its contents aren't changed until the information is safely on disk. Transactions can continue to write redo information to the rest of the redo log buffer (the portion that isn't being written to disk and therefore isn't fenced off by Oracle). In a busy database, transactions may generate enough redo to fill the remaining unfenced portion of the redo log buffer before the I/O to the disks for the fenced area of the redo log buffer is complete. If this happens, the transactions will have to wait for the I/O to complete because there is no more space in the redo log buffer. This situation can impact performance. The statistic "redo buffer allocation retries" can be used to understand this situation. It is available through V$SYSSTAT and is an indication of how often a session waited for space in the redo log buffer. An example of the query you may use to obtain the statistic is:

```
SELECT name, value FROM V$SYSSTAT
    WHERE name = 'redo buffer allocation retries';
```

You would monitor these statistics over a period of time to gain insight into the trend. The values at one point in time reflect the cumulative totals since the instance was started and aren't necessarily meaningful as a single data point. Note that this is true for all statistics used for performance tuning. Ideally, the value of "redo buffer allocation retries" should be close to 0. If you observe the value rising during the monitoring period, you would increase the size of the redo log buffer by resetting the LOG_BUFFER initialization parameter.

Query results caching

One of the most significant performance features in Oracle Database 11g can be used to help improve the performance of repeated queries. Oracle caches database and index blocks, eliminating the need to perform resource-intensive disk reads. Oracle caches SQL plans, eliminating the need to reparse and optimize queries. But prior to Oracle Database 11g, a cached SQL plan would still have to execute and assemble a result set.

The new feature allows Oracle Database 11g to cache the completed result set in the shared pool. This new functionality means that a repeated query requesting the same result set can simply take that result set completely from memory. Since the result sets have to be the same for this feature to work, the query results cache has the biggest impact on situations like web page serving, where the same page is being retrieved repeatedly. This feature also works on the results of PL/SQL functions.

Oracle Database 11g also includes the ability to cache query result sets on the client, while automatically keeping the result set consistent with any changes that could affect it. This feature gives the performance benefits of query result set caching on the server while eliminating network roundtrips as an added benefit.

How Oracle Uses the Program Global Area

Each server has a Program Global Area (PGA), which is a private memory area that contains information about the work the server process is performing. There is one PGA for each server process. The total amount of memory used for all the PGAs is a function of the number of server processes active as part of the Oracle instance. The larger the number of users, the higher the number of server processes and the larger the amount of memory used for their associated PGAs. Using the Multi-Threaded Server (known as the shared server from Oracle9i on) reduces total memory consumption for PGAs because it reduces the number of server processes.

The PGA consists of a working memory area for things such as temporary variables used by the server process, memory for information about the SQL the server process is executing, and memory for sorting rows as part of SQL execution. The initial size of the PGA's working memory area for variables, known as *stack space*, cannot be directly controlled because it's predetermined based on the operating system you are using for your database server. The other areas within the PGA can be controlled as described in the following sections.

Memory for SQL statements

When a server process executes a SQL statement for a user, the server process tracks the session-specific details about the SQL statement and the progress by executing it in a piece of memory in the PGA called a *private SQL area*, also known as a *cursor*. This area should not be confused with the shared SQL area within the shared pool. The shared SQL area contains shareable details for the SQL statement, such as the optimization plan. Optimizers and optimization plans are discussed in Chapter 4.

The private SQL area contains the session-specific information about the execution of the SQL statement within the session, such as the number of rows retrieved so far. Once a SQL statement has been processed, its private SQL area can be reused by another SQL statement. If the application reissues the SQL statement whose private SQL area was reused, the private SQL area will have to be reinitialized.

Each time a new SQL statement is received, its shared SQL area must be located (or, if not located, loaded) in the shared pool. Similarly, the SQL statement's private SQL area must be located in the PGA or, if it isn't located, reinitialized by the server process. This reinitialization is relatively expensive in terms of CPU resources.

A server process with a PGA that can contain a higher number of distinct private SQL areas will spend less time reinitializing private SQL areas for incoming SQL statements. If the server process doesn't have to reuse an existing private SQL area to accommodate a new statement, the private SQL area for the original statement can be kept intact. Although similar to a larger shared pool, a larger PGA avoids memory churn within the private SQL areas. Reduced private SQL area reuse, in turn, reduces the associated CPU consumption, increasing performance. There is, of course, a trade-off between allocating memory in the PGA for SQL and overall performance.

OLTP systems typically have a "working set" of SQL statements that each user submits. For example, a user who enters car rental reservations uses the same forms in the application repeatedly. Performance will be improved if the user's server process has enough memory in the PGA to cache the SQL those forms issue. Application developers should also take care to write their SQL statements so that they can be easily reused, by specifying bind variables instead of different hardcoded values in their SQL statements.

Memory for sorting within the PGA

Each server process uses memory in its PGA for sorting rows before returning them to the user. If the memory allocated for sorting is insufficient to hold all the rows that need to be sorted, the server process sorts the rows in multiple passes called *runs*. The intermediate runs are written to the temporary tablespace of the user, which reduces sort performance because it involves disk I/O.

Sizing the sort area of the PGA was a critical tuning point in Oracle database releases prior to Oracle Database 10g. A sort area that was too small for the typical amount of data requiring sorting would result in temporary tablespace disk I/O and reduced performance. A sort area that was significantly larger than necessary would waste memory.

As of Oracle Database 10g, the database provides automatic sizing for the PGA. By default, this memory management is enabled, and sizing for PGA work areas is based on 20 percent of the SGA memory size. By using automatic sizing for the PGA, you eliminate the need to size individual portions of the PGA, such as SORT_AREA_SIZE.

Oracle Database 11g introduced automatic memory management that spans both the SGA and the PGA. By setting a single MEMORY_TARGET initialization parameter (given that the PGA size can be based on a percentage of the SGA memory size), the PGA and SGA will be automatically set to appropriate initial values. Oracle then tunes memory for optimal SGA and PGA performance on an ongoing basis.

TimesTen

In 2005, Oracle acquired the leading in-memory database TimesTen. *In-memory databases* provide optimal performance by reducing data retrieval latency. The optimizer used with the TimesTen database is aware of the memory location of the data, and creates execution plans to take advantage of this residency. In addition, the actual number of machine instructions is significantly reduced, since there is no need for code to handle situations where data resides only on disk. TimesTen is most appropriate for a high-load OLTP environment that requires extremely high throughput and real-time responsiveness.

A TimesTen instance can be used as a cache for an Oracle database. You load a subset of Oracle tables into the TimesTen instance, and the Cache Connect to Oracle feature keeps the data synchronized.

You can also enable replication between TimesTen instances on different machines for load sharing and higher availability. For more information on TimesTen, please refer to the relevant pages on the Oracle Technology Network.

Oracle and CPU Resources

The Oracle database shares the CPU(s) with all other software running on the server. If there is a shortage of CPU power, reducing Oracle or non-Oracle CPU consumption will improve the performance of all processes running on the server.

If all the CPUs in a machine are busy, the processes line up and wait for a turn to use the CPU. This is called a *run queue* because processes are waiting to run on a CPU. The busier the CPUs get, the longer processes can spend in this queue. A process in the queue isn't doing any work, so as the run queue gets longer, response times degrade.

 You can use the standard monitoring tools for your particular operating system to check the CPU utilization for that machine.

Tuning CPU usage is essentially an exercise in tuning individual tasks: it reduces the number of commands required to accomplish the tasks and/or reduces the overall number of tasks to be performed. You can do this tuning through workload balancing, SQL tuning, or improved application design. This type of tuning requires insight into what these tasks are and how they're being executed.

As mentioned earlier, an in-depth discussion of all the various tuning points for an Oracle database is beyond the scope of this book. However, there is a set of common tasks that typically result in excess CPU consumption. Some of the usual suspects to examine if you encounter a CPU resource shortage on your database server include the following:

Bad SQL

Poorly written SQL is the number one cause of performance problems. An Oracle database attempts to optimally execute the SQL it receives from clients. If the SQL contained in the client applications and sent to the database is written so that the best optimization plan Oracle can identify is still inefficient, Oracle will consume more resources than necessary to execute the SQL. Tuning SQL can be a complex and time-consuming process because it requires an in-depth understanding of how Oracle works and what the application is trying to do. Initial examinations can reveal flaws in the underlying database design, leading to changes in table structures, additional indexes, and so on. Changing the SQL requires retesting and a subsequent redeployment of the application—until Oracle Database 10g.

Oracle Database 10g introduced the SQL Tuning Advisor, a tool that can not only recognize poorly written SQL, but also create an optimizer plan to circumvent the problem and replace the standard optimization plan with the improved plan. With this capability, you can improve the performance of poorly written

SQL without changing any code in the application. The SQL Advisor in Oracle Database 11g combines the functionality of the SQL Tuning Advisor, the SQL Access Advisor, and the Partition Advisor.

In Oracle Database 11g, the database can automatically spot the SQL queries with the largest loads and automatically create SQL profiles to improve their performance, if appropriate. This process can also result in advice on new indexes that could improve the performance of these statements.

Oracle Database 11g also tracks changes in execution plans for SQL statements, described in Chapter 4. The optimizer can maintain the history of execution plans, and when a new plan is detected, the optimizer uses the old plan and evaluates the performance of the new plan. Once the optimizer verifies that the new plan can deliver the same performance, the old plan is replaced. This feature does not directly relate to bad SQL, but rather to the occasional effects of plan changes, which can result in unplanned performance degradation.

Excessive parsing

As we discussed in the section "Memory for SQL statements," Oracle must parse every SQL statement before it's processed. Parsing is very CPU-intensive, involving a lot of data dictionary lookups to check that all the tables and columns referenced are valid. Complex algorithms and calculations estimate the costs of the various optimizer plans possible for the statement to select the optimal plan. If your application isn't using bind variables (discussed in Chapter 9), the database will have to parse every statement it receives. This excessive and unnecessary parsing is one of the leading causes of performance degradation. Another common cause is a shared pool that's too small, as discussed previously in the section "The shared pool." Keep in mind that you can avoid the creation of execution plans by using stored outlines, as described in Chapter 4. And, as of Oracle9i, you also have the ability to edit the hints that make up a stored outline. As described earlier, Oracle Database 11g includes the ability to cache complete result sets, which can minimize the impact of repeated execution of identical queries.

Database workload

If your application is well designed and your database is operating at optimal efficiency, you may experience a shortage of CPU resources for the simple reason that your server doesn't have enough CPU power to perform all the work it's being asked to do. This shortage may be due to the workload for one database (if the machine is a dedicated database server) or to the combined workload of multiple databases running on the server. Underestimating the amount of CPU resources required is a chronic problem in capacity planning. Unfortunately, accurate estimates of the CPU resources required for a certain level of activity demands detailed insight into the amount of CPU power each transaction will consume and how many transactions per minute or second the system will process, both at peak and average workloads. Most organizations don't have the time or resources for the system analysis and prototyping required to answer these questions. This is perhaps why CPU shortages are so common, and why the equally common solution is to simply add more CPUs to the machine until the problem goes away. Real Application Clusters and the grid are attempts to at least make adding more CPU horsepower easier.

Nondatabase workload

Not all organizations have the luxury of dedicating an entire machine to an Oracle database to ensure that all CPU resources are available for that database. Use operating system utilities to identify the top CPU consumers on the machine. You may find that non-Oracle processes are consuming the bulk of the CPU resources and adversely impacting database performance.

Database Resource Manager

The previous section described some of the ways that you can end up with poor performance through a lack of CPU resources. The Database Resource Manager (DRM) was first introduced in Oracle8*i* and can help you automatically avoid some of these problems.

DRM works by leveraging consumer groups you've identified and enabling you to place limits on the amount of computer resources that can be used by that group. Implementing the DRM ensures that one group or member of a group does not end up using an excessive amount of any one resource, as well as acting to deliver guaranteed service levels for different sets of users. You can create DRM hierarchies in which you specify the amount of resources for groups within groups.

The following DRM features can be combined to protect against poor performance:

Predicting resource utilization

The DRM can leverage the query optimizer cost computations to predict the amount of resources that a given query will take and the query execution time. Note that, by default, the query optimizer uses a CPU + I/O cost model since Oracle Database 10*g*. In Oracle9*i*, the query optimizer used an I/O cost model based on single block reads.

Switching consumer groups

The DRM can switch consumer groups dynamically. You might want to give a particular consumer group a high allocation of CPU resources. But if a single query from that group looks as if it will take up too many CPU resources and affect the overall performance of the machine, the consumer group can be switched to another group that has a smaller CPU allocation—for example, a consumer group designed for batch operations.

Limiting number of connections

The DRM can limit the number of connections for any particular consumer group. If the limit on connections for a group has been reached and another connection request comes in, the connection request is queued until an existing connection is freed. By limiting the overall number of connections for a consumer group, you can place some rough limits on the overall resources that particular group might require.

In Oracle Database 11g, the database installs with a default DRM plan. The default plan is designed to limit the amount of resources used by automated maintenance tasks such as optimizer statistics gathering, the Automatic Segment Advisor, and the Automatic SQL Tuning Advisor.

CHAPTER 8

Oracle Multiuser Concurrency

Sharing data is at the center of all information systems. As systems provide higher and higher levels of functionality, we can sometime forget that the ability to efficiently share data is the underlying governor of overall system performance. At the same time, database systems must protect the integrity of the data, as the value of that data is directly proportional to the correctness of the data. Database systems must protect data integrity, while still providing high levels of performance for multiuser access. These two forces sometimes conflict and shape some of the core technology in any database system.

Data integrity must always come first. As Ken Jacobs, vice president at Oracle, put it in his classic paper entitled "Transaction Control and Oracle7," a multiuser database must be able to handle concurrently executing transactions in a way that "ensure(s) predictable and reproducible results." This goal is the core issue of data integrity, which, in turn, is the foundation of any database system.

When multiple users access the same data, there is always the possibility that one user's changes to a specific piece of data will be unwittingly overwritten by another user's changes. If this situation occurs, the accuracy of the information in the database is compromised, which can render the data useless or, even worse, misleading. At the same time, the techniques used to prevent this type of loss can dramatically reduce the performance of an application system, as users wait for other users to complete their work before continuing. These techniques act like a traffic signal, so you can't solve this type of performance problem by increasing the resources available to the database. The problem isn't due to a lack of horsepower—it's caused by a red light.

Although concurrency issues are central to the success of applications, they are some of the most difficult problems to predict because they can stem from such complex interactive situations. The difficulties posed by concurrent access continue to increase as the number of concurrent users increases. Even a robust debugging and testing environment may fail to detect problems created by concurrent access, since these problems are created by large numbers of users who may not be available in a test environment. Concurrency problems can also pop up as user access patterns change throughout the life of an application.

If problems raised by concurrent access aren't properly handled by a database, developers may find themselves suffering in a number of ways. They will have to create their own customized solutions to these problems in their software, which will consume valuable development time. They will frequently find themselves adding code during the late stages of development and testing to work around the underlying deficiencies in their database systems, which can undercut the design and performance of the application. Worst of all, they may find themselves changing the optimal design of their data structures to compensate for weaknesses in the capabilities of the underlying database.

There is only one way to deal successfully with the issues raised by concurrent data access. The database that provides the access must implement strategies to transparently overcome the potential problems posed by concurrent access. Fortunately, Oracle has excellent methods for handling concurrent access.

This chapter describes the basics of concurrent data access and gives you an overview of the way that Oracle handles the issues raised by concurrent access. If you've worked with large database systems in the past and are familiar with concurrent user access, you might want to skip the first section of this chapter.

Basics of Concurrent Access

Before you can understand the problems posed by multiuser concurrent access to data, you need to understand the basic concepts that are used to identify and describe those potential concurrency issues.

Transactions

The *transaction* is the bedrock of data integrity in multiuser databases and the foundation of all concurrency schemes. A transaction is defined as a single indivisible piece of work that affects some data. All of the modifications made to data within a transaction are uniformly applied to a database with a COMMIT statement, or the data affected by the changes is uniformly returned to its initial state with a ROLLBACK statement. Once a transaction is committed, the changes made by that transaction become permanent and are made visible to other transactions and other users.

Transactions always occur over time, although most transactions occur over a very short period of time. Since the changes made by a transaction aren't official until the transaction is committed, each individual transaction must be isolated from the effects of other transactions. The mechanism used to enforce transaction isolation is the lock.

Locks

A database uses a system of *locks* to prevent transactions from interfering with each other. A lock prevents users from modifying data. Database systems use locks to keep one transaction from overwriting changes added by another transaction.

Figure 8-1 illustrates the potential problems that could occur if a system did not use locks. Transaction A reads a piece of data; Transaction B reads the same piece of data and commits a change to the data. When Transaction A commits the data, its change unwittingly overwrites the changes made by Transaction B, resulting in a loss of data integrity.

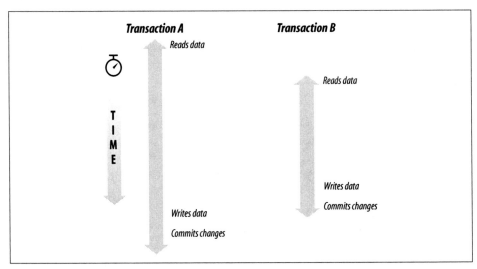

Figure 8-1. Transactions over time

Two types of locks are used to avoid this type of problem. The first is called a *write lock*, or an *exclusive lock*. An exclusive lock is applied and held while changes are made to data in the course of a transaction and released when the transaction is ended by either a COMMIT or a ROLLBACK statement. A write lock can be held by only one user at a time, so only one user at a time can change that data.

Some databases also use *read locks*, or *shared locks*. A read lock can be held by any number of users who are merely reading the data, since the same piece of data can be shared among many readers. However, a read lock prevents a write lock from being placed on the data, as the write lock is an exclusive lock. In Figure 8-1, if a read lock were placed on the data when Transaction A began, Transaction B would be able to read the same data but would be prevented from acquiring a write lock on the data until Transaction A ended.

Oracle uses read locks only when a SQL operation specifically requests them with the FOR UPDATE clause in a SELECT statement. You shouldn't use the FOR UPDATE clause routinely because it unduly increases the probability that readers will interfere with writers—a situation that normally never occurs with Oracle, as you will see shortly.

Concurrency and Contention

A system of locks enforcing isolation between concurrent users of data can lead to its own problems. As you can see from the example described above, a single transaction can cause significant performance problems as the locks it places on the database prevent other transactions from completing. The interference caused by conflicting locks is called *contention*. More contention in a database slows response times and lowers the overall throughput.

In most other databases, increased concurrent access to data results in increased contention and decreased performance. Oracle's multiversion read concurrency scheme can greatly reduce contention, as you will see later in this chapter.

Integrity Problems

Some basic integrity problems can result if transaction isolation isn't properly enforced. Four of these problems are common to many databases:

Lost updates
> The most common type of integrity problem occurs when two writers are both changing the same piece of data, and one writer's changes overwrite the other writer's changes. This is the problem that exclusive locks are designed to prevent.

Dirty reads
> Occur when a database allows a transaction to read data that has been changed by another transaction but hasn't been committed yet. The changes made by the transaction may be rolled back, so the data read may turn out to be incorrect. Many databases allow dirty reads to avoid the contention caused by read locks.

Nonrepeatable reads
> Occur as a result of changes made by another transaction. One transaction makes a query based on a particular condition. After the data has been returned to the first transaction, but before the first transaction is complete, another transaction *changes* the data so that some of the previously retrieved data no longer satisfies the selection condition. If the query were repeated in the same transaction, it would return a different set of results, so any changes made on the basis of the original results may no longer be valid. Data that was read once can return different results if the data is read again later in the same transaction.

Phantom reads

Also occur as a result of changes made by another transaction. One transaction makes a query based on a particular condition. After the data has been returned to the first transaction, but before the first transaction is complete, another transaction inserts into the database new rows that meet the selection criteria for the first transaction. If the first SQL statement in a transaction returned the number of rows that initially satisfied the selection criteria, and then performed an action on the rows that satisfied the selection criteria later in the transaction, the number of rows affected would be different from the initial number of rows indicated, based on the inclusion of new phantom rows.

Serialization

The goal of a complete concurrency solution is to provide the highest level of isolation between the actions of different users accessing the same data. As defined by the SQL92 standard, this highest level is called *serializable*. As the name implies, serializable transactions appear as though they have been executed in a series of distinct, ordered transactions. When one transaction begins, it is isolated from any changes that occur to its data from subsequent transactions.

To the user, a serializable transaction looks as though it has the exclusive use of the database for the duration of the transaction. Serializable transactions are predictable and reproducible, the two cardinal virtues of data integrity.

Of course, it's not trivial to have a database server support thousands of users while each one thinks he is the only one. But Oracle manages to pull off this quietly dramatic feat.

Oracle and Concurrent User Access

Oracle solves the problems created by concurrent access through a technology called *multiversion read consistency*, sometimes referred to as MVRC. Multiversion read consistency guarantees that a user sees a consistent view of the data she requests. If another user changes the underlying data during the query execution, Oracle maintains a version of the data as it existed at the time the query began. If there were transactions underway but uncommitted at the time the query began, Oracle will ensure that the query ignores the changes made by those transactions. The data returned to the query will reflect all committed transactions at the time the query started.

This feature has two dramatic effects on the way queries impact the database. First, Oracle doesn't place any locks on data for read operations. This means that a read operation will never block a write operation. Even where the database places a single lock on a single row as part of a read operation, a single lock can still cause contention in the database, especially since most database tables tend to concentrate update operations around a few "hot spots" of active data.

Second, a user gets a complete "snapshot" view of the data, accurate at the point in time that the query began. Other databases may reduce the amount of contention in the database by locking an individual row only while it's being read, rather than over the complete duration of the row's transaction. A row that's retrieved at the end of a result set may have been changed since the time the result set retrieval began. Because rows that will be read later in the execution of the query weren't locked, they could be changed by other users, which would result in an inconsistent view of the data.

Oracle's Isolation Levels

Oracle, like many other databases, uses the concept of *isolation levels* to describe how a transaction will interact with other transactions and how it will be isolated from other transactions. An isolation level is essentially a locking scheme implemented by the database that guarantees a certain type of transaction isolation.

An application programmer can set an isolation level at the session level (ALTER SESSION) or transaction level (SET TRANSACTION). More restrictive isolation levels will cause more potential contention, as well as delivering increased protection against data integrity problems.

Two basic isolation levels are used frequently within Oracle: READ COMMITTED and SERIALIZABLE. (A third level, READ ONLY, is described later in this section.) Both of these isolation levels create serializable database operations. The difference between the two levels is in the duration for which they enforce serializable operations:

READ COMMITTED
> Enforces serialization at the statement level. This means that every statement will get a consistent view of the data as it existed at the start of that statement. However, since a transaction can contain more than one statement, it's possible that nonrepeatable reads and phantom reads can occur within the context of the complete transaction. The READ COMMITTED isolation level is the default isolation level for Oracle.

SERIALIZABLE
> Enforces serialization at the transaction level. This means that every statement within a transaction will get the same consistent view of the data as it existed at the start of the transaction.

Because of their differing spans of control, these two isolation levels also react differently when they encounter a transaction that blocks their operation with an exclusive lock on a requested row. Once the lock has been released by the blocking transaction, an operation executing with the READ COMMITTED isolation level will simply retry the operation. Since this operation is concerned only with the state of data when the statement begins, this is a perfectly logical approach.

On the other hand, if the blocking transaction commits changes to the data, an operation executing with a SERIALIZABLE isolation level will return an error indicating that it cannot serialize operations. This error makes sense, because the blocking transaction will have changed the state of the data from the beginning of the SERIALIZABLE transaction, making it impossible to perform any more write operations on the changed rows. In this situation, an application programmer will have to add logic to his program to return to the start of the SERIALIZABLE transaction and begin it again.

 There are step-by-step examples of concurrent access later in this chapter (in the "Concurrent Access and Performance" section) that illustrate the different ways in which Oracle responds to this type of problem.

One other isolation level is supported by Oracle: you can declare that a session or transaction has an isolation level of READ ONLY. As the name implies, this level explicitly prohibits any write operations and provides an accurate view of all the data at the time the transaction began.

Oracle Concurrency Features

Three features are used by Oracle to implement multiversion read consistency:

Rollback segments

Rollback segments are structures in the Oracle database that store "undo" information for transactions in case of rollback. This information restores database rows to the state they were in before the transaction in question started. When a transaction starts changing some data in a block, it first writes the old image of the data to a rollback segment. The information stored in a rollback segment provides the information necessary to roll back a transaction and supports multiversion read consistency.

A rollback segment is different from a redo log. The redo log is used to log all transactions to the database and recover the database in the event of a system failure, while the rollback segment provides rollback for transactions and read consistency.

Blocks of rollback segments are cached in the System Global Area just like blocks of tables and indexes. If rollback segment blocks are unused for a period of time, they may be aged out of the cache and written to disk.

System Change Number (SCN)

To preserve the integrity of the data in the database and enforce any type of serialization, it is critical to keep track of the order in which actions were performed. Oracle uses the System Change Number as an absolute determinant of the order of transactions.

The SCN is a logical timestamp that tracks the order in which transactions begin. Oracle uses the SCN information in the redo log to reproduce transactions in the original and correct order when applying redo. Oracle also uses the SCN to determine when to clean up information in rollback segments that are no longer needed, as you will see in the following sections.

 Since Oracle Database 10g, there is a pseudocolumn on each row that contains the SCN, ORA_ROWSCN. You can use this to quickly determine if a row has been updated since it was retrieved by comparing the value read from this pseudocolumn at the start of a transaction with the value read from this pseudocolumn at the end of the transaction.

Locks in data blocks

A database must have a way of determining if a particular row is locked. Most databases keep a list of locks in memory, which are managed by a lock manager process. Oracle keeps locks with an area of the actual block in which the row is stored. A data block is the smallest amount of data that can be read from disk for an Oracle database, so whenever the row is requested, the block is read, and the lock is available within the block. Although the lock indicators are kept within a block, each lock affects only an individual row within the block.

In addition to the above features, which directly pertain to multiversion read consistency, another implementation feature in Oracle provides a greater level of concurrency in large user populations:

Nonescalating row locks

To reduce the overhead of the lock-management process, other databases will sometimes *escalate* locks to a higher level of granularity within the database. For example, if a certain percentage of rows in a table are locked, the database will escalate the lock to a table lock, which locks all the rows in a table, including rows that aren't specifically used by the SQL statement in question. Although lock escalation reduces the number of locks the lock manager process has to handle, this escalation causes unaffected rows to be locked. With Oracle, the lock indicator is stored within the data block itself, so there is no increase in overhead for a lock manager when the number of locks increases. Consequently, there is never any need for Oracle to escalate a lock.

A lock manager called the Distributed Lock Manager (DLM) has historically been used with Oracle Parallel Server to track locks across multiple instances of Oracle. This is a completely different and separate locking scheme that doesn't affect the way Oracle handles row locks. The DLM technology used in Oracle Parallel Server was improved and integrated into a core product in Oracle9i, Real Application Clusters. Real Application Clusters are described in more detail in Chapter 9.

How Oracle Handles Locking

If you've read this chapter from the beginning, you should now know enough about the concepts of concurrency and the features of Oracle to understand how the Oracle database handles multiuser access. However, to make it perfectly clear how these features interact, we'll walk you through three scenarios: a simple write to the database, a situation in which two users attempt to write to the same row in the same table, and a read that takes place in the midst of conflicting updates.

For the purposes of these examples, we'll use the scenario of one or two users modifying the EMP table, a part of the standard sample Oracle schema that lists data about employees via a form.

A Simple Write Operation

This example describes a simple write operation, in which one user is writing to a row in the database. In this example, an HR clerk wants to update the name for an employee. Assume that the HR clerk already has the employee record on-screen. The steps from this point are as follows:

1. The client modifies the employee name on the screen. The client process sends a SQL UPDATE statement over the network to the server process.

2. The server process obtains a System Change Number and reads the data block containing the target row.

3. The server records row lock information in the data block.

4. The server writes the old image of the data to the redo buffers in memory, and then writes the changes to a rollback segment and modifies the employee data, which includes writing the SCN to the ORA_ROWSCN pseudocolumn in Oracle Database 10g or newer database releases.

5. The server process writes the redo buffers to disk, and then writes the rollback segments and the changed data to disk. The rollback segment changes are part of the redo, since the redo log stores all changes coming from the transaction.

6. The HR clerk commits the transaction.

7. Log Writer (LGWR) writes the redo information for the entire transaction, including the SCN that marks the time the transaction was committed, from the redo log buffer to the current redo log file on disk. When the operating system confirms that the write to the redo log file has successfully completed, the transaction is considered committed.

8. The server process sends a message to the client confirming the commit.

Oracle Database 10g Release 2 introduced the ability to have the server process return control to the client without waiting for all the redo information to be written. The plus side of this enhancement is that high-volume OLTP applications may benefit from improved performance. The downside of this feature is that it opens a window of vulnerability—the database could crash after a transaction had been committed, but before the redo was written, which would make it impossible to recover the committed transaction, so this feature should be used with caution.

A Conflicting Write Operation

The write operation previously described is a little different if there are two users, Client A and Client B, who are trying to modify the same row of data at the same time. The steps are as follows:

1. Client A modifies the employee name on the screen. Client A sends a SQL UPDATE statement over the network to the server process.

2. The server process obtains an SCN for the statement and reads the data block containing the target row.

3. The server records row lock information in the data block.

4. The server process writes the changes to the redo log buffer.

5. The server process copies the old image of the employee data about to be changed to a rollback segment. Once the server process has completed this work, the process modifies the employee data, which includes writing the SCN to the ORA_ROWSCN pseudocolumn in Oracle Database 10g or newer database releases.

6. Client B modifies the employee name on the screen and sends a SQL UPDATE statement to the server.

7. The server process obtains an SCN and reads the data block containing the target row.

8. The server process sees that there is a lock on the target row from the information in the header of the data block, so it takes one of two actions. If the isolation level on Client B's transaction is READ COMMITTED, the server process waits for the blocking transaction to complete. If the isolation level for Client B's transaction is SERIALIZABLE, an error is returned to the client.

9. Client A commits the transaction, the server process takes the appropriate action, and the server sends a message to Client A confirming the commit.

10. If Client B executed the SQL statement with the READ COMMITTED isolation level, the SQL statement then proceeds through its normal operation.

The previous example illustrates the default behavior of Oracle when it detects a problem caused by a potential lost update. Because the SERIALIZABLE isolation level has a more drastic effect when it detects a write conflict than the READ COMMITTED isolation level, many developers prefer the latter level. They can avoid some of the potential conflicts by either checking for changes prior to issuing an update (by comparing values in a row or using the Oracle Database 10g or later row SCN) or using the SELECT FOR UPDATE syntax in their SQL to avoid the problem altogether.

A Read Operation

You can really appreciate the beauty of Oracle's read consistency model by looking at the more common scenario of one user reading data and one user writing to the same row of data. In this scenario, Client A is reading a series of rows from the EMP table, while Client B modifies a row before it is read by Client A, but after Client A begins her transaction:

1. Client A sends a SQL SELECT statement over the network to the server process.

2. The server process obtains an SCN for the statement and begins to read the requested data for the query. For each data block that it reads, it compares the SCN of the SELECT statement with the SCNs for any transactions for the relevant rows of the data block. If the server finds a transaction with a later SCN than the current SELECT statement, the server process uses data in the rollback segments to create a "consistent read" version of the data block, current as of the time the SELECT was issued. This is what provides the multiversion read consistency (MVRC) and avoids the need for Oracle to use read locks on data. If a row has been updated since the transaction started, Oracle simply gets the earlier version of the data for a consistent view.

3. Client B sends a SQL UPDATE statement for a row in the EMP table that has not yet been read by Client A's SELECT statement. The server process gets an SCN for the statement and begins the operation.

4. Client B commits his changes. The server process completes the operation, which includes recording information in the data block that contained the modified row that allows Oracle to determine the SCN for the update transaction.

5. The server process for Client A's read operation comes to the newly modified block. It sees that the data block contains changes made by a transaction that has an SCN that is later than the SCN of the SELECT statement. The server process looks in the data block header, which has a pointer to the rollback segment that contains the data as it existed when Client A's transaction started. The rollback segment uses the old version of the data to create a version of the block as it existed when the SELECT statement started. Client A's SELECT statement reads the desired rows from this consistent version of the data block.

Figure 8-2 illustrates the process of reading with multiversion read consistency.

We explained how MVRC works with two users for the sake of clarity. But imagine a database supporting one or more enterprise applications, with hundreds of simultaneous users. Oracle's concurrency handling could avoid an enormous amount of contention and performance degradation in a heavy use scenario—in fact, the greater the workload, the greater the benefits of MVRC.

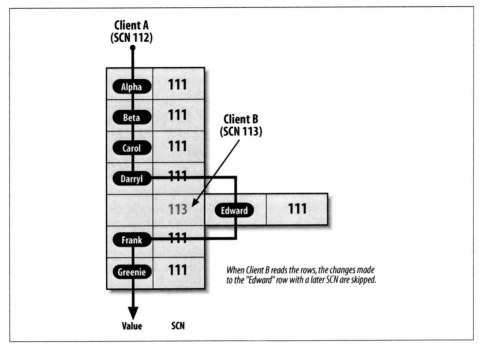

Figure 8-2. Multiversion read consistency

Concurrent Access and Performance

When you read through all the steps involved in the above processes, you might think that Oracle would be a very slow database. This is not at all true. Oracle has consistently turned in benchmarks that make it one of the fastest databases, if not the fastest, on the market today.

Oracle provides good performance while implementing multiversion read consistency by minimizing and deferring unnecessary I/O operations. To assure the integrity of the data in a database, the database must be able to recover in the event of a system failure. This means that there must be a way to ensure that the data in the database accurately reflects the state of the committed data at the time of the crash. Oracle can do this by writing changed data to the database whenever a transaction commits. However, the redo log contains much less information than the entire data block for the changed data, so it's much "cheaper" to write to disk. Oracle writes the redo information to disk as soon as a transaction commits and defers writing the changed data blocks to the database until several sets of changed blocks can be written together. Oracle can restore the database using the redo logs, and these procedures cut down on time-consuming I/O operations.

However, when you're considering the performance of a database, you have to think about more than simple I/O operations. It doesn't really matter how fast your database runs if your transaction is waiting for another transaction to release a lock. A faster database may complete the blocking transaction faster, but your transaction is still at a dead stop until the blocking transaction completes.

Because most databases perform a mixture of reading and writing, and because Oracle is one of the only databases on the market that doesn't use read locks, Oracle will essentially always deliver the lowest amount of database contention. Less contention equals greater throughput for a mixed application load.

There is also more than one type of performance. Performance for database operations is measured in milliseconds; performance for application developers is measured in months. Because Oracle provides much less contention with its read consistency model, developers have to spend less time adding workarounds to their applications to handle the results of contention.

It's not as though Oracle is the only database to give you a concurrency solution you can use to implement applications that provide adequate data integrity. But the multiversion read consistency model makes it easy for you to get a consistent view of data without excessive contention and without having to write workarounds in your application. If it sounds as if we're big fans of Oracle's locking scheme, well—we are.

Workspaces

Oracle9*i* introduced a new feature that relates to concurrency, Workspace Manager.

A *workspace* is a way to isolate data from changes in the general database environment. Workspace Manager accomplishes this by creating workspace-specific versions of data. When you create a workspace, you essentially create a snapshot of the data in the workspace at a specific point in time. Further changes to that data from outside the workspace do not affect the view of the data in the workspace, and changes made to data within the workspace are not seen by users outside the workspace. And changes to data within a workspace are visible only to other workspace users.

Workspaces allow you to essentially create separate data environments for specialized usage. You can capture data at a certain point in time for historical analysis and can also perform various types of "what-if" analysis, testing to see how changes would affect the overall composition of the data without disturbing the main production database. Both of these options would normally require you to create a duplicate database, so workspaces can save you time and resources.

Workspace Implementation

The key to workspaces is the support of multiple versions of the same data. To use workspaces to version data in a table, you must first enable the table for versioning. Workspace Manager can version-enable one or more user tables in the database. The unit of versioning is a row. When a table is version-enabled, all rows in the table can support multiple versions of the data. Versioned rows are stored in the same table as the original rows. The versioning infrastructure is not visible to the users of the database, and application SQL statements to select, insert, modify, and delete data continue to work in the usual way with version-enabled tables. Workspace Manager version-enables a table by renaming the table, adding a few columns to the table to store versioning metadata, creating a view on the version-enabled table using the original table name, and defining INSTEAD OF triggers on the view for SQL DML operations.

The workspace keeps changes to the data only to minimize the size of the workspace data and avoid data duplication.

You can have a hierarchy of workspaces, and a workspace can have more than one parent. All workspace operations, described in the next sections, affect a workspace and its parent workspaces. Multiple levels of workspaces can give you finer granularity on the isolation of changes for workspace-enabled tables.

Oracle implements workspaces by adding metadata to the rows of a table. This metadata can include a timestamp as to when a change was made, which can help in analysis of workspace activity. This option works with savepoints to provide a history of changes made to each row version created by a savepoint. The timestamp allows users in a workspace to go back to any point in time and view the database from the perspective of changes made in that workspace up to another point in time. You can think of this as a type of Flashback (described in Chapter 3) for a limited set of tables.

In addition, you can specify that a particular version of data in a workspace is valid only for a specific time period. For instance, you could make a change to data that would be visible to workspace users for the next 24 hours and that would then disappear.

Workspaces have their own locking mechanisms that apply only to other workspace users. You can exclusively lock a row of data in a workspace, but this lock prevents access only to that row for other workspace users. The underlying data could still be accessed or changed by users who are not part of the workspace. This additional locking makes sense, since both locks and workspaces are meant to isolate data from changes. A workspace exists outside the boundaries of the standard database, so workspace locks and standard database locks do not directly interact.

Workspace Operations

There are three basic operations that apply to workspaces:

Rollback

You can roll back changes to a workspace to return the workspace to the point in time when the workspace was created. You can also designate savepoints, which allow you to roll back the changes in a workspace to a subsequent point in time.

Refresh

Refreshing a workspace means bringing the data in a workspace into agreement with the same data in the overall database. This capability could be used if you chose to create a workspace with a snapshot of the data at the end of a day. At midnight, you would refresh the workspace to make the workspace reflect the data from the previous day.

Merge

A merge operation rolls changes made in a workspace into its parent workspace.

As you can imagine, both the refresh and the merge operations could end up with conflicts between data values in the workspace and its parent. Workspace management keeps track of conflicts on a per-table basis; you can resolve the conflicts manually.

Workspace Enhancements

Workspace Manager is tightly integrated with the Oracle database. Oracle Database 10g Workspace Manager enhancements included the ability to export and import version-enabled tables, to use SQL*Loader to bulk-load data into version-enabled tables, to trigger events based on workspace operations, and to define workspaces that are continually refreshed.

Oracle Database 11g continues the stream of enhancements to workspaces, providing support for optimizer hints and more data maintenance operations on workspace-enabled tables.

CHAPTER 9

Oracle and Transaction Processing

The value of information systems is clear from the ever-increasing number of transactions processed by the world's databases. Transactions form the foundation of business computing systems. In fact, transaction processing (TP) was the impetus for business computing as we know it today. The batch-oriented automation of core business processes like accounting and payroll drove the progress in mainframe computing through the 1970s and 1980s. Along the way, TP began the shift from batch to users interacting directly with systems, and online transaction processing (OLTP) was born. In the 1980s the computing infrastructure shifted from large centralized mainframes with dumb terminals to decentralized client/server computing with graphical user interfaces (GUIs) running on PCs and accessing databases on other machines over a network.

The client/server revolution provided a much better user interface and reduced the cost of hardware and software, but it also introduced additional complexity in systems development, management, and deployment. After a decade of use, system administrators were being slowly overwhelmed by the task of managing thousands of client machines and dozens of servers, so the latter half of the 1990s saw a return to centralization, including the grid (introduced in Chapter 1). Throughout all of these shifts, Oracle databases have continued to use their inherent architecture and constant enhancements to service the ever-growing load of transactions.

This chapter looks at all of the features of the Oracle database that contribute to its ability to handle large transaction loads. Although many of the specific features covered in this chapter are touched upon in other chapters of this book, this chapter examines all of these features in light of their use in large OLTP systems.

OLTP Basics

Before we discuss how Oracle specifically handles OLTP, we'll start by presenting a common definition of online transaction processing.

What Is a Transaction?

The concept of a transaction and the relevant Oracle mechanics for dealing with transactions were discussed in Chapter 8. To recap that discussion, a *transaction* is a logical unit of work that must succeed or fail in its entirety. Each transaction typically involves one or more Data Manipulation Language (DML) statements such as INSERT, UPDATE, or DELETE, and ends with either a COMMIT to make the changes permanent or a ROLLBACK to undo the changes.

The industry bible for OLTP, *Transaction Processing: Concepts and Techniques,* by Jim Gray and Andreas Reuter (Morgan Kaufmann; see Appendix B), introduced the notion of the *ACID* properties of a transaction. A transaction must be the following:

Atomic
    The entire transaction succeeds or fails as a complete unit.

Consistent
    A completed transaction leaves the affected data in a consistent or correct state.

Isolated
    Each transaction executes in isolation and doesn't affect the states of others.

Durable
    The changes resulting from committed transactions are persistent.

If transactions execute serially—one after the other—their use of ACID properties can be relatively easily guaranteed. Each transaction starts with the consistent state of the previous transaction and, in turn, leaves a consistent state for the next transaction. Concurrent usage introduces the need for sophisticated locking and other coordination mechanisms to preserve the ACID properties of concurrent transactions while delivering throughput and performance. Chapter 8 covered Oracle's handling of locking and concurrency in depth.

What Does OLTP Mean?

Online transaction processing can be defined in different ways: as a type of computing with certain characteristics, or as a type of computing in contrast to more traditional batch processing.

General characteristics

Most OLTP systems share some of the following general characteristics:

High transaction volumes and large user populations
    OLTP systems are the key operational systems for many companies, so these systems typically support the highest volume and largest communities of any systems in the organization.

Well-defined performance requirements

OLTP systems are central to core business operations, so users must be able to depend on a consistent response time. OLTP systems often involve Service Level Agreements that state the expected response times.

High availability

These systems are typically deemed mission-critical with significant costs resulting from downtime.

Scalability

The ability to increase transaction volumes without significant degradation in performance allows OLTP systems to handle fluctuations in business activity.

In short, OLTP systems must be able to deliver consistent performance at any time, regardless of system load. Anything that affects these core systems can produce a ripple effect throughout your entire organization, affecting both revenue and profitability.

Online versus batch

Online transaction processing implies direct and conversational interaction between the transaction processing system and its users. Users enter and query data using forms that interact with the backend database. Editing and validation of data occur at the time the transactions are submitted by users.

Batch processing occurs without user interaction. Batches of transactions are fed from source files to the operational system. Errors are typically reported in exception files or logs and are reviewed by users or operators later on. Virtually all OLTP systems have a batch component: jobs that can execute in off-peak hours for reporting, payroll runs, posting of accounting entries, and so on.

Many large companies have batch-oriented mainframe systems that are so thoroughly embedded in the corporate infrastructure that they cannot be replaced or removed. A common practice is to "frontend" these legacy systems with OLTP systems that provide more modern interfaces. Users interact with the OLTP system to enter transactions. Batch files are extracted from the OLTP system and fed into the downstream legacy applications.

Once the batch processing is done, extracts are produced from the batch systems and are used to refresh the OLTP systems. This extraction process provides the users with a more sophisticated interface with online validation and editing, but it preserves the flow of data through the entrenched batch systems. While this process seems costly, it's typically more attractive than the major surgery that would replace older systems. To compound the difficulty, in some cases the documentation of these older systems is incomplete and the employees who understand the inner workings have retired or moved on.

The financial services industry is a leader in information technology for transaction processing, so this notion of feeding legacy downstream applications is very common in banks and insurance companies. For example, users often enter insurance claims into frontend online systems. Once all the data has been entered, if the claim has been approved, it's extracted and fed into legacy systems for further processing and payment.

Oracle features such as transportable tablespaces and Streams, discussed in Chapter 13 of this book, are aimed in part at providing the functionality required by distributed OLTP systems in a more timely fashion than traditional batch jobs.

OLTP Versus Business Intelligence

Mixed workloads—OLTP and reporting—are the source of many performance challenges and the topic of intense debate. The data warehousing industry had its genesis in the realization that OLTP systems could not realistically provide the needed transaction throughput while supporting the enormous amount of historical data and ad hoc query workload that business analysts needed for things like multiyear trend analysis.

The issue isn't simply one of adequate machine horsepower; rather, it's the way data is modeled, stored, and accessed, which is typically quite different. In OLTP, the design centers on analyzing and automating business processes to provide consistent performance for a well-known set of transactions and users. The workload revolves around large numbers of short and well-defined transactions—with a fairly significant percentage of write transactions.

Business intelligence typically operates on larger data stores that frequently are assembled from multiple data sources and contain long histories. The schema design for data warehouses is usually very different from the fully normalized design best suited for OLTP data stores. And data warehouses can support ad hoc queries that, because of their complexity and the amount of data accessed, can place significant loads on a system with only a handful of requests.

Reporting and query functions are part of an OLTP system, but the scope and frequency are typically more controlled than in a data warehouse environment. For example, a banking OLTP system will include queries for customer status and account balances, but not multiyear transaction patterns.

The OLTP system typically provides forms that allow well-targeted queries that are executed efficiently and don't consume undue resources. However, hard and fast rules—for example, that OLTP systems don't include extensive query facilities—don't necessarily hold true. The I/O performed by most OLTP systems tends to be approximately 70–80 percent read and 20–30 percent write. Most transactions involve the querying of data, such as product codes, customer names, account balances, inventory levels, and so on. Users submitting tuned queries for specific business functions are a key part of OLTP. Ad hoc queries across broad data sets are not.

Business intelligence data warehousing systems and OLTP systems could access much of the same data, but these types of systems also typically have different requirements in terms of CPU, memory, and data layout, which makes supporting a mixed workload less than optimal for both types of processing. Real Application Clusters, with dynamic service provisioning since Oracle Database 10g, makes it possible to allocate individual nodes for individual workloads. It also makes it more feasible to deploy these mixed workloads to a single database (albeit with multiple database instances).

Oracle's OLTP Heritage

Oracle has enjoyed tremendous growth as the database of choice for OLTP in the midrange-computing environment. Oracle6 introduced nonescalating row-level locking and read consistency (two of the most important of Oracle's core OLTP features), but Oracle7 was really the enabler for Oracle's growth in OLTP. Oracle7 introduced many key features, including the following:

- Multi-Threaded Server (MTS), now known as shared server
- Shared SQL
- Stored procedures and triggers
- XA support
- Distributed transactions and two-phase commits
- Data replication
- Oracle Parallel Server (OPS)*

Oracle8 enhanced existing functionality and introduced additional OLTP-related features including the following:

- Connection pooling
- Connection multiplexing
- Data partitioning
- Advanced Queuing (AQ)
- Index organized tables
- Internalization of the Distributed Lock Manager (DLM) for Oracle Parallel Server
- Internalization of the triggers for replicated tables and parallel propagation of replicated transactions

---

* OPS was actually available for DEC VMS in 1989 and for NCR Unix with the last production release of Oracle6 (version 6.0.36), but it became widely available, more stable, and more popular in Oracle7.

Oracle8*i* provided the following additional enhancements and technologies for OLTP:

- Support for Java internally in the database kernel
- Support for distributed component technologies: CORBA V2.0 and Enterprise JavaBeans (EJB) v1.0
- Publish/subscribe messaging based on Advanced Queuing
- Online index rebuild and reorganization
- Database Resource Manager (DRM)
- Use of a standby database for queries
- Internalization of the replication packages used to apply transactions at the remote sites

Oracle9*i* continued this trend, with the introduction of Real Application Clusters, which extended the benefits of Oracle Parallel Server to OLTP applications. Since Oracle Database 10*g*, the capabilities of Real Application Clusters support deployment to a new computing model, grid computing. But many of the capabilities that enable OLTP with Oracle have been core to the database product for many years.

The remainder of this chapter examines many of these features in more depth.

Architectures for OLTP

Although all OLTP systems are oriented toward the same goals, there are several different underlying system architectures that you can use for the deployment of OLTP, including the traditional two-tier model, a three-tier model, and a centralized model that encompasses the use of the Web and the grid.

Traditional Two-Tier Client/Server

The late 1980s saw the rise of two-tier client/server applications. In this configuration, PCs acted as clients accessing a separate database server over a network. The client ran both the GUI and the application logic, giving rise to the term *fat clients*. The database server processed SQL statements and returned the requested results back to the clients. While database servers were relatively simple to develop using visual tools, client/server systems were difficult to deploy and maintain—they required fairly high-bandwidth networks and the installation and regular upgrading of specific client software on every user's PC.

Figure 9-1 illustrates the two-tier architecture.

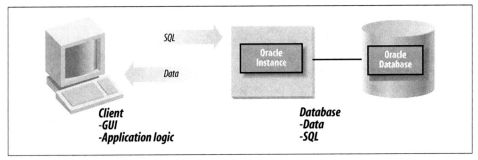

Figure 9-1. Two-tier client/server architecture

Stored Procedures

Oracle7 introduced stored procedures written in PL/SQL, Oracle's proprietary language for writing application logic. These procedures are stored in the database and executed by clients issuing remote procedure calls (RPCs) as opposed to executing SQL statements. Instead of issuing multiple SQL calls, occasionally with intermediate logic to accomplish a task, the client issues one procedure call, passing in the required parameters. The database executes all the required SQL and logic using the parameters it receives.

Stored procedures can also shield the client logic from internal changes to the data structures or program logic. As long as the parameters the client passed in and received back don't change, no changes are required in the client software. Stored procedures move a portion of the application logic from the client to the database server. By doing so, stored procedures can reduce the network traffic considerably. This capability increases the scalability of two-tier systems. Figure 9-2 illustrates a two-tier system with stored procedures.

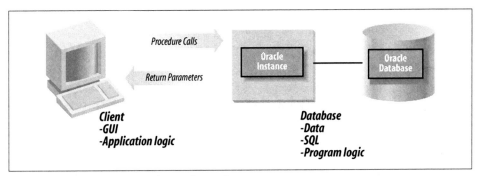

Figure 9-2. Two-tier system with stored procedures

Three-Tier Systems

The OLTP systems with the largest user populations and transaction throughput are typically deployed using a three-tier architecture. In the past, the three-tier architecture involved a transaction processing monitor, but now more frequently uses an application server. Clients access a transaction processing (TP) monitor or application server in the middle tier that, in turn, accesses a database server on the backend. The notion of a TP monitor dates back to the original mainframe OLTP systems. Of course, in the mainframe environment all logic ran on one machine. In an open system environment, application servers typically run on a separate machine (or machines), adding a middle tier between clients and the database server.

There are various classes of application servers:

- Older, proprietary servers such as Tuxedo from BEA Systems on Unix and Windows, or CICS from IBM on mainframes
- Industry-standard application servers based on Java 2 Enterprise Edition (J2EE)
- The Microsoft .NET application server environment as part of the Windows operating systems for servers, for example, Windows 2000 or Windows 2003

Application servers provide an environment for running services that clients call. The clients don't interact directly with the database server. Some examples of calling services provided by a TP monitor on a remote machine seem similar in many ways to the stored procedure architecture described in the previous section, which is why stored procedure-based systems are sometimes referred to as "TP-Lite."

Application servers provide additional valuable services, such as:

Funneling
> Like Oracle's shared servers, application servers leverage a pool of shared services across a larger user population. Instead of each user connecting directly to the database, the client calls a service running under the TP monitor or application server's control. The application servers invoke one of its services; the service interacts with the database.

Connection pooling
> The application server maintains a pool of shared, persistent database connections used to interact with the database on behalf of clients in handling their requests. This technique avoids the overhead of individual sessions for each client.

Load-balancing
> Client requests are balanced across the multiple shared servers executing on one or more physical machines. The application servers can direct client service calls to the least-loaded server and can spawn additional shared servers as needed.

Fault-tolerance

The application server acts as a transaction manager; the monitor performs the commit or rollback of the transaction.* The underlying database becomes a resource manager, but doesn't control the transaction. If the database server fails while executing some transaction, the application server can resubmit the transaction to a surviving database server, as control of the transaction lies with the application server.

This type of transaction resiliency is a hallmark of the older TP monitors such as Tuxedo, and the newer application servers and standards offer similar features.

Transaction routing

The logic in the middle tier can direct transactions to specific database servers, increasing scalability.

Heterogeneous transactions

Application servers can manage transactions across multiple heterogeneous database servers—for example, a transaction that updates data in Oracle and DB2.

While developing three-tier OLTP systems is complex and requires specialized skills, the benefits are substantial. Systems that use application servers provide higher scalability, availability, and flexibility than the simpler two-tier systems. Determining which architecture is appropriate for an OLTP system requires (among other things) careful evaluation and consideration of costs, available skills, workload profiles, scalability requirements, and availability requirements.

Figure 9-3 illustrates a three-tier system using an application server.

Application Servers and Web Servers

The middle tier of web-based systems is usually an application server and/or a web server. These servers provide similar services to the application server previously described, but are more web-centric, dealing with HTTP, HTML, CGI, and Java.

J2EE and .NET application servers have evolved a great deal in the last decade and are the clear inheritors of the TP monitor legacy for today's *N*-tier systems. Different companies have different standards and preferences—the proprietary nature of .NET leads some firms to J2EE, while others prefer the tight integration of Microsoft's offerings. A detailed discussion of the relative merits of J2EE and .NET, and application server technology in general, is beyond the scope of this book. Suffice to say that application servers play an extremely important role in today's systems environment, and database management personnel need to understand *N*-tier systems architecture.

---

* TP monitors usually control transactions using the X/Open Distributed Transaction Processing standard published by the X/Open standards body. A database that supports the XA interface can function as a resource manager under control of a TP monitor, which acts as a transaction manager.

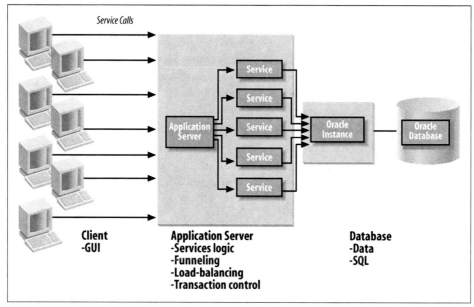

Figure 9-3. Three-tier architecture

Figure 9-4 depicts an *N*-tier system with a client, web server, application server, and DBMS server.

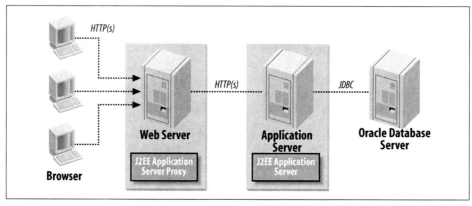

Figure 9-4. An N-tier system

The Grid

Oracle Database 10g introduced focus on another architecture variation, grid computing. The actual topology of the grid is not relevant to the discussion in this chapter, because the point of the grid is to provide an extremely simple user interface that transparently connects to a highly flexible source of computing power.

In this way, the grid gives IT departments the ability to achieve the benefits of more complex architectures while not imposing undue complexity on users, and OLTP applications are deployed using grid computing resources.

Oracle Features for OLTP

Oracle has many features that contribute to OLTP performance, reliability, scalability, and availability. This section presents the basic attributes of many of these features. This section is by no means exhaustive; it's only intended to be an introduction. Please see the relevant Oracle documentation and third-party books for more information.

General Concurrency and Performance

As discussed in Chapter 8, Oracle has excellent support for concurrency and performance in OLTP systems. Some of the key features relevant to OLTP are as follows:

Nonescalating row-level locking
> Oracle locks only the rows a transaction works on and never escalates these locks to page-level or table-level locks. In some databases, which escalate row locks to page locks when enough rows have been locked on a page, contention can result from false lock contention when users want to work on unlocked rows but contend for locks that have escalated to higher granularity levels.

Multiversion read consistency
> Oracle provides statement-level and transaction-level data consistency without requiring read locks. A query is guaranteed to see only the data that was committed at the time the query started. The changes made by transactions that were in-flight but uncommitted at the time the query started won't be visible. Transactions that began after the query started and were committed before the query finishes also won't be seen by the query. Oracle uses rollback segments to reproduce data as it existed at the time the query started. This capability avoids the unpleasant choice between allowing queries to see uncommitted data (known as dirty reads) or having readers block writers (and vice versa). It also provides a consistent snapshot view of data at a single point in time.

Shared SQL
> The parsing of a SQL statement is fairly CPU-intensive. Oracle caches parsed and optimized SQL statements in the shared SQL area within the shared pool. If another user executes a SQL statement that is cached, the parse and optimize overhead is avoided. The statements must be identical to be reused; no extra spaces, line feeds, or differences in capitalization are allowed. OLTP systems involve a large number of users executing the same application code. These systems provide an ideal opportunity for reusing shared SQL statements.

Stored outlines

Oracle8*i* added support of execution-plan stability, sometimes referred to as *bound plans*, with stored outlines. The route a SQL statement takes during execution is critical for high performance. Once application developers and DBAs have tuned a SQL statement for maximum efficiency, they can force the Oracle optimizer to use the same execution plan regardless of environmental changes. This provides critical stability and predictability in the face of software upgrades, schema changes, data-volume changes, and so on. Oracle9*i* added the capability for administrators to edit stored outlines.

Since Oracle Database 10*g*, you can select better execution plans for the optimizer to use in conjunction with poorly written SQL to improve OLTP performance without having to rewrite the SQL. The SQL Tuning Advisor performs these advanced optimizations on SQL statements, and can then create an improved SQL Profile for the statement. This profile is used instead of the original optimization plan at runtime.

Scalability

Both the shared server and the Database Resource Manager help Oracle support larger or mixed user populations.

Multi-Threaded Server/shared server

Oracle7 introduced the Multi-Threaded Server (MTS, renamed the shared server in Oracle9*i*) (described in Chapter 2) to allow Oracle to support larger user populations. While shared server and MTS reduced the number of server processes, each client still used its own physical network connection. The resources for network connections aren't unlimited, so Oracle8 introduced two solutions for increasing the capabilities of the actual network socket layer at the operating-system level:

Oracle Net connection pooling

Allows the client population to share a pool of shared physical network connections. Idle clients transparently "time out," and their network connections are returned to the pool to be used by active clients. Each idle client maintains a virtual connection with Oracle and will get another physical connection when activity resumes. With the Oracle security model, authentication is separate from a specific connection, so a single pooled connection can represent different users at different times. Connection pooling is suitable for applications with clients that connect but aren't highly active (for example, email systems).

Oracle Net Connection Manager

Reduces the number of network connections used on the database server. Clients connect to a middle-tier machine running the Oracle Net Connection

Manager (CMAN). The Connection Manager multiplexes the traffic for multiple clients into one network connection per Oracle Net dispatcher on the database server. Unlike connection pooling, there is no notion of "time-out" for a client's virtual network connection. The Oracle network topology can include multiple machines running the Connection Manager to provide additional scalability and fault-tolerance.

In terms of scalability, you can think of connection pooling as the middleweight solution and multiplexing via Connection Manager as the heavyweight solution. Figure 9-5 illustrates these two network-scaling technologies.

Connection Manager has become more flexible in Oracle Database 10g, with the added ability to dynamically alter configuration parameters without shutting down Connection Manager and improved access rules to filter CMAN traffic.

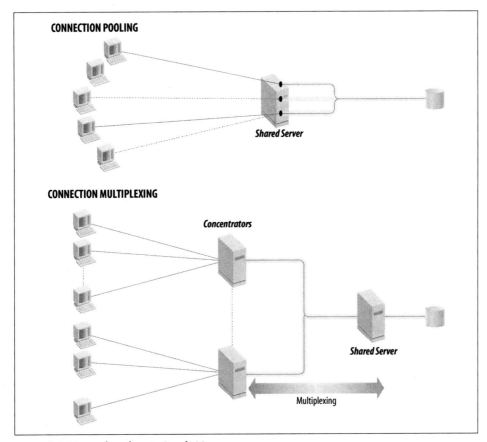

Figure 9-5. Network scaling in Oracle Net

Bind Variables and Shared SQL

As we've mentioned, Oracle's shared SQL is a key feature for building high-performance applications. In an OLTP application, similar SQL statements may be used repeatedly, but each SQL statement submitted will have different selection criteria contained in the WHERE clause to identify the different sets of rows on which to operate. Oracle can share SQL statements, but the statements must be absolutely identical.

To take advantage of this feature for statements that are identical except for specific values in a WHERE clause, you can use bind variables in your SQL statements. The values substituted for the bind variables in the SQL statement may be different, but the statement itself is the same.

Consider an example application for granting raises to employees. The application submits the following SQL:

```
UPDATE emp SET salary = salary * (1 + 0.1)
        WHERE empno = 123;
UPDATE emp SET salary = salary * (1 + 0.15)
        WHERE empno = 456;
```

These statements are clearly different; they update different employees identified by different employee numbers, and the employees receive different salary increases. To obtain the benefits of shared SQL, you can write the application to use bind variables for the percentage salary increase and the employee numbers, such as:

```
UPDATE emp SET salary = salary * (1 + :v_incr)
        WHERE empno = :v_empno;
UPDATE emp SET salary = salary * (1 + :v_incr)
        WHERE empno = :v_empno;
```

These statements are recognized as identical and would therefore be shared. The application would submit different values for the two variables :v_incr and :v_empno, a percentage increase of 0.1 for employee 123 and 0.15 for employee 456. Oracle substitutes these actual values for the variables in the SQL. The substitution occurs during the phase of processing known as the *bind phase*, which follows the *parse phase* and *optimize phase*. For more details, see the relevant Oracle guide for your development language.

Oracle Database 10g and more recent versions include tuning tools that can easily spot this type of potential application optimization.

Database Resource Manager

Oracle8i introduced the Database Resource Manager (DRM) to simplify and automate the management of mixed workloads in which different users access the same database for different purposes. You can define different consumer groups to contain different groups of users. The DRM allocates CPU and parallelism resources to consumer groups based on resource plans. A resource plan defines limits for the amount of a particular computer resource a group of users can use. This allows the

DBA to ensure that certain types of users receive sufficient machine resources to meet performance requirements.

For example, you can allocate 80 percent of the CPU resources to order-entry users, with the remaining 20 percent allocated to users asking for reports. This allocation prevents reporting users from dominating the machine while order-entry users are working. If the order-entry users aren't using all the allocated resources, the reporting users can use more than their allotted percentage. If the order-entry workload increases, the reporting users will be cut back to respect their 20 percent allocation. In other words, the order-entry users will get up to 80 percent of CPU time, as needed, while the users asking for reports will get at least 20 percent of the CPU time, and more depending on how much the order-entry group is using. With the DRM, you can dynamically alter the details of the plan without shutting down the instance.

Oracle9*i* added a number of significant improvements to the Database Resource Manager. The DRM now allows a DBA to specify the number of active sessions available to a consumer group. Any additional connection requests for the consumer group are queued. By limiting the number of active connections, you can start to avoid the situation where a request comes in that pushes the resource requirements for a group over the limit and affects all the other users in that group.

Oracle9*i* also added to the Database Resource Manager the ability to proactively estimate the amount of CPU that an operation will require. If an operation looks as if it will exceed the maximum CPU time specified for a resource group, the operation will not be executed, which can prevent inappropriately large operations from even starting.

Finally, since Oracle9*i*, the DRM can also automatically switch a consumer group to another consumer group if that group is active for too long. This feature could be used to automatically switch a consumer group oriented toward short OLTP operations to another group that would be more appropriate for batch operations.

Since Oracle Database 10*g*, you can define a consumer group by the service name, application, host machine, or operating system username of a user.

Real Application Clusters

Arguably, the biggest advance in Oracle9*i* was a feature called Real Application Clusters. Real Application Clusters (RAC) was a new version of technology replacing Oracle Parallel Server (OPS).

In the first edition of this book, we described OPS as a feature that could be used for improving performance and scalability for certain data warehouse-style applications—applications in which data could be partitioned in logical ways and applications that primarily supported read activity. The reason why use of OPS was mostly limited to data warehousing implementations was the phenomenon known as *pinging*.

In the world of both OPS and RAC, multiple machines access the same database files on shared disk (either physically attached or appearing as physically attached through software), as shown in Figure 9-6.

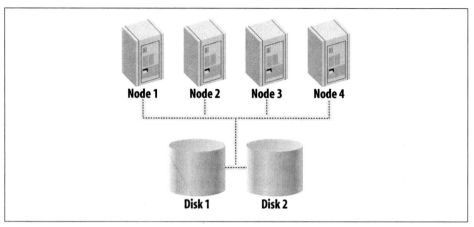

Figure 9-6. RAC architecture

This architecture allows you to add more machines to a cluster of machines, which in turn adds more overall horsepower to the system. But there was a problem with the implementation of this architecture for OPS, stemming from the fact that a page can contain more than a single row. If one machine in a cluster wanted to modify a row in a page that was already being modified by another machine, that page had to be flushed to the database file on the shared disk—a scenario that was termed a *ping*. This chain of events caused extra disk I/O, which in turn decreased the overall performance of the solution.

The traditional way around this problem was simply to avoid it—to use OPS only when a database would not cause pings with a lot of write operations, or to segregate writes so that they would not require data in use on another node. This limitation required you to carefully consider the type of application to which you would deploy OPS and sometimes forced you to actually modify the design of your application to work around OPS's limitations.

With Real Application Clusters, the problem caused by pings was eliminated. RAC fully supports the technology known as Cache Fusion. Cache Fusion makes all the data in every cache on every machine in a Real Application Cluster available to every other machine in the cluster. If one machine needs a block that is either being used by another machine or simply residing in the cache of another machine, the block is directly shipped to the requesting machine, usually over a very high-speed interconnect.

Cache Fusion means that you do not have to work around the problems of pinging. With Real Application Clusters you will be able to see significant scalability improvements for most all applications, without any modifications. With that said, for OLTP applications deployed to RAC (where there are frequent modifications to indexes within a small set of leaf blocks), reverse key indexes might be used to distribute inserts across leaf keys in the index and eliminate possible performance issues for this special situation (see Chapter 4 for an explanation of reverse key indexes).

Real Application Clusters also deliver all the availability advantages that were a part of OPS. Because all the machines in a Real Application Cluster share the same disk, the failure of a single machine does not mean that the database as a whole has failed. The users connected to the failed machine have to be failed over to another machine in the cluster, but the database server itself will continue to operate.

As of Oracle Database 10g, the model implemented with RAC has been extended beyond clusters to grid computing. Oracle now offers all the components you need to use to implement clusters on several operating system platforms as part of the Oracle software stack, including a volume manager and clusterware. In Oracle 10g Release 2, Oracle made it possible to monitor the different nodes in a cluster and to issue advisories to ensure better load balancing across the nodes.

High Availability

From an operational perspective, OLTP systems represent a company's electronic central nervous system, so the databases that support these systems must be highly available. Oracle has a number of features that contribute to high availability:

Standby database
>   Oracle can provide database redundancy by maintaining a copy of the primary database on another machine, usually at another site. Redo logs from the primary server are shipped to the standby server and applied there to duplicate the production activity. Oracle8i introduced the automated shipping of redo logs to the standby site and the ability to open the standby database for read-only access for reporting.
>
>   Oracle9i Release 2 introduced the concept of *logical standby*. With a logical standby database the changes are propagated with SQL statements, rather than redo logs, which allow the logical standby database to be used for other database operations.

Transparent Application Failover (TAF)
>   TAF is a programming interface that automatically connects a user session to another Oracle instance should the primary instance fail. Any queries that were in process are resumed from the point of the last row fetched for the result set.

Oracle Streams/Advanced Queuing (AQ)

AQ in Oracle Streams provides a method for asynchronous, or deferred, intersystem communication, allowing systems to operate more independently. Avoiding direct system dependencies can help to avoid "cascading" failures, allowing interconnected systems to continue to operate even if one system fails. For example, Streams can enable change data capture among Oracle databases and can be used with non-Oracle databases by leveraging gateways. These capabilities are described in more detail in the following section and in Chapter 13.

Oracle Streams Replication

You can use Oracle's built-in replication functionality to provide data redundancy. Changes made by transactions are replicated synchronously or asynchronously to other databases. If the primary database fails, the data is available from the other databases. As of Oracle9*i* Release 2, log-based replication is included as part of Streams. Replication is described in more detail in Chapter 13.

Real Application Clusters

Real Application Clusters can increase the scalability of the Oracle database over multiple nodes in a cluster. But by supporting multiple instances with full access to the same database, RAC also provides the highest levels of availability for protection from the failure of a node in a clustered environment. If one node fails, the surviving nodes provide continued access to the database. Grid computing deployment further extends availability capabilities.

Oracle Database 11g provides a number of high availability enhancements, including the ability to easily capture diagnostic information about database failures. For a more detailed discussion of high availability, see Chapter 11.

Oracle Streams and Advanced Queuing

Messaging technology has existed for quite some time and is common in OLTP applications. Typical messaging technologies provide a reliable transport layer for shipping messages from one machine to another over a network. Oracle8 introduced Advanced Queuing (AQ) as an integrated database service. Oracle9*i* Release 2 combined AQ with log-based replication in the creation of Oracle Streams.

Oracle Streams AQ provides the benefits of simple messaging products but adds the value of database-resident queues. The information in message queues represents critical business events and should be stored in a reliable, scalable, secure, and recoverable place. Placing the queues in the database extends the core benefits of a database to the queues themselves.

The data that flows through queues represents the ebb and flow of business activity. Analyzing the types and volumes of message traffic can help to identify how different business functions are operating and interacting and this, in turn, can provide valuable insights into the operation of your business. AQ supports the notion of *message warehousing*, in which the content and details of the queues can be queried and analyzed because they're already in the database. Oracle can dequeue messages but can leave historical data in the queues for subsequent analysis.

Applications can enqueue and dequeue messages as part of a transaction or as a separate event that occurs as soon as the specific enqueue or dequeue statement is issued. Queue actions included in the scope of a transaction are committed or rolled back with that transaction. Should a failure occur, the queue activities are recovered along with the rest of the database activity.

Oracle can propagate messages from one queue to another by providing a routing engine for message traffic. Figure 9-7 illustrates the use of queuing and propagation.

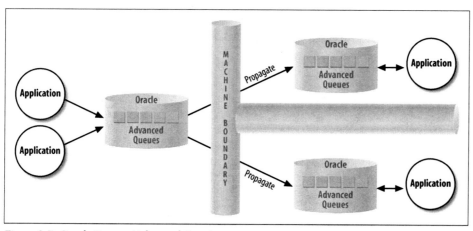

Figure 9-7. Oracle Streams/Advanced Queuing

Oracle Database 10g and more recent versions make it easier to implement Streams programmatically, by allowing you to enqueue and dequeue batches of messages and by reducing the amount of coding required to interact with queues.

Streams for System Interfaces

Implementing OLTP systems invariably involves interfaces with other systems in the enterprise or in other companies. The effort to design, create, and manage these interfaces is substantial and can easily account for 40 percent to 60 percent of the cost of large-scale ERP implementations. Furthermore, adding other systems to the mix or changing existing systems entails reworking the interfaces, resulting in an increasing and ongoing burden.

Oracle Streams can help companies solve the integration problem when implementing a "hub-and-spoke" architecture using a combination of messaging, routing, and transformation technologies. Traditionally, you would develop a specific interface between two systems. As you added a third system to the mix, you would have to create more specific interfaces between each of the systems. The more systems you attempt to integrate, the more custom interfaces you would be responsible for developing and the greater the development and maintenance burden would be.

Using these components, individual systems can connect to a hub via the spokes, thus avoiding direct system-to-system interfaces. The spokes send and receive messages, while the hub provides routing and transformation services. This reduces the number of interfaces required to connect a set of systems. You don't need a specific interface for every specific system pair. Adding systems to existing systems doesn't require development of many new interfaces. You connect the new system to the hub and leverage the routing and transformation services. Figure 9-8 contrasts the custom approach with the hub-and-spoke approach.

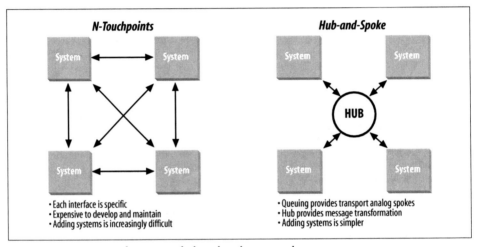

Figure 9-8. Custom interfaces versus hub-and-spoke approach

Oracle and Publish-Subscribe Technology

Oracle8*i* enhanced Advanced Queuing to include publish-subscribe functionality. Applications can subscribe to a message queue by specifying the attributes of messages they're interested in receiving. When another application publishes a message by placing it in a queue, Oracle evaluates the contents of the message to determine which of the subscribing applications are interested and notifies those applications. For example, a shipping application can subscribe to a queue used for orders and specify that only messages for orders with a status of "Ready to Ship" are of interest. As messages representing these orders flow through the queue, the shipping application will receive only the desired messages. This publish-subscribe functionality, coupled with message propagation for routing, provides a very powerful messaging backbone for information flow between systems.

Object Technologies and Distributed Components

In theory, the greater the amount of information, the more intelligence that can be extracted from it. Integrating information from separate systems can be an enormous task, especially because the complexity of integration increases geometrically as more systems are added to the mix.

While messaging technologies can assist with interfacing different systems, online interaction is often needed as well. For example, if the Human Resources system maintains information about the company's employees (such as the department in which they work and their role), ideally the Purchasing system could access the data in the HR system online at the time purchases are being made. At this point, the Purchasing system could determine the spending limits of the purchaser and to what department the accounting should be tied. In practice, these online interfaces are difficult to build because they require the systems to agree, and remain in agreement, about how to communicate. Each system has proprietary application programming interfaces (APIs) that allow other systems to communicate with them. These specific, and often conflicting, APIs limit the reuse of the functionality within each system.

Object technologies offer one solution: systems communicate by invoking methods on objects instead of by calling specific APIs. For example, if you want to check the department of a user, you make a standard object call to the employee object managed by the HR system.

Oracle8*i* and later versions support a number of object technologies, including Java for use as an object-oriented programming language. Oracle's object-oriented support is described in more detail in Chapter 14. More recently, the focus on developing applications and code for reuse now includes the concept of a Service-Oriented Architecture (SOA) and web services, described in Chapter 15.

CHAPTER 10

Oracle Data Warehousing and Business Intelligence

Although a database is general-purpose software, it provides a solution for a variety of technical requirements, including:

Recording and storing data
Reliably storing data and protecting each user's data from the effects of other users' changes

Reading data for online viewing and reports
Providing a consistent view of the data

Analyzing data
Summarizing data, detecting trends and data relationships, and forecasting

The last two solutions can be deployed as a *data warehouse*, part of an infrastructure that provides *business intelligence* used in strategic and tactical management of the corporation or organization. Such solutions expose valuable business information embedded in an organization's data stores.

Data warehousing and business intelligence solutions are now widely deployed and new projects continue to be extremely popular. There is a very simple reason behind this trend: such projects are seen as core to the business and provide a return on investment that can be grasped by the business community.

The trend is not new. Oracle began adding data warehousing features to Oracle7 in the early 1990s. Additional features for warehousing and business intelligence appeared in subsequent releases, enabling better performance, functionality, scalability, and management. Oracle also offers tools for building and using a business intelligence infrastructure, including data movement and business analyses tools and applications.

A business intelligence infrastructure can enable business analysts to determine:

- How a business scenario compares to past business results
- New solutions by looking at the data differently

- What could happen in the future
- How business actions could be changed to impact the future

This chapter introduces the basic concepts, technologies, and tools used in data warehousing and business intelligence. To help you understand how Oracle addresses infrastructure and analyses issues, we'll first describe some of the basic terms and technologies.

Business Intelligence Basics

Why build a data warehouse or business intelligence solution? Why is the data in an online transaction processing (OLTP) database part of only a business intelligence solution? Data warehouses are often designed with the following in mind:

Strategic and tactical analyses can discern trends in data
> Data warehouses often are used in creation of simple reports based on aggregate values culled from enormous amounts of data. If OLTP databases were used to create such aggregates on the fly, the database resources used would impact the ability to process transactions in a timely manner. These ad hoc queries often leverage compute-intensive analytic functions embedded in the database.

A significant portion of the data in a data warehouse is often read-only, with infrequent updates
> Leveraging database manageability features can make it possible to deploy warehouses holding hundreds of terabytes of data, even where near real-time updates of some of the data is occurring.

The data in OLTP systems is not "clean" or consistent across systems
> Data input to OLTP systems, if not carefully controlled, is likely to contain errors and duplication. Often, a key portion of the data warehouse loading process involves elimination of these errors. In addition, since multiple OLTP systems might differ in common data definitions, the loading process can be used to consolidate this data into a single definition.

The design required for an efficient data warehouse differs from the standard normalized design for a relational database
> Queries are typically submitted against a fact table, which may contain summarized data. The schema design often used, a *star schema*, lets you access facts quite flexibly along key dimensions or "lookup" values. (The star schema is described in more detail later in this chapter.) For instance, a data warehouse user may want to compare the total amount of sales, which comes from a fact table, by region, store in the region, and items, all of which can be considered key dimensions. Today's data warehouses often feature a *hybrid schema* that is a combination of the star schema common in previous-generation data marts with third normal form schema for detailed data that is common in OLTP systems and enterprise data warehouses.

The Evolution of Business Intelligence

Gathering business intelligence is not a new idea. The use of corporate data for strategic decision-making beyond simple tracking and day-to-day operations has been going on for almost as long as computing itself.

Quite early, builders and users of operational systems recognized potential business benefits of analyzing the data in complementary systems. In fact, much of the early growth in personal computers was tied to the use of spreadsheets that performed analyses using data downloaded from the operational systems. Business executives began to direct IT efforts toward building solutions to better understand the business using such data leading to new business strategies. Today, solutions are commonly provided in business areas such as customer relationship management, sales and marketing campaign analysis, product management and packaging, financial analysis, supply chain analysis, and risk and fraud analysis.

In the 1980s, many organizations began using dedicated servers for these applications, collectively known then as *decision support systems* (DSS), supplementing their management information systems. Decision-support queries tended to be particularly CPU and memory intensive using read-only data, whereas traditional OLTP was typically I/O intensive with a large number of updates to data. The characteristics of queries were much less predictable (e.g., more "ad hoc") than what had been experienced in OLTP systems. This led to the development of data stores for decision support apart from those for OLTP.

When Bill Inmon (whose books are noted in Appendix B) and others popularized the term "data warehouse" in the early 1990s, a formalized common infrastructure for building a solution came into being. The topology of business intelligence solutions continued to evolve, as the next section illustrates. Today's business intelligence solutions often include infrastructure that exposes data from data warehouses and also OLTP systems in reports. Underlying hardware has evolved such that I/O is now a more important design consideration for data warehousing hardware platforms (see Chapter 12).

A Topology for Business Intelligence

The classic data warehouse topology, serving as an enterprise-wide source of information, is represented by the multitier topology shown in Figure 10-1.

This topology developed over many years for a variety of reasons. Initial efforts at creating a single enterprise warehouse often resulted in "analysis paralysis." Just as efforts to define an enterprise-wide OLTP model can take years (due to cross-departmental politics and the scope of the effort), similar attempts in data warehousing also took much longer than business sponsors were willing to accept. These efforts were further hampered by the continually changing analysis requirements necessitated by a changing marketplace. While the data elements and

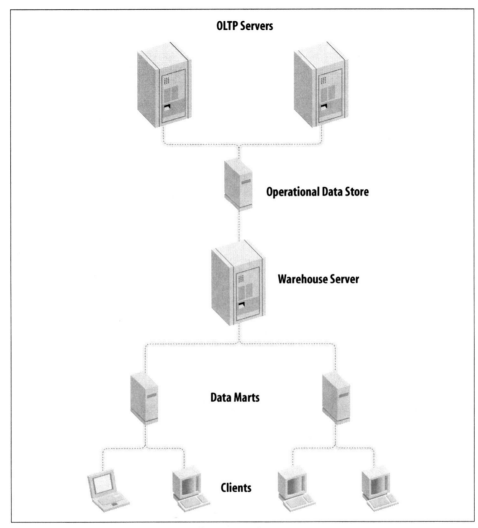

Figure 10-1. Typical initial business intelligence topology

requirements for operational systems can remain relatively stagnant over time, understanding business trends can be like trying to catch lightning in a bottle.

Consequently, attempts at building such enterprise-wide models that would satisfy everyone often satisfied no one.

Data Marts

When some large-scale, enterprise-only data warehouse efforts ended in dismal failure, frustration and impatience followed. Some reacted and built department-focused independent *data marts* by extracting data from the appropriate operational source systems. Many data marts were initially quite successful because they fulfilled a specific business need relatively quickly.

However, problems began to surface. There was often no coordination between departments regarding basic definitions, such as "customer." If a senior manager asked the same question of multiple departments, the answers provided by these independent data marts were often different, thus calling into question the validity of all of the marts. Many departments also encountered ongoing difficulty in managing these multiple data marts and in maintaining extractions from operational sources (which were often duplicated across multiple departments).

As architects took another look at their solutions, they began to realize that it was very important to have a consistent view of the detailed data at an enterprise data warehouse level. They also saw that data marts could solve business problems and provide return on investment in an incremental fashion. Today, most successful implementers simultaneously grow dependent data marts one business solution at a time while growing the enterprise warehouse server in an incremental fashion.

The currently accepted definition of a data mart is simply a subject- or application-specific data warehouse, usually implemented within a department. Typically, these data marts are built for performance and may include a large number of summary tables. Data marts were initially thought of as being small, since not all the detail data for a department or data from other departments need be loaded in the mart. However, some marts get quite large as they incorporate data from outside sources (sometimes purchased) that isn't relevant in other parts of the business.

In some organizations, data marts are deployed to meet specific project goals with models optimized for performance for that particular project. Such data marts are retired when the project is completed and the hardware is reused for other projects. As the analysis requirements for a business change, the topology of any particular data warehouse is subject to evolution over time, so developers must be aware of this possibility.

Increasing focus on cost savings, manageability, and compliance are leading many to reexamine the wisdom of having a large number of physically separate data marts. As a result, consolidation of marts into the enterprise warehouse is a common trend. More recent versions of Oracle enable effective management of different user communities, helping to make such consolidation possible.

Operational Data Store and Enterprise Warehouse

The *operational data store* (ODS) concept also grew in popularity in the 1990s. The ODS may best be described as a distribution center for current data. Like the OLTP servers, the schema is highly normalized and the data is recent. The ODS serves as a consolidation point for reporting and can give the business one location for viewing current data that crosses divisions or departments. The popularity of the ODS grew

in part as a result of companies in the midst of acquisitions
nizations often face mixed-application environments. The (
location that can be used as the source for further transform.
house or into data marts.

The warehouse server, or *enterprise data warehouse*, is a multisι
mation store usually supporting multiple departments and (
corporate database of record. When an ODS is established, th
often extracts data from the ODS. When an ODS isn't present,
house is directly extracted and transformed from operational souι
may also feed the warehouse server.

As noted previously, platform consolidation is popular within these tiers today. The
enterprise data warehouse can be the point of consolidation for the ODS and multiple data marts. Although different logical models remain, they are consolidated to a
single platform and database.

OLTP Systems and Business Intelligence

True real-time data resides in the OLTP systems. Organizations can provide reporting out of such transaction processing systems side-by-side in portals or dashboards
with information from data warehouse systems. A key to providing meaningful dashboards is to provide high-quality data with consistent meaning. The quality of data
in OLTP systems is directly related to controlling data input to eliminate duplicate or
error-prone entries.

Consistent meaning can be resolved using master data management (MDM) solutions. MDM solutions consist of data hubs that serve as a common reference point
for data supporting key business measurements such as customers, products, or
finance. Oracle offers a number of data hubs for these and other business areas to
enable building out of such an infrastructure.

Projects that leverage data from data warehouses, OLTP systems, and MDM solutions are called data integration projects. Most business intelligence deployments, at
the time of publication of this edition, use just the data warehouse infrastructure as
the primary source of historic data for business intelligence. The extraction, transformation, and loading (ETL) techniques applied to the data warehouse are designed to
resolve differences in common data elements, to cleanse the data, and to provide a
historical database of record.

Data Warehouse Design

The database serves as the foundation of the business intelligence infrastructure: it is
the place where the data is stored. But there is more to business intelligence than
data—the infrastructure becomes useful only when business users use the data to

t. This may seem like a trivial point, but we've seen numerous companies
elegant infrastructure without consulting business users to determine business
ds or key performance indicators (KPIs) to be measured. Often, such deployed
projects end up supporting very few users, generate little activity, and little business
intelligence is gained.

Assuming that your infrastructure is well planned and there is a demand for the data,
your next challenge will be to figure out how to handle the demand. You will be
faced with the need to design your data warehouse and other infrastructure components to deliver appropriate performance to your users—performance that may
initially seem far beyond your capabilities, since the information needed can involve
comparisons of massive amounts of detailed data.

When you start your design, also remember that this infrastructure will never be considered finished. When the business needs change, so too must components in the
infrastructure. Thus, the ability to track changes through metadata stored in a repository often becomes critical as part of the design work.

Various design tools can provide this capability. Oracle's Warehouse Builder
(OWB), included with Oracle Enterprise Edition, Standard Edition, and Standard
Edition One databases (since 2006), provides a metadata repository and also the
capability to import metadata from operational tables and then forward-engineer
new schema and tables. A data warehouse designer creates columns for the new
tables and builds constraints for the new schema. Maps are then created between
source and target columns with appropriate transformations. DML scripts for creation of new tables, and PL/SQL or SQL*Loader scripts for ETL are automatically
generated.

As noted previously, data warehouses historically have had a different set of usage
characteristics from those of an OLTP database. One aspect that makes it easier to
meet data warehousing performance requirements is the high percentage of read
operations. Oracle's locking model, described in detail in Chapter 8, is ideally suited
for data warehouse operations. Oracle doesn't place any locks onto data that's being
read, thus reducing contention and resource requirements for situations where there
are a lot of database reads. Since locks don't escalate, Oracle is also extremely appropriate for near real-time data feeds into the warehouse in a scenario not unlike OLTP
workloads.

Warehousing usage characteristics lead to deploying different types of schema. In
OLTP databases, transaction data is usually stored in multiple tables and data items
are stored only once. If a query requests data from more than one transaction table,
the tables are joined together. Typically, the database query optimizer decides which
table to use as the starting point for the join, based on the assumption that the data
in the tables is essentially equally important.

Although Oracle-based data warehouses are sometimes modeled as third normal form (3NF) (described in Chapter 4), when business users need an understandable schema to formulate their own ad hoc queries or analytical processing is required, key transaction data can be more appropriately stored in a central fact table, surrounded by dimension or lookup tables, as shown in Figure 10-2. The fact table can contain summarized data for data items duplicated elsewhere in the warehouse, and dimension tables can contain multiple hierarchies. As noted previously, when organizations consolidate their data marts into enterprise data warehouses, many now deploy a variation called a hybrid schema, a mixture of third normal form and star schema.

Ralph Kimball, author of the widely read book *The Data Warehouse Toolkit* (Wiley; see Appendix B for details), is largely credited with discovering that users of data warehouses typically pose their queries in such a manner that a star schema, illustrated in Figure 10-2, is an appropriate model to use. A typical query might be something such as the following:

> Show me how many sales of computers (a product type) were sold by a store chain (a channel) in Wisconsin (a geography) over the past 6 months (a time).

The schema in Figure 10-2 shows a relatively large sales transactions table (called a *fact table*) surrounded by smaller tables (called *dimensions* or *lookup tables*). The query just described is often called *multidimensional*, since several dimensions are included (and time is almost always one of them). Because these queries are typical in a data warehouse, the recognition of the star schema by Oracle's cost-based optimizer can deliver enormous performance benefits.

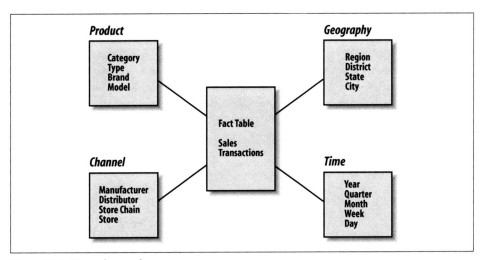

Figure 10-2. Typical star schema

Query Optimization

Oracle first provided the ability to recognize a star schema in the query optimizer in Oracle7 and has focused on making its cost-based query optimizer smarter in response to business intelligence queries in subsequent database releases. Further improving optimizer prediction accuracy, since Oracle Database 10g, optimizer predictions are compared to actual runtime performance, and any errors are subsequently corrected automatically. The optimizer also can provide query rewrite transparently to summary levels commonly deployed with star schema through materialized views. Oracle Database 11g added query rewrite for the OLAP Option as well as improved solving of queries containing inline views.

How does the optimizer handle a query against a star schema? First, it finds a sales transactions fact table (shown in Figure 10-2) with a lot more entries than the surrounding dimension tables. This is the clue that a star schema exists. As Oracle7 evolved, the optimizer began to produce much smarter plans. The optimizer for a standard relational database typically would have tried to join each of the dimension tables to the fact table, one at a time. Because the fact table is usually very large, using the fact table in multiple joins takes a lot of time.

Cartesian product joins were added to Oracle7 to first join the dimension tables, with a subsequent single join back to the fact table in the final step. This technique works relatively well when there are not many dimension tables (typically six or fewer, as a rule of thumb, to keep the Cartesian product small) and when data is relatively well populated.

In some situations, there are a fairly large number of dimension tables or the data in the fact table is sparse. For joining such tables, a parallel bitmap star join may be selected by the optimizer.

In earlier releases of the Oracle database, DBAs had to set initialization parameters (e.g., STAR_TRANSFORMATION) and gather statistics, enabling the optimizer to recognize the best methods for solving such queries. Today, needed parameters are preset upon installation and statistics are automatically gathered by the Oracle database.

Bitmap Indexes and Parallelism

Bitmap indexes, described in Chapter 4, were first introduced in Oracle7 to speed up the type of data retrieval and joins in data warehousing queries. Bitmap indexes in Oracle are typically considered for columns in which the data has low cardinality. *Cardinality* is the number of different values in an index divided by the number of rows. There are various opinions about what low cardinality actually is. Some consider cardinality as high as 10% to be low, but remember that if a table has a million rows, that "low" cardinality would mean 100,000 different values in a column!

In a bitmap index, a value of 1 in the index indicates that a value is present in a particular row and 0 indicates that the value is not present. A bitmap is built for each of the values in the indexed columns. Because computers are built on a concept of 1s and 0s, this technique can greatly speed up data retrieval. In addition, join operations such as AND become a simple addition operation across multiple bitmaps. A side benefit is that bitmap indexes can provide considerable storage savings.

Figure 10-3 illustrates the use of a bitmap index in a compound WHERE clause. Bitmap indexes can be used together for even faster performance. The bitmap indexes are essentially stacked together, as a set of punch cards might be. Oracle simply looks for those parts of the stack with all the bits turned on (indicating the presence of the value), in the same way that you could try to stick a knitting needle through the portions of the card stack that were punched out on all of the cards.

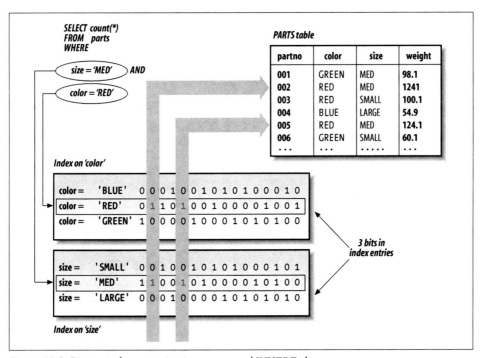

Figure 10-3. Bitmap index operation in a compound WHERE clause

In Oracle, star-query performance is improved when bitmap indexes are created on the foreign-keys columns of the fact table that link to the surrounding dimension tables. A parallel bitmap star join occurs in which the bitmaps retrieve only the necessary rows from the fact table and the rows are joined to the dimension tables. During the join, sparseness (i.e., a large quantity of empty values) is recognized inherently in the bitmaps, and the number of dimension tables isn't a problem. This algorithm can also efficiently handle a *snowflake schema*, which is an extension of a standard star schema in which there are multiple tables for each dimension.

To further speed queries, Oracle9*i* added a bitmap join index from fact tables to dimension tables. A bitmap join index is simply the bitmap index of a join of two or more tables. The speedup in performance comes from avoiding actual table joins or reducing the amount of data joined by taking into account restrictions in advance of the joining of data. Performance speedup for star queries with multiple dimension tables can be greatly improved since bitwise operations in star transformations can now be eliminated.

Performing queries in parallel also obviously improves performance. Joins and sorts are frequently used to solve decision-support queries. Parallelism is described in Chapter 7. That chapter lists functions that Oracle can perform in parallel (see "What Can Be Parallelized?").

Real Application Clusters, which replaced Oracle Parallel Server as of Oracle9*i*, further expands parallelism by enabling queries to transparently scale across nodes in clusters or in grids of computer systems.

Remember that these Oracle features use the cost-based optimizer and, prior to Oracle Database 10*g*, you should run statistics periodically (using the ANALYZE command) on the tables to ensure good performance. Statistics gathering can be done in parallel.

Since Oracle Database 10*g*, statistics gathering is automatic and populates the Automatic Workload Repository. For example, the SQL Access Advisor leverages this information when making tuning recommendations.

Summary Tables

Data within dimensions is usually hierarchical in nature (e.g., in the time dimension, day rolls up to week, which rolls up to month, which rolls up to quarter, which rolls up to year). If the query is simply looking for data summarized at a monthly level, why should it have to sort through more detailed daily and weekly data? Instead, it can simply view data at or above that level of the hierarchy. Formerly, data warehousing performance consultants designed these types of summary tables—including multiple levels of precalculated summarization. For example, all the time periods listed in Figure 10-2 can be calculated on the fly using different groupings of days. However, to speed queries based on a different time series, a data warehouse can have values precalculated for weeks and months and stored in summary tables to which queries can be redirected.

Materialized Views

Oracle8*i* introduced the concept of *materialized views* for the creation of summary tables for facts and dimensions that can represent rollup levels in the hierarchies. A materialized view provides precomputed summary data; most importantly, a materialized view is automatically substituted for a larger detailed table when appropriate. The cost-based query optimizer can perform query rewrites to these summary tables and rollup levels in the hierarchy transparently, often resulting in dramatic increases in performance. For instance, if a query can be answered by summary data based on sales by month, the query optimizer will automatically substitute the materialized view for the more granular table when processing the query. A query at the quarter level might use monthly aggregates in the materialized view, selecting the months needed for the quarter(s). Oracle Database 10g added query rewrite capabilities such that the optimizer can make use of multiple appropriate materialized views.

Materialized views can be managed through Oracle Enterprise Manager (see also Chapter 5). The SQL Advisor accessible in Enterprise Manager includes a SQL Access Advisor that can recommend when to create materialized views.

Analytics, OLAP, and Data Mining in the Database

Analysis of large data sets is faster when it takes place in the database where the data is stored. This section describes the database functions and other features available for analytics and statistics, online analytical processing (OLAP) multidimensional deployment choices, and data mining.

It is worth noting here that the growing use of Oracle for statistical computations led to support for floating-point number types providing the precision outlined in the IEEE 754-1985 standard (with minor differences). These are provided in the datatypes BINARY_FLOAT and BINARY_DOUBLE in Oracle Database 10g and more recent database releases.

Analytic and Statistical Functions

Oracle releases dating back to Oracle8i have continued to add new analytic and statistical functions as SQL extensions to the core Oracle Enterprise Edition and Standard Edition databases. These analytic functions now include:

Ranking functions
> Used to compute a record's rank with respect to other records. Functions include RANK, DENSE_RANK, CUME_DIST, PERCENT_RANK, NTILE, and ROW_NUMBER. Hypothetical ranking is supported.

Windowing aggregate functions
> Used to compute cumulative and moving averages. Functions include SUM, AVG, MIN, MAX, COUNT, VARIANCE, STDDEV, and FIRST_VALUE, LAST_VALUE.

LAG/LEAD functions
> Often used to compare values from similar time periods, such as the first quarter of 2006 and the first quarter of 2007.

Reporting aggregate functions
> Include SUM, AVG, MIN, MAX, COUNT, VARIANCE, STDDEV, and RATIO_TO_REPORT.

Linear regression functions
> Include REGR_COUNT, REGR_AVGX and REGR_AVGY, REGR_SLOPE, REGR_INTERCEPT, REGR_R2, and other functions used in regression line fitting for a set of numbers in pairs (e.g., having X and Y values).

Also supported in Oracle are pivoting operations, histograms (using WIDTH_BUCKET), CASE expressions, filling gaps in data, and time-series calculations.

The database includes a statistics package, DBMS_STATS_FUNCS. Functions in the statistics package support linear algebra, frequent itemsets, descriptive statistics, hypothesis testing (T-test, F-test, Binomial test, Wilcoxon Signed Ranks Test, One-Way ANOVA, Chi-square, Mann Whitney, Kolmogorov-Smirnov), crosstab statistics (% statistics, chi squared, phi coefficient, Cramer's V, contingency coefficient, and Cohen's kappa), and nonparametric correlation (Pearson's correlation coefficients, and Spearman's and Kendall's).

MODEL Clause in SELECT

The SQL MODEL clause first appeared in Oracle Database 10g as an extension to the SELECT statement. This clause enables relational data to be treated as multidimensional arrays (much like spreadsheets) and is also used to define formulas for the arrays, avoiding multiple joins and UNION clauses.

MODEL supports analytical queries that include prior-year comparisons and share of ancestor, and it is particularly useful in budgeting, forecasting, and other statistical applications. Example MODEL usages include calculating sales differences in two geographies, calculating percentage change, and calculating net present value. The SQL MODEL clause can also use simultaneous equations and regression in calculations.

OLAP and Data Mining Capabilities

For stored cubes (objects with predefined multidimensional joins), facts, and dimensions in the relational database, Oracle introduced the OLAP Option to the Oracle9i database. OLAP database capabilities are most commonly accessed althrough SQL, though there is also a Java API. Oracle Database 11g added support for OLAP SQL query rewrite.

As an OLAP alternative, Oracle now offers a technology that is relational database-agnostic: Essbase, from Hyperion (acquired by Oracle in 2007) is an OLAP engine that can extract data from Oracle and other databases. This OLAP solution is especially popular for Hyperion's financial applications and in cases where business

---

analysts want to generate their own cubes. Essbase cubes can also be accessed using Oracle Business Intelligence Enterprise Edition (OBI EE) tools.

Data-mining algorithms were first embedded in the Oracle9*i* database in the Data Mining Option. These were initially accessible via a Java API, but Oracle later added a PL/SQL API.

For applications-based data mining independent of underlying database technology, the OBI EE tools can utilize data-mining algorithms Oracle acquired with Sigma Dynamics in 2006. This technology is known as Real-Time Decisions (RTD).

We describe OLAP and data mining in the database and Oracle's business intelligence tools in the following sections.

Database Extensibility and the Data Warehouse

A growing trend in data warehousing is the storage of multiple datatypes within the database. These extended database capabilities are described in Chapter 14, but we'll quickly mention here how these options might be useful in data warehousing.

Multimedia

The Multimedia feature set (formerly knows as *inter*Media) opens up the possibilities of including documents, audio, video, and some locator functions in the warehouse. Of these, text retrieval (Oracle Text) is most commonly used in warehouses today. However, the number of organizations storing other types of data, such as images, is growing. Often, storage of these types of data is driven by a need to provide remote users with access.

Spatial Option

The Spatial Option is also relevant in a data warehouse in which data is retrieved based on proximity to certain locations. Spatial data includes some type of geographic coordinates. Typically, companies use add-on products in conjunction with Oracle's Spatial Option. An example of this option's use for data warehousing is a marketing analysis application that determines the viability of retail outlets at various locations.

XML

Oracle added native XML datatype support to the Oracle9*i* database, along with XML and SQL interchangeability for searching. Oracle provided key technology in the development of the XQuery standard, and began shipping a production version of XQuery with Oracle Database 10*g* Release 2. XML database performance was greatly improved in Oracle Database 11*g* through the introduction of binary XML. Oracle estimates that binary XML offers performance gains of up to 15 times compared to the XML LOBs that were previously available.

Managing the Data Warehouse

Once you've built a data warehouse topology, you could deploy multiple Oracle databases to implement the data warehouse and its data marts. Enterprise-wide warehouses are common on Unix servers, but are also appearing on clustered (RAC) Linux platforms. Smaller data marts are common on Windows and Linux. Many organizations are consolidating data marts and enterprise data warehouses on the more scalable platforms.

Oracle Enterprise Manager provides a common GUI for managing these multiple instances regardless of the underlying operating system. EM is browser-based with a multiuser repository for tracking and managing the Oracle instances. (EM is discussed in much more detail in Chapter 5.)

In warehousing, in addition to basic management, ongoing tuning for performance is crucial. Enterprise Manager supports many of the automated diagnostics and tuning features added in Oracle Database 10g and more recent releases.

Within the largest warehouses and data marts, you may want to manage or maintain availability to some of the data even as other parts of the database are moved offline. Oracle's Partitioning Option enables data partitions based on business value ranges (such as date) or discrete values for administrative flexibility, while enhancing query performance through the cost-based optimizer's ability to eliminate access to non-relevant partitions. For example, "rolling window" administrative operations can be used to add new data and remove old data using time ranges. A new partition can be added, loaded, and indexed in parallel, and optionally removed, all without impacting access to existing data.

Range partitioning first became available in the Oracle8 Partitioning Option. *Hash partitioning* was added to the Oracle8i Partitioning Option enabling the spread of data evenly based on a hash algorithm for performance. Hashing may be used within range partitions (*composite partitioning*) to increase the performance of queries while still maintaining the manageability offered by range partitioning. Oracle9i introduced *list partitioning*—partitions based on discrete values such as geographies. A composite partitioning type, *range-list partitioning*, which allows you to partition by dates within geographies, was added in Oracle9i Release 2. More composite types were added in Oracle Database 11g including *list-hash*, *list-list*, *list-range*, and *range-range partitioning*. *Interval partitioning* was also added in Oracle Database 11g, providing automatic creation of range partitions when needed.

Other Software for the Data Warehouse

A data warehouse isn't necessarily built with a single software product, nor is it simply a database. In addition to the database capabilities we've described, if you're going to build an effective data warehouse topology like the one we've outlined, your software will provide the following functionality:

Data Warehouses and Backups

Early data warehousing practitioners often overlooked the need to perform backups. Their belief was that since data for the warehouse was extracted from operational systems, the warehouses could easily be repopulated from those same systems if needed. However, as warehouses grew and the transformations needed to create and refresh them evolved, it became evident that backups of data warehouses were necessary because the transformation process had grown extremely complicated and time-consuming. Today, planning for warehouse availability includes not only an understanding of how long loading will take, but also backup and recovery operations. Due to the tactical nature of such warehouses, planning often also includes designs for high availability, disaster recovery, and lifecycle information management.

Extraction of data from operational data sources
> The movement of needed data from source systems for the purpose of loading a data warehouse. This process might involve extracting a large amount of bulk data or a steady stream of incremental changes.

Transformation and/or cleansing of data
> Because the data in a data warehouse can come from many different sources, the data must frequently be converted into a common format. Original data might also need to be cleansed to eliminate or correct invalid values.

Loading the data warehouse/marts
> This process might also occur in bulk or a steady stream.

Basic reporting
> Standard reports should be easily accessible by nontechnical business analysts in a browser-based portal or dashboard and could be published.

Ad hoc query and analysis
> Tools business analysts can use for picking and choosing data items and building their own queries. The results can be published into reports.

Advanced OLAP for multidimensional analysis
> More advanced analysis capability needed to spot business changes and trends typically where a large number of dimensions are present.

Data mining
> Usually used where there are a large number of variables present to determine a best model for known outcomes and then used to predict future results where outcomes are not known.

Metadata management
> Store descriptive business and technical data and enable extended management services such as versioning and impact analysis.

The following sections provide descriptions of how Oracle can deliver such functionality in various tools and database features and options.

Extraction, Transformation, and Loading

The first three requirements described in the previous list are often handled by what are called ETL tools (for extraction, transformation, and loading). Those who are experienced in data warehouse solutions realize that the process of understanding the data sources, designing the transformations, testing the loading process, and debugging is often the most time-consuming part of deployment. Transformations generally remove bogus data (including erroneous entries and duplicate entries), convert data items to an agreed-upon format, and filter data not considered necessary for the warehouse. These operations not only improve the quality of the data, but frequently reduce the overall amount of data, and that, in turn, improves data warehouse performance.

The frequency of extraction and loading is largely determined by the required timeliness of the data in the warehouse. Most extraction and loading takes place on a "batch" basis with a known time delay (typically subhourly or hourly or daily today). Many first-generation warehouses were completely refreshed during the loading process. As data volumes grew, this became impractical due to the limited time frames available for loading. Today, updates to tables are most common. When a need for near real-time data exists, warehouses can be loaded nearly continuously using a *trickle feed*.

Is Cleanliness Best?

Once the data in the warehouse is "clean," is this version of the true nature of the data propagated back to the originating OLTP systems? This is an important issue for data warehouse implementation. In some cases, a "closed loop" process is implemented whereby updates are provided back to the originating systems. In addition to minimizing some of the cleansing that takes place during future extractions, operational reports become more accurate.

Another viable option is to avoid cleansing by improving the quality of the data at the time of its input into the operational system. As noted previously in this chapter, this is critical if OLTP systems are to be directly accessed for business intelligence. Improving data quality at the source also enables high-speed loading techniques to be used in near real-time data warehouses (since transformations can be eliminated).

Improving data quality at the source can sometimes be accomplished by not allowing a "default" condition as allowable input into a data field. Presenting the data-entry person with an array of valid options, one of which *must* be selected, is often a way to ensure the most consistent and valid responses. Many companies also provide education to the data-entry people, showing them how the data they're keying in will be used and what the significance of it is.

Simple extraction and transportation of data is possible using one of several Oracle database features:

Transparent Gateways and Heterogeneous Services
> Provide a bridge to retrieve data from non-Oracle sources using Oracle SQL to load an Oracle database. Heterogeneous Services provide ODBC connectivity to non-Oracle relational sources. Gateways can optionally provide a higher level of performance when extracting data from non-Oracle sources.

Transportable Tablespaces
> Another feature for data movement, Transportable Tablespaces enable rapid data movement between Oracle instances without export/import. Metadata (the data dictionary) is exported from the source and imported to the target. The transferred tablespace can then be mounted on the target. Oracle Database 10g introduced cross-platform Transportable Tablespaces, which can move a tablespace from one type of system (e.g., Solaris) to another (e.g., Linux).

Oracle Streams
> Streams have been bundled with Oracle since Oracle9i Release 2. Oracle Streams include Oracle's log-based replication, Advanced Queues (AQ), and since Oracle Database 10g, includes Transportable Tablespaces. Streams are often used for near real-time data movement. Oracle Database 10g added support for downstream capture, which allows changed data to be collected from log files, eliminating overhead, RMAN and Transportable Tablespaces for instantiation, support for LONG, LONG RAW, and NCLOB datatypes, and asynchronous change data capture that uses Streams to transport only changed records from a source database to a target.

Data Pump Fast Import/Export
> Added in Oracle Database 10g and enabled via external table support, Data Pump is a newer import/export format. Parallel direct path loading and unloading are supported.

Each of these database features is typically used for high-performance data transfers and not (by themselves) for difficult transformations. Oracle Warehouse Builder (OWB) is the Oracle database's ETL tool used for building maps from extraction sources, through predefined or custom transformations to target tables. OWB then can be used to automatically generate the scripts needed to perform the ETL. More than just an ETL tool, OWB also can be used as a data warehouse design tool and provides a metadata repository. Designs may also be imported from a variety of design tools such as Oracle Designer, CA's ERwin, Sybase PowerDesigner, and Business Objects Designer.

In most warehouse building, metadata is first imported that describes source tables, including Oracle (via database links) and other RDBMS systems (through ODBC or gateways) and flat files. Target tables are designed or imported, and source metadata is mapped to target metadata, including transformations. OWB's basic set of transformations include a name and address cleansing operator for use with Oracle partners' libraries and applications that perform "householding," matching, and merging of data. Advanced features such as support for slowly changing dimensions and pluggable mappings are available in the OWB Enterprise Option. The OWB Data Quality Option includes support for data profiling and data rules.

OWB can validate the source-to-target mappings (see Figure 10-4). Once validated, you can then generate any of the following:

- DDL if target tables are to be created
- SQL*Loader control files for the loading of flat files
- PL/SQL scripts for ETL from relational sources

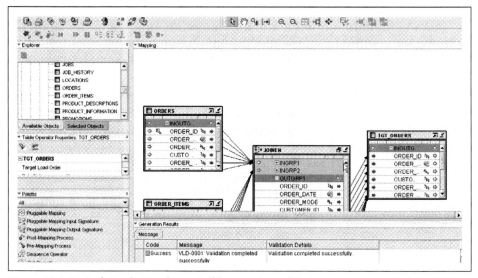

Figure 10-4. Typical Oracle Warehouse Builder mapping validation

Scripts are deployed to and run at the target data warehouse, typically scheduled using the Enterprise Manager job scheduler. In this way, OWB is more of an "ELT" tool since the transformations leverage the target database engine. For more complex scheduling of ETL jobs where certain prerequisites must be met, OWB leverages Oracle Workflow components.

OWB provides access to a number of other non-Oracle sources. Connectors for the E-Business Suite and PeopleSoft provide access to technical and business metadata and enable inclusion of objects from those ERP applications into mappings and process flows. The SAP Connector is similar but also includes an ABAP code generator used to build access to any SAP table on any database, including cluster tables, through an RFC connection.

For high-speed loading of flat files, Oracle SQL*Loader's *direct path load* option provides rapid loading by bypassing the buffer cache and rollback mechanism and writing directly to the datafile. You can run SQL*Loader sessions in parallel to further speed the table-loading process (as many warehouses need to be loaded in a limited "window" of time). Many popular extraction tools, including OWB, generate SQL*Loader scripts.

Oracle9i first added key ETL functionality in the core database engine, including support for external tables, table functions, merge (i.e., insert or update depending on whether a data item exists), multitable inserts, change data capture, and resumable statements. Today, OWB can be used to leverage this functionality. Additionally, OWB can create trickle feeds through the use of Streams and Advanced Queues.

For ETL into both Oracle databases and non-Oracle targets, Oracle offers a product named Oracle Data Integrator (ODI). This product was acquired in 2007 and was formerly known as Sunopsis. ODI features Knowledge Modules that define integration capabilities including extraction with change data capture, loading and unloading utilities, SQL-based loading and unloading, and transformation logic SQL. The Knowledge Modules are modifiable. The product architecture includes a development environment that makes use of the Knowledge Modules as templates in declarative design processes and an orchestration agent.

In addition to providing heterogeneous ETL, ODI can be used to deploy and integrate data and transformation services in a Service-Oriented Architecture (SOA) infrastructure. ODI is a key component in Oracle MDM solutions and in some of Oracle's emerging business intelligence applications.

Reporting and Ad Hoc Query Tools

Marketing, financial, and other business analysts are rarely interested in the storage and schema that hold their information. Their interest level rises when the discussion turns to the tools they'll be using. Business intelligence tools are often evaluated and purchased within individual business areas, sometimes without close IT coordination. For implementations leveraging Oracle databases, you have a choice between suites of Oracle business intelligence tools or popular independent vendors' products, such as Business Objects, Cognos, and MicroStrategy.

Oracle's business intelligence tools are bundled in three suites today: Oracle Business Intelligence Enterprise Edition, Standard Edition One, and Standard Edition. In addition, Oracle has obtained through acquisition the Hyperion Intelligence Server and Client products now bundled in Oracle Business Intelligence Enterprise Edition Plus. Oracle's most strategic offerings are the Enterprise Edition Plus and Standard Edition One, although development and support continues for all of the other products.

Oracle Business Intelligence Enterprise Edition (OBI EE) contains the former Siebel Analytics tools and Oracle BI Publisher (previously XML Publisher). It includes optimizations for Oracle and non-Oracle databases. Included in the suite are:

Interactive Dashboards

Provide interactive browser-based collection of content from other OBI EE components such as Answers. This content can include guided analytics to help less-sophisticated business users explore the right additional information available.

Answers

Thin client (DHTML) interactive tool for generating ad hoc queries and analysis. Answers can be used directly against relational databases and MOLAP data stores. Generated reports can be posted to the dashboard or serve as input to BI Publisher.

Reporting and Publishing (BI Publisher)

Template-based publishing solution that incorporates XML data extracts and produces reports in various output formats including PDF, RTF, HTML, Excel, XML, and eText. Report editors include popular desktop tools such as Adobe Acrobat and Microsoft Word.

Delivers

Infrastructure built by defining "iBot" alerts that trigger based on user-specified conditions. Delivers can set up publish-and-subscribe mechanisms to email, dashboard alerts, SMS text messaging, and other such notifications. It can also be linked to business process flows generated using Oracle's Business Process Execution Language (BPEL).

Disconnected Analytics

Enables a business analyst to leverage the suite of tools disconnected from the network by accessing local data on a laptop. Resynchronization occurs when the analyst reconnects to his network.

Office Plug-in

Supports access to the BI Server from popular Microsoft tools such as Excel.

BI Server

Middle-tier for the previously described components that provides a business model and extraction layer, caching services, calculation and integration engine, and optimized data access into supported sources. Supported databases include the Oracle database and Oracle OLAP Option (analytic workspaces), Microsoft SQL Server and Analysis Services, IBM DB2, Teradata, and other ODBC sources. Other sources can include Oracle Business Intelligence (BI) Applications, PeopleSoft EPM, E-Business Suite, Siebel, Fusion Business Intelligence Applications, and SAP.

BI Server Administrator

Used in managing the presentation layer, business model and mapping, and physical layer defined in the BI Server. Business analyst and user access and groupings are configured through this tool.

In the OBI EE Plus packaging, Hyperion components were added; these include the Hyperion Foundation Services, Interactive Reporting, SQR production reporting, Financial Reporting, Smartview for Office, and Web Analysis.

Figure 10-5 illustrates a typical query formulation using Answers in the OBI EE Suite.

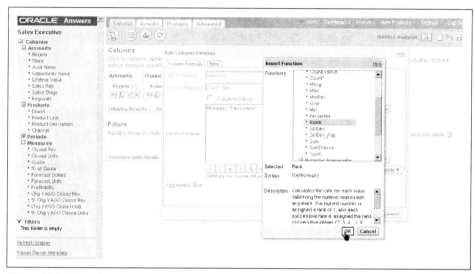

Figure 10-5. Typical query using Answers to produce ranked results

Figure 10-6 illustrates the query output as viewed in Answers.

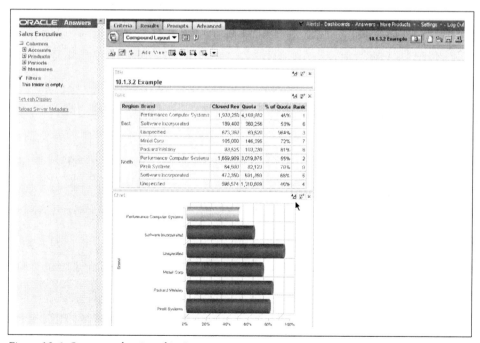

Figure 10-6. Query results viewed in Answers

The Oracle Business Intelligence Standard Edition One packaging includes a subset of the above and is intended for small and medium-sized implementations (e.g., deployed on a maximum of two CPUs or four cores and supporting from 5 to 50 users). Components include Oracle Dashboards, Answers, BI Publisher, BI Server, and BI Server Administrator. In addition, OBI SE One includes the Oracle Database Standard Edition One and Oracle Warehouse Builder.

Oracle's previous-generation business intelligence tools, targeting Oracle databases only, are bundled in the Oracle Business Intelligence Standard Edition (OBI EE SE) and in the Oracle Application Server. The tools include the following:

Discoverer Plus

> Easy-to-use Java applet-based frontend for picking and choosing data items used in building queries by business users. Discoverer is designed to access Oracle relational databases and the Oracle OLAP Option (analytic workspaces). Users can generate their own reports and deploy them to the Web as HTML files. Discoverer has a query governor that can predict the amount of time a query will take based on comparisons in records of previous queries kept in the database server.

Discoverer Viewer

> Thin client used most often to view Discoverer reports. It provides a subset of the functionality of Discoverer Plus.

Discoverer Portlet Provider

> Used for embedding Discoverer reports into enterprise portal solutions such as Oracle Portal.

Discoverer Administration Edition

> Used for managing the Discoverer End User Layer (EUL), maintaining business areas and mapping relevant database tables and views, and controlling tasks available to business analysts and users.

Reports

> Wizard-based frontend for building reports that can then be deployed to the Web for access as Adobe Acrobat, plain text, or HTML files. With this tool, you can cache reports on a middle-tier server for better performance. The tool also provides some limited drill-down search capabilities, in which a user can ask for more detail about a particular portion of a report.

Oracle has enterprise portal offerings (Oracle Portal, and more recently WebCenter) available as part of the Oracle Application Server. These provide an integration point for custom-built business intelligence applications using Oracle Business Intelligence tools. For example, Answers can publish portlets to an enterprise portal via the JSR specification. An enterprise portal can also provide access to a number of other applications and web sites through its interface, and it is highly customizable by users.

OLAP and OLAP Applications Building

As business users become more sophisticated, their questions evolve from "what happened" to "what trends are present and what might happen in the future?" *OLAP tools* provide the ability to handle time-series and mathematical analysis for understanding past trends and forecasting the future.

OLAP initially grew around the early inability of relational databases to effectively handle multidimensional queries (described previously in the section "Data Warehouse Design"). This led to OLAP tools packaged with their own data "cubes" where data is downloaded from relational sources into the cubes.

These separate database engines are called Multidimensional Online Analytical Processing engines, or *MOLAP engines*. Examples include Oracle's Express Server and Oracle's Hyperion Essbase, as well as the Microsoft Analysis Services. Such MOLAP engines handle queries extremely quickly and work best when the data is not updated frequently (because the cube-generation process takes time). Oracle's Essbase offering provides a MOLAP engine that can be used in conjunction with a variety of relational database engines.

OLAP functionality became more common in relational databases since star schema containing summary levels are supported to various degrees in many databases and because there is an increased need for very frequently updated data. When used in this fashion, the interaction is called *ROLAP*, which stands for Relational Online Analytical Processing. Tools that can work against either relational databases or MOLAP engines are sometimes referred to as *hybrid tools*. For ROLAP deployment, Oracle's Business Intelligence tools and several other tools can leverage ANSI standard analytic functions built into the database as SQL extensions and can also access the OLAP Option, a MOLAP cube within the relational database, via SQL.

Oracle Database 11g significantly improved the flexibility of accessing the Oracle database OLAP Option. Although queries were accessible via SQL in the past, business users needed to specifically point their queries to OLAP Option cubes. When deployed in Oracle Database 11g, the OLAP cubes can be used transparently as an alternative to materialized views since Oracle's SQL query rewrite recognizes the cubes. The materialized view refresh can refresh OLAP cubes as of Oracle Database 11g.

OLAP Option cubes are deployed in what are called *analytic workspaces*. They can be created using Oracle Warehouse Builder or using a simplified logical dimensional modeling tool called the Analytic Workspace Manager (AWM). Both tools provide interfaces for creation of the cubes and for building maps from relational tables into the cubes.

Custom OLAP applications can be built using Oracle's JDeveloper and *business intelligence beans*, although this is much less common than using off-the-shelf tools.

The Java beans provide prebuilt components for manipulating tables, crosstabs, and graphs and for building queries and calculations similar to the functionality previously found in Express. JDeveloper generates Java code utilizing these building blocks that maps to the Java OLAP API provided by Oracle's OLAP Option.

Data Mining

Data mining, an often overused and misunderstood term in data warehousing, is the use of mathematical algorithms to model relationships in the data that wouldn't be apparent by using other tools. Most companies shouldn't approach data mining unless analysts have met the following criteria:

- An understanding of the quality and meaning of the data in the warehouse.
- Business insight gained using other tools and the warehouse.
- An understanding of a business issue being driven by too many variables to model outcomes in any other way.

In other words, data-mining tools are not a replacement for the analytical skills of data warehouse users.

The data-mining tools themselves can rely on a number of techniques to produce the relationships, such as:

- Extended statistical algorithms, provided by statistical tools vendors, that can highlight statistical variations in the data.
- Clustering techniques that show how business outcomes can fall into certain groups, such as insurance claims versus time for various age brackets. In this example, once a low-risk group is found or classified, further research into influencing factors or "associations" might take place.
- Logic models (if A occurs, then B or C are possible outcomes) validated against small sample sets and then applied to larger data models for prediction, commonly known as *decision trees*.
- Neural networks "trained" against small sets, with known results to be applied later against a much larger set.
- Anomaly detection used to detect outliers and rare events.
- Visualization techniques used to graphically plot variables and understand which variables are key to a particular outcome.

Data mining is often used to solve difficult business problems such as fraud detection and churn in micro-opportunity marketing, as well as in other areas where many variables can influence an outcome. Companies servicing credit cards use data mining to track unusual usage—for example, the unexpected charging to a credit card of expensive jewelry in a city not normally traveled to by the cardholder. Discovering clusters of unusual buying patterns within certain small groups might also drive micro-opportunity marketing campaigns aimed at small audiences with a high probability of purchasing products or services.

A recent trend among relational database providers is tighter integration of data-mining algorithms into the relational database. Oracle's data-mining strategy initially included a client/server product called Oracle Darwin to provide algorithms for modeling associations, neural networks, classification and regression trees, and clusters against Oracle tables or flat files. Oracle began to embed algorithms packaged as the Data Mining Option into the Oracle9*i* database. Algorithms now in the Data Mining Option include Naïve Bayes, Associations, Adaptive Bayes Networks, Clustering, Support Vector Machines (SVM), Nonnegative Matrix Factorization (NMF), Decision Trees, and Generalized Linear Models (as of Oracle Database 11g, supporting Binary Logistic Regression and Multivariate Linear Regression). The algorithms are accessible via Java and PL/SQL APIs. Other data mining capabilities available include text mining (providing document clustering and classification) and BLAST similarity searches leveraging the SVM algorithms (common in genetic research).

Data mining applications can be custom-built using Oracle's Data Miner tool. Data Miner is used to develop, test, and score the models. Generally, the data must first be prepared for mining by binning, normalizing, and adjusting for missing values. The Data Mining Option in Oracle Database 11g added the capability to automate this data preparation process in the database. Data Miner provides the ability to define metadata, tune the generated Java code, view generated XML files, and test application components. Data-mining analysts can also use tools such as InforSense or SPSS Clementine to build models that leverage the Oracle Data Mining Option algorithms and manage the development process.

Business Intelligence Applications

Business intelligence applications are prebuilt solutions providing extended reporting and "dashboard-like" interfaces to display business trends. These applications directly access OLTP schema (Oracle's Daily Business Intelligence) or more commonly access solutions with infrastructure similar to traditional data warehouses. Examples of product suites that take the latter approach include Oracle Business Intelligence Applications, PeopleSoft EPM, and SAP's Business Warehouse, all often deployed on Oracle databases.

The business intelligence applications often focus on specific areas of the business, such as marketing or financial analysis. For example, Oracle's Hyperion Financial Performance Management applications address financial planning and budgeting. Such applications include predefined queries, reports, and charts that deliver the kind of information required for a particular type of business analysis while sparing the business user the complexity of creating these objects from scratch. The data warehousing type of solutions also include prebuilt ETL from supported data sources.

Oracle E-Business Suite's Daily Business Intelligence (DBI) provides access into Oracle transactions tables and materialized views. Access is through prebuilt Oracle Business Intelligence workbooks containing prepopulated business metadata. The most recent Oracle toolset supported is OBI EE. Oracle DBI modules include Compliance, Customer Support, Financials, Human Resources, Procurement, Product Lifecycle, Projects, Marketing, Maintenance, Sales, Supply Chain, and others.

Oracle Business Intelligence Applications include more than 2500 KPIs in OBI EE and prebuilt mappings for ETL from Siebel, Oracle E-Business Suite, PeopleSoft, SAP, and other applications. Formerly known as the Siebel Analytics applications, the applications cover the areas of Sales, Service and Contact Center, Marketing, Financial, Supply Chain, and Workforce. Oracle Business Intelligence Applications have been designated as Oracle's flagship business intelligence horizontal applications offering. As such, Oracle is continuing to extend the KPIs provided, the ETL mappings, and the business areas covered.

The PeopleSoft EPM offering includes more than 1,200 metrics with prebuilt mappings from PeopleSoft and JD Edwards applications. EPM packaged warehouses include Human Capital Management, Financials, Campus Solutions, Supply Chain, and Customer Relationship Management. These applications also support OBI EE as a frontend tool.

The promise of such prebuilt solutions is that they provide easier-to-deploy solutions with more out-of-the-box functionality. While some customization will probably always be needed, the time required to deploy an initial and useful solution can be substantially reduced.

The Metadata Challenge

On the one hand, *metadata*—or descriptive data about data—is incredibly important. Virtually all types of interactions with a database require the use of metadata, from datatypes of the data to business meaning and history of data fields.

On the other hand, metadata is useful only if the tools and clients who wish to use it can leverage it. One of the great challenges is to create a set of common metadata definitions that allows tools and databases from different vendors to interact.

There have been a number of attempts to reach an agreement on common metadata definitions. In 2000, a standard was ratified that defines a common interface for interchange of metadata implementations. Named the Common Warehouse Metadata Interchange (CWMI) by the Object Management Group (OMG), this standard is based on XML interchange. Oracle was one of the early proponents and developers of the technology in this standard. For example, Oracle has a CWM bridge for exchanging metadata stored in the Oracle Warehouse Builder repository. OWB also includes a metadata viewer for more detailed metadata reports, and a viewer for data lineage and impact analysis diagrams.

As noted earlier in this chapter, an emerging complementary solution—one in which ETL into a single data warehouse is not the entire solution—is the leveraging of master data management and data hub solutions. Today, most organizations are still a long way from consolidated metadata, and when they have tried to do this as an IT best-practice project, they generally have not been successful. Such projects are usually adopted only when delivered within a business intelligence project that delivers business value.

Best Practices

Those experienced in business intelligence generally agree that the following are typical reasons why these projects fail:

Failure to involve business users, IT representatives, sponsoring executives, and anyone else with a vested interest throughout the project process
Not only do all of these groups provide valuable input for creating a business intelligence solution, but lack of support by any of them can cause a project to fail.

Overlooking the key reasons for the business intelligence infrastructure
During the planning stages, IT architects can lose sight of the forces driving the creation of the solution.

Overlooked details and incorrect assumptions
A less-than-rigorous examination of the environment can doom the project to failure.

Unrealistic time frames and scope
As with all projects, starting the creation of a business intelligence solution with too short a time frame and too aggressive a scope will force the team to cut corners, resulting in the mistakes previously mentioned.

Failure to manage expectations
Data warehouses and business intelligence solutions, like all technologies, are not a panacea. You must make sure that all members of the team, as well as the eventual users of the solution, have an appropriate set of expectations.

Tactical decision-making at the expense of long-term strategy
Although it may seem overly time-consuming at the start, you must keep in mind the long-term goals of your project, and your organization, throughout the design and implementation process. Failing to do so has two results: it delays the onset of problems, but it also increases the likelihood and severity of those problems.

Failure to leverage the experience of others
There's nothing like learning from those who have succeeded on similar projects. It's almost as good to gain from the experience of others who have failed at similar tasks; at least you can avoid the mistakes that led to their failures.

Successful business intelligence projects require the continuous involvement of business analysts and users, sponsoring executives, and IT. Ignoring this often-repeated piece of advice is probably the single biggest cause of many of the most spectacular failures. Establishing this infrastructure has to produce a clear business benefit and an identifiable return on investment (ROI). Executives are key throughout the process because business intelligence coordination often crosses departmental boundaries, and funding likely comes from high levels.

Your business intelligence project should provide answers to business problems that are linked to key business initiatives. Ruthlessly eliminate any developments that take projects in another direction. The motivation behind the technology implementation schedule should be the desire to answer critical business questions. Positive ROI from the project should be demonstrated during the incremental building process.

Common Misconceptions

Having too simplistic a view during any part of the building process (a view that overlooks details) can lead to many problems. Here are just a few of the typical (and usually incorrect) assumptions people make in the process of implementing a business intelligence solution:

- Sources of data are clean and consistent.
- Someone in the organization understands what is in the source databases, the quality of the data, and where to find items of business interest.
- Extractions from operational sources can be built and discarded as needed, with no records left behind.
- Summary data is going to be adequate, and detailed data can be left out.
- IT has all the skills available to manage and develop all the necessary extraction routines, tune the database(s), maintain the systems and the network, and perform backups and recoveries in a reasonable time frame.
- Development is possible without continuous feedback and periodic prototyping involving analysts and possibly sponsoring executives.
- The warehouse won't change over time, so "versioning" won't be an issue.
- Analysts will have all the skills needed to make full use of the infrastructure or the business intelligence tools.
- IT can control what tools the analysts select and use.
- The number of users is known and predictable.
- The kinds of queries are known and predictable.
- Computer hardware is infinitely scalable, regardless of choices made.

- If a business area builds a data mart or deploys an appliance independently, IT won't be asked to support it later.
- Consultants will be readily available in a pinch to solve last-minute problems.
- Metadata or master data is not important, and planning for it can be delayed.

Effective Strategy

Most software and implementation projects have difficulty meeting schedules. Because of the complexity in business intelligence projects, they frequently take much longer than the initial schedule, and that is exactly what executives who need the information to make vital strategic decisions don't want to hear! If you build in increments implementing working prototypes along the way, the project can begin showing positive return on investment, and changes in the subsequent schedule can be linked back to real business requirements, not just back to technical issues (which executives don't ordinarily understand).

You must avoid scope creep and expectations throughout the project. When you receive recommended changes or additions from the business side, you must confirm that these changes provide an adequate return on investment or you will find yourself working long and hard on facets of the infrastructure without any real payoff. The business reasoning must be part of the prioritization process; you must understand why trade-offs are made. If you run into departmental "turf wars" over the ownership of data, you'll need to involve key executives for mediation and guidance.

The pressure of limited time and skills and immediate business needs sometimes leads to making tactical decisions in establishing a data warehouse at the expense of a long-term strategy. In spite of the pressures, you should create a long-term strategy at the beginning of the project and stick to it, or at least be aware of the consequences of modifying it. There should be just enough detail to prevent wasted efforts along the way, and the strategy should be flexible enough to take into account business acquisitions, mergers, and so on.

Your long-term strategy must embrace emerging trends, such as the need to meet compliance initiatives or the need for highly available solutions. The rate of change and the volume of products being introduced sometimes make it difficult to sort through what is real and what is hype. Most companies struggle with keeping up with the knowledge curve. Traditional sources of information include vendors, consultants, and data-processing industry consultants, each of which usually has a vested interest in selling something. The vendors want to sell products; the consultants want to sell skills they have "on the bench," and IT industry analysts may be reselling their favorable reviews of vendors and consultants to those same vendors and consultants. Any single source can lead to wrong conclusions, but by talking to multiple sources, some consensus should emerge and provide answers to your questions.

The best place to gain insight is discussing business intelligence projects with other similar companies—at least at the working-prototype stage—at conferences. Finding workable solutions and establishing a set of contacts to network with in the future can make attendance at these conferences well worth the price—and can be more valuable than the topics presented in the standard sessions.

CHAPTER 11

Oracle and High Availability

The data stored in your databases is one of your organization's most valuable assets. Protecting and providing timely access to this data when it is needed for business decisions is crucial for any Oracle site.

As a DBA, system administrator, or system architect, you'll probably use a variety of techniques to ensure that your data is adequately protected from catastrophe. Of course, implementing proper backup operations is the foundation of any availability strategy, but there are other ways to avoid a variety of possible outages that could range from simple disk failures to a complete failure of your primary site.

Computer hardware is, by and large, extremely reliable, and that can tempt you to postpone thinking about disaster recovery and high availability. Most software is also very reliable, and the Oracle database protects the integrity of the data it holds even in the event of software failure. However, hardware and software will fail occasionally. The more components involved, the greater the likelihood of downtime at the worst time.

The difference between inconvenience and disaster is often the presence or absence of adequate recovery plans. This chapter should help you understand all of the options available when deploying Oracle so you can choose the best approach for your site.

With Oracle, you can guarantee that your precious data is highly available by leveraging built-in capabilities such as instance recovery or options such as Real Application Clusters. However, equally important in deploying a high-availability solution is the implementation of the appropriate procedures to safeguard your data. This chapter covers these various aspects of high availability.

What Is High Availability?

Before we can begin a discussion of how to ensure a high level of availability for your data, you need to understand the exact meaning of the term *availability*.

Availability can mean different things for different organizations. For this discussion, we'll consider a system to be available when it is *up* (meaning that the database can be accessed by users) and *working* (meaning that the database is delivering the expected functionality to business users at the expected performance).

Most businesses depend on data availability. More recently, accessibility to data via web-based solutions means that database failures can have an even more dramatic impact on business. Failures of such systems accessed by a wider community outside of company boundaries are, unfortunately, immediately and widely visible and can seriously impact a company's financial health and image. Consider the web-based customer service provided by package shipping companies that enable customers to perform package tracking. As these customers come to depend on such service, interruptions in that service can cause these same customers to move to competitors.

Taking this a step further, consider complexities in accessing data that resides in multiple systems. Integrating multiple systems can increase chances of single failure and could cause access to an entire supply chain to be unavailable.

To implement databases that are highly available, you must design an infrastructure that can mitigate downtime, such as by deploying redundant hardware. You must also embrace techniques that allow recovery from disasters, such as by implementing appropriate backup routines.

Measuring and Planning Availability

Most organizations initially assume that they need data access 24/7, meaning that the system must be available 24 hours a day, 7 days a week. Quite often, this requirement is stated with little examination of the business functions the system must support. As the cost of technology components declines and reliability increases, many feel that achieving very high levels of availability should be simple and cheap.

Unfortunately, while many components are becoming cheaper and more reliable, component availability doesn't equate to system availability. The complex layering of hardware and software in today's two- and three-tier systems introduces multiple interdependencies and points of failure. Achieving very high levels of availability for a system with varied and interdependent components is not usually simple or inexpensive.

To provide some perspective, consider Table 11-1, which translates the percentage of system availability into days, minutes, and hours of annual downtime based on a 365-day year.

Table 11-1. System availability

% availability	System downtime per year		
	Days	Hours	Minutes
95.000	18	6	0
96.000	14	14	24
97.000	10	23	48
98.000	7	7	12
99.000	3	16	36
99.500	1	20	48
99.900	0	9	46
99.990	0	1	53
99.999	0	0	5

Large-scale systems that achieve over 99 percent availability can cost millions of dollars to design and implement and can have correspondingly high ongoing operational costs. Marginal increases in availability can require large incremental investments in system components. Moving from 95 to 99 percent availability is likely to be costly, while moving from 99 to 99.99 percent will probably be costlier still.

Another key aspect of measuring availability is the definition of *when* the system must be available. A required availability of 99 percent of the time during normal working hours (e.g., from 8 a.m. to 5 p.m.) is very different from 99 percent availability based on a 24-hour day. In the same way that you must carefully define your required levels of availability, you must also consider the hours during which availability is measured. For example, a lot of companies take orders during "normal" business hours. The cost of an unavailable order-entry system is very high during the business day, but drops significantly after hours. Thus, scheduled downtime can make sense after hours that will, in turn, help reduce unplanned failures during business hours. Of course, in some multinational companies and the world of the Internet, a global reach implies that the business day never ends.

That initial requirement that a system be available 24/7 must be put in the context of the cost in deploying and maintaining such a system. An examination of the complexity and cost of very high availability will sometimes lead to compromises reducing goals and budgets for system availability.

The costs of achieving high availability are certainly justified in some cases. It might cost a brokerage house millions of dollars for each hour that key systems are down. A less-demanding business, such as catalog sales, might lose only thousands of dollars an hour by using a less-efficient manual system that acts as a stopgap measure. But, regardless of the cost of lost business opportunity, an unexpected loss of availability can cut into the productivity of employees and IT staff alike.

Causes of Unplanned Downtime

There are many different causes of unplanned downtime. You can prevent some very easily, while others require significant investments in site infrastructure, telecommunications, hardware, software, and skilled employees. Figure 11-1 summarizes some of the more common causes of system failures.

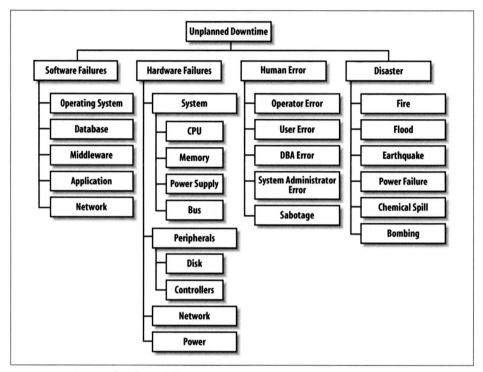

Figure 11-1. Causes of unplanned downtime

When creating a plan to guarantee the availability of your application, you should consider all of the items shown in this chart as well as other potential causes of system interruption that are specific to your own circumstances. As with all planning, it's much better to consider all options, even if you quickly dismiss them, than to be caught off guard when an unexpected event occurs.

System Availability Versus Component Availability

A complete system is composed of hardware, software, and networking components operating as a technology *stack*. Ensuring the availability of individual components doesn't necessarily guarantee system availability. Different strategies and solutions exist for achieving high availability for each of the system components. Figure 11-2 illustrates the technology stack used to deliver a potential system.

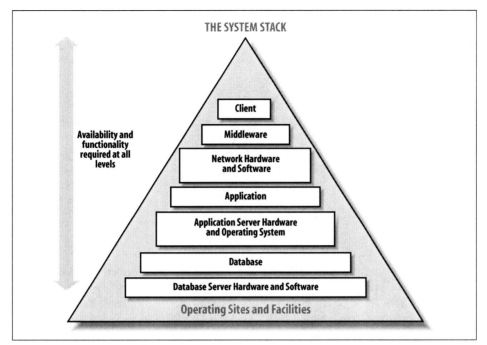

Figure 11-2. Components of a system

As this figure shows, a variety of physical and logical layers must cooperate to deliver an application. Some systems may involve fewer components; for example, a two-tier client/server system would not have the additional application server components.

Failures in the components above the database can effectively prevent access to the database even though the database itself may be available. The database server and the database itself serve as the foundation for the stack. When a database fails, it immediately affects the higher levels of the stack. If the failure results in lost or corrupted data, the overall integrity of the application may be affected.

The potential threats to availability span all of the components involved in an application system, but in this chapter we'll examine only availability issues relating specifically to the database.

System Failure

The abrupt failure of the server machine running the database is one of the most common causes of unplanned downtime. A server may crash because of hardware problems, such as the failure of a power supply, or because of software problems, such as a process that begins to consume all the machine's CPU resources. Even if the underlying server platform is fine, the Oracle instance itself can fail. Whatever the cause of the crash, the effect on Oracle is the same—the instance cannot deliver its promised functionality. Remember that when an Oracle database crashes, it is the instance that crashes, not the database (as described in Chapter 2). Even if the system fails, the failure will not imperil any data that's already safely stored within the disk files used by the Oracle database.

The impact of a crash will depend on the activity in progress at the time of the crash. Any connected sessions will no longer have a server process to which to talk. All active queries and transactions will be abruptly terminated. The process of cleaning up the resulting mess is called *instance recovery* or *crash recovery*.

Telltale Error Messages

The following two error messages are often good indicators that an Oracle instance is down:

```
ORA-03113: End-of-file on communication channel
```

This message is usually received by clients that try to resubmit an operation that failed due to an instance failure. The message is somewhat cryptic but becomes clear if you interpret it very literally. Oracle works using a pipe to communicate between the client application and its associated server process in the Oracle instance. When the instance fails, the client's server process ceases to exist, so there is no one listening on the other end of the pipe. The communication channel between the client and the server is no longer valid.

```
ORA-01034: Oracle not available
```

This terse message means that when the client requested a connection to the Oracle instance, the instance was not there. Clients that try to connect to a failed instance will typically get this message. The client can connect to the Listener, but when the Listener attempts to hand the client off to the requested Oracle instance, the ORA-01034 condition results.

What Is Instance Recovery?

When you restart an Oracle instance after a failure, Oracle detects that a crash occurred using information in the control file and the headers of the database files. Oracle then performs instance recovery automatically and uses the online redo logs to guarantee that the physical database is restored to a consistent state as it existed at the time of the crash. This includes two actions:

- All committed transactions will be recovered.
- In-flight transactions will be rolled back or undone.

Note that an in-flight transaction might be one that a user didn't commit or one that was committed by the user but not confirmed by Oracle before the system failure. A transaction isn't considered committed until Oracle has written the relevant details of the transaction to the current online redo log and has sent back a message to the client application confirming the committed transaction.

Phases of Instance Recovery

Instance recovery has two phases: rollforward and rollback.

Recovering an instance requires the use of the redo logs, described in Chapter 2. The redo logs contain a recording of all the physical changes made to the database as a result of transactional activity, both committed and uncommitted.

 The introduction of delayed redo log writes for committed transactions as an option in Oracle Database 11g could create a scenario where a transaction appears to have been committed but could still not be recovered.

The checkpoint concept, also described in Chapter 2, is critical to understanding crash recovery. When a transaction is committed, Oracle writes all associated database block changes to the current online redo log. The actual database blocks may have already been flushed to disk, or may be flushed at some later point. This means that the online redo log can contain changes not yet reflected in the actual database blocks stored in the datafiles. Oracle periodically ensures that the data blocks in the datafiles on disk are synchronized with the redo log to reflect all the committed changes up to a point in time. Oracle does this by writing all the database blocks changed by those committed transactions to the datafiles on disk. This operation is called a *checkpoint*. Completed checkpoints are recorded in the control file, datafile headers, and redo log.

Rollforward

At any point in time, the online redo logs will be ahead of the datafiles by a certain amount of time or number of committed transactions. Instance recovery closes this gap and ensures that the datafiles reflect all committed transactions up to the time the instance crashed. Oracle performs instance recovery by rolling forward through the online redo log and replaying all the changes from the last completed checkpoint to the time of instance failure. This operation is called the *rollforward* phase of instance recovery.

While implementing rollforward recovery, Oracle reads the necessary database blocks into the System Global Area and reproduces the changes that were originally applied to the blocks. This process includes reproducing the undo or rollback information, in addition to the data changes. Rollback segments are composed of extents and data blocks just like tables, and all changes to rollback segment blocks are part of the redo for a given transaction. For example, suppose that a user changed an employee name from "John" to "Jonathan." As Oracle applies the redo log, it will read the block containing the employee row into the cache and redo the name change. As part of recovering the transaction, Oracle will also write the old name "John" to a rollback segment, as was done for the original transaction.

When the rollforward phase is finished, all the changes for committed and uncommitted transactions have been reproduced. The uncommitted transactions are in-flight once again, just as they were at the time the crash occurred. This leads to the next logical phase of instance recovery—rollback. But before we discuss rollbacks themselves, we need to look at how Oracle uses checkpoints and how the timing of checkpoints can affect recovery time.

Fast-start fault recovery and bounded recovery time

Checkpoints cause an increase in I/O since the database writer flushes all the database blocks to disk to bring the datafiles up to the time of the checkpoint. Prior to Oracle8, DBAs controlled checkpoint frequency by setting the initialization file parameters LOG_CHECKPOINT_INTERVAL (number of redo blocks between checkpoints) and LOG_CHECKPOINT_TIMEOUT (in seconds) and setting the size of the redo log files. In addition, Oracle always performs a checkpoint whenever a log file switch occurs.

Reducing the checkpoint interval or timeout would result in smaller amounts of data between checkpoints and lead to faster recovery times, but could also introduce the overhead of more frequent checkpoints and their associated disk activity. A common strategy for minimizing the number of checkpoints was to set the initialization file parameters so that checkpoints would occur only with log switches.

Oracle8i introduced an initialization file parameter to provide a simpler and more accurate way to control recovery times: FAST_START_IO_TARGET. The bulk of recovery activity involves performing I/O for reading database blocks into the cache so that redo can be applied to them. This parameter set a target ceiling on how many database blocks Oracle would have to read in applying redo information. Oracle would dynamically vary the checkpoint frequency in an attempt to limit the number of blocks that will need to be read for recovery to the value of this parameter.

Oracle9i further sped this recovery process. Beginning at the last checkpoint, the redo log was scanned for data blocks that contain unsaved changes and need to be recovered. In the subsequent scan, changes are applied only where needed. Because the subsequent scan is a sequential read and reading unnecessary blocks (random I/O) is eliminated, the recovery time is reduced.

Oracle9i introduced an important fast-start time-based recovery feature. DBAs specify a target for recovery time in seconds (in the FAST_START_MTTR_TARGET initialization parameter, where MTTR stands for Mean Time to Recover) in order to meet Service Level Agreements and other requirements. The database automatically determines values for FAST_START_IO_TARGET and LOG_CHECKPOINT_ INTERVAL. Estimated MTTR values are calculated and placed in V$INSTANCE_ RECOVERY, thereby providing a means for real-world calibration and more accurate estimates over time.

Today, this is all much simpler through Fast-Start Fault Recovery. The Oracle database automatically bounds recovery time at startup using self-tuned checkpoint processing, first introduced in Oracle Database 10g.

Rollback improvements

The rollforward phase re-creates uncommitted transactions and their associated rollback information. These in-flight transactions must be rolled back to return to a consistent state.

In Oracle releases prior to Version 7.3, the database wasn't available until all uncommitted transactions rolled back. Although a DBA could control the checkpoint frequency and therefore control the time required for the rollforward phase of instance recovery, the number of uncommitted transactions at the time of the crash varied tremendously so the time needed for rollback could not really be accurately controlled or predicted. In a busy OLTP system, there are typically a fair number of in-flight transactions requiring rollback after a crash. This situation led to variable and unpredictable times for crash recovery.

The solution to this problem, *deferred rollback*, was introduced in Oracle 7.3. Oracle opens the database after the rollforward phase of recovery and performs the rollback of uncommitted transactions in the background. This process reduces database downtime and helps to reduce the variability of recovery times by deferring the rollback phase.

But what if a user's transaction begins working in a database block that contains some changes left behind by an uncommitted transaction? If this happens, the user's transaction will trigger a foreground rollback to undo the changes and will then proceed when rollback is complete. This action is transparent to the user—he doesn't receive error messages or have to resubmit the transaction.

Oracle8i further optimized the deferred rollback process by limiting the rollback triggered by a user transaction to the block in which the transaction is interested. For example, suppose there is a large uncommitted transaction that affected 500 database blocks. Prior to Oracle8i, the first user transaction that touched one of those 500 blocks would trigger a foreground rollback and absorb the overhead of rolling back the entire transaction. Leveraging fast-start rollback, the user's transaction would roll back only the changes to the block in which it was interested. New transactions would not have to wait for the complete rollback of large uncommitted transactions.

Today, rollback management is made simpler by automated features in the database. For example, as of Oracle Database 10g, automatic undo retention tuning occurs controlling the amount of undo information held in rollbacks. The Redo Logfile Size Advisor determines the optimal smallest redo logfile size based on the FAST_START_MTTR_TARGET setting and database statistics gathered.

Protecting Against System Failure

There are a variety of approaches you can take to help protect your system against the ill effects of system crashes and failures, including the following:

- Providing component redundancy
- Using Real Application Clusters
- Using Transparent Application Failover software services

Component Redundancy

As basic protection, the various hardware components that make up the database server itself must be fault-tolerant. *Fault-tolerance*, as the name implies, allows the overall hardware system to continue to operate even if one of its components fails. This, in turn, implies redundant components and the ability to detect component failure and seamlessly integrate the failed component's replacement. The major system components that should be fault-tolerant include the following:

- Disk drives
- Disk controllers
- CPUs
- Power supplies
- Cooling fans
- Network cards
- System buses

Disk failure is the largest area of exposure for hardware failure, since disks have the shortest mean times to failure of any of the components in a computer system. Disks also present the greatest variety of redundant solutions, so discussing that type of failure in detail should provide the best example of how high availability can be implemented with hardware.

Disk redundancy

Although the mean time to failure of an individual disk drive is very high, the ever-increasing number of disks used for today's very large databases results in more frequent failures. Protection from disk failure is usually accomplished using RAID

(Redundant Array of Inexpensive Disks) technology. The use of redundant storage has become common for systems of all sizes and types for two primary reasons: the real threat of disk failure and the proliferation of packaged, relatively affordable RAID solutions.

RAID technology uses one of two concepts to achieve redundancy:

Mirroring
> The actual data is duplicated on another disk in the system.

Striping with parity
> Data is striped on multiple disks, but instead of duplicating the data itself for redundancy, a mathematical calculation termed *parity* is performed on the data and the result is stored on another disk. You can think of parity as the sum of the striped data. If one of the disks is lost, you can reconstruct the data on that disk using the surviving disks and the parity data. The lost data represents the only unknown variable in the equation and can be derived. You can conceptualize this as a simple formula:
>
> ```
> A + B + C + D = E
> ```
>
> in which A–D are data striped across four disks and E is the parity data on a fifth disk. If you lose any of the disks, you can solve the equation to identify the missing component. For example, if you lose the B drive you can solve the formula as:
>
> ```
> B = E - A - C - D
> ```

There are a number of different disk configurations or types of RAID technology, which are formally termed *levels*. The basics of RAID technology were introduced in Chapter 7, but Table 11-2 summarizes the most relevant levels of RAID in a bit more detail, in terms of their cost, high availability, and the way Oracle uses each RAID level.

Which RAID Levels Should You Use with Oracle?

Some people say that you should never use RAID-5 for an Oracle database because of the degraded write performance of this level of RAID. RAID-1 and RAID-0+1 offer better performance, but at double the cost of disk storage. RAID-5 offers a cheaper and reasonable solution, provided that you can meet performance requirements despite the extra write overhead for maintaining parity data. Use these generic guidelines to help determine the appropriate uses of different RAID levels:

- Use RAID-1 for redo log files.
- Use RAID-5 for database files, provided that the write overhead is acceptable and adequate I/O is available.
- Use RAID-1 or RAID-0+1 for database files if RAID-5 write overhead is unacceptable.

Table 11-2. RAID levels relevant to high availability

Level	Disk configuration	Cost	Comments	Oracle usage
0	Simple striping, no redundancy	Same cost as unprotected storage.	The term RAID-0 is used to describe striping, which increases read and write throughput. However, this is not really RAID, as there is no actual redundancy.	Striping simplifies administration for Oracle datafiles. Suitable for all types of data for which redundancy isn't required.
1	Mirroring	Twice the cost of unprotected storage.	Same write performance as a single disk. Read performance may improve through servicing reads from both copies.	Lack of striping adds complexity of managing a larger number of devices for Oracle. Often used for redo logs, since the I/O for redo is typically relatively small sequential writes. Striped arrays are more suited to large I/Os or to multiple smaller, random I/Os.
0+1	Striping and mirroring	Twice the cost of unprotected storage.	Best of both worlds— striping increases read and write performance and mirroring for redundancy avoids "read-modify-write" overhead of RAID-5.	Same usage as RAID-0, but provides protection from disk failure.
5	Striping with rotating or distributed parity	Storage capacity is reduced by 1/N, where N is the number of disks in the array. For example, the storage is reduced by 20%, or 1/5 of the total disk storage, for a 5-disk array.	Parity data is spread across all disks, avoiding the potential bottleneck found in some other types of RAID arrays. Striping increases read performance. Maintaining parity data adds additional I/O, decreasing write performance. For each write, the associated parity data must be read, modified, and written back to disk. This is referred to as the "read-modify-write" penalty.	Cost-effective solution for all Oracle data except redo logs. Degraded write performance must be taken into account. Popular for reads where adequate I/O is provided. Write penalties may slow loads and index builds. Often avoided for high-volume OLTP due to write penalties. Some storage vendors, such as EMC, have proprietary solutions (RAID-S) to minimize parity overhead on writes.

Figure 11-3 illustrates the disk configurations for various RAID levels.

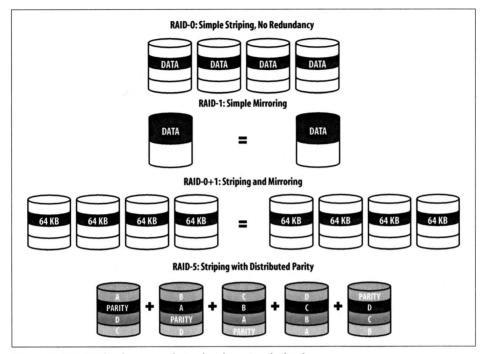

Figure 11-3. RAID levels commonly used with an Oracle database

Automatic Storage Management

Oracle Database 10g and more recent database releases include Automatic Storage Management (ASM). We introduced ASM in Chapter 5 and described its manageability considerations. ASM enables you to create a pool of storage on disk groups and then manages the placement of database files on the storage. ASM features enable it to replace non-Oracle file systems and logical volume managers for files managed by the Oracle database. An ASM instance manages each of the disks in the disk group, and one ASM instance is provided for each database node in a RAC environment.

ASM provides "Striping and Mirroring Everything" (SAME) for many types of disks, including "Just a Bunch of Disks" (JBOD) arrays. You can specify groups of disks, and designate a failure group to be used in the result of a disk failure. Mirroring can also be set up on a per-file basis, and you can specify one or two mirrors. ASM includes the ability to detect disk "hot spots" and redistribute data to avoid disk bottlenecks, as well as the capability of adding disks to a disk group without any interruption in service. DBAs add the disks to disk groups or remove disks from disk groups using Oracle Enterprise Manager.

Stored data is automatically rebalanced when disks are added or removed. When a drive fails, remirroring to remaining drives is automatic. These features make ASM ideal for managing a database storage grid and allow you to use cheaper disk systems while obtaining higher levels of availability and performance.

Oracle Database 11g introduced a fast mirror resynchronization capability enabling faster recovery from transient failures. ASM can now be set to only resynchronize changed ASM disk extents for limited duration failures.

Simple Hardware Failover

Oracle recovers automatically from a system crash. The automatic recovery protects data integrity, critical in a relational database, but also results in downtime as the database recovers from a crash. When a hardware failure occurs, the ability to quickly detect a system crash and initiate recovery is crucial to minimizing the associated downtime.

When an individual server fails, the instance running on that node fails as well. Depending on the cause, the failed node may not return to service quickly or be noticed immediately. Either way, companies that wish to protect their systems from the failure of a node typically employ a cluster of machines to achieve simple hardware *failover*. Failover is the ability of a surviving node in a cluster to assume the responsibilities of a failed node. Although failover doesn't directly address the issue of the reliability of the underlying hardware, automated failover can reduce the downtime from hardware failure.

The concept is very simple: a combination of software and hardware "watches" over the cluster. Typically, this monitoring is done by regularly checking a *heartbeat*, which is a message sent between machines in the cluster. If Machine A fails, Machine B will detect the failure through the loss of the heartbeat and will execute scripts to take over control of the disks, assume Machine A's network address, and restart the processes that failed with Machine A. From an Oracle database perspective, the entire set of events is identical to an instance crash followed by an instance recovery. The instance uses the control files, redo log files, and database files to perform crash recovery. The fact that the instance is now running on another machine is irrelevant—the various Oracle files on disk are the key.

Most failover solutions include software that runs on the machine to monitor specific processes, such as the background processes of the Oracle instance. If the primary node itself has not failed but some process has, the monitoring software will detect the failure of the process and take some action based on scripts set up by the system administrator. For example, if the Oracle instance fails, the monitoring software may attempt to restart the Oracle instance three times. If all three attempts are unsuccessful, the software may initiate physical hardware failover, transferring control to the alternate node in the cluster.

Figures 11-4 and 11-5 illustrate the process of implementing a simple failover.

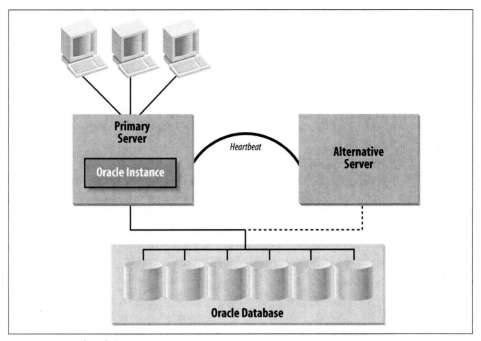

Figure 11-4. Before failover

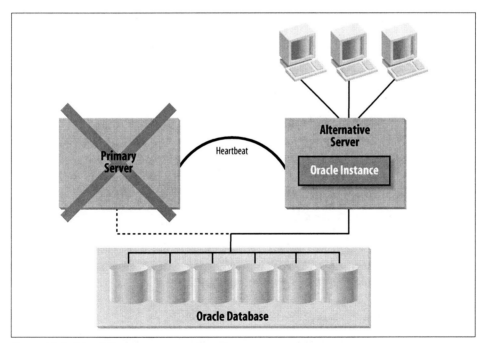

Figure 11-5. After failover

Outage duration for hardware failover

The time for failover to take effect, and therefore the length of the associated database downtime, depends on the following intervals:

Time for the alternate node to detect the failure of the primary node
> The alternate node monitors the primary node using a heartbeat mechanism. The frequency of this check is usually configurable—for example, every 30 seconds—providing control over the maximum time that a primary-node failure will go undetected.

Time for the alternate node to execute various startup actions
> The time needed for such actions (e.g., assuming control of the disks used to store the Oracle database) may vary by system and should be determined through testing. One important consideration is the time required for a filesystem check. The larger the database, the larger the number of filesystems that may have been used. When the alternate node assumes control of the disks, it must check the state of the various filesystems on the disks.

Time for Oracle crash recovery
> As we mentioned, you can effectively control this time period using checkpoints. Oracle provides a simple way to control recovery times using the initialization parameter FAST_START_IO_TARGET or the more recently introduced FAST_START_MTTR_TARGET parameter.

When the instance fails, users will typically receive some type of error message and will typically attempt to log in again. Application developers can deal with this sequence of failover events with generic or specific error handling in their applications, or they can use the Transparent Application Failover functionality described later in this chapter.

Failover and operating system platform

This type of failover capability has been available for many years. On Unix-based platforms, vendors typically offer a simple failover solution that includes two machines, a private network between them to monitor the heartbeat, shared disk, and cluster software. No additional software is required from Oracle.

On Windows, Oracle includes Fail Safe, software that provides a GUI interface for configuring the Oracle database for hardware failover that leverages Microsoft's Cluster Server. The mechanics of the failover are the same—a GUI is provided for administrative convenience. (In recent releases, the Fail Safe Manager and Real Applications Cluster Guard Manager have merged.)

Real Application Clusters

Oracle introduced Oracle Parallel Server (OPS), the predecessor to Real Application Clusters, in 1989 on Digital Equipment Corporation's VAX clusters running the

VMS operating system, and on Unix in 1993. OPS clusters were often deployed to assure a highly available database. Real Application Clusters followed, in Oracle9i, and was first made generally available in 2001.

At first glance, Real Application Clusters (RAC) may look similar to the clustered solutions described earlier in the "Simple Hardware Failover" section. Both failover and Real Application Clusters involve clustered hardware with access to disks from multiple nodes. The key difference is that with simple hardware failover only one node is an active instance. With RAC, the Oracle database is spread across multiple nodes and each node has an active Oracle instance. Clients can connect to any of the instances to access the same database.

Because each Oracle instance runs on its own node, if a node fails, the instance on that node also fails. The overall Oracle database remains available since surviving instances are still running on other working nodes.

Figure 11-6 illustrates Real Application Clusters on a cluster.

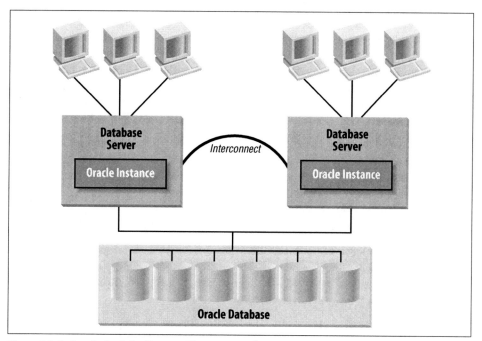

Figure 11-6. Oracle Real Application Clusters on a cluster

Real Application Clusters and hardware failover

The Real Application Clusters option can typically provide higher levels of availability than simple hardware failover. This option can also provide additional flexibility for scaling database applications across multiple machines, and manageability was simplified as of Oracle Database 10g when Enterprise Manager Grid Control was introduced.

Real Application Clusters increases availability by enabling avoidance of complete database blackouts. With simple hardware failover, the database is completely unavailable until node failover, instance startup, and crash recovery are complete. With RAC, clients can connect to a surviving instance any time. Clients may be able to continue working with no interruption, depending on whether the data they need to work on was under the control of the failed instance. You can think of the failure of a Real Application Clusters instance as a potential database "brownout," as opposed to the guaranteed blackout caused by hardware failover.

Some other key differences between hardware failover and Real Application Clusters include the following:

- The Real Application Clusters option avoids the various activities involved in disk takeover: mounting volumes, validating filesystem integrity, opening Oracle database files, and so on. Not performing these activities can significantly reduce the time required to achieve full system availability.

- The Real Application Clusters option doesn't require the creation and maintenance of the complex scripts typically used to control the activities for hardware failover. For example, there is no need to script which disk volumes will be taken over by a surviving node. The automatic nature of Real Application Clusters avoids the complex initial system administration to set up the failover environment, as well as the ongoing administration needed as additional disk volumes are used. In fact, adding disk volumes to your database but forgetting to add the volumes to the various failover scripts can cause a hardware failover solution to fail itself!

In a simple two-way cluster used for hardware failover, both machines should have equal processing power and should be sized so that each can handle the entire workload. This equivalence is clearly required since only one node of the cluster is used at any point for the entire workload. If one node fails, the other should be capable of running the same workload with equal performance.

With Real Application Clusters, you can use both nodes of the cluster concurrently to spread the workload, reducing the load on one machine or node. You must still make sure that each machine will be powerful enough to adequately handle the entire workload (albeit at a reduced performance level) to meet basic business requirements when a node is not available.

Of course, using Real Application Clusters to spread the workload over several machines will result in a lower percentage of each machine's resources being used in normal operating conditions, typically more expensive than using fully utilized machines. Each machine in the cluster must devote some overhead to maintaining its role in the cluster, although this overhead is minimal. You will have to weigh the benefits of carrying on with some performance degradation in the event of a node failure versus the cost of buying more nodes or more powerful machines. The economics of your situation may dictate that a decrease in performance in the event of a node failure is more palatable than a larger initial outlay for more nodes or larger systems.

Much of the complexity of tuning and programming for scalability has been removed since Oracle9i. Deployment was simplified in Oracle Database 10g when integrated clusterware was first introduced. Interested readers can find more details about Real Application Clusters scalability in the Oracle documentation and in Chapter 9 of this book.

Node failure and Real Application Clusters

The database instances provide protection for each other—if an instance fails, one of the surviving instances will detect the failure and automatically initiate RAC recovery. This type of recovery is different from the hardware failover discussed previously. No actual "failover" occurs—no disk takeover is required, since all nodes already have access to the disks used for the database. There is no need to start an Oracle instance on the surviving node or nodes, since Oracle is already running on all the nodes. The Oracle software performs the necessary actions without using scripts; the required steps are an integral part of Real Application Clusters software.

The phases of Real Application Clusters recovery are the following:

Cluster reorganization
> When an instance failure occurs, Real Application Clusters must first determine which nodes of the cluster remain in service. Oracle9i introduced a disk-based heartbeat in which each database group member votes on what members are part of the current group. Based on arbitration, a correct current group configuration is established. The time required for this operation is very brief.

Lock database rebuild
> The lock database, which contains the information used to coordinate Real Application Clusters traffic, is distributed across the multiple active instances. Therefore, a portion of that information is lost when a node fails. The remaining nodes have sufficient redundant data to reconstruct the lost information. Once the cluster membership is determined, the surviving instances reconstruct the lock database. The time for this phase depends on how many locks must be recovered, as well as whether the rebuild process involves a single surviving node or multiple surviving nodes. Oracle speeds the lock remastering process by allowing optimization of lock master locations in the background while users are accessing the system. In a two-node cluster, node failure leaves a single surviving node that acts as a dictator and processes the lock operations very quickly.

Instance recovery
> Once the lock database is rebuilt, the redo logs from the failed instance perform crash recovery. This is similar to single-instance crash recovery—a rollforward phase followed by a nonblocking, deferred rollback phase. The key difference is that the recovery isn't performed by restarting a failed instance. Rather, it's performed by the instance that detected the failure.

While Real Application Clusters recovery is in progress, clients connected to surviving instances remain connected and can continue working. In some cases users may experience a slight delay in response times, but their sessions aren't terminated. Clients connected to the failed instance can reconnect to a surviving instance and can resume working. Uncommitted transactions will be rolled back and will have to be resubmitted. Queries that were active will also have been terminated; however, Transparent Application Failover (TAF) can be used to automatically continue query processing on a surviving node without requiring users to resubmit their queries. You can also use TAF to resubmit transactions without user intervention.

Parallel Fail Safe/RACGuard

Oracle Parallel Fail Safe was renamed RACGuard in Oracle9*i* and integrated into the core RAC product in Oracle Database 10*g*. Prior to Oracle Database 10*g*, it was a feature in Real Application Clusters that leveraged the clustering software from systems vendors. As of Oracle Database 10*g*, the database includes a cluster filesystem.

RACGuard supported such features as:

- Automated, fast, and bounded recovery times from Oracle instance crashes
- Automatic capture of diagnostic data
- Guaranteed primary and secondary configuration
- Support for features such as Transparent Application Failover (described in the next section)
- Client preconnection to secondary instances to speed reconnection

Oracle Transparent Application Failover

Oracle introduced the Transparent Application Failover (TAF) capability in the first release of Oracle8. As the name implies, TAF provides a seamless migration of users' sessions from one Oracle instance to another. You can use TAF to mask the failure of an instance for transparent high availability or to migrate users from an active instance to a less active one. Figure 11-7 illustrates TAF with Real Application Clusters.

As shown in this figure, TAF can automatically reconnect clients to another instance of the database, which provides access to the same database as the original instance. The high-availability benefits of TAF include the following:

Transparent reconnection
> Clients don't have to manually reconnect to a surviving instance. You can optimally reconfigure TAF to preconnect clients to an alternate instance in addition to their primary instance when they log on. Preconnecting clients to an alternate instance removes the overhead of establishing a new connection when automatic

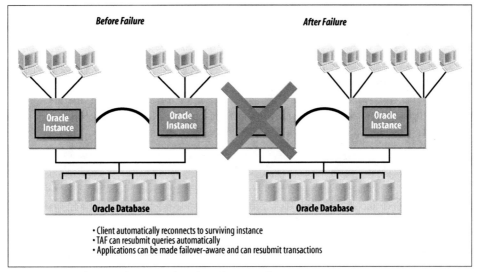

Figure 11-7. Failover with TAF and Real Application Clusters

failover takes place. For systems with a large number of connected clients, this preconnection avoids the overhead and delays caused by flooding the alternate instance with a large number of simultaneous connection requests.

Automatic resubmission of queries

TAF can automatically resubmit queries that were active at the time the first instance failed and can resume sending results back to the client. Oracle will reexecute the query as of the time the original query started. Oracle's read consistency will therefore provide the correct answer regardless of any activity since the query began. However, when the user requests the "next" row from a query, Oracle will have to process through all rows from the start of the query until the requested row, which may result in a performance lag.

Callback functions

Oracle8*i* enhanced TAF by enabling the application developer to register a "callback function" with TAF. Once TAF has successfully reconnected the client to the alternate instance, the registered function will be called automatically. The application developer can use the callback function to reinitialize various aspects of session state as desired.

Failover-aware applications

Application developers can leverage TAF by writing "failover-aware" applications that resubmit transactions that were lost when the client's primary instance failed, further reducing the impact of failure. Note that unlike query resubmission, TAF itself doesn't automatically resubmit the transactions that were in-flight. Rather, it provides a framework for a seamless failover that can be leveraged by application developers.

How TAF works

TAF is implemented in the Oracle Call Interface (OCI) layer, a low-level API for establishing and managing Oracle database connections. When the instance to which a client is connected fails, the client's server process ceases to exist. The OCI layer in the client can detect the absence of a server process on the other end of the channel and automatically establish a new connection to another instance. The alternate instance to which TAF reconnects users is specified in the Oracle Net configuration files, which are described in the Oracle Net documentation.

Because OCI is a low-level API, writing programs with OCI requires more effort and sophistication on the part of the developer. Fortunately, Oracle uses OCI to write client tools and various drivers, so that applications using these tools can leverage TAF. Support for TAF in ODBC and JDBC drivers is especially useful; it means that TAF can be leveraged by any client application that uses these drivers to connect to Oracle. For example, TAF can provide automatic reconnection for a third-party query tool that uses ODBC. To implement TAF with ODBC, set up an ODBC data source that uses an Oracle Net service name that is configured to use TAF in the Oracle Net configuration files. ODBC uses Oracle Net and can therefore leverage the TAF feature.

TAF and various Oracle configurations

Although the TAF-Real Application Clusters combination is the most obvious combination for high availability, TAF can be used with a single Oracle instance or with multiple databases, each accessible from a single instance. Some possible configurations are as follows:

- TAF can automatically reconnect clients back to their original instances for cases in which the instance failed but the node did not. An automated monitoring system, such as Oracle Enterprise Manager, can detect instance failure quickly and restart the instance. The fast-start recovery features in Oracle enable very low crash recovery times. Users that aren't performing heads-down data entry work can be automatically reconnected by TAF and might never be aware that their instance failed and was restarted.

- In simple clusters, TAF can reconnect users to the instance started by simple hardware failover on the surviving node of a cluster. The reconnection cannot occur until the alternate node has started Oracle and has performed crash recovery.

- When there are two distinct databases, each with a single instance, TAF can reconnect clients to an instance that provides access to a different database running in another data center. This clearly requires replication of the relevant data between the two databases. Oracle fortunately provides automated support for data replication, which is covered in the later section entitled "Complete Site Failure."

Recovering from Failures

Despite the prevalence of redundant or protected disk storage, media failures can and do occur. In cases in which one or more Oracle datafiles are lost due to disk failure, you must use database backups to recover the lost data.

There are times when simple human or machine error can also lead to the loss of data, just as a media failure can. For example, an administrator may accidentally delete a datafile, or an I/O subsystem may malfunction, corrupting data on the disks. The key to being prepared to handle these types of failures is implementing a good backup-and-recovery strategy and understanding the power of Oracle's newer features such as Flashback.

Developing a Backup-and-Recovery Strategy

Proper development, documentation, and testing of your backup-and-recovery strategy is one of the most important activities in implementing an Oracle database. You must test every phase of the backup-and-recovery process to ensure that the entire process works, because once a disaster hits, the complete recovery process *must* work flawlessly.

Some companies test the backup procedure but fail to actually test recovery using the backups taken. Only when a failure requires the use of the backups do companies discover that the backups in place were unusable for some reason. It's critical to test the entire cycle from backup through restore and recovery.

Taking Oracle Backups

Two basic types of backups are available with Oracle:

Hot backup
> The datafiles for one or more tablespaces are backed up while the database is active.

Cold backup
> The database is shut down and all the datafiles, redo log files, and control files are backed up.

With a hot backup, not all of the datafiles must be backed up at once. For instance, you may want to back up a different group of datafiles each night. You must be sure to keep backups of the archived redo logs that date back to your oldest backed-up datafile, since you'll need them if you have to implement rollforward recovery from the time of that oldest datafile backup.

Some DBAs with very large databases back up the various datafiles over several runs. Some DBAs back up the datafiles that contain data subject to frequent changes more frequently (for example, daily), and back up datafiles containing more static data less often (for example, weekly). There are commands to back up the control file as well; this should be done after all the datafiles have been backed up.

If the database isn't archiving redo logs (this is known as running in NOAR-CHIVELOG mode and is described in Chapter 2), you can take only complete cold backups. If the database is archiving redo logs, it can be backed up while running.

Regardless of backup type, you should also back up the *INIT.ORA* or *SPFILE* file and password files—these are key files for the operation of your Oracle database. While not required, you should also back up the various scripts used to create and further develop the database. These scripts represent an important part of the documentation of the structure and evolution of the database.

For more information about the different types of backups and variations on these types, please refer to your Oracle documentation as well as the third-party books listed in Appendix B.

Using Backups to Recover

Two basic types of recovery are possible with Oracle, based on whether or you are archiving the redo logs:

Complete database recovery
> If the database did not archive redo logs, only a complete cold backup is possible. Correspondingly, only a complete database recovery can be performed. You restore the database files, redo logs, and control files from the backup. The database is essentially restored as of the time of the backup. All work done since the time of the backup is lost and a complete recovery must be performed even if only one of the datafiles is damaged. The potential for lost work, coupled with the need to restore the entire database to correct partial failure, are reasons most shops avoid this situation by running their databases in ARCHIVELOG mode. Figure 11-8 illustrates backup and recovery for a database without archived redo logs.

Partial or targeted restore and rollforward recovery
> When you're running the Oracle database in ARCHIVELOG mode, you can restore only the damaged datafile(s) and can apply redo log information from the time the backup was taken to the point of failure. The archived and online redo logs reproduce all the changes to the restored datafiles to bring them up to the same point in time as the rest of the database. This procedure minimizes the time for the restore and recovery operations. Partial recovery like this can be done with the database down. Alternatively, the affected tablespace(s) can be placed offline and recovery can be performed with the rest of the database available. Oracle9*i* improved the granularity of the recovery process by also enabling restore and recovery of individual data blocks instead of providing restore and recovery only of entire datafiles. Figure 11-9 illustrates backup and recovery with archived redo logs.

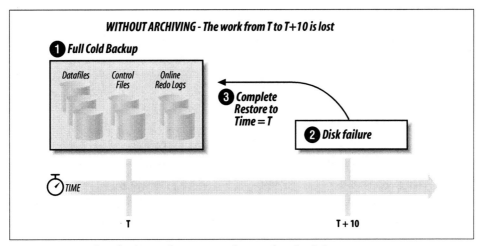

Figure 11-8. Database backup and recovery without archived redo logs

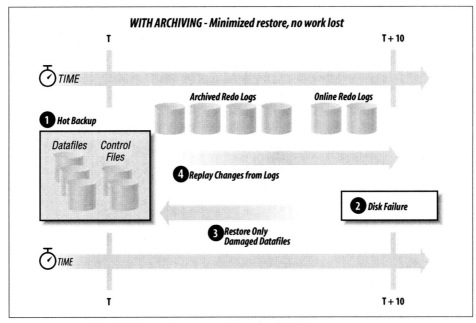

Figure 11-9. Database backup and recovery with archived redo logs

Obviously, the redo logs are extremely important. Oracle first enabled analysis of these files through the LogMiner tool in Oracle8*i*. Since Oracle9*i*, the LogMiner is accessible through an Oracle Enterprise Manager GUI, and it provides log analysis for all datatypes. If the redo log has become corrupted, the LogMiner can now read past corrupted records as desired in order to analyze the impact on transactions after the corruption.

Recovery Manager

Recovery Manager (RMAN), first available with Oracle8, provides server-managed online backup and recovery. RMAN does the following:

- Backs up one or more datafiles to disk or tape
- Backs up archived redo logs to disk or tape
- Restores datafiles from disk or tape
- Restores and applies archived redo logs to perform recovery
- Automatically parallelizes both the reading and writing of the various Oracle files being backed up

RMAN performs the backup operations and updates a catalog (stored in an Oracle database) with the details of what backups were taken and where they were stored. You can query this catalog for critical information, such as datafiles that have not been backed up or datafiles whose backups have been invalidated through NOLOGGING operations performed on objects contained in those datafiles.

RMAN also uses the catalog to perform incremental backups. RMAN will back up only database blocks that have changed since the last backup. When RMAN backs up only the individual changed blocks in the database, the overall backup and recovery time can be significantly reduced for databases in which a small percentage of the data in large tables changes. Since Oracle Database 10g, RMAN can apply incremental backups to an image backup of the database. Improvements in methods used by RMAN in recent Oracle releases have greatly enhanced performance for incremental backups.

RMAN reads and writes Oracle blocks, not operating system blocks. While RMAN is backing up a datafile, Oracle blocks can be written to it, but RMAN will read and write in consistent Oracle blocks, not operating system blocks within an Oracle block.

The following list summarizes the RMAN capabilities that enable high availability:

- Automated channel failover during backup and restore
- Automated failover to a previous backup during restore when the current backup is missing or corrupt
- Automated new database and temporary file creation during recovery
- Automated recovery to a previous point in time
- Block media recovery while the datafile is online
- Block change tracking for fast incremental backups
- Merged incremental backups
- Backup and restore of required files only

- Retention policy ensuring that relevant backups are available
- Resumable backup and restore if operations failed
- Automatic backup of the control file and server parameter file

Since Oracle Database 10g, RMAN is also used to support automated disk-based backup. Disk-based strategies have an advantage over tape: they enable random access to any data such that only changes need be backed up or recovered. RMAN can be set up to run a backup job to disk at a specific time. RMAN manages the deletion of backup files that are no longer necessary. In combination with ASM, RMAN will write all backups, archive logs, control file autobackups, and datafile copies to a designated disk group. The single storage location is referred to as the Flash Recovery Area.

More recently, Oracle introduced the Information Lifecycle Management (ILM) Assistant for managing online data and allocating data to appropriate tiers of disk performance. In Oracle Database 11g, the Flashback data archive feature has been added to ILM, enabling the storing and tracking of all transactional changes to a record. This feature, available through Oracle's Total Recall Option, allows you to gain access to previous database records.

Read-Only Tablespaces

Oracle 7.3 introduced read-only tablespaces. Using the ALTER TABLESPACE command in SQL, you can mark a tablespace as read-only. No changes are possible to the objects stored in a read-only tablespace. You can toggle a tablespace between read/write and read-only states as you wish.

Once a tablespace is in read-only mode, it can be backed up once and doesn't have to be backed up again, since its contents cannot change unless it's placed in read/write mode. Marking a tablespace as read-only allows entire sections of a database to be marked read-only, backed up once, and excluded from regular backups thereafter.

If a datafile of a read-only tablespace is damaged, you can restore it directly from the backup without any recovery. Because no changes were made to the datafiles, no redo log information needs to be applied. For databases with significant static or historical data, this option can significantly simplify and streamline backup and restore operations.

Read-only tablespaces, combined with Oracle's ability to partition a table on a range or list of column values (for example, a date) provide powerful support for the rolling windows common to data warehouses (described in Chapter 10). Once a new month's data is loaded, indexed, and so on, the relevant tablespaces can be marked read-only and backed up once, removing the tablespaces datafile(s) from the cycle of ongoing backup and significantly reducing the time required for those backup operations.

Point-in-Time Recovery

Oracle 7.3 introduced point-in-time recovery (PITR) for the entire database. Point-in-time recovery allows a DBA to restore the datafiles for the database and apply redo information up to a specific time or System Change Number (SCN). This limited type of recovery is useful for cases in which an error occurred—for example, if a table was dropped accidentally or a large number of rows were deleted incorrectly. The DBA can restore the database to the point in time just prior to the event to undo the results of the mistake.

A difficulty with database-level point-in-time recovery is that the entire database has to be restored. In response to this limitation, Oracle8 introduced point-in-time recovery at the tablespace level within the database. Point-in-time recovery based on a tablespace allows a DBA to restore and recover a specific tablespace or set of tablespaces to a particular point in time. Only the tablespace(s) containing the desired objects need to be recovered. This has been a very useful improvement given the ever-increasing size of today's databases.

However, this tablespace feature needs to be used carefully, since objects in one tablespace may have dependencies, such as referential integrity constraints, on objects in other tablespaces. For example, suppose that Tablespace1 contains the EMP table and Tablespace2 contains the DEPT table, and a foreign key constraint links these two tables together for referential integrity. If you were to recover Tablespace2 to an earlier point than Tablespace1, you might find that you had rows in the EMP table that contained an invalid foreign key value, since the matching primary key entry in the DEPT table had not been rolled forward to the place where the primary key value to which the EMP table refers had been added. The newer Flashback capability (described in the next section), particularly the Flashback Table feature, now provides an easier-to-use alternative for table recovery.

Flashback

Oracle9*i* introduced a recovery approach called *Flashback*, which was designed to help in recovering from user errors. Flashback Query was the first example of this feature made available by Oracle. The concept behind a Flashback Query is simple. You can execute a query against the database as of a particular time or System Change Number (SCN). Oracle delivers the result set as it would have appeared if the query were run at that time, using the undo log information segments to reconstruct the data, which can then be used to correct the results of the errant action.

Oracle Database 10*g* added a much wider range of flashback capabilities, including:

Flashback Versions Query
  Returns all the versions of rows in a particular query over a span of time.

Flashback Transaction Query
  Returns all the changes made by a specific transaction.

Flashback Drop
> When an object is dropped, it is placed in a Recycle Bin, so a user can simply un-drop the object to restore it.

Flashback Table
> Returns a table to a specific point in time.

Flashback Database
> Returns the entire database to a particular point in time. Can be used instead of point-in-time recovery in some situations.

Flashback Restore Points
> Enables canceling of planned database changes using user-defined labels (instead of SCNs or timestamps). Can also be used with Data Guard and RMAN to resynchronize a clone database.

Oracle Database 11g adds a Flashback Transaction command for backing out an individual transaction and its dependent transactions by utilizing undo data to revert data to its original state.

As we noted earlier in this chapter, Oracle now provides a Flashback Data Archive capability through the Oracle Database 11g Total Recall Option. This data archive is established for a defined retention period. Update and delete operations are then recorded in tables that map to the database tables being tracked. If you have specified an "AS OF" clause in your SQL specifying a particular moment it time, you will then have access to the data as it appeared at that moment. The updates and deletes are rolled back, as appropriate, and show you what the data looked like at the specified point in time.

Complete Site Failure

Protection from the complete failure of your primary Oracle site poses significant challenges. Your organization must carefully evaluate the risks to its primary site. These risks include physical and environmental problems as well as hardware risks. For example, is the data center in an area prone to floods, tornadoes, or earthquakes? Are power failures a frequent occurrence? Earlier versions of this book treated events such as "a terrorist attack or an airplane crash into the data center" as remote possibilities, but, unfortunately, these scenarios no longer seem so implausible.

Protection from primary site failure involves monitoring of and redundancy controls for the following:

- Data center power supply
- Data center climate control facilities
- Database server redundancy
- Database redundancy
- Data redundancy

The first three items on the list are aimed at preventing the failure of the data center. Data server redundancy, through simple hardware failover or Real Application Clusters, provides protection from node failure within a data center but not from complete data center loss.

Should the data center fail completely, the last two items—database redundancy and data redundancy—provide for disaster recovery.

Emerging Technologies: Clusters Across a Distance

Some vendors are now offering clustering solutions that allow the nodes of the cluster to be separated by enough distance to allow one node to survive the failure of the data center that contains the other node. In fact, it is anticipated that many grid computing deployments will occur this way in the future. The clustering of nodes separated by a few kilometers is becoming possible using sophisticated interconnect technologies that can function over greater distances. The disks are mirrored with a copy at each site to allow each site to function in the event of a complete failure of the other site.

These solutions are intriguing because they can provide data server redundancy and data center redundancy in a single solution. If one node (or the data center containing it) fails, the node in the other data center provides failover.

A simpler approach often used in data warehousing is to create duplicate grid implementations at primary and secondary sites. Extraction scripts from the source systems load both data warehouses simultaneously. If one of the target sites fails, ETL remains queued such that the failed system can be updated once it is recovered.

Oracle Data Guard: Standby Database for Redundancy

Oracle's physical standby database functionality was introduced in Oracle 7.3 to provide database redundancy. In Oracle9*i*, this concept was extended to include support for a logical standby database. The enhanced feature set is called Oracle Data Guard.

The concept of a physical standby database is simple—keep a copy of the database files at a second location, ship the redo logs to the second site as they are filled, and apply them to the copy of the database. This process keeps the standby database "a few steps" behind the primary database. If the primary site fails, the standby database is opened and becomes the production database. The potential data loss is limited to the transactions in any redo logs that have not been shipped to the standby site. Figure 11-10 illustrates the standby database feature.

The physical standby database can be used to offload reporting, such as end-of-day reports, from the primary server to the standby server. The ability to offload reporting requests provides flexibility for reporting and queries and can help performance on the primary server while making use of the standby server.

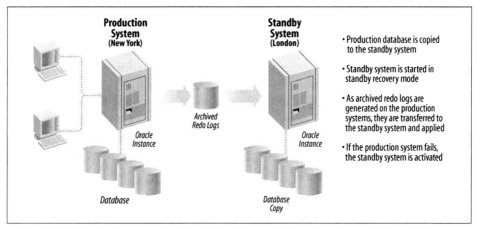

Figure 11-10. Standby database

When the standby database was being used for reporting, archived redo information from the primary site could not be applied prior to Oracle Database 10g. Recovery could only continue when the standby database was closed again. This factor had important implications for the time it took to recover from an outage with the standby database. Oracle Database 10g introduced a real-time apply, enabling redo data to be applied at the standby as soon as it was received.

The physical standby database is still more useful as of Oracle Database 11g since by deploying the Active Data Guard Option you can query the standby database while the redo apply is active. The implication of all of these enhancements is that you can use your disaster recovery database to handle some of your query workload, as a site for database backups, and as a site to test database changes.

Logical standby database

Oracle Data Guard also offers a logical standby database capability. With this capability, the standard Oracle archive logs are transformed into SQL transactions, and these are applied to an open standby database. The logical standby database is different physically from the primary standby database and can be used for different tasks. For example, the primary database might be indexed for transaction processing while the standby database might be indexed for data warehousing. Although physically different from the primary database, the secondary database is logically the same and can take over processing in case the primary fails. As archive logs are shipped from the primary to the secondary, undo records in the shipped archive log can be compared to the logical standby undo records to guard against potential corruption. As of Oracle Database 10g, you can instantiate the logical standby database without quiescing the primary.

Oracle Data Guard management

The Oracle Data Guard broker provides monitoring and control for physical and logical standby databases and components. A single command can be used to perform failover. Oracle Enterprise Manager provides a Data Guard Manager GUI for setting up, monitoring, and managing the standby database. SQL*Plus also provides an interface for Data Guard SQL statements and initialization parameters as of Oracle Database 11*g*.

The Oracle Database 10*g* Data Guard broker added support for creating and managing configurations containing RAC primary and standby databases. The Data Guard broker now leverages the Cluster Ready Services.

Possible Causes of Lost Data with a Physical Standby Database

There is a possibility that you will lose data, even if you use a physical standby database. There are three possible causes of lost data in the event of primary site failure:

- Archived redo logs have not been shipped to the standby site.
- Filled online redo logs have not been archived yet.
- The current online redo log is not a candidate for archiving until a log switch occurs.

These three potential problems are addressed in different ways, as described in the following sections.

Copying archived redo logs to a standby site

Prior to Oracle8*i*, copying of archived redo logs from the primary to the standby site was not automated. You were free to use any method to copy the files across the network. For example, you could schedule a batch job that copies archived logs to the standby site every *N* minutes. If the primary site fails, these copies would limit the lost redo information (and therefore the lost data) to a maximum of *N* minutes of work plus whatever was in the currently active log.

Oracle8*i* first provided support for the archiving of redo logs to a destination on the primary server as well as on multiple remote servers. This feature automates the copying and application of the archived redo logs to one or more standby sites. The lost data is then limited to the contents of any filled redo logs that have not been completely archived, as well as the current online redo log. Oracle also automatically applies the archived redo logs to the standby database as they arrive.

Oracle9*i* added the option to specify zero data loss to a standby machine. In this mode, all changes to a local log file are written synchronously to a remote log file. This mode guarantees that switching over to the standby database will not result in any lost data. As you might guess, this mode may impact performance, as each log write must also be completed to a remote log file. Oracle provides an option that will wait to write to a remote log only for a specified period of time, so that a network failure will not bring database processing to a halt.

If some data loss is allowable within certain limits, Oracle Database 11g enables a fast-start failover to occur provided that redo loss exposure does not exceed the limits the administrator sets. As noted earlier, a physical standby database is also more useful as of Oracle Database 11g since it is now possible to query the standby while redo apply is active.

Unarchived redo information and the role of geo-mirroring

If you require primary site failure not to result in the loss of *any* committed transactions, and do not choose to use the zero data loss option of Data Guard, the solution is to mirror all redo log and control file activity from the primary site to the standby site.

You can provide this level of reliability by using a remote mirroring technology sometimes known as *geo-mirroring*. Essentially, all writes to the online redo log files and the control files at the primary site must be mirrored synchronously to the standby site. For simplicity, you can also geo-mirror the archived log destination, which will duplicate the archived logs at the remote site, in effect copying the archived redo logs from the primary to the standby site. This approach can simplify operations; you use one solution for all the mirroring requirements, as opposed to having Oracle copy the archived logs and having geo-mirroring handle the other critical files.

Geo-mirroring of the online redo logs results in every committed transaction being written to both the online redo log at the primary site and the copy of the online redo log at the standby site. This process adds some time to each transaction for the mirrored write to reach the standby site. Depending on the distance between the sites and the network used, geo-mirroring can hamper performance, so you should test its impact on the normal operation of your database.

Geo-mirroring provides the most complete protection against primary site failure and, accordingly, it is a relatively expensive solution. You will need to weigh the cost of the sophisticated disk subsystems and high-speed telecommunication lines needed for nonintrusive geo-mirroring against the cost of losing the data in any unarchived redo logs and the current online redo log. See Appendix B for where to find more information about geo-mirroring.

Data Redundancy Solutions

Redundant data is another option for dealing with primary site failure. Implementing a redundant data approach differs from using a standby database, which duplicates the entire primary database. Data redundancy is achieved by having a copy of your critical data in an entirely separate Oracle database with a different structure.

The data, not the database itself, is redundant. If the primary site fails, users can continue working using the redundant data in the secondary database.

Oracle provides automated synchronous and asynchronous data-replication features to support data redundancy. For simplicity, in the following sections we'll examine replication using a simple two-site example—a primary and a secondary. Oracle can, however, perform *N*-way or multimaster replication involving more than two sites with all sites replicating to all others.

Data Replication—Synchronous and Asynchronous

Whenever you have a data replication scenario, you always have a primary site, from which the replication originates, and a secondary site, which is the recipient of the data replication. (In a multimaster scenario, you can have more than one master site, and a single machine can be a master for one replication plan and a secondary site for another.) When you design your replication plan, you must consider the degree to which data at the secondary site can differ for a period of time from the data at the primary site. This difference is referred to as *data divergence*. When you implement replication, Oracle generates triggers on all specified tables. These triggers are fired as part of the primary site transactions. The triggers either update the secondary site's data as part of the same transaction (*synchronous replication*) or place an entry in a deferred transaction queue that will be used later to update the secondary site (*asynchronous replication*).

Oracle's replication capabilities are delivered today in the Oracle Streams product. Streams includes log-based replication and Advanced Queues and is covered in more detail in Chapter 13.

Key considerations in setting up a replication environment include the following:

Tolerance for data divergence
> The smaller the data divergence, the more individual replication actions will have to be performed. You will reduce the resources needed to implement the replication by increasing the data divergence.

Performance requirements
> Since replication requires resources, it can have an impact on performance. However, since Oracle Database 10g, Oracle Streams can capture change data from log files, which greatly reduces the performance impact of replication on an active database.

Network bandwidth
> Since replication uses network bandwidth, you have to consider the availability of this resource.

Distance between sites
> The more distance between sites, the longer the physical transfer of data will take and the longer each application will take.

Site and network stability

If a site or a network goes down, all replications that use that network or are destined for that site will not be received. When either of these resources comes back online, the stored replication traffic can have an impact on the amount of time it takes to recover the site.

Experience level of your database administrators

Even the most effective replication plan can be undone by DBAs who aren't familiar with replication.

Figure 11-11 illustrates synchronous and asynchronous replication.

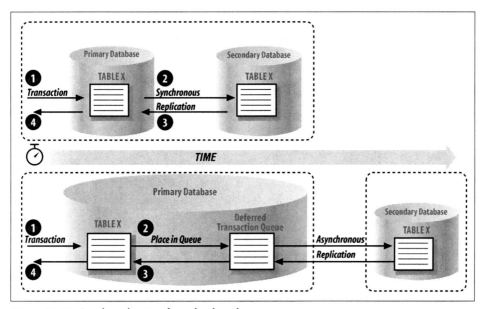

Figure 11-11. Oracle replication for redundant data

Synchronous, or real-time, replication can be used when there is no tolerance for data divergence or lost data. The data at the secondary site *must* match the primary site at all times and reflect all committed transactions. Each transaction at the primary site will fire triggers that call procedures at the secondary site to reproduce the transaction. Synchronous replication uses distributed transactions that will add overhead to every transaction at the primary site. Whether this additional overhead is acceptable will clearly depend on your specific requirements. Synchronous replication introduces system interdependencies—the secondary site and the network connecting the sites must be up or the primary site will not be able to perform transactions.

You can also use asynchronous, or deferred, replication to provide redundant data. With asynchronous replication, transactions are performed at the primary site and replicated some time later to the secondary site. Until the deferred transaction queue is "pushed" to the secondary site, replicating the changes, the data at the secondary site will differ from the primary site data. If the primary database is irrevocably lost, any unpushed transactions in the deferred queue will also be lost.

The extent of the data divergence and potential data loss resulting from the divergence is a very important consideration in configuring asynchronous replication. In addition, asynchronous replication allows the primary site to function when the network or the secondary site is down, while synchronous replication *requires* that the secondary site be available. Asynchronous replication adds overhead to transactions at the primary site, so once again, you'll need to carefully consider throughput requirements and perform appropriate testing. Typically, asynchronous replication adds less overhead than synchronous replication, since the replication of changes can be efficiently batched to the secondary site. However, asynchronous replication will still add some overhead to the operation of the primary site, so you should consider and test the effect of both types of replication on your database environment.

Old-Fashioned Data Redundancy

You can also achieve data redundancy using Oracle's standard utilities. Historically, one of the most common backup methods for Oracle was simply to export the contents of the database into a file using the Oracle Export utility. This file could then be shipped in binary form to any platform Oracle supports and subsequently imported into another database with Oracle's Import utility. This approach can still provide a simple form of data redundancy if the amount of data is manageable.

Oracle 7.3 introduced a *direct path export* feature that runs about 70 percent faster than a traditional export. The direct path export avoids some of the overhead of a normal export by directly accessing the data in the Oracle datafiles. Oracle Database 10*g* and newer database releases provide a much higher speed export/import than in the earlier Oracle version. This latest version, often called the *Data Pump*, is about 60 percent faster for export and 15 to 20 times faster for import per stream.

Another export option is to unload data from the desired tables into simple flat files by spooling the output of a SELECT statement to an operating system file. You can then ship the flat file to the secondary site and use Oracle's SQL*Loader utility to load the data into duplicate tables in the secondary database. For cases in which a significant amount of data is input to the primary system using loads, such as in a data warehouse, a viable disaster-recovery plan is simply to back up the load files to a secondary site on which they will wait, ready for reloading to either the primary or secondary site, should a disaster occur.

While these methods may seem relatively crude, they can provide simple data redundancy for targeted sets of data. Transportable tablespaces can also be used to move entire tablespaces to a backup platform. Transportable tablespaces in Oracle Database 10*g* and newer releases let you transport tablespaces from one type of system to another, increasing their flexibility for implementing redundancy, moving large amounts of data, and migrating to another database platform.

Export/Import, Standby Database, or Replication?

All the choices we've discussed in this chapter offer you some type of protection against losing critical data—or your entire database. But which one is right for your needs?

To quote the standard answer to so many technical questions, "it depends." Export/import, whether in its original form or in the Oracle Data Pump, provides a simple and proven method, but the time lag involved with this method typically leaves larger time periods where data is lost in the event of a failure. Transportable tablespaces can provide the same functionality with better performance, but are less granular. A physical standby database typically leaves smaller data gaps or, in the case since introduction of Oracle9*i* zero-data loss, no data gap; however, this solution does require the expense of redundant hardware. More recent database releases somewhat mitigate this as the standby database can be used for queries. Streams replication also requires redundant hardware and ensures consistent and complete data on both the primary and backup server, but this solution is the most resource-intensive of the three.

You should carefully balance the cost, both in extra hardware and performance, of each of these solutions, and balance them against the potential cost of a database or server failure. Of course, any one of these solutions is infinitely more valuable than not implementing any of them and simply hoping that a disaster never happens to you.

Rolling Upgrades

Thus far, we have focused on preventing unplanned downtime. But much of the availability planning in the past included defining planned downtime for system maintenance operations. Today, such downtime has largely disappeared with Oracle's extensive online management capabilities. For example, Oracle provides online reorganization capabilities in recent releases, a task that often required extensive planning in the past.

The one remaining area that posed an availability challenge until recently is the need to perform upgrades. Today, where RAC configurations leverage ASM, rolling upgrades (introduced in Oracle Database 10*g* Release 2) are entirely feasible with no downtime. Among the tasks that can be accomplished are system and hardware upgrades, operating system upgrades, patching, and storage migration.

Other Oracle features can minimize downtime for non-RAC or ASM configurations. Data Guard can be used to minimize downtime for system, database, and patch set upgrades. Transportable tablespaces and Oracle Streams are useful in speeding database upgrades and platform migrations.

CHAPTER 12

Oracle and Hardware Architecture

In Chapter 2, we discussed the architecture of the Oracle database, and in Chapter 7, we described how Oracle uses hardware resources. How hardware architectures are chosen and deployed can ultimately determine the specific scalability, performance tuning, management, and reliability options available to you. In fact, systems are sometimes badly configured without consideration of the proper balance of CPUs, memory, and I/O for projected workloads. This can limit options for database tuning if performance later becomes an issue.

Over the years, Oracle has developed new features to address specific platforms and, with Oracle Database 11g, continues this process by building on a commitment to grid computing and information appliance-like configurations. This chapter discusses the various hardware architectures to provide a basis for understanding how Oracle leverages each of these. It covers the following types of hardware systems and how Oracle takes advantage of the features inherent in each of the platforms:

- Uniprocessors (including multicores)
- Symmetric Multiprocessing (SMP) systems
- Clusters
- Non-Uniform Memory Access (NUMA) systems
- Grid computing

We'll also discuss the use of different disk technologies and how to choose the hardware system that's most appropriate for your purposes.

System Basics

Any discussion of hardware systems begins with a review of the components that make up a hardware platform and the impact these components have on the overall system. You'll find the same essential components under the covers of any computer system:

- One or more CPUs, which execute the basic instructions that make up computer programs, possibly with multiple cores to provide added processing power
- Memory, storing recently accessed instructions and data
- An input/output (I/O) system, that typically consists of some combination of disk storage, device controllers for pulling data and programs off physical media, and network controllers for connecting the system to other systems on the network

The number of each of these components and the capabilities of the individual components themselves determine the ultimate cost and scalability of a system. A machine with four processors is typically more expensive and capable of doing more work than a single-processor machine; new versions of components, such as CPUs, are typically faster and often less expensive than older versions.

Online transaction processing (OLTP) systems are most often designed for throughput. In business intelligence or data warehousing systems, it is often assumed that CPU and memory are the performance-limiting components. However, CPU processing power and memory capacity constraints have greatly risen in recent years (especially in the time period since we wrote earlier editions of this book), and providing adequate I/O now deserves special attention for these systems as well.

Each system component has a time to access and transport data, or a *latency cost*. The latency cost of a component is the amount of latency the use of that component introduces into the system; in other words, how much slower each successive level of a component is than its previous level (e.g., Level 2 versus Level 1; see Table 12-1). Each component also has limited capacity.

The CPU and the Level 1 (L1) memory cache on the CPU have the lowest latency, as shown in Table 12-1, but also the least capacity. Disk has the most capacity but the highest latency.

 There are several different types of memory: an L1 cache, which is on the CPU chip; an L2 (Level 2) cache on the CPU surface, an L3 cache on the same board as the CPU; and main memory, which is the remaining memory on the system accessible through the memory bus.

Table 12-1. Typical sizes and latencies of system components

Element	Typical storage capability	Typical latency
CPU	None	None
L1 cache (on CPU)	10s to 100s of KBs	10 nanoseconds
L2 cache (on CPU surface)	Single MBs	40–60 nanoseconds
L3 cache (on same board)	10s of MBs	120 nanoseconds
Main memory	MBs to TB+	1,000 - 10,000 nanoseconds
Disk	GBs to hundreds TBs	1-10 million nanoseconds

An important part of tuning any Oracle database involves reducing the need to read data from sources with the greatest latency (e.g., disk) and, when a disk must be accessed, ensuring that there are as few bottlenecks as possible in the I/O subsystem. As the Oracle database accesses a greater percentage of its data from memory rather than disk, the overall latency of the system is correspondingly decreased and performance increases. For more information about tuning concepts, see Chapter 7.

Uniprocessor Systems

Uniprocessor systems, such as the one shown in Figure 12-1, are the simplest systems in terms of architecture. Each of these systems (typically a standard personal computer) contains a single CPU and a single I/O channel and is made entirely with industry-standard components. They are most often used as single-user machines (for example, for database development or providing browser access over a network). Some uniprocessor machines are also used as small servers for databases, especially where multicore processors are installed.

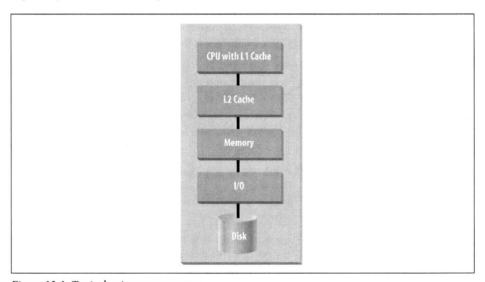

Figure 12-1. Typical uniprocessor system

Until the 1990s, uniprocessor systems were frequently used as servers because of their low price and the limited ability of relational databases to fully utilize other types of systems. However, Oracle evolved to take advantage of systems containing multiple CPUs through improved parallelism and more sophisticated optimization. At the same time, the price points of Symmetric Multiprocessing systems (described in the next section) have plummeted dramatically, making SMP systems the database hardware servers of choice.

Even in a uniprocessor system, the server operating systems used by these systems support multiple threads. The multicore processors are becoming common to further enable simultaneous processing of multiple tasks. Multicore processors are integrated circuits that contain two or more processors. Hardware platform vendors are racing to provide more cores to differentiate their platforms.

Each thread in a server operating system can be used to support a concurrent process, which can execute in parallel. By default, the PARALLEL_THREADS_PER_CPU parameter in the initialization file is set at 2 for most platforms on which Oracle runs. Oracle can further determine the degree of parallelism based on parameters set in the initialization file or using the adaptive degree of parallelism feature, described in Chapter 7. This adaptive multiuser feature makes use of algorithms that take into account the number of threads. Additional tuning parameters can also affect parallelism, although the need for tuning of such parameters is much diminished in recent Oracle releases.

Symmetric Multiprocessing Systems

One of the early limiting factors for a uniprocessor system was the ultimate speed of its processor—all applications have to share this one resource. Symmetric Multiprocessing (SMP) systems were invented in an effort to overcome this limitation by adding CPUs to the memory bus, as shown in Figure 12-2.

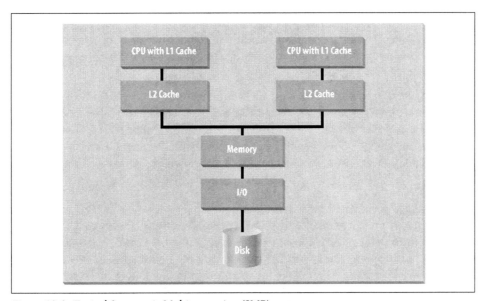

Figure 12-2. Typical Symmetric Multiprocessing (SMP) system

Each CPU has its own memory cache. Data resident in the cache of one CPU is sometimes needed for processing by a second CPU. Because of this potential sharing of data, the CPUs for such machines must be able to "snoop" the memory bus to determine where copies of data reside and whether the data is being updated. This snooping is managed transparently by the operating system that controls the SMP system. Oracle Standard Edition One, Standard Edition, or Enterprise Edition can be used on these platforms. (Oracle limits the number of CPUs you can deploy using Standard Edition One and Standard Edition while placing no limit on the number of CPUs for Enterprise Edition.)

SMP platforms have been available since the 1980s as midrange platforms, primarily as Unix-based machines. Today, there is a category of entry-level servers featuring mostly 64-bit CPUs (replacing previous-generation 32-bit CPUs). The most popular operating systems in this category are Windows variations and Linux.

SMP servers that can scale to larger sizes from platform vendors such as HP, IBM, and Sun feature variations on this basic design. For example, SMP systems might include multicore CPUs, a larger L2 cache, faster memory bus and/or multiple higher-speed I/O channels. Each enhancement is intended to remove potential bottlenecks that can limit performance. Unix and Linux are the most common operating systems used in Oracle implementations on high-end SMP servers.

The number of CPUs possible in a SMP system is limited by scalability of the system (memory) bus. As more CPUs are added to the bus, the bus itself can become saturated with traffic between CPUs attached to the bus.

Systems featuring 64-bit CPUs can handle large amounts of data more efficiently than previous 32-bit CPUs; they support dozens of CPUs on a single system with hundreds of gigabytes of memory.

Of course, the database must have parallelization features to take full advantage of the SMP architecture. Oracle operations such as query execution and other DML activity and data loading can run as parallel processes within the Oracle server, allowing Oracle to take advantage of the benefits of multiprocessor systems. Oracle, like all software systems, benefits from parallel operations, as shown by "Amdahl's Law."

Total execution time = (parallel part / number of processors) + serial part

Amdahl's Law, formulated by mainframe pioneer Gene Amdahl in 1967 to describe performance in mixed parallel and serial workloads, clearly shows that moving an operation from the serial portion of execution to a parallel portion provides the performance increases expected with the use of multiple processors. In the same way, the more serial operations that make up an application, the longer the execution time will be because the sum of the execution time of all serial operations can offset any performance gains realized from the use of multiple processors. In other words, you cannot speed up a serial operation or a sequence of serial operations by adding more processors.

Each subsequent release of Oracle has added more parallelized features to speed up the execution of queries as well as the tuning and maintenance of the database. For an extensive list of Oracle operations that can be parallelized, see the section "What Can Be Parallelized?" in Chapter 7.

Oracle's parallel operations take advantage of available CPU resources. If you're working with a system on which the CPU resources are already being completely consumed, this parallelism will not help improve performance; in fact, it could even hurt performance by adding the increased demands for CPU power required to manage the parallel processes. Oracle's adaptive degree of parallelism automatically can reduce the degree of parallelism for an operation to prevent this situation.

Clusters

Clustered systems have provided a highly available and highly scalable solution since initially appearing in the 1980s in the DEC VAXcluster configuration. Clusters can combine all the components of separate machines, including CPUs, memory, and I/O subsystems, into a single hardware entity. However, clusters are typically built by using shared disks linked to multiple "nodes" (computer systems). A high-speed interconnect between systems provides a means of exchanging data and instructions without writing to disk (see Figure 12-3). Each system runs its own copy of an operating system and Oracle instance. Grids, described later in this chapter, are typically made up of a few very large clusters.

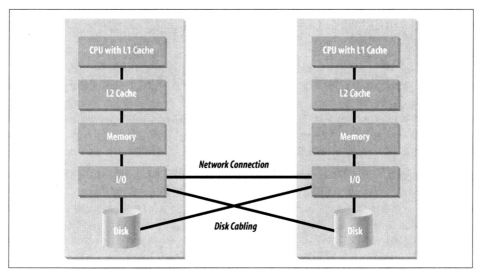

Figure 12-3. Typical cluster (two systems shown)

Oracle's support for clusters dates back to the VAXcluster. Oracle provided a sophisticated locking model so that the multiple nodes could access the shared data on the disks. Clusters require such a locking model because each machine in the cluster must be aware of the data locks held by other, physically separate machines in the cluster.

Today, that Oracle solution has evolved into Real Application Clusters (RAC) (replacing the Oracle Parallel Server (OPS) that was available prior to Oracle9i). RAC is most frequently used for Windows, Linux, or Unix-based clusters. Oracle provides an integrated lock manager that mediates between different servers, or nodes, that seek to update data in the same block.

RAC introduced full support of Cache Fusion, where locks are maintained in memory without frequent writing to disk. Cache Fusion is different from the standard locking mechanisms that are described in Chapter 8, in that it applies to blocks of data, rather than rows. The mediation is necessary since two different nodes might try to access different rows in the same physical block, which is the smallest amount of data that can be used by Oracle.

Cache Fusion initially greatly increased performance for read/write operations compared to the previous OPS and later added improved performance for write/write operations in Oracle9i RAC. Today, Oracle supports Sockets Direct Protocol (SDP) and asynchronous I/O protocols, lighter-weight transports than those used in previous traditional TCP/IP based RAC implementations. More recent database releases further improved performance by leveraging faster interconnects such as Infiniband networks through support of Reliable Datagram Sockets (RDS). For example, Infiniband node-to-node latency is about a tenth of the latency in Gigabit Ethernet (typically about 70-80 microseconds).

Prior to Real Application Clusters, you would configure clusters to deliver higher throughput or greater availability for the system. In the high-availability scenario, if a single node fails, a secondary node attached to the shared disk can get access to the same data. Queries can run to completion without further intervention through transparent client failover. RAC provides both availability and scalability since each node in a cluster can act as a failover node for all the other nodes in the cluster.

Real Application Clusters are increasingly used in Windows and Linux environments where a single platform cannot scale adequately or as an alternative to higher-cost Unix high-end solutions. Clustered solutions might also be deployed where high availability is desired. On Windows clustered platforms, Oracle Fail Safe might be chosen as an alternative to RAC, although data is not shared by the two systems and the second system provides only standby access to this data. Because concurrent access isn't provided, the Fail Safe solution doesn't offer the scalability that Real Application Clusters can provide.

In earlier editions of this book, we described a very high-end variation of clusters known as a massively parallel processing (MPP) system. Such systems were essentially a cluster in a box with nodes connected via very high-speed and proprietary networks (see Figure 12-4). Open-systems vendors now rarely sell such platforms since clusters of lower-cost system components (nodes) have displaced them in the broader marketplace.

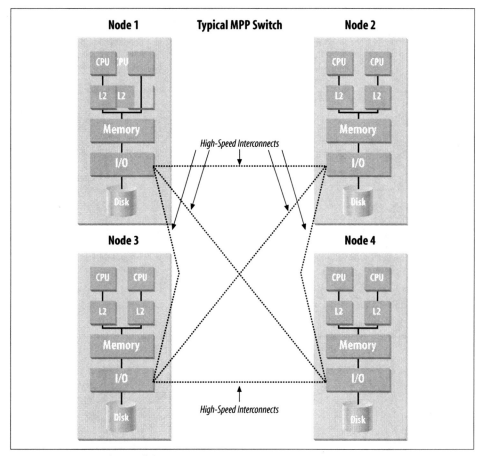

Figure 12-4. Massively parallel processing (MPP) system

Non-Uniform Memory Access Systems

Non-Uniform Memory Access (NUMA) computers, introduced in the mid-1990s, provide even greater throughput than SMP by linking multiple SMP components via distributed memory, as shown in Figure 12-5. Like clusters, these systems provide scaling of memory and I/O subsystems in addition to CPUs. A key difference is the single operating system copy that manages the entire platform and a directory-based cache coherency scheme to keep data synchronized. Memory access between nodes is in the hundreds of microseconds, which is much faster than going to disk in clustered configurations, and only slightly less swift than local memory bus speeds in a single SMP system. Memory capacities can range into multiple terabytes.

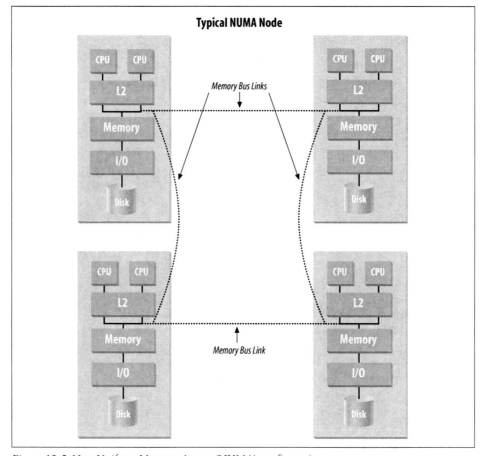

Figure 12-5. Non-Uniform Memory Access (NUMA) configuration

This enables NUMA to have some major advantages over cluster solutions:

- Parallel versions of applications don't need to be developed or certified to run on these machines (though additional performance gains may be realized when such applications can be tuned for NUMA).

- Management is much simpler on NUMA systems than on clusters because there is only one copy of the operating system to manage and only one database instance is typically deployed.

Today, the Hewlett Packard Superdome is an example of a NUMA system with demonstrated scalability in production databases that scale into dozens of terabytes of data. Since this platform behaves like, and is managed the same as, SMP systems, NUMA and SMP systems have similar tradeoffs (although NUMA systems tend to be higher priced).

Grid Computing

The "g" in Oracle's database nomenclature since Oracle Database 10g signifies the company's focus on enabling grid computing. *Grids* are simply pools of computers that provide needed resources for applications on an as-needed basis. The goal is to provide computing resources that transparently scale to the user community, much as an electrical utility company can deliver power to meet peak demand by accessing energy from other power providers' plants via a power grid. Computing grids enable this dynamic provisioning of CPU and data resources (shown in Figure 12-6). The Oracle database with RAC forms the foundation for the provisioning of these resources.

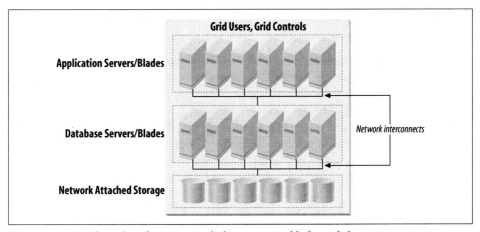

Figure 12-6. Sample grid configuration, including computer blades and cluster

Oracle Database 10g introduced several important features that enable the delivery of resources when needed via a grid:

Dynamic Service Provisioning
> This feature automatically allocates and reallocates server resources based on configuration and failover rules. Service requests are automatically routed to the server with the least load. If a server fails, the surviving services are automatically reallocated to the available servers.

Web services
> Web services are also an inherent part of the grid landscape, because applications running on the grid want to use the same type of transparent access to components (or services) that users have to applications. Database web services provide support for queries, messaging, and DML, can access Java and PL/SQL, and can provide full XML support.

Rolling upgrades
> A rolling upgrade allows you to bring down some of the nodes in the grid, upgrade their software, and then bring them back online as part of the grid. You can then repeat this procedure with the other nodes. The end result is that you can achieve a complete upgrade of your Oracle database software without having to bring down the database.

Automatic Storage Management
> The ASM system also enables management of large numbers of nodes by implementing automatic data rebalancing across disks, as well as easy addition of new disks to the overall pool of storage.

Enterprise Manager Grid Control
> Enterprise Manager Grid Control manages a grid infrastructure from a central location, including RAC databases, storage, Oracle Application Servers/Fusion Middleware, and network services.

Oracle Database 11g includes multitier service management and improvements to ASM including support for rolling upgrades, automatic bad block detection and repair, and fast mirror resynchronization. The Automatic Database Diagnostics Monitor (ADDM) for RAC determines the most globally significant performance issues for a multi-instance database, including the global cache interconnect, lock manager congestion, global resource contention (such as I/O), high-load SQL across the instances, and skew in instance response times. Hot database patching can now be applied to any Oracle database, including RAC implementations.

Disk and Storage Technology

The discussion of hardware architectures and performance in this chapter so far has centered on ways of increasing performance by increasing available system resources such as CPUs, memory, and I/O subsystems and on the parallelism that can take advantage of these resources. An important way to increase hardware performance is to tune for I/O, which includes spreading data across disks and providing an adequate number of access paths to the data. As a rule of thumb, your I/O should deliver 1 GB per second of throughput for every 4 CPUs with a minimum of 2 GB per second delivered. Since disk access has the greatest latency, another focus of I/O tuning is keeping data retrieved from disk in memory.

Oracle refers to proper configurations—those that feature proper I/O (especially spindles that provide access paths to storage), memory, and CPUs—as *balanced configurations*. As noted previously, Oracle Database 10g and later releases now include ASM for disk, greatly simplifying day-to-day management for storage. However, working with hardware vendors in order to get proper storage configurations has sometimes proven difficult, especially for data warehousing. Also, as disk capacities have grown, improvements in access times have not kept pace. This has led Oracle to develop reference configurations with several key hardware platform and storage vendors to help provide more accurate initial sizing through an Information Appliance Initiative.

 The Oracle Optimized Warehouse Initiative is a series of Oracle-based data warehousing reference configurations, with key platform and storage providers such as HP, IBM, Sun, and EMC/Dell. Several of Oracle's platform partners have also announced Oracle Optimized Warehouses that are pretested hardware configurations with preinstalled Oracle databases. The reference configurations include a variety of node, system, and storage configurations offering a variety of upgrade paths. As a starting point, you should understand the complexity of queries in the workload, the amount of data, and the number of concurrent users. Oracle and its partners continue to update these configurations as hardware platforms are improved. For more information, search on "Optimized Warehouse" on Oracle's main web site.

Disk Deployment Strategies

Disks are often directly attached to systems—more expensive systems offer faster disk controllers and I/O. As network bandwidth has improved, Network Attached Storage (NAS) and Storage Area Networks (SAN) have appeared as cost-effective alternatives. Disks are also configured in a variety of ways for redundancy, eliminating the possibility of single points of disk failure resulting in loss of access to data.

Disk is commonly deployed in arrays, the industry standard being RAID (Redundant Array of Inexpensive/Independent Disks). You can use RAID as a part of any of the configurations we've discussed to provide higher performance and reliability. RAID disk arrays were introduced in this book in Chapter 7 and discussed in the context of their use in high-availability scenarios in Chapter 11. Please refer to those chapters for more information about RAID disk arrays. In addition, since Oracle

Database 10g, Automatic Storage Management (ASM) delivers much of the functionality of a RAID array, such as striping and mirroring, with a collection of commodity disks. ASM is further described in Chapter 5.

Oracle9i introduced table compression in the database as a means of decreasing disk storage requirements primarily in data warehousing. Duplicate values in a data block are eliminated because values that are duplicated are stored in a symbol table at the beginning of the block, and all additional occurrences are replaced with a short reference to the symbol table. Oracle Database 11g also features an Advanced Compression Option for insert, update, and delete operations important in OLTP operations. Data compression of 50 percent is commonly observed today. In addition to reducing disk storage, compressed data can also be advantageous for performance when it fits entirely into cache (instead of requiring disk access).

Since storage capacities are growing and disk is available at lower cost points, many organizations are now storing all relevant data online in disk storage for data warehousing and business intelligence implementations. Given that disks delivering the best performance are typically more expensive and of lower capacity, many now deploy such disks in combination with higher capacity but lower performing (and cheaper) disk for less frequently accessed data. Information Lifecycle Management (ILM) in the Oracle database, particularly the ILM Assistant, first available in 2007, provide the capability to manage such an environment.

Which Platform Deployment Solution?

In a world in which there was no limit to the amount of money you could spend on hardware, you could make a simple decision about the most appropriate hardware: simply choose the level of throughput and reliability you need, and go buy it! Unfortunately, we have yet to discover the location of this kind of world, so your choice of a hardware solution will often be a compromise. But since this book was first written, relative price points have continued to collapse making this selection much easier.

Platform Comparison

The most commonly implemented hardware platform for an Oracle server is the SMP system, which strikes a nice balance between power and price. SMP systems are popular for the following reasons:

- SMP systems offer more and simpler scalability options for the future than uniprocessor systems.

- 64-bit processors and operating systems with large memory support enable SMP systems to handle the needs of very large databases (even containing dozens of terabytes of data).

- SMP systems have a single operating system and a single Oracle instance to manage and maintain, unlike clusters.

- More applications are certified to run on SMP systems than clusters.

- SMP systems can be less expensive than NUMA, clusters, or grid configurations in similar CPU configurations because memory and I/O subsystems are not duplicated to the same degree

This is not to say that other configurations should not be considered. Certainly, if scalability demands exceed the capabilities of SMP machines, clusters or a grid may provide the only viable solution. Clusters can prove cheaper through use of "commodity" nodes in RAC configurations. With careful planning and an enterprise-computing management style, such configurations do provide powerful and highly available solutions.

 Today, one of the key tradeoffs in determining the type of system to deploy is the cost associated with deploying multicore CPUs versus CPUs consisting of single cores. This analysis extends beyond simply hardware costs since database vendors have adopted new pricing models to take this technology into account. Oracle's pricing policy has changed in reaction to accepted industry practices in this regard. Many organizations purchase CPU-based licenses of Oracle based on the number of CPUs in their platforms. However, where multicore CPUs are deployed, the incremental Oracle license price is not at a 1:1 ratio with the number of additional cores. This is because platform vendors and Oracle Corporation recognize there is overhead associated with multicore technology, so Oracle license prices increase incrementally based on expected performance gains. Of course, technologies and industry pricing practices often change more frequently than major database releases, and that is one of the reasons why we don't dwell on pricing in this book. To figure out current tradeoffs, you will likely need the help of both your platform provider and Oracle.

Table 12-2 provides a comparison of the relative strengths of the different deployment platforms for scalability, manageability, and availability.

Table 12-2. Relative strengths of deployment platforms

Ranking	Scalability	Manageability	Availability
Best	Grid	Uniprocessor	Grid
	Cluster	SMP	Cluster
	SMP	Grid	SMP
Worst	Uniprocessor	Cluster	Uniprocessor

You should select a storage technology based on your performance and recovery requirements and budget. In general, more expensive solutions offer better performance and more flexible availability options. Be sure to consider throughput requirements as you choose storage.

Approaches to Choosing Platforms

When selecting a solution for deployment, most organizations choose systems that will meet anticipated performance and scalability needs for the near future, taking into account management and availability requirements. However, there are two additional approaches to be considered.

First is the truism with which we're all familiar—the longer you wait, the cheaper computer hardware (and related components) get. According to Moore's Law, credited by Intel to Gordon Moore in 1965 (and proven many times over since then), each chip will double in computing power every 18–24 months, each time providing huge leaps in performance. Today, such performance increases are driven by increased clock speeds and the introduction of more cores in the processors.

This continual reduction in price and increase in performance characteristics is an ongoing fact of life in the computer hardware industry. But how can you use this fact in planning deployment strategies for your organizational system architecture?

Buy what you need, when you need it, and plan for the obsolescence of hardware by recycling it into the organization when it no longer meets the needs of an individual application. For instance, today's departmental server may turn into tomorrow's web server. With grid deployment, you might continue to leverage older hardware as part of the existing computing solution.

Second, remember to consider the effect of hardware upgrades, particularly CPU upgrades, in nongrid solutions. SMP systems and nodes require that all CPUs be identical within them, so if you upgrade one you will have to upgrade all of them. At some point the vendor will recommend a new system anyway because other internal features (e.g., memory and I/O bus technologies) will have improved, partly to match the increased capabilities of the new CPUs.

The grid is tempting to consider since new machine types can be added to the grid as they become available. Oracle's self-tuning and advanced management capabilities available in Oracle Database 10g and further improved in Oracle Database 11g make grid computing more practical by eliminating difficult manual tuning efforts that formerly needed to take into account variations in systems.

CHAPTER 13

Oracle Distributed Databases and Distributed Data

Data in large and mid-sized companies can be spread over many different databases. The data can be on different servers running different operating systems or even different database management systems. The data needed to answer any specific business question may need to be accessed from more than one server. A user may need to access this separate data on several servers simultaneously, or the data required for an answer may need to be moved to a local server. Inserts, updates, or deletions of data across these distributed servers may also be necessary.

There are two basic ways to deal with data in distributed databases: as part of a single distributed entity in which the distributed architecture is transparent, or by using a variety of replication techniques to create copies of the data in more than one location. This chapter examines both of these options and the technologies associated with each solution.

Accessing Multiple Databases As a Single Entity

Users sometimes need to query or manipulate data that resides in multiple Oracle databases or in a mixture of Oracle and non-Oracle databases. This section describes a number of techniques and architectures you can use to interact with data in a distributed environment.

Distributed Data Access Across Multiple Oracle Databases

For many years, Oracle has offered access to distributed data residing on multiple Oracle database servers on multiple systems or *nodes*. Users don't need to know the location of the data in distributed databases. Data is accessed using a unique identifier to a specific table name. Administrators can create simple identifiers so that data in an Oracle table in a separate machine can appear to users to be part of a single logical database.

Developers can create connections between individual databases by creating database links in SQL. These connections form a distributed database. The statement:

```
CREATE PUBLIC DATABASE LINK employees.northpole.bigtoyco.com
```

creates a path to a remote database containing a table with Bigtoyco's North Pole employees. Any application or user attached to a local employees database can access the remote North Pole database by using the global access name (employees. northpole.bigtoyco.com) in SQL queries, inserts, updates, deletions, and other statements. Oracle Net (previously known as Net8 or SQL*Net in older database releases) handles the interaction with any network protocols used to communicate with the remote database transparently.

Although the database link makes data access transparent to users, Oracle still has to treat interactions over distributed databases differently. Let's look briefly at how queries and updates issued for distributed Oracle databases differ from those issued for a single Oracle database. When using distributed data in a query, your primary concern is to properly optimize the retrieval of data for a query. Queries in a single Oracle database are optimized for performance, most frequently using the cost-based optimizer, as discussed in Chapter 4. Oracle7 added global cost-based optimization for the improvement of query performance across distributed databases as well. For example, the cost-based optimizer considers indexes on remote databases when choosing a plan, whereas the rule-based optimizer does not. The cost-based optimizer also considers statistics on remote databases. Improvements to the Oracle8i optimizer included optimizing for join and set operations to be performed on the nodes offering the best performance and also minimizing the amount of data sent between systems. Since Oracle Database 10g, the cost-based optimizer is Oracle's only recommended optimizer for single and for distributed databases.

When a user wants to write data back to a distributed database, the issue becomes a bit more complicated. As we've mentioned before, a transaction is an atomic logical unit of work that typically contains one or more SQL statements. These statements write data to a database and must either be committed or rolled back as a unit. Distributed transactions can take place across multiple database servers. When distributed transactions are committed via the SQL COMMIT statement, Oracle uses a two-phase commit protocol to ensure transaction integrity and consistency across multiple systems. This protocol is further described in this chapter's "Two-Phase Commits" section.

Access to and from Non-Oracle Databases

Oracle's Transparent Gateways (illustrated in Figure 13-1) are Oracle software products that provide users with access to non-Oracle databases via Oracle SQL. Oracle SQL is automatically translated into the SQL of the target database, allowing applications developed for Oracle to be used against non-Oracle databases. You can also use native SQL syntax for the target database, which can be sent directly to the target without translation. Oracle datatypes such as NUMBER, CHAR, and DATE are converted into the datatypes of the target. Oracle data dictionary views are provided for target data store objects. As with Oracle databases, heterogeneous databases can be linked to Oracle through database links to create a distributed database. The gateways can be deployed in a two-tier architecture in the Oracle database or in a middle tier (Oracle Application Server).

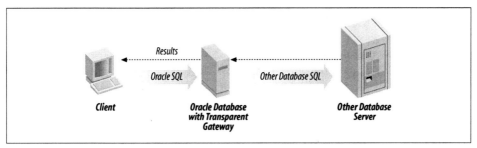

Figure 13-1. Typical configuration and use of Transparent Gateways

There are four basic types of database connectivity provided:

Open Database Connectivity
Generic ODBC and OLE DB interfaces are free and are bundled with the Oracle database. Open Systems Gateways provide access to Informix, Microsoft SQL Server, Sybase, and other databases on Unix and Windows platforms. These interfaces and gateways leverage Heterogeneous Services included in the Oracle database, which determine optimal SQL strategies for the remote site. Additionally, starting with Oracle Database 10g, Oracle's OLAP Option provides OLE DB for OLAP (ODBO) enabling access from a variety of analysis tools.

Transparent Gateways
Transparent Gateways exist for dozens of non-Oracle data stores. Mainframe Integration Gateways provide access to DB2 on mainframes. Enterprise Integration Gateways provide access to IBM AS/400 and via IBM Distributed Relational Database Architecture (DRDA) connections. Finally, Oracle offers the EDA/SQL Gateways for a number of other sources. Transparent Gateway performance improved in Oracle8 by moving Heterogeneous Services from the Transparent Gateway layer into the database kernel. Performance was further improved in the Oracle8i release with the introduction of multithreading for these services, in Oracle9i with multithreaded agent support, and in Oracle Database 11g with parallel data retrieval from non-Oracle databases. Oracle Database 10g added support for remote functions in non-Oracle databases embedded in SELECT statements. Oracle Database 11g adds new Gateways to connect to Adabas, IMS, and VSAM data stores.

Procedural Gateways
Procedural Gateways implement remote procedure calls (RPCs) to applications built on non-Oracle data stores. The Gateway for APPC, the standard IBM protocol for RPCs, is used when Oracle applications need procedural access to

applications built on CICS, DB2, IMS, VSAM, and other data stores on the mainframe and applications that use SNA LU6.2 to communicate to the mainframe. The Oracle Procedural Gateway for IBM MQSeries allows Oracle-based applications to exchange messages with applications that communicate via MQSeries message queues. Both are included with the Oracle Enterprise Integration Gateways.

Access Manager

An access manager provides access to Oracle from non-Oracle based applications. The Oracle Access Manager for AS/400 resides on the AS/400 and provides AS/400 applications written in RPG, C, or COBOL access to Oracle running on any platform. You can access Oracle from these applications through ANSI-standard SQL or through Oracle DML or DDL. Because PL/SQL is also supported, AS/400 applications can call Oracle stored procedures. TCP/IP and LU6.2 are supported for connectivity (via Oracle Net). The Oracle Access Manager for AS/400 is included with the Oracle Enterprise Integration Gateways.

Two-Phase Commits

One of the biggest issues associated with the use of distributed databases is the difficulty of guaranteeing the same level of data integrity for updates to distributed databases. Because a transaction that writes data to multiple databases must depend on a network for the transmission of information, it is inherently more susceptible to lost information than a single Oracle instance on a single machine. And since a transaction must guarantee that all writes occur, this increased instability could adversely affect data integrity.

The standard solution for this problem is to use two message-passing phases as part of a transaction commit; hence, the protocol used is referred to as a *two-phase commit*. The main database first polls each of the participants to determine if they are ready; if they are, the transactional updates are tentatively sent to them. In the second phase, if all the participants are in agreement that the messages have properly been received, the changes are committed. If any of the nodes involved in the transaction cannot verify receipt of the changes, the transactions are rolled back to their original state.

For example, if a transaction is to span databases on machines A, B, and C, in the first phase of the commit operation, each of the databases is sent the appropriate transactional update. If each of these machines acknowledges that it has received the update, the second phase of the update executes the COMMIT command. By separating the transmission of the data for the update from the actual COMMIT operation, a two-phase commit greatly decreases the possibility of distributed data losing its integrity.

You can compare this approach to a single-phase update in which the COMMIT command is sent along with the transactional update information. There is no way of knowing whether the update ever reached all the machines, so any sort of interruption in the delivery of the update to any of the machines would cause the data to be in an inconsistent state. When a transaction involves more than one machine, the possibility of the loss of an update to one of the machines increases greatly, which, in turn, mandates the use of the two-phase commit protocol. Of course, since the two-phase commit protocol requires more messaging to be passed between machines, a two-phase commit can take longer than a standard commit; however, the corresponding gain in all-important data integrity more than makes up for the decrease in performance.

Transaction Processing Monitors

In 1991, the X/Open standards group defined an open systems standard interface through which transaction processing (TP) monitors could communicate with XA-compliant resource managers, such as the Oracle RDBMS and other XA-compliant databases. Several popular TP monitors that support XA are in production, including BEA Tuxedo and IBM's CICS and Encina.

Oracle added an Oracle Manager for Microsoft Transaction Server (MTS) to Oracle8*i* for Windows NT. Since that time, Microsoft has superseded its COM architecture with the .NET architecture. Release 2 of Oracle9*i* added .NET support enabling .NET transactional applications to use Oracle as a resource manager.

We have mentioned TP monitors in previous chapters in connection with their role in online transaction processing. Among their other duties, TP monitors assure that transactions between multiple applications and resources complete properly. As noted previously, Oracle provides its own two-phase commit protocol for distributed transactions, a capability once available only with a TP monitor. Standalone TP monitors are also used less frequently today for workload management (see Figure 13-2), as this capability is now built into middle-tier applications.

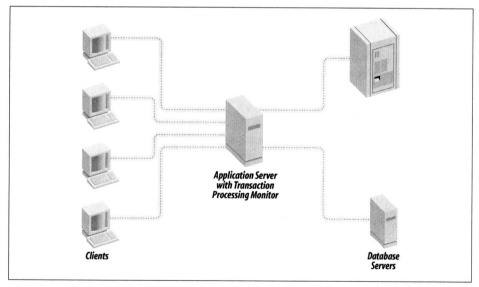

Figure 13-2. Application server with TP monitor

If you are still considering the use of TP monitors, you likely have one of these scenarios:

- Migration of legacy applications (usually originally written using CICS and COBOL for a mainframe) to CICS on Unix or Windows NT
- Need for two-phase commits between Oracle and other XA-compliant databases

Moving Data Between Distributed Systems

The previous section discussed the use of multiple database servers acting together as part of a single logical database for users. The following situations call for the contents of a database to be duplicated and moved between systems:

- When data available locally eliminates network bandwidth issues or contention for system resources
- When mobile database users can take their databases with them and operate disconnected from the network
- When redundant databases can help to deliver higher levels of reliability, as each database can be used as a backup for other databases

In many grid implementations, the ability to share resources across the grid can also require data to be replicated to multiple servers within the grid.

The biggest issue facing users of multiple identical or similar databases is how to keep the data on all of the servers in sync as the data is changed over time. As a user inserts, updates, or deletes data on one database, you need to have some way to get this new data to the other databases. In addition, you will have to deal with the possible data-integrity issues that can crop up if the changes introduced by distributed users contend with each other.

Oracle offers a number of strategies to address this situation. With Oracle9*i* Release 2, these strategies were rolled into a single component, Oracle Streams. However, the different strategies within Streams still have their own characteristics, which are discussed separately in the following sections.

Advanced Replication

The copying and maintaining of database tables among multiple Oracle databases on distributed systems is known as *replication*. Changes that are applied at any local site are propagated automatically to all of the remote sites. These changes can include updates to data or changes to the database schema. Replication is frequently implemented to provide faster access for local users at remote sites or to provide a disaster-recovery site in the event of loss of a primary site. Oracle's Advanced Replication features support both asynchronous replication and synchronous replication. Oracle also supports heterogeneous replication to DB2 through its Replication Services, bundled in the Mainframe Integration Gateways.

Replication services have been in the Oracle database for a long time, but have been continually evolving. Oracle8 moved execution of replication triggers to the database kernel and enabled automatic parallelization of data replication to improve performance. Oracle8*i* added replication triggered by changes to selected rows or columns of a table. Oracle9*i* replication added support for object datatypes and multitier updateable materialized views. Release 2 of Oracle9*i* added log-based replication via Oracle Streams. Although Oracle continued to support the previous generation Advanced Replication in newer database releases, we recommend that for new implementations you use Streams for replication. Nevertheless, we'll describe replication basics here and some of the features of Advanced Replication for completeness before we cover Streams.

Asynchronous replication is the storage of changes locally for subsequent forwarding to a remote site. Some types of asynchronous replication include read-only snapshots replicated from a single updateable master table and updateable snapshots that, though disconnected, can also be updated.

In the Standard Edition of Oracle, you can have only one master site, which replicates changes to its child sites. In the Enterprise Edition, multiple master sites can exist and updates can take place at any of these sites. The updates to these sites must be *synchronized*, meaning that an update is not completed until all of the target sites have been updated; otherwise, conflicts can remain unresolved.

Conflicts can occur when more than one site updates the same data element during the same replication interval. Changes are propagated using deferred remote procedure calls (RPCs) based on events or at points in time when connectivity is available or communications costs are minimal.

Several conflict-resolution routines provided with Enterprise Edition can be automatically used to resolve replication conflicts. An administrator can simply choose which conflict-resolution strategy he wishes to use for a particular replication. For updates that may affect a column or groups of columns, standard resolution choices include the following:

Overwrite and discard value
Used when there is a single master (originating) site for new values to update current values at destination sites.

Minimum and maximum value
Minimum compares the new value at the originating site and the current value at the destination and applies the new value only if it is less than the current value.

Maximum compares the new value at the originating site and the current value at the destination and applies the new value only if it is greater than the current value.

Earliest and latest timestamp value (with designation of a column of type DATE)
> Earliest dictates that when there are multiple new values, the value used for updates will be in the row with the earliest timestamp.

> Latest dictates that when there are multiple new values, the value used for updates will be in the row with the latest timestamp.

Additive and average value for column groups with single numeric columns
> Additive takes the difference of new and old values at the originating site and adds them to the current value at the destination site.

> Average takes the current value at the destination and the new value at the originating site, divides by 2, and applies the new value.

Priority groups and site priority
> When priority levels are assigned to columns and multiple new values occur, higher priority columns will update columns with lower priority.

Uniqueness conflict-resolution routines are used to resolve conflicts that result from the distributed use of primary key and unique constraints. The built-in routines include the following:

Append site name to duplicate value
> Appends the global database name of the originating site to the replicated column.

Append sequence to duplicate value
> Appends a generated sequence number to the column value.

Discard duplicate value
> Discards the row at the originating site that causes errors.

You can also write your own custom conflict-resolution routines and assign them if your business requirements are not addressed by the standard routines.

Managing Advanced Replication

You can manage replication through Oracle Enterprise Manager. Administrators can configure database objects that need to be replicated, schedule replication, troubleshoot error conditions, and view the deferred transaction queue at each location through this central interface. A deferred transaction queue is a queue holding transactions that will be replicated (and applied) to child sites.

For example, to set up a typical multimaster replication, you must first define master groups and tables and objects to be replicated in each of the databases.

You define a connection to the master definition site, and then create one or more master groups for replicating tables and objects to the multiple master sites. Next, you assign conflict-resolution routines for replicated tables in each master group. Finally, you grant appropriate access privileges to users of applications that access the data at the multiple sites.

Advanced Queuing

In the 1980s, *message-oriented middleware* (MOM) gained popular usage. MOM uses *messages* to transmit information between systems. It doesn't require the overhead of a two-phase commit because the MOM itself guarantees the delivery of all messages. Products such as IBM's MQSeries store control information (message destination, expiration, priority, and recipients) and the message contents in a file-based queue. Delivery is guaranteed in that the message will remain in the queue until the destination is available and the message is forwarded.

Oracle's Advanced Queuing (AQ) facility, first introduced with Oracle8 Enterprise Edition and now part of Oracle Streams, provides a complete queuing environment by storing the queue in the Oracle relational database. Advanced queues are Oracle database tables that support queuing operations—in particular, *enqueue* to create messages and *dequeue* to consume them. These messages, which can either be unstructured (raw) or structured (as Oracle objects, which are described in Chapter 14), correspond to rows in a table. Messages are stored in normal queues for normal message handling or in exception queues if they cannot be retrieved for some reason.

Queue creation and management

Queues are created through PL/SQL commands or the Java API. An administrator creates a queue by following these steps:

1. Create a queue table.
2. Create and name the queue.
3. Specify the queue as a normal queue or an exception queue.
4. Specify how long messages remain in the queue: indefinitely, for a fixed length of time, until a particular time elapses between retries, or based on the number of retries.

Queues can be started and stopped by the administrator, who also grants users the privileges necessary for using the queue and revokes those privileges when necessary.

Producers of messages specify a queue name, enqueue options, message properties, and the payload to be put into the queue, which is then handled by a producer agent. Consumer agents listen for messages in one or more queues that are then dequeued so users can use the contents. Notification of the existence of messages in the queue can occur via the Oracle Call Interface (OCI; described in Chapter 1) callback registration or through a listen call that can be used by applications to monitor for messages in multiple queues.

Because messages are stored persistently in queues in the database, a number of message-management features are available. End-to-end tracking is enabled since each message carries its history with it, including location and state of the message, nodes visited, and previous recipients. Messages that don't reach subscribers within a defined lifetime are moved to the exception queue, from which they can be traced. Messages that successfully reach subscribers may be retained after consumption for additional analysis, including enqueue and dequeue times. As messages may be related (for example, one message might be caused by the successful execution of two other messages), retaining the messages can be useful in tracking sequences.

Oracle Database 10g Release 2 introduced the ability to use nonpersistent message queuing for better performance in situations where there is not a need for the capabilities provided by data-based queues.

Queue management through Oracle Enterprise Manager includes the following capabilities:

- Creating, dropping, starting, and stopping queues.
- Adding and removing subscribers.
- Scheduling message propagation from local to remote queues.
- Displaying queue statistics, including the average queue length, the number of messages in the wait state, the number of messages in the ready state, and the number of expired messages.

Oracle9i introduced several new AQ capabilities:

- XML-based messaging over HTTP enables support across firewalls; requests may be through the XML-based Internet Document Access Protocol (iDAP).
- AQ policies and services can be defined using Dynamic Services.
- AQ agents can be defined in and managed through the Oracle Internet Directory (OID).

Oracle9i (and beyond) AQ includes a built-in message transformation for PL/SQL and XSLT. A messaging gateway is also available for propagation to other systems, such as MQSeries and TIBCO.

Publish-and-subscribe capabilities

Oracle8i Enterprise Edition introduced publish-and-subscribe capabilities to Advanced Queuing. As illustrated in Figure 13-3, a *publisher* puts a message onto a queue, while a *subscriber* receives messages from a queue. The publisher and subscriber interact separately with the queue, and neither party needs to know of the existence of the other. Publishers decide when, how, and what to publish, while subscribers express an interest. Messages can be published and subscribed to using the subject name or content (through filtering rules). Asynchronous notification is enabled when subscribers register callback functions.

You can use Advanced Queuing and its publish-and-subscribe features for additional notification of database events that, in turn, improve the management of the

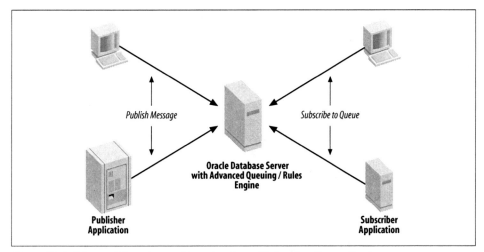

Publish Message

Subscribe to Queue

Oracle Database Server
with Advanced Queuing / Rules
Engine

Publisher
Application

Subscriber
Application

Figure 13-3. Advanced Queuing configuration for publish-subscribe applications

database or business applications. Database events such as DML (inserts, updates, deletions) and system events (startup, shutdown, and so on) can be published and subscribed to. As an example, an application may be built to automatically inform a subscriber when a shipment occurs to certain highly valued customers; the subscriber would then know that she should begin to track the shipment's progress and alert the customer that it is in transit.

Oracle Database 11g includes several enhancements to Oracle's messaging server that increase the performance and reliability of the server.

Oracle Streams

Oracle9i Release 2 introduced Oracle Streams, which folded the capabilities of Advanced Replication and Advanced Queuing into a single product family and added a method of sharing data and events within a database or between databases. Streams enable the propagation of changes via a capture-and-apply process, including Oracle's change data capture. Changes can be propagated between Oracle instances, from Oracle instances to non-Oracle instances (via Transparent Gateways), and from non-Oracle databases to Oracle (via messaging gateways in combination with custom code on the non-Oracle source to collect changes). Streams leverages log-based procedures to capture DML or DDL changes or synchronous capture for DML changes and then uses queuing procedures as part of the staging. User-supplied "apply" rules define consumption.

When changes are captured from an Oracle source database redo log or changes in rows are gathered from synchronous capture, a background database process creates a logical change record (LCR). LCR and user message events are enqueued in a

Streams queue. Events are propagated from source to target queues and then, via a background process, dequeued in the target database and applied. Since Oracle Database 10g, downstream capture of changes and enqueue/dequeue of messages in batch are supported.

Also, since Oracle Database 10g, Streams can be configured to provide Database Change Notification via email, HTTP, and PL/SQL. This feature can send notifications to a client whenever the data in a query result set has changed. Oracle Database 11g enhances this feature enabling notification for individual row changes, rather than just a single notification whenever any row in the result set changes.

As of Oracle Database 10g Release 2, Streams can be managed through Oracle Enterprise Manager. A migration tool is available to aid migration from Advanced Replication to Streams.

Streams and Grid Computing

Oracle Streams provides key functionality in grid computing implementations. By its nature, grid computing can consist of widely distributed data, users, and platforms. Streams enables the movement of data when and where it is needed, as well as message sharing, notification or invocation of user procedures on events, message and database change subscriptions, and interoperation with other platforms. Streaming databases can offload processing to replica databases by creating operational data stores, or can create replicas and apply changes from replicas or data transformations to the production database.

As of Oracle Database 11g, Streams can mine active online log files for DML and DDL, enabling low-latency change propagation among RAC instances. Streams runs from a single RAC instance identified as the primary for queues and processes. A secondary instance can be identified to provide a more highly available solution.

Streams can also play a role in database migrations to grid computing and newer Oracle versions. When the new database is installed and while the original database remains in production, Streams can be used to capture changes on the original database that are then applied to the new database as migration nears completion.

Transportable Tablespaces

The previous sections focused on sharing data between distributed databases when the data is "live"—making sure changes are propagated to other databases in real time. *Transportable tablespaces* are a way to speed up the distribution of complete tablespaces between multiple databases while the tablespaces are not active.

Transportable tablespaces were introduced with Oracle8*i* Enterprise Edition to rapidly copy and distribute tablespaces among database instances. Previously, tablespaces needed to be exported from the source database and imported at the target (or unloaded and loaded). Transportable tablespaces enable copies to be moved simply through the use of file transfer commands such as *ftp*.

Before you copy and move a copy of the tablespace, you should make the tablespace read-only to avoid inadvertently changing it. Data dictionary information needs to be exported from the source prior to transfer, then imported at the target.

Some of the most popular reasons to use transportable tablespaces include:

- Rapid copying of tablespaces from enterprise data warehouses to data marts
- Copying of tablespaces from operational systems to operational data stores for use in consolidated reporting
- Publishing of tablespaces for distribution on CD-ROM
- Use of backup copies for rapid point-in-time tablespace recovery

Oracle9*i* eliminated the restriction that Oracle block sizes needed to be the same in both the source and target databases. Oracle Database 10*g* eliminated the restriction that the source and target databases needed to be running on the same operating system platform.

CHAPTER 14

Oracle Extended Datatypes

The Oracle database has a rich set of native datatypes, but you may sometimes need to go beyond their capabilities, depending on the specifics of your development and deployment requirements. You can use traditional datatypes, such as those described in Chapter 4, to represent a portion of the information that your organization needs to store and manage. Introduction of the XML datatype (described in Chapter 4) and support for features such as XMLSchema, an XML DB repository (enabling URL-based access to XML documents stored in Oracle), and SQL/XML (for generating XML documents from SQL) have extended Oracle's ability to function as a "XML database." Oracle also provides datatypes that are specifically designed to provide optimal storage, performance, and flexibility for other specific types of data, the focus of this chapter.

Real-world information used in business, such as purchase orders, claims forms, shipping forms, and so on, may sometimes be best represented as object types, which are more complex than the simple atomic datatypes discussed in Chapter 4. Location-oriented data may best be represented using spatial coordinates. Documents, images, video clips, and audio clips have their own special requirements for storage and retrieval.

Oracle has extended the functionality of its basic relational database engine to support the storage and manipulation of these nontraditional datatypes through the introduction of additional features and options. Oracle has also extended the types of data, the SQL that manipulates that data, and the basic Oracle service framework so that you can modify the data and extend its capabilities even further.

Object-Oriented Development

An object-oriented approach to software development shifts the focus from building computing procedures that operate on sets of data to modeling business processes. Building software components that model business processes with documented interfaces makes programming more efficient and allows applications to offer more flexible deployment strategies. It also makes applications easier to modify when business conditions change. In addition, since the modeling reflects real business use, application performance may improve as objects are built that do not require excessive manipulation to conform to the real-world behavior of the business processes they represent.

Oracle chose to take an evolutionary approach to object technology by allowing *data abstraction*, or the creation of user-defined datatypes as objects and collections as extensions to the Oracle relational database. The Objects and Extensibility features, included with the database since Oracle8*i*, position Oracle as an object-relational database.

Support of the Java language complements this approach. The JVM (formerly JServer) feature is a Java Virtual Machine integrated with the database. It supports the building and running of Java components, as well as Java stored procedures and triggers, in the server.

The Promise of Code Reuse

Although a number of object-oriented approaches and technologies have been introduced since the 1980s, many of the promised improvements in software development efficiency have largely been unrealized. One of the reasons that these productivity improvements have failed is the difficulty many developers have had in making the adjustment to building reusable components. In addition, the need to learn new languages (such as C++) and technologies (object-oriented databases, CORBA, DCOM, and .NET) slowed the adoption of object-oriented development. Developers did become more familiar with these techniques and skills as Java moved into the mainstream of development. Interestingly, Oracle leverages many of these object features itself in development of new database capabilities.

However, the benefits of code reuse are more likely to be realized in deployment of a Service-Oriented Architecture (SOA) today, which is described in more detail in Chapter 15. Oracle's Application Server/Fusion Middleware is a key component. The database has also evolved in providing web services as we describe in this chapter.

Object-Relational Features

This section describes the major object-relational features available in Oracle.

Objects in Oracle

Objects created in Oracle are reusable components representing real-world business processes. The objects created using the database Objects and Extensibility features occupy the same role as the table in a standard relational model: the object is a template for the creation of individual "instances" of the object, which take the same role as rows within a table. An object is "instantiated" using Oracle-supplied "constructors" in SQL or PL/SQL.

An *object* consists of a name, one or more attributes, and methods. *Attributes* model the structure and state of the real-world entity, while *methods* model the operations of the entity. Methods are functions or procedures, usually written either in PL/SQL or Java or externally in a language such as C. Methods make up the interface between an object and the outside programming environment. Each method is identified by the name of the object that contains the method and a method name. Each method can have one or more *parameters*, which are the vehicles for passing data to the method from the calling application.

For example, a purchase order can be represented as an object. Attributes can include a purchase order number, a vendor, a vendor address, a ship-to address, and a collection of items (with their associated quantity and price). You can use a method to add an item to the purchase order, delete an item from the purchase order, or return the total amount of the purchase order.

You can store objects as rows in tables or as values in columns. Each row object has a unique object identifier (OID) created by Oracle. Row objects can be referred to from other objects or relational tables. The REF datatype represents such references. For column objects, Oracle adds hidden columns for the object's attributes.

Object views provide a means of creating virtual object tables from data stored in the columns of relational tables in the database. These views can also include attributes from other objects. Object views are created by defining an object type, writing a query defining the mapping between data and tables containing attributes for that type, and specifying a unique object identifier. When the data is stored in a relational table, the unique identifier is usually the primary key. This implementation means that you can use object-oriented programming techniques without converting existing relational tables to object-relational tables. The tradeoff when using this approach is that performance may be less than optimal, since the data representing attributes for an object may reside in several different tables. Hence, it may make sense to convert the relational tables to object tables in the future.

Objects that share the same attributes and methods are said to be in the same datatype or *class*. For example, internal and external purchase orders can be in the same class as purchase orders. *Collection types* model a number of objects of the same datatype as varying arrays (VARRAYs) if the collection of objects is bounded and ordered or as nested tables if the collection is unbounded and unordered. If a collection has fewer than 4,000 bytes, it is stored as part of the database table; if it is larger, it is stored as a Binary Large Object (BLOB) in a segment separate from the table that is considered "out-of-line" storage. Nested table rows are stored in a separate table identified through a hidden NESTED_TABLE_ID by Oracle. Typically, VARRAYs are used when an entire collection is being retrieved and nested tables are used when a collection is being queried, particularly if the collection is large and only a subset is needed.

An application can call object methods through SQL, PL/SQL, Pro*C/C++, Java, OCI, and the Oracle Type Translator (OTT). The OTT provides client-side mappings to object types by generating header files containing C structure declarations and indicators. Developers can tune applications by using a client-side object cache to improve performance.

Inheritance, or the use of one class of objects as the basis for another, more specific class, is one of the most powerful features of object-oriented design. The child class inherits all the methods and attributes of the parent class and also adds its own methods and attributes to supplement the capabilities of the parent class. The great power of inheritance is that a change in a parent class automatically ripples down to the child classes. Object-oriented design supports inheritance over many levels of parent, child, and grandchild classes.

Polymorphism describes the ability of a child class to supersede or "override" the operation of a parent method by redefining the method on its own. Once a method has been replaced in a child class, subsequent changes to the method in the parent class don't ripple down to the child class or its descendants. In the purchase order example, as shown in Figure 14-1, purchase orders from contracted suppliers and suppliers not under contract inherit the methods and attributes of external purchase orders. However, the procedure for placing the order can exhibit polymorphism because additional approvals may be required for ordering from suppliers not under contract.

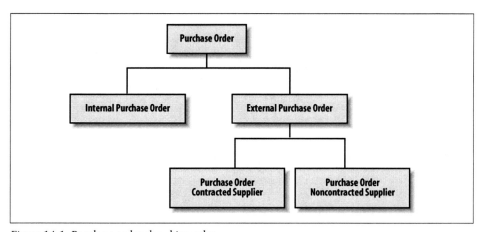

Figure 14-1. Purchase order class hierarchy

Inheritance and polymorphism were not supported in Oracle8*i* objects, though the Oracle8*i* database could act as persistent storage for objects, and an application interface in an object-oriented language such as C++ or Java could add these features to the client-side implementation of objects. Oracle9*i* added SQL type inheritance to the database, as well as object view hierarchies, type evolution, generic and transient datatypes, function-based indexes for type method functions, and multilevel collections. Oracle Database 10g added support for remote access to object types. Oracle Database 11g added an ANSI SQL feature that provides a method invocation scoping operator.

Other extensibility features

Several other extensibility features are included in the Objects and Extensibility features. These include:

- The ability to create new index types by defining the structure of the index
- The ability to store the index data inside or outside the Oracle database
- The ability to create user-defined operators for use in standard SQL statements
- An interface to the cost-based optimizer to extend support for user-defined object types and indexes

The use of object-relational features is most common today among software developers who are building database extensions. Oracle itself has made use of these features in the creation of many of the database features—for example, in the Spatial and Multimedia capabilities.

Java's Role and Web Services

Java has gained wide acceptance as an application language, particularly for building web-based applications, due to its portability and availability on a wide variety of platforms.

For Java developers wanting to use the Oracle database as a backend to their applications, Oracle first offered support for JDBC 3.0 in Oracle Database 10g and continued to offer support for the two common approaches to accessing the database from a Java program: JDBC and SQLJ. Both of these approaches are based on industry-standard application program interfaces (APIs):

JDBC
> More commonly used since it can be used where SQL is dynamic, or when a developer wants explicit control over interactions with the database.

SQLJ
> An industry standard typically used when static SQL statements have been embedded into a Java program. SQLJ is similar to other Oracle precompilers in that Java source files are created with calls to the SQLJ runtime (as well as to additional profile files). The Java source code is then compiled, and the application is run with the SQLJ runtime library.

SQLJ and JDBC can be mixed in the same program when some SQL is static and other SQL is dynamic.

The Oracle JVM in Oracle9*i* and later releases (formerly JServer in Oracle8*i*) introduced additional component- and object-based development options. Oracle9*i* and subsequent versions feature a tightly integrated Java Virtual Machine (hence the JVM name) and support for Java stored procedures in the database; these enable component-based development to take place through the use of Enterprise JavaBeans (EJBs). Java Messaging Support (JMS) is provided through Oracle Streams.

Oracle Database 10*g* added web services used in triggering database operations via nonconnected clients. Web services capabilities in the database include SQL, PL/SQL, embedded Java, JDBC, HTTP client, and SOAP client, and are combined with those in Oracle Application Server (Java, J2EE, JDBC, HTTP, SOAP server, and XML). The database can act as a web services consumer or provider and can be exposed using JPublisher, Oracle's utility for generating Java classes that represent user-defined database entities.

As of Oracle Database 11*g*, the database can be treated as a service provider in a Service-Oriented Architecture (SOA) environment using the XDB HTTP Server for SOA. PL/SQL packages, procedures, and functions can be exposed as web services. Dynamic SQL and XQuery queries can be executed when deploying the database in this manner.

Enterprise JavaBeans

Server-side Java components are referred to as Enterprise JavaBeans (EJB) in contrast to client-side reusable interface components, which are referred to as simply JavaBeans. You can deploy EJBs in the database server or with Oracle Application Server. The tight integration of the Java Virtual Machine in the database makes use of database System Global Area (SGA) memory-management capabilities to provide EJB server scalability beyond what would be expected in most JVM implementations. For example, each client within the JVM requires only about 50-150 KB of memory for session state.

In its initial release, Oracle8*i* supported the *session bean*, which is an EJB created by a specific call from the client that usually exists only during a single client/server session. Session beans may be *stateless*, allowing the EJB server to reuse instances of the bean to service clients, or *stateful* (i.e., bound to clients directly). Database cache information maintained by stateful session beans is synchronized with the database when transactions occur by using JDBC or SQLJ. *Entity Java beans*, also known as *persistent beans* (because they remain in existence through multiple sessions), were not supported in Oracle8*i* but are supported in Oracle9*i* and subsequent database JVMs. The third type of EJB is the *message-driven bean*, designed to receive asynchronous Java Message Services (JMS) messages and supported via Oracle's more recent Applications Servers that support EJB 3.0.

Extensibility Features and Options

Oracle's extensibility features and options extend SQL to perform tasks that can't otherwise be easily programmed in a relational database. These include manipulation of text, multimedia and content, and spatial data. These features are typically used by application developers but are sometimes bundled with applications sold by Oracle partners.

Oracle Multimedia and Oracle Text

Oracle Multimedia (formerly known as *inter*Media) has been included with the database since version 8.1.6 of Oracle8*i*. In Oracle9*i*, the product's text features became known as Oracle Text. These features were available as options in previous versions of Oracle:

- The Text Management feature was formerly known as the ConText Option.
- The Location Services evolved from the Spatial Option and supports the location queries and the geocoding described later, in the "Oracle Spatial" section.
- Image storage and manipulation features were formerly bundled in the Image Option.

Additionally, the product extensions enable the storage and manipulation of audio and video clips including extraction of content and organizing metadata as a CLOB in XML format. Oracle has positioned Oracle Multimedia and Oracle Text as being useful features for applications that typically include multiple media types since the features integrate all of these key datatypes and their associated functions. Oracle Multimedia and Oracle Text utilize a number of underlying database storage options, which are described in Table 14-1.

Table 14-1. Storage options for Oracle Multimedia and Oracle Text

Type	Storage options
Text/images	VARCHAR2
	BLOB
	CLOB
	VARCHAR
	CHAR
	LONG
	LONG RAW
	Object attribute
	Master-detail stores (in which the master table identifies the text or image and the detail table contains the content)
	BFILEs
	URLs that point to content
	DICOM

Table 14-1. Storage options for Oracle Multimedia and Oracle Text (continued)

Type	Storage options
Audio and video clips	BLOB
	BFILE
	URLs that point to content
Locator ordinates	VARRAYs

Oracle Database 10*g* was enhanced to store large documents of up to 128 terabytes in LOBs. Oracle Database 11*g* Multimedia object type media size limits are extended to those of BLOBs (between 8 and 128 terabytes). Also introduced in this version of Multimedia is a new, higher-performing BLOB implementation accessible via Oracle's SecureFiles.

Oracle Multimedia and Oracle Text support a number of commonly used formats:

- Documents can be indexed while stored in formats such as ASCII, Microsoft Word, Excel, and PowerPoint, WordPerfect, HTML, XML, and Adobe Acrobat (PDF).

- Audio formats supported include AU, AIFF, AIFF-C, WAV, MPEG1, MPEG2, and MPEG4 audio formats.

- Video formats supported include Apple QuickTime 3.0, AVI, video MPEG formats (MPEG and MP4), and Real Networks Real video format (RMFF).

- Image formats supported include BMPF, CALS, FPIX, GIFF (gif), JFIF (jpeg), PBMF, PGMF, PPMF, PPNF, PCXF (pcx), PICT, PNGF, RPIX, RASF, TGAF, TIFF, and WBMP. Image-compression formats supported include ASCII encoding, BMPRLE, DEFLATE, DEFLATE-ADAM7, FAX3, FAX4, GIFLZW, GIFLZW-INTERLACED, HUFFMAN3, JPEG, JPEG-PROGRESSIVE, LZW, LZWHDIFF, NONE, PACKBITS, PCXRLE, RAW, SUNRLE, and TARGARLE.

- As of Oracle Database 11*g*, Digital Imaging and Communications in Medicine (DICOM) version 3, a medical imaging standard, is supported. The database includes support for single-frame and multiframe images, waveforms, 3-D volume slices, video segments, and structured support. Methods and functions are available to convert DICOM to JPEG, GIF, PNG, TIFF, and other formats. Metadata can be extracted into XML documents or custom mappings can be created.

With Oracle's text-management capabilities, you can identify the strongest theme (or *gist*) of a document and generate document summaries based on that theme. Oracle Database 10*g* additions included theme (NEAR) proximity searching and the ability to determine the character set and language of documents with unknown content. Searching capabilities include full-text searches for word and phrase matching, theme searches, and mixed searches for both text and nontext data. As of Oracle Database 10*g*, native indexing columns of type XMLType using Oracle Text are supported.

Since typical users of Oracle text management are often news services that publish news items to interested users via the Web, recent database releases include an algorithm for determining the popularity rankings of web pages and content. Also included since Oracle Database 10g is an easy, custom text application building interface through JDeveloper with a text application generator, a catalog search application generator wizard, and a classification training set wizard.

Image support in the Oracle database includes conversion among image and compression formats, access to raw pixel data, and support for basic image-manipulation functions such as scaling and cropping.

Clients can access audio and video files through Java Media Framework (JMF) players. (Java Advanced Imaging in Oracle9i and more recent releases also provide image support through JMF.) Streaming servers such as the Real Networks Server can also deliver audio and video content on demand.

You can also access images, audio, and video stored in Oracle and Multimedia through C++, Java, OCI, or PL/SQL. Oracle Database 10g and newer database release image object types support the SQL/MM Still Image standard, ISO/IEC 13249-5 SQL and support for the Sun Microsystems Java Advanced Imaging (JAI) package for storing and processing content. DICOM content stored in Oracle Database 11g is accessible using Java and PL/SQL APIs.

Audio, video, and images stored using Multimedia might also be included as part of a web site using a variety of web-authoring tools. Content services are provided to the Portal in Oracle Application Server, Oracle JDeveloper, and various Oracle partners.

Oracle Content Management

Oracle's Content Database Suite provides core document services in the Oracle database and the infrastructure needed to build document management applications. Content DB provides the repository and the Content Server manages the documents. The suite can be used for file server consolidation, management of document policies and procedures, document sharing and collaboration, and as a content repository for applications.

In 2007, Oracle completed the acquisition of Stellent and began providing a more complete content management framework and suite of applications called Universal Content Management (UCM). UCM consists of an enterprise content management suite that supports document management, web content management, digital asset management, and records management.

A third pillar in Oracle's content management offerings is Imaging and Process Management (IP/M) supporting process-oriented imaging applications for Oracle's E-Business Suite, PeopleSoft, and JD Edwards products. Modules supported include accounts payable and receivable automation, travel and expense automation, and HR and application processing.

When deploying such an infrastructure, extensive records management and security are often stated requirements. Oracle's Universal Records Management (URM) provides unified consistent records and central policy retention management for Oracle's enterprise content management solutions. The content repositories are accessed through adapters. For example, URM in combination with a Content DB adapter is a replacement for Oracle's earlier Records DB offering.

Information Rights Management (IRM) can be deployed to issue Secure Keys from an IRM Server, controlling access to and securing sensitive content. IRM enables management of centralized policies, auditing, monitoring, encryption, and rights revocation.

Oracle Ultra Search

Ultra Search provides search and location information for text in Oracle databases, other ODBC-accessible databases, Oracle Portal repositories, IMAP mail servers, HTML documents available from web servers, and other files. Oracle database version 8.1.7 introduced Ultra Search, leveraging Oracle Text. Today, Ultra Search is included with the Oracle database and the Oracle Application Server.

Ultra Search gathers information using a Java process *crawler* started by Oracle on a set schedule. The crawler indexes the documents residing on various servers using Oracle Text, and then stores this information in an Oracle database. The Ultra Search administration tool is a J2EE-compliant web application. Application builders can invoke Ultra Search using PL/SQL or Java procedures and use the APIs to make crawler results "searchable."

In Oracle Application Server, Ultra Search is located in the metadata repository. Application Server users can search and receive a list of results through a portlet that can be accessed through Oracle Portal.

In a secure search, document retrieval is based on user access rights. An access control list (ACL) is evaluated during such a secure search. The ACLs are stored in XML DB.

 Ultra Search requires management skills commonly found where Oracle databases and Application Servers are deployed. For organizations wanting to deploy content search without those skills, Oracle offers Secure Enterprise Search (SES) with plug-ins for a wide variety of data sources and commonly deployed Internet directories.

Oracle Spatial Option

Spatial data is data that contains location information. The Oracle Spatial Option provides the functions and procedures that allow spatial data to be stored in an Oracle database and then accessed and analyzed according to location comparisons.

An example of using spatial query functions to combine spatial and standard relational conditions would be to "find all homes within two square miles of the intersection of Main Street and First Avenue in which the residents' income is greater than $100,000, and show their location." This query might return a list of home addresses or, when used with a Geographic Information System (GIS), plot the home locations on a map, as shown in Figure 14-2. Geocoding matches references such as addresses, phone numbers (including area codes), and postal codes (with longitude and latitude), which are then stored in the database.

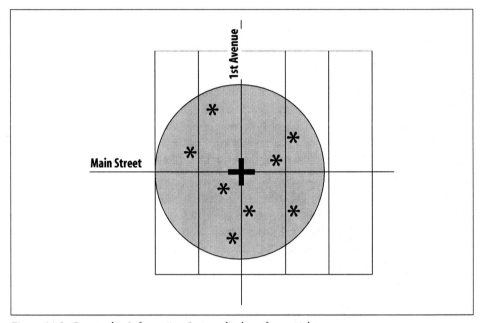

Figure 14-2. Geographic Information System display of a spatial query

Multiple geometric forms are supported by the Oracle Spatial Option to represent many different types of spatial data, including points and point clusters, lines and line strings, polygons and complex polygons with holes, arc strings, line strings, compound polygons, and circles. You can determine the interaction of these features through the use of operators such as touch, overlap, inside, and disjoint.

Data that shares the same object space and coordinates but represents different characteristics (such as physical and economic) is often modeled in layers. Each layer is divided into tiles representing smaller subareas within the larger area. A representation of this tile is stored with a spatial index that provides for quick lookups of multiple characteristics in the same tile. The Spatial Option uses these representations to rapidly retrieve data based on spatial characteristics. For example, you can perform a query against a physical area to examine where pollutants, minerals, and water are present. Each of these characteristics is likely to be stored in a separate layer, but they can be quickly mapped to their common tiles. The designers of these spatial-based databases can increase the resolution of the maps by increasing the number of tiles representing the geography.

The Spatial Option fully leverages Oracle's object features through the use of a *spatial object type* that represents single or multielement geometries. Spatial coordinates are stored in VARRAYs.

Oracle Database 10g introduced the GeoRaster for storing, indexing, querying, analyzing, and delivering raster image data, associated spatial vector geometry data, and metadata. This feature enables storage of multidimensional grid layers and digital images in an object-relational schema that are referenced to coordinate systems. Oracle Database 11g added three-dimensional geometry objects and enhanced web services support including business directory, Web Feature Service (WFS), Catalog Services for the Web (CSW), and OpenLS support.

In the real world, most spatial implementations in business aren't custom-built from SQL, but instead utilize purchased GIS solutions that are built on top of databases. Many of these GIS providers include Oracle Spatial technology as part of their product bundles.

Using the Extensibility Framework in Oracle

Oracle allows users to extend the basic functionality of the database. Oracle's extensibility framework provides entry points in which developers can add their own features to the existing feature set. By using this framework you can do the following:

Add new relational or set operators for use in SQL statements
These operators can be useful when working with extended datatypes, such as multimedia or spatial data. You can create relational operators that relate specifically to a particular datatype, such as the relational operator CLOSER TO, which you can use in SQL statements that access spatial data.

Create cooperative indexing
Cooperative indexing is a scheme in which an external application is responsible for building and using an index structure that you can use with complex datatypes. The indexes created are known as *domain indexes*.

Extend the optimizer
If you use extended indexes, user-defined datatypes, or other features, you can extend the statistics-collection process or define selectivity and cost functions for these extended features. The cost-based optimizer can then use these to choose an appropriate query plan.

Add cartridge services

These are services used by Oracle database extensions (such as the spatial capabilities) providing memory management, context management, parameter management, string and number manipulation, file I/O, internationalization, error reporting, and thread management. These services are available to software developers to provide a means to create uniform integration of extensions with the Oracle database.

With these features, the extensibility framework enables you or a third-party software developer to integrate additional functionality into the main Oracle database while still using the core features of the database, such as security management, backup and recovery, and the SQL interface.

CHAPTER 15

Beyond the Oracle Database

As we have mentioned (just a few times before!), the Oracle database is a deep and wide product, providing vast realms of capabilities. Until now, though, this book has focused on Oracle as a database—a place to store, retrieve, and manipulate data. As such, your Oracle database is an integral part of your overall infrastructure.

This chapter goes beyond this core functionality to explore features of Oracle beyond its data-centric core. This chapter focuses on three main areas:

- Application Express, a browser-based declarative development tool. Application Express, commonly referred to as ApEx, is a free add-on to an Oracle database that you can use to create applications.

- Fusion Middleware, which encompasses the functionality of Oracle Application Server and more.

- Oracle SOA Suite, which provides the Service-Oriented Architecture (SOA), a group of features and offerings that allow your Oracle database to deliver specific functionality in an easy-to-integrate form.

Application Express

In Chapter 1, we provided a basic overview of various development tools that could be used with the Oracle database and stated that we would not delve further into the development area. This section makes an exception to that rule by covering Application Express (commonly known as ApEx), a development tool that comes with the Oracle database and simplifies HTML application development. We discuss ApEx here because the tool can be downloaded for free and installed on an Oracle database installation without any other software, and because the tool creates applications by generating PL/SQL packages that are stored in the Oracle database.

The Application Express product was previously known at HTML-DB, which itself sprung from WebDB. All of these products had the same basic development methodology—browser-based wizards that helped you create application components that also ran in a browser.

ApEx creates components as PL/SQL packages that produce the browser-based user interface. ApEx components can include forms, reports, and charts. The ApEx development environment gives you the ability to create rich applications, and that environment is too robust to fully describe in this brief section. The following points emerge as some of the more interesting aspects of ApEx:

- ApEx is data-centric, which means that links can be built into reports and charts. The automatic links make it easy to drill down into data for more detail.
- You can use a web service to provide data for ApEx forms and reports.
- You can import data from a spreadsheet into an Oracle table with an easy utility, or export the contents of a report or page to a spreadsheet.
- You can export any report to a PDF, making the report available outside the ApEx environment.
- ApEx allows you to specify basic look-and-feel specifications for all the pages in your application.
- SQL Workshop, a component of ApEx, gives you a graphical interface to use in creating and managing your Oracle data.
- Oracle Technology Network offers a hosted version of ApEx that you can use from any browser.
- You can create your own security schemes for limiting access to pages within an application.
- You can add JavaScript logic to extend your ApEx application.
- The latest release of ApEx includes an Access migration tool that will help you move your data from an Access application into your Oracle database. Once the data is in Oracle, you can quickly generate an ApEx application for the data.

Oracle Fusion Middleware

At the most basic level, users do not care where the computing resources that handle their requirements come from. The first edition of this book came out at a time when the overall computing environment was moving from a client/server model, where computing operations were split between a client computer and a server, and the dawn of the Internet age, where the "new" paradigm of on-demand computing allowed access to applications without depending on client-side resources. Of course, this change was just another swing of the pendulum, from the days when the computing environment was dumb clients and centralized mainframes.

The current IT landscape uses multiple tiers of servers. Many organizations have a database tier, full of servers that handle the Oracle software, and an intermediate tier of application servers. These servers typically are used to deploy applications, acting as a pool of resources that sit between the user and the database tier.

As this multitier architecture grew in popularity, so too did the functionality provided by these application servers. More and more components, which provided a broader reach of prebuilt functional areas, were added to the application servers. Oracle Application Server (AS), the focus of the following sections, is one of the leading examples of application servers available today, based on both the amount of functionality and the sales of the product.

Oracle Application Server, which, prior to Oracle Database 10*g* was known as Oracle *i*AS, is the other major component of the "Oracle platform." Oracle Application Server has continually grown in the number of components it includes and the scope of functionality those components address. AS both complements and supplements the capabilities of the Oracle database, combining to create a highly integrated yet open infrastructure.

The main component of Oracle's Fusion Middleware is Oracle Application Server 10*g* or a more current release (depending on when you are reading this book). Fusion Middleware also encompasses the Oracle SOA Suite, covered in the next section, and other components more recently introduced to the Oracle stack. The remainder of this section focuses on the components of Fusion Middleware that come with Oracle Application Server.

Oracle Application Server Editions

Oracle Application Server comes in four separate editions, as of the release of Oracle Database 11*g*:

Java Edition
> Contains the HTTP Server, Java Containers for J2EE, JDeveloper, Oracle Application Development Framework, Toplink, Oracle Business Rules (described as part of the Oracle SOA Suite later in this chapter), MapViewer, and Enterprise Manager.

Standard Edition One
> A counterpart to Oracle Database Standard Edition One, AS SE1 contains all the capabilities of Standard Edition but is limited to deployment on a single server with no more than two CPUs. This edition also includes a limited-use licence for Oracle Internet Directory.

Standard Edition
> Contains everything in Java Edition as well as Portal, Web Cache, single sign-on capabilities, and the Content Management SDK. Also includes Oracle Internet Directory.

Enterprise Edition

Contains everything in Standard Edition with these additional components:

- Reporting and Forms services
- Oracle Business Intelligence Discoverer
- Personalization
- Wireless
- Oracle Sensor Edge Server
- Integration components
- Oracle Enterprise Service Bus described as part of the Oracle SOA Suite below

You can optionally add Oracle WebCenter, Oracle Business Activity Monitoring, and Oracle BPEL Manager to the Enterprise Edition, and Oracle Service Registry to all editions of AS. WebCenter is described in this section, while the other three options are covered in the section on the Oracle SOA Suite later in this chapter.

Oracle Application Server Installation

You can see from the brief list of functionality in the previous section that Oracle Application Server is a broad product. You can configure AS as part of the installation process to provide different types of functionality, including J2EE Server, Web Cache, Portal, Wireless, Business Intelligence, and Forms.

Oracle Application Server Components

The following subsections discuss the various functional components of Oracle Application Server. Services, which affect the overall operation of AS, are described in the later section, "Oracle Application Server System Services."

HTTP Server

The Oracle HTTP Server (OHS) that is part of Oracle Application Server is the same basic product that we described in earlier sections as part of the database. OHS in AS is based on Apache, but provides some additional modules, known as *mod*s, including:

mod_oc4j

Directs requests for Java modules to the Oracle Containers for Java component, described below

mod_jserv

Used for Java Server Pages

mod_webdav
> Supports versioning through web-based Distributed Authoring and Versioning (WebDAV)

mod_osso
> Provides built-in single sign-on functionality

You can add other mods to OHS, but Oracle Support may ask you to remove unsupported modules if a problem occurs.

Oracle HTTP Server includes the ability to use server-side includes, which can be used to add code to the headers and footers of all pages served to implement standardized behaviors and look-and-feel.

OHS provides virtual host capabilities, which let you use a single instance of OHS to map to multiple hostnames. OHS can act as a proxy server or a reverse proxy server, and it can also support URL rewriting, which allows administrators to change the location of a page without requiring users to change the way they access the page. OHS includes a proxy plug-in for Internet Information Server and SunONE server, enabling requests to these servers to be automatically rerouted to OHS. These plug-ins can provide the load balancing functionality, described in the later section, "Clustering," for Oracle Containers for J2EE (described in the following section).

Containers for J2EE (OC4J)

The core Java capabilities of Oracle Application Server are provided by Oracle Application Server Containers for J2EE, also known as OC4J. This component is a Java virtual machine, providing support for a wide range of Java 1.3 standards, including session beans, entity beans (with both bean-managed and session-managed persistence), and message-driven Java beans, Java Server Pages 1.2 and Servlets 2.3, and Java Message Service.

You can scale OC4J by having multiple instances of OC4J on a single machine as well as having multiple threads, each running a single application module, in an individual OC4J instance.

OC4J also implements JDBC connections to the Oracle database, which can include connection pooling.

TopLink

TopLink provides object-relational mapping, the ability to associate object attributes with relational tables and columns. Because TopLink performs this mapping, a developer can change the mapping without changing the Java code that accesses the underlying data.

TopLink also provides caching and optimization to reduce database and network traffic.

Development tools

Oracle Application Server 10g includes several development kits:

Application Development Framework (ADF)
> Meant to simplify Java development by including a wide variety of prebuilt services and libraries to allow rapid implementation of core Java services.

XML Development Kit
> Provides components, tools, and utilities for working with XML in applications.

Content Management Kit
> Integrates with Oracle content management products in Collaboration Suite and provides a variety of capabilities, including security, versioning, workflow, and search and retrieval operations.

MapViewer
> Makes it easier to build maps to represent themes or locations.

WebCenter
> A component in Oracle Application Server since Application Server 10g Release 3. Designed to bring together the worlds of Java, AJAX, business intelligence, content management, and collaboration services. Oracle has stated that WebCenter will be the "default user environment for the next generation of Oracle Applications called Fusion Applications," so it seems that this environment will become more prominent as we move forward.

The increased need for integration of diverse applications has thrust web services to the forefront of application development. Oracle Application Server supports a range of web service standards, including SOAP, WSDL, and UDDI. AS includes the ability to easily publish both stateful and stateless J2EE classes as web services, automatically generating WSDL descriptions and client-side proxy stubs.

Naturally, the course of standards bodies, like that of true love, never runs smooth. AS already provides integration between .NET SOAP and Java SOAP, and Oracle has stated its intention to continue this type of integration.

Development servers

Oracle's traditional development tools, including Oracle Forms Developer (formerly known as Developer), Oracle Reports, and JDeveloper, are part of the Oracle Developer Suite of products, as are Oracle Designer and Discoverer. However, AS includes runtime services for Forms and Reports.

Oracle Application Server, Enterprise Edition, comes with a Forms Services component. This component allows a user to run the user interface to a Forms application as a Java applet on the client. The Forms Service creates a server process to handle HTTP requests from the Java client.

AS Enterprise Edition also includes a Reports Server used in deploying Oracle's previous-generation Reports product. The Reports Server creates and manages reports processes to handle user requests. Reports can be cached for a specified length of time, so that subsequent requests are satisfied by retrieving the report, rather than by running the queries for the report again. Reports can be scheduled to run and be delivered to multiple recipients.

Portal

Oracle Application Server Portal has gone through some significant changes in its history. When it was first released under the name of WebDB, as part of the Oracle database, Portal was viewed as a tool to create HTML-based applications, a role subsequently taken by HTML DB, and later ApEx, described earlier in this chapter. WebDB was renamed Oracle Portal, and the aim of the product was changed to focus on bringing together separate sources of information into a common desktop. Entire books have been written on Portal alone, so the description in this section is, of necessity, a very brief overview of the range of Portal capabilities.

Portal uses *pages*, which can consist of static or dynamic information, and which use a theme for overall look and feel. Portal includes wizards for easy creation of pages.

Portlets are applications that can get information from a wide variety of sources, from a database to a web source, and can be plugged into the Portal framework. The Portal framework provides a look and feel as well as navigation controls for all the information displayed in it.

Developers can allow users to customize some parts of portlet and page display, and Portal will automatically save these customizations. Portal provides a single sign-on capability to identify users and secure content.

A user can search across all information in a portal with a built-in search mechanism. Developers can also add categorization to pages to aid in searches. A single Portal deployment can also deploy multiple versions of pages in different languages.

Oracle Application Server 10g Release 2 introduced a new feature called Instant Portal, which creates a portal, including relevant portlets, with a single click on installation. The release also added the Oracle Portlet Factory, created to make it easy to build portlets against a variety of data sources, most notably SAP.

Wireless

OracleAS Wireless is a set of services and applications that form a development platform that can be used to create applications to address a variety of mobile devices and forms, including PDAs, cell phones, and other wireless devices. OracleAS Wireless supports three modes:

Pull mode
> In this mode, a wireless user requests information.

Push mode
> In this mode, information is sent to a wireless user.

Persistent mode
> In this mode, a wireless user can maintain an application even when he or she is out of wireless contact.

This component also includes a set of mobile enablers, which provide services that wireless applications commonly need. These enablers include:

- Content and data syndication, which translates web and WAP content for mobile devices
- Location services
- Personalization
- Analytics, used to understand user behaviors
- Commerce, used for mobile wallets and payment integration
- Provisioning, used for phone and device settings
- Synchronization, used for phones and devices, as well as data synchronization with Oracle Lite
- Notification, used to provide multichannel conditional and time-based alerts

OracleAS Wireless also includes three mobile applications:

- Mobile Office, which includes basic productivity applications for mobile devices
- Multichannel messaging, which lets you send a message to different mobile devices
- Mobile Location, which helps to add location awareness with driving directions, a business finder, and maps

Security

Security features are used to limit access to data, applications, and computing resources. The Oracle database has a complete security system, described in Chapter 6. Oracle Application Server can be used to authenticate users, store security credentials, and implement identity management.

Identity management allows an administrator to establish and maintain a security identity for a user and enforce it across an entire set of computing components, such as databases, application servers, and applications. Oracle Application Server uses the Oracle Internet Directory (OID) to store security information and provide user authentication. OID is an Lightweight Directory Access Protocol (LAPD) compliant store of information. Any application can access OID, including the Oracle database.

Identity management also includes a number of other features, including:

- A user provisioning framework that can be integrated with other applications, such as the HR system, provided with OID
- Directory integration tools, provided with OID
- PKI certificate management, provided with AS Certificate Authority, now a part of OID
- Tools for managing security, implemented as part of Enterprise Manager

In addition, Oracle Application Server provides a single sign-on capability. As the name implies, this service allows a user to log on once; the user's information is then used by various computing entities to retrieve the authenticated identity of the user.

Oracle's identity management solution can also be integrated with other third-party identity management products.

Oracle Application Server 10g Release 3 added security features and includes the Oracle Security Developer Toolkit, enabling developers to implement a variety of cryptographic and security features. The range of Oracle identity management capabilities added support for heterogeneous security sources. The Oracle Certificate Authority is now included as part of a larger set of modules called Oracle Identity Management Control.

Business intelligence

Business intelligence can encompass a wide spectrum of options. Oracle's acquisition of technologies from Siebel and Hyperion enabled Oracle to offer a full suite of best-of-breed business intelligence ad-hoc query, analysis, and reporting tools. As Oracle reintroduced these products in the Oracle family, Oracle's previous-generation business intelligence tools remained a part of the Oracle Application Server 10g release. These included:

Reports services
  These services are discussed earlier in the "Development tools" section.

Discoverer
  Discover is a tool that business analysts use to obtain business intelligence data from an Oracle database. The analysts use Discoverer to query and retrieve data via a browser-based interface and to manipulate it in a variety of ways, including drill down, pivoting, and changing the layout and presentation of data into various forms, such as tabular and crosstab forms. Administrators set up an End User Layer to simplify complex access to multiple data sources, complete with appropriate aggregation. Because Discoverer can also present data in a graphical format, Figure 15-1 is worth the remaining thousand words of description. Discoverer is also available as part of the Oracle Business Intelligence Suite.

We cover all of Oracle's current business intelligence tools and the Oracle database as used for data warehousing in more depth in Chapter 10.

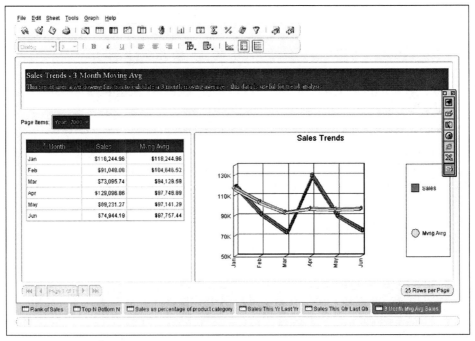

Figure 15-1. Typical Discover output

Integration

Integration is a broad area that encompasses bringing together information from different sources. The Oracle database has a number of features for integration, including Streams and Heterogeneous Gateways. Oracle Application Server 10*g* Release 1 included the following set of features for integration, including:

Integration Modeler
  This is an HTML-based tool that can model business processes and map data transformations. The results of this tool are stored in a repository, and they can be changed at any time.

Integration Manager
  This tool handles the runtime processes used for integration.

Adapters
  Oracle Application Server includes a set of adapters for packaged applications, such as SAP and Peoplesoft, as well as other databases and messaging systems. You can also create your own adapters with an Adapter SDK.

In Oracle Application Server 10*g* Release 2, AS's integration components were refactored to include Oracle Integration Interconnect (which is designed to make integration of different sources easier), BPEL Process Manager and Business Activity Monitor (described later in the "Oracle SOA Suite" section), and integration with Data Hubs (designed to give a single view of different data sources).

Oracle Application Server System Services

The remaining areas of Oracle Application Server capabilities provide services that affect more than one of the functional areas described in earlier sections:

- Management capabilities address the entire AS stack.
- Caching improves performance across many areas of functionality.
- AS allows for several types of clustering and load balancing for scalability and reliability.
- RFID-handling capabilities are provided via Oracle Sensor Edge Server.

The following sections describe these areas.

Management

With the Oracle Database 10g release, the scope of Enterprise Manager was broadened to encompass AS. Enterprise Manager (described in Chapter 5) now provides availability and performance tracking for both Oracle Application Server and the Oracle database. For instance, Enterprise Manager automatically provides information on the web pages that take the longest to serve, and it does this by mining the log files for AS, so there is virtually no impact on performance.

AS now lets you archive the configuration of an individual instance either to act as a backup before making configuration changes or to apply to any other instance.

Oracle Application Server 10g Release 2 added an implementation for management beans, based on the JMX standard, that provides management and deployment functionality for JavaBeans based on OC4J.

In Oracle Application Server 10g Release 3, Oracle introduced a new management capability with Dynamic Resource Monitor (DRM). The monitor is designed to watch resource utilization across nodes and dynamically allocate these resources, based on policies created by the system manager.

Caching

Caching is a standard concept in computing; caching speeds up the retrieval of frequently used information by saving it in a location where it can be rapidly retrieved. In the database, this means keeping frequently used data in memory, rather than retrieving it from disk. For Reports Server, described earlier, this means saving a report rather than running it again.

Oracle Application Server includes two specific components meant to provide additional caching capabilities: Web Cache and Java Object Cache.

The idea behind Web Cache is fairly simple—maintain copies of frequently requested information in a cache so the information does not have to be retrieved every time it is requested. Web Cache works on HTML pages and parts of pages. It can cache either static or dynamic data and includes validation routines that you can implement to specify when the data should be refreshed. Web Cache is aware of individual user and application dependencies on data, so it automatically caches and delivers situation-specific information.

HTML code uses Edge Side Includes to indicate where partial page content goes, and Web Cache will use those directives to assemble pages with cached data. Web Cache can also cache images, audio, video, Java, and search results.

Web Cache also compresses web pages, which can speed delivery to clients. Both cache validation rules and compression rules can be implemented with regular expressions for flexibility.

Web Cache instances can be on the same node as Oracle Application Server instances, or on their own servers, as shown in Figure 15-2. Web Cache instances can be clustered with a load balancer or use a built-in clustering capability. This capability provides a shared distributed cache, where each cache instance is aware of the contents of the other cache instances. Web Cache can be used with Forms and Reports.

Web Cache includes a technology Oracle refers to as *surge protection*. Surge protection proactively monitors the load on each server and implements actions to prevent the servers from being overwhelmed by a spike in traffic or a denial-of-service attack.

In Oracle Application Server 10g, Web Cache is used to collect the data on page service times that are used by Enterprise Manager's Application Performance Monitoring feature.

The Java Object Cache is implemented with a set of Java classes. As its name implies, this cache stores frequently used Java objects in memory or disk. Developers use a set of attributes associated with a Java object to define how an object is loaded into the cache, where an object is stored, and validation rules that specify when an object is moved out of the cache.

Clustering and load balancing

Oracle Application Server instances can be clustered together, for higher performance and availability. You can cluster Web Cache, Java Container, Portal, Forms Service, Report Servers (deprecated in Oracle Application Server 10g Release 2), or OID instances. In addition, you can use Real Application Clusters to provide clustering capabilities for the AS infrastructure or Portal. A multitier set of clusters is shown in Figure 15-2.

mod_oc4j, which directs requests to the Oracle Container for Java from the Oracle HTTP Server, provides load balancing across multiple instances of the Java Container, based on several different types of schemes, including varieties of random assignment, round robin, and metric-based. With Oracle Application Server 10g

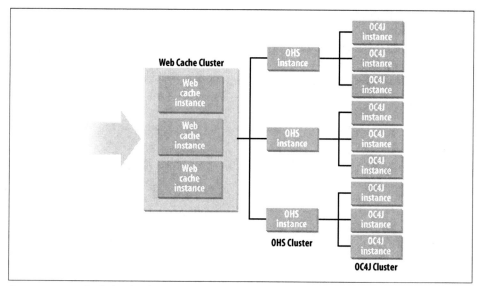

Figure 15-2. Multiple levels of clustering in Oracle Application Server

Release 2, an OC4J instance can host clustered and nonclustered applications at the same time.

You can implement load balancing for either stateless requests or requests that carry state. State-based load balancing is implemented with cookies and can be done either explicitly or with Java Object Cache. Oracle Java Containers are aware of nodes that share state information, so they can provide high availability for stateful load balancing by redirecting requests to a failed node to another node that shared application state with the failed node. In Oracle Application Server 10*g*, you can create policies that can reallocate a node from one cluster to another without having to restart the cluster.

Oracle Application Server includes a high availability framework, which monitors instances for their health, informs the system of problems, and automatically attempts to restart failed instances. Each node in a cluster contains its own configuration information, so if the node containing the repository that describes the cluster becomes unavailable, the node can continue to run. Oracle HTTP Server (OHS) can rebuild the repository on a designated backup node, eliminating this potential single source of failure.

Oracle Application Server 10*g* Release 3 added a Flashback capability giving administrators the ability to revert to earlier versions of configuration and system files, and Application Server Guard used to verify and synchronize standby servers. Of course, since AS is focused on running applications rather than storing data, these functions are not nearly as complex as the similar functionality available for the database, which must support thousands of potential users.

AS can be installed to use underlying hardware cluster functionality in what is called a *Cold Failover Cluster*. This configuration uses a shared disk attached to multiple machines. If the primary server should fail, operations fail over to a backup server. Oracle Application Server 10g also supports *Active Failover Clusters* (AFCs) (although the initial release of AS 10g did not support this configuration in a production environment). AFCs require a load balancer in front of the active nodes, but both nodes can operate at the same time, providing scalability with high availability. Figure 15-3 shows the differences between these two types of failover configurations.

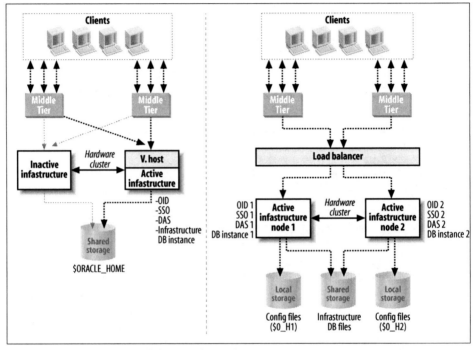

Figure 15-3. Cold Failover and Active Failover Clusters

 Of course, many uses of Oracle Application Server involve multiple services, such as Java, identity management, and database access. To use clustering for high availability, you must avoid single points of failure for all of these services. This can require careful planning and multiple clustering and failover schemes.

For easier creation of clusters, AS comes with a feature called Distributed Configuration Management (DCM), which simplifies creating clones of existing nodes and redistributes J2EE components to the new node.

Oracle Application Server 10g and newer releases also leverage a feature in the database called *failover notification*. Prior to AS 10g, an AS instance had to wait for a TCP/IP timeout to know that a database server node had failed. With this new release, the cluster management software for the database cluster proactively informs the AS instance of a failure, reducing failover time.

RFID handling in Oracle Sensor Edge Server

The Oracle Sensor Edge Server component of Oracle Application Server is used to process and dispatch RFID sensor information. The component captures RFID data close to the source, eliminates redundant or nonrelevant events, and forwards the appropriate events on to other processes.

Oracle SOA Suite

The Oracle SOA Suite pulls together a number of software offerings that can address issues related to a Service-Oriented Architecture (SOA), one of the hot buzzwords in the industry as of 2007.

The buzz that surrounds SOA is not there because the concepts or implementation are, for the most part, new. The core idea behind SOA is easy reuse and sharing of application functionality—a goal that organizations have been striving toward for decades. SOA reinvigorates the quest for these virtues with the new elements added by the Web.

The Web provides two key ingredients to the SOA story. First, there are new widely adopted standards such as XML and BPEL (which uses XML as its dialect). Standardization provides a common language at some levels of the application stack, reducing the overhead required for translation between applications.

Second, the Web expanded the reach of IT, in the sense that the user community breached the organizational walls that used to limit the scope of applications. When you can get valued functionality from outside your own solution set, the benefits that come from reuse and integration are correspondingly multiplied.

A Service-Oriented Architecture exposes applications, modules, and data as web services—essentially, an Application Program Interface (API) for logic and data access. This interface can help standardize functionality and data access, which will help to overcome some of the issues that have acted as roadblocks to reuse and integration in the past.

The components of the Oracle SOA Suite are described in the following sections.

Oracle BPEL Process Manager

BPEL stands for Business Process Engineering Language. As its name implies, BPEL is a standard language that helps to "orchestrate" or "choreograph" web services to act together. The concept of orchestration is implemented through BPEL as workflows that describe the order and conditions under which different web services interact. Orchestration requires explicit definitions of business processes, since the interaction is controlled by a central process. With choreography, multiple processes act as peers, so less information is required about the different business processes, making this technique more appropriate for use with web services from multiple external sources.

Oracle BPEL Process Manager is a plug-in for either Oracle's JDeveloper product or the Eclipse framework. The Process Manager gives users a graphical interface to describe process steps and interactions, as well as an engine for executing and monitoring steps in a process.

Business Activity Monitoring

Oracle Business Activity Monitoring (BAM) is used to create dashboards, which give quick graphical indications of progress on key business indicators (KPIs). Oracle says that their BAM implementation links back to the processes that create the information used for the KPIs, which means that a collection of issues that stem from the same process failure will not overwhelm an administrator.

Oracle BAM also has the ability to collect information from a variety of sources in real-time, giving more timely information and providing users with more time to address the issues that have generated the alerts.

Business Rules

Business rules are implementations of logic separate from, but used by, multiple applications. The use of business rules provides flexible reuse of business logic and, perhaps more importantly, consistent implementation of that logic. This consistency is increasingly important in today's business climate, where legislation can require that companies prove how they are making business decisions. By delegating specific implementation of business logic to a separate system, you can ensure that all applications that require this logic do so consistently, and you can point to the specifics in the standard implementation to satisfy audit requirements.

The Oracle Business Rules component of Oracle Application Server combines a Rule Authoring tool (which lets users create rules using English-like syntax), a Rules Engine (which executes the called rules), and a Rules SDK (for programmatic access to rules and the rules repository).

Enterprise Service Bus

In order for an SOA solution to work, all the services must be able to communicate freely with each other. This simple task is complicated by multiple communications protocols and the need to connect the service descriptions (in Web Services Definition Language, or WSDL) between all the players in the environment.

Oracle's Enterprise Service Bus (ESB) provides this capability and more. The ESB also delivers the ability to transform messages and data between consumers using Oracle Adapters (explained below) to connect to hundreds of data sources, model interactions between service providers, and implement efficient message routing and monitoring in the runtime environment.

Web Services Manager

When you start to use web services from an extremely wide range of sources, you are running the risk that your overall operations could be compromised by any of these sources. Oracle Web Services Manager is designed to define security and monitoring on web services, providing the safety required by enterprises and the proof of compliance that audit committees may demand.

Oracle Web Services Manager gives you the ability to define and manage security policies for web services. You can also monitor the use of web services and store the security rules in UDDI-compliant registries for proof of compliance.

Oracle JDeveloper

Oracle JDeveloper is Oracle's Java development environment. Oracle JDeveloper was introduced by Oracle in 1998 to enable developing of basic Java applications without writing code. JDeveloper is now available for free and can be downloaded from the Oracle Technology Network, as well as being included as part of the Oracle SOA Suite. Oracle Application Server 10g Release 3 introduced a new look and feel for JDeveloper.

Oracle JDeveloper includes wizards for generating data forms, JavaBeans, and BeanInfo, and for deploying your Java applications. JDeveloper includes database development features such as various Oracle drivers, a Connection Editor to hide the JDBC API complexity, database components to bind visual controls, and a SQLJ precompiler for embedding SQL in Java code that you can then use with Oracle.

The final JDeveloper application is written in Java code, even though you may have developed large parts of the application using wizards.

Adapters

Oracle Adapters provide a standards-based (Web Services Invocation Framework, or WSIF) interface to established external applications and protocols. There are Oracle Adapters available for more than 300 packaged applications and a variety of protocols, including CICS, Tuxedo, and FTP. You can see any of these targets as data sources with Oracle Adapters.

Oracle Service Registry

Oracle Service Registry is not a part of Oracle SOA Suite, but is a useful component in an SOA solution. The Service Registry is a repository for information about all services, so you can use it both to discover information about external services for your use and to publish information about your own services for others.

Oracle Service Registry is integrated with the components of the SOA Suite to act as the official repository of services for those components. However, Oracle Service Registry has been a component of Oracle Application Server since Oracle Application Server 10g.

What's New in This Book for Oracle Database 11g

When we wrote the first edition of *Oracle Essentials* in 1999, our goal was to offer a new kind of book about Oracle, one that would clearly and concisely cover all of the essential features and concepts of the Oracle database. In order to keep our focus on those essentials, we limited the scope of the book.

For instance, we decided not to cover SQL, or PL/SQL, in depth; these complex topics would have required a level of detail that would have run counter to the purpose of our book, and they are amply described in other books.

The latest release of the Oracle database, Oracle Database 11g, contains many new features. Most of these features build on the existing foundation of Oracle database technology.

We have tried to add details about these features in the chapters in which their discussion seemed most appropriate, but there are of course some enhancements in the new release that are outside the scope of this book.

The following sections summarize the new features of Oracle Database 11g that are covered in this new edition, chapter by chapter. Although many of these features are mentioned in multiple chapters, they are listed here according to where the most relevant discussion occurs.

Chapter 1: Introducing Oracle

This introductory chapter was extensively updated to reflect the packaging changes in Oracle Database 11g. It also briefly mentions features described in more detail in other chapters.

Chapter 2: Oracle Architecture

This chapter describes the initialization parameters that must be specified in Oracle Database 11g, database and instance characteristics, and background processes. New features include:

Automatic memory management
> Provides automatic distribution of memory among SGA and PGA instance components.

PL/SQL Function Result Cache in shared pool area
> Improves performance in cases where PL/SQL functions use the same parameters.

Chapter 3: Installing and Running Oracle

Although the standard installation and runtime operations of the Oracle database remain essentially the same, a few Oracle Database 11g enhancements are covered in this chapter:

Oracle Internet Directory
> This product is now part of the Fusion Middleware product stack.

Automated memory management of SGA and PGA size
> Enabled by default when you set the MEMORY_MANAGEMENT parameter.

Flashback transaction
> Continues to expand the flashback capabilities of the Oracle database by giving you the ability to reverse the effects of individual transactions.

Chapter 4: Data Structures

This chapter covers the basic data structures and optimization technology in the Oracle database. New features include:

Virtual columns
> These columns, defined as the results of an expression, are not stored in the database, but are accessible to users with appropriate security clearance at runtime.

Invisible indexes
> You can remove an index from consideration by the optimizer by making it invisible—you know, like a ghost.

Interval partitioning
> Gives Oracle Database 11g the ability to create a new partition with a fixed interval when data to be inserted does not fit in any existing partitions.

Composite partitioning (additional types)
> New composite partitioning types include list-range, list-hash, and list-list. Partitioining can also be based on functions or virtual columns.

Partition pruning
> Gives applications the ability to control partition pruning.

Partition Advisor
> Gives users an analysis of when partitions could improve performance.

Sequences in PL/SQL
> Allows the use of sequences in PL/SQL expressions.

Compound triggers
> You can now combine triggers with different timing options into a single compound trigger, which can help improve performance.

Database replay
> Captures workloads on production systems and allows you to replay them on other systems, such as test environments.

SQL Advisor
> Combines SQL Tuning Advisor, SQL Access Advisor, and Partition Advisor (mentioned above). Covered in more detail in Chapter 7.

Chapter 5: Managing Oracle

This chapter covers Oracle Enterprise Manager improvements and manageability offered in Oracle Database 11g. New features include:

SQL Performance Impact Advisor
> Forecasts how system changes will impact SQL performance.

Undo Advisor
> Enables automatic undo management.

Health Monitor infrastructure
> Components enable a Support Workbench and include the SQL Test Case Builder, SQL Repair Advisor, and Data Recovery Advisor.

Real Applications Testing Option
> Enables capture of a production workload for replay in a test database environment.

Chapter 6: Oracle Security, Auditing, and Compliance

This chapter is new in this edition, although some of the material was covered in Chapter 5 in previous versions of the book. The chapter also covers some significant new features available with Oracle Database 11g:

Prompting for default security settings
To improve security "out of the box," Oracle Database 11g installation procedures prompt you to determine whether you want to keep the default security settings.

Tablespace encryption
You can use Transparent Data Encryption to encrypt entire tablespaces.

Auditing on by default
The default setting for database auditing is ON.

Flashback Data Archive
Gives you a way to see all the changes that have happened to a record over the course of its lifetime, which is very useful for compliance.

Chapter 7: Oracle Performance

This chapter covers enhancements that provide better performance and performance analysis in the latest release:

Automatic Database Diagnostic Monitor for clusters
ADDM can now be used with clusters.

SQL Advisor
Combines the SQL Tuning Advisor, SQL Access Advisor, and Partition Advisor (previously described). Also mentioned in Chapter 4.

Automatic Workload Repository baselines
Can create baselines for AWR to cover specific time periods.

Very large file backups
Backups can now include very large files.

Query results caching
Oracle Database 11g can cache entire result sets, which can improve the performance of repeated queries.

Automatic profiling
The Oracle database can automatically spot and profile queries that require lots of resources, and this can improve their performance. This feature can also produce advice on new indexes to help enhance performance on queries using these indexes.

Default Database Resource Manager (DRM) plan
The default plan is designed to limit the resources used by automated maintenance tasks, such as gathering statistics.

Chapter 8: Oracle Multiuser Concurrency

The ability to handle very large groups of users without excessive contention, while protecting data integrity, has long been one of the best features of the Oracle database. This capability has been a core part of the Oracle database for 20 years, but this chapter also covers workspaces, which have changed a bit in the latest release:

Workspace enhancements
 Provide support for optimizer hints for workspaces and a wider range of data maintenance operations on workspace-enabled tables.

Chapter 9: Oracle and Transaction Processing

Oracle has been one of the leading databases for OLTP for many years. Although Oracle Database 11*g* includes many enhancements to improve the performance and manageability of the Oracle database when used for OLTP, there were no significant new features covered in this chapter.

Chapter 10: Oracle Data Warehousing and Business Intelligence

In addition to covering the database and data warehousing, this chapter describes Oracle's current suites of business intelligence tools and business intelligence applications. New features in the database for data warehousing include:

Database OLAP Option query rewrite and improved manageability
 The OLAP Option is now refreshed similarly to materialized views, and the database optimizer can transparently redirect SQL queries to the OLAP Option stored summaries.

Binary XML
 Performance of binary XML is up to 15 times that of XML LOBs stored in Oracle.

Partitioning enhancements
 There are new composite types (list-hash, list-list, list-range, and range-range) and a new partitioning type, interval partitioning, that automatically creates range partitions as needed.

Data Mining Option enhancements
 This option now provides generalized Linear Model algorithms and automated data preparation.

Chapter 11: Oracle and High Availability

This chapter describes the Oracle characteristics that keep your database up and highly available. New features include:

Automatic Storage Management Fast Mirror Resynchronization
Resynchronizes only changed ASM disk extents for faster recovery.

Flashback Transaction command
Backs out an individual transaction and dependent transactions.

Total Recall Option
Provides a Flashback Data Archive capability to query data as of a previous date.

Active Data Guard Option
You can now query your standby database while redo apply is active; fast-start failover is also possible.

Data Guard Management
SQL*Plus can be used as an interface for Data Guard SQL statements and initialization parameters.

Chapter 12: Oracle and Hardware Architecture

New coverage in this chapter's description of various hardware architectures includes the implications of multicore CPUs and an introduction to Oracle's Optimized Warehouse Initiative. A new option in this chapter is:

Advanced Compression Option
Provides compression for insert, update, and delete operations.

Chapter 13: Oracle Distributed Databases and Distributed Data

This chapter focuses on using Oracle as the core database for accessing data stored in non-Oracle databases, as well as using Oracle as a distributed database. New features include:

Transparent Gateway query performance
Oracle Database 11g supports parallel retrieval for queries against non-Oracle databases through Transparent Gateways.

Extended Transparent Gateway targets
Provides new Gateways for ADABAS, IMS, and VSAM.

Messaging server
These enhancements improve the performance and reliability of the server.

Database Change Notification
You can now enable notification when individual rows change.

Oracle Streams enhancements
It is now possible to log active online log files for DDL and DML and to run from a single Real Application Clusters (RAC) node for the entire RAC cluster.

Chapter 14: Oracle Extended Datatypes

This chapter describes capabilities beyond Oracle's standard set of datatypes. New features enhancing Oracle's support of extended datatypes include:

Object-relational enhancements
A method invocation scoping operator is now available.

Database as a Service-Oriented Architecture (SOA) services provider
PL/SQL packages, procedures, and functions are now exposed as web services.

Multimedia (formerly interMedia) enhancements
These include media size limits extended to those of BLOBs, a higher-performing BLOB implementation accessible via SecureFiles, and DICOM medical imaging support.

Spatial enhancements
Support for three-dimensional geometry objects and enhanced web services.

Chapter 15: Beyond the Oracle Database

This chapter covers the world beyond the boundaries of the Oracle database. The chapter now describes Application Express (ApEx), an HTML-based development tool that can be used to create applications that run from the Oracle database platform. It also includes Fusion Middleware, which has combined the software stack of Oracle Application Server as well as additional components, and the Oracle SOA Suite, aimed at SOA developers.

Additional Resources

In this concise volume, we have attempted to give you a firm grounding in all the basic concepts you need to understand Oracle and use it effectively. We hope we have accomplished this goal. At the same time, we realize that there is more to using a complex product such as Oracle than simply understanding how and why it works the way it does. Although you can't use Oracle without a firm grasp of the foundations of the product, you will still need details if you're actually going to implement a successful system.

This appendix lists two types of additional sources of information for the topics covered in this book—relevant web sites, which act as a constantly changing resource for a variety of information, and a chapter-by-chapter list of relevant books, articles, and Oracle documentation.

For the chapter-by-chapter list, the sources fall into two basic categories: Oracle documentation and third-party sources. Typically, the Oracle documentation provides the type of hands-on information you will need regarding syntax and keywords, and the third-party sources cover the topics in a more general and problem-solving way. We have listed the third-party sources first and ended each listing with the relevant Oracle documentation. Also note that some of the volumes listed here include previous Oracle release names in their titles. You can assume that by the time you are reading this, similar volumes exist (or will soon exist) for whatever version of Oracle you may be using (for example, Oracle Database 11g).

Web Sites

Oracle Corporation: http://www.oracle.com
> The home of the company. Latest information and marketing, as well as some good technical and packaging information.

Oracle Technology Network: http://otn.oracle.com

The focal point of Oracle Corporation's attempt to reach a wider audience of developers. You can find tons of stuff at the Oracle Technology Network (OTN), including low-cost developer versions or free downloads of most Oracle software and lots of information and discussion forums.

International Oracle Users Group (IOUG): http://www.ioug.org

The International Oracle Users Group web site includes information on meetings, links to Oracle resources, a technical repository, discussion forums, and special interest groups.

OraPub, Inc.: http://www.orapub.com

Craig Shallahamer's site devoted to all things Oracle. Craig was a long-time Oracle employee in the performance analysis group and technical reviewer for various editions of this book.

Quest Software: http://www.quest.com

The Quest Software site for all things PL/SQL-oriented, as well as information on Oracle database administration, Java database programming, and other topics.

O'Reilly Media, Inc.: http://www.oreilly.com

The O'Reilly web site, which contains web pages for each book and a variety of other helpful information. See *http://www.oreilly.com/catalog/oressentials4/* for errata and other information for this book.

Books and Oracle Documentation

The following books and Oracle documentation provide additional information for each chapter of this book.

Chapter 1: Introducing Oracle

Ellison, Lawrence. *Oracle Overview and Introduction to SQL*. Belmont, CA: Oracle Corporation, 1985.

Greenwald, Rick et al. *Professional Oracle Programming*, Indianapolis, IN: Wrox/ John Wiley & Sons, 2005.

Kreines, David, and Brian Laskey. *Oracle Database Administration: The Essential Reference*. Sebastopol, CA: O'Reilly Media, Inc., 1999.

Loney, Kevin, and Bob Bryla. *Oracle10g DBA Handbook*. New York, NY: McGraw-Hill, 2005.

Ralston, Anthony, ed. *Encyclopedia of Computer Science and Engineering*. New York, NY: Nostrand Reinhold Company, 1983.

Thome, Bob. *Achieving a 24x7 e-Business Leveraging the Oracle Database.* Belmont, CA: Oracle Corporation, 2000.

Flashback Data Archive (An Oracle White Paper). Redwood Shores, CA: Oracle Corporation, 2007.

Oracle Database 11g Concepts. Redwood Shores, CA: Oracle Corporation, 2007.

Oracle Database New Features Guide 11g Release 1. Redwood Shores, CA: Oracle Corporation, 2007.

Oracle Database 11g: Real Application Testing and Manageability Overview (An Oracle White Paper). Redwood Shores, CA: Oracle Corporation, 2007.

Chapter 2: Oracle Architecture

Kreines, David, and Brian Laskey. *Oracle Database Administration: The Essential Reference.* Sebastopol, CA: O'Reilly Media, Inc., 1999.

Loney, Kevin. *Oracle Database 10g The Complete Reference.* New York, NY: McGraw-Hill, 2004.

Oracle Database Concepts. Redwood Shores, CA: Oracle Corporation, 2007.

Chapter 3: Installing and Running Oracle

Kreines, David, and Brian Laskey. *Oracle Database Administration: The Essential Reference.* Sebastopol, CA: O'Reilly Media, Inc., 1999.

Toledo, Hugo, and Jonathan Gennick. *Oracle Net8 Configuration and Troubleshooting.* Sebastopol, CA: O'Reilly Media, Inc., 2000.

Oracle Database Concepts. Redwood Shores, CA: Oracle Corporation, 2007.

Oracle Database Installation Guide. 11g Release for Microsoft Windows. Redwood Shores, CA: Oracle Corporation, 2007.

Oracle Database Net Services Administrators Guide. Redwood Shores, CA: Oracle Corporation, 2007.

Oracle Enterprise Manager Basic Installation and Configuration. Redwood Shores, CA: Oracle Corporation, 2007.

Chapter 4: Data Structures

Date, C.J., *The Relational Database Dictionary.* Sebastopol, CA: O'Reilly Media, Inc., 2006.

Ensor, Dave, and Ian Stevenson. *Oracle Design.* Sebastopol, CA: O'Reilly Media, Inc., 1997.

Harrington, Jan L. *Relational Database Design Clearly Explained*. San Francisco, CA: AP Professional, 1998.

Oracle Database Concepts. Redwood Shores, CA: Oracle Corporation, 2007.

Chapter 5: Managing Oracle

Feuerstein, Steven, with Bill Pribyl. *Oracle PL/SQL Programming*, Fourth Edition. Sebastopol, CA: O'Reilly Media, Inc., 2005.

Greenwald, Rick, and David Kreines. *Oracle in a Nutshell: A Desktop Quick Reference*. Sebastopol, CA: O'Reilly Media, Inc., 2002.

Himatsingka, Bhaskar, and Juan Loaiza. "How to Stop Defragmenting and Start Living: The Definitive Word on Fragmentation." Paper no. 711. Belmont, CA: Oracle Corporation, 1998.

Kuhn, Darl, and Scott Schulze. *Oracle RMAN Pocket Reference*. Sebastopol, CA: O'Reilly Media, Inc., 2002.

Manning, Paul, and Angelo Pruscino. *Simplify your Job—Automatic Storage Management (Oracle White Paper)*. Redwood Shores, CA: Oracle Corporation, 2003.

Legato Storage Manager Administrator's Guide. Belmont, CA: Oracle Corporation, 1999.

Oracle Database Administrator's Guide. Redwood Shores, CA: Oracle Corporation, 2007.

Oracle Database Backup and Recovery Basics. Redwood Shores, CA: Oracle Corporation, 2007.

Oracle Database Concepts. Redwood Shores, CA: Oracle Corporation, 2007.

Oracle Database Storage Administrator's Guide. Redwood Shores, CA: Oracle Corporation, 2007.

Oracle Database VLDB and Partitioning Guide. Redwood Shores, CA: Oracle Corporation, 2007.

Oracle Enterprise Manager Concepts. Redwood Shores, CA: Oracle Corporation, 2007.

Feature Overview: Oracle Enterprise Manager EM2Go. Redwood Shores, CA: Oracle Corporation, 2003.

Managing the Complete Oracle Environment with Oracle Enterprise Manager (Oracle White Paper). Redwood Shores, CA: Oracle Corporation, 2003.

Chapter 6: Oracle Security, Auditing, and Compliance

Knox, David *Effective Oracle Database 10g Security by Design*. New York, NY: McGraw-Hill, 2005.

Feurstein Steven, and Bill Pribyl. *Oracle PL/SQL Programming*. Sebastopol, CA: O'Reilly Media, Inc., 2005.

Nanda, Arup, and Steven Feuersten. *Oracle PL/SQL for DBAs*. Sebastopol, CA: O'Reilly Media, Inc., 2005.

Oracle Database Advanced Security Administrator's Guide. Redwood Shores, CA: Oracle Corporation, 2003.

Oracle Database Label Security Administrator's Guide. Redwood Shores, CA: Oracle Corporation, 2003.

Oracle Database Security Guide. Redwood Shores, CA: Oracle Corporation, 2007.

Oracle Database 2 Day + Security Guide. Redwood Shores, CA: Oracle Corporation, 2007.

Chapter 7: Oracle Performance

Millsap, Cary, with Jeff Holt. *Optimizing Oracle Performance*. Sebastopol, CA: O'Reilly Media, Inc., 2003.

Niemiec, Rich et al. *Oracle Database 10g Performance Tuning Tips & Techniques*. New York, NY: McGraw-Hill, 2007.

Oracle Database Concepts. Redwood Shores, CA: Oracle Corporation, 2007.

Oracle Database Performance Tuning Guide. Redwood Shores, CA: Oracle Corporation, 2007.

Oracle Real Application Clusters Administration. Redwood Shores, CA: Oracle Corporation, 2007.

Chapter 8: Oracle Multiuser Concurrency

Oracle Database Concepts. Redwood Shores, CA: Oracle Corporation, 2007.

Chapter 9: Oracle and Transaction Processing

Gray, Jim, and Andreas Reuter. *Transaction Processing: Concepts and Techniques*. San Francisco, CA: Morgan Kaufmann Publishers, 1992.

Edwards, Jeri, with Deborah DeVoe. *3-Tier Client/Server at Work*. New York, NY: John Wiley & Sons, 1997.

Oracle Database 10g Application Developer's Guide—Fundamentals. Redwood Shores, CA: Oracle Corporation, 2003.

Oracle8i Call Interface Programmer's Guide. Belmont, CA: Oracle Corporation, 1999.

Oracle Database Concepts Guide. Redwood Shores, CA: Oracle Corporation, 2007.

Oracle Database Java Developer's Guide. Redwood Shores, CA: Oracle Corporation, 2007.

Oracle Database Net Services Reference Guide. Redwood Shores, CA: Oracle Corporation, 2007.

Oracle Real Application Clusters Administration and Deployment Guide. Redwood Shores, CA: Oracle Corporation, 2003.

Oracle Streams Advanced Queuing Users Guide and Reference. Redwood Shores, CA: Oracle Corporation, 2007.

Chapter 10: Oracle Data Warehousing and Business Intelligence

Berry, Michael J.A., and Gordon Linoff. *Data Mining Techniques.* New York, NY: John Wiley & Sons, 1997.

Dodge, Gary, and Tim Gorman. *Oracle8 Data Warehousing.* New York, NY: John Wiley & Sons, 1998.

Hobbs, Lilian et al. *Oracle9iR2 Data Warehousing.* Oxford, UK: Butterworth-Heinemann, 2003.

Inmon, W.H. *Building the Data Warehouse.* New York, NY: John Wiley & Sons, 1996.

Kelly, Sean. *Data Warehousing, The Route to Mass Customisation.* Chichester, England: John Wiley & Sons, 1996.

Kimball, Ralph. *The Data Warehouse Toolkit.* New York, NY: John Wiley & Sons, 1996.

Peppers, Don, and Martha Rogers. *Enterprise One to One.* New York, NY: Currency Doubleday, 1997.

Peppers, Don, Martha Rogers, and Bob Dorf. *One to One Fieldbook.* New York, NY: Currency Doubleday, 1999.

Stackowiak, Robert et al. *Oracle Data Warehousing and Business Intelligence Solutions.* Indianapolis, IN: John Wiley & Sons, 2007.

Stackowiak, Robert. "Why Bad Data Warehouses Happen to Good People." *The Journal of Data Warehousing,* April 1997.

Oracle Data Mining Concepts. Redwood Shores, CA: Oracle Corporation, 2007.

Oracle Database Concepts. Redwood Shores, CA: Oracle Corporation, 2007.

Oracle Database Data Warehousing Guide. Redwood Shores, CA: Oracle Corporation, 2007.

Oracle Database 2 Day + Data Warehousing Guide. Redwood Shores, CA: Oracle Corporation, 2007.

Oracle OLAP User's Guide. Redwood Shores, CA: Oracle Corporation, 2007.

Oracle Warehouse Builder User's Guide. Redwood Shores, CA: Oracle Corporation, 2007.

Chapter 11: Oracle and High Availability

Chen, Lee et al. "RAID: High Performance, Reliable Secondary Storage." *ACM Computing Surveys*, June 1994.

Peterson, Erik. "No Data Loss." *Standby Database*. Belmont, CA: Oracle Corporation and Paul Manning, EMC Corporation, 1998.

Oracle Database Backup and Recovery Basics. Redwood Shores, CA: Oracle Corporation, 2007.

Oracle Database Concepts. Redwood Shores, CA: Oracle Corporation, 2007.

Oracle Data Guard Concepts and Administration. Redwood Shores, CA: Oracle Corporation, 2007.

Oracle High Availability Overview. Redwood Shores, CA: Oracle Corporation, 2007.

Oracle Streams Replication Administrator's Guide. Redwood Shores, CA: Oracle Corporation, 2007.

Chapter 12: Oracle and Hardware Architecture

Morse, H. Stephen. *Practical Parallel Computing*. Cambridge, MA: AP Professional, 1994.

Pfister, Gregory. *In Search of Clusters*. Upper Saddle River, NJ: Prentice Hall PTR, 1995.

Oracle Grid Computing (An Oracle Business White Paper). Redwood Shores, CA: Oracle Corporation, 2003.

Chapter 13: Oracle Distributed Databases and Distributed Data

Cerutti, Daniel, and Donna Pierson. *Distributed Computing Environments*. New York, NY: McGraw-Hill, 1993.

Dye, Charles. *Oracle Distributed Systems*. Sebastopol, CA: O'Reilly Media, Inc., 1999.

Ortalie, Robert, Dan Harkey, and Jeri Edwards. *The Essential Distributed Objects Survival Guide*. New York, NY: John Wiley & Sons, 1996.

Oracle Streams Advanced Queuing User's Guide and Reference. Redwood Shores, CA: Oracle Corporation, 2007.

Oracle Database Concepts. Redwood Shores, CA: Oracle Corporation, 2007.

Oracle Database Heterogeneous Connectivity Administrator's Guide. Redwood Shores, CA: Oracle Corporation, 2007.

Oracle Streams Advanced Queuing User's Guide. Redwood Shores, CA: Oracle Corporation, 2007.

Oracle Streams Replication User's Guide. Redwood Shores, CA: Oracle Corporation, 2007.

Chapter 14: Oracle Extended Datatypes

Bales, Donald. *Java Programming with Oracle JDBC*. Sebastopol, CA: O'Reilly Media, Inc., 2001.

Siegal, Jon. *CORBA Fundamentals and Programming*. New York, NY: John Wiley & Sons, 1996.

Taylor, David A. *Object-Oriented Technology: A Manager's Guide*. Alameda, CA: Servio Corporation, 1990.

Oracle Database Concepts. Redwood Shores, CA: Oracle Corporation, 2007.

Oracle Multimedia User's Guide. Redwood Shores, CA: Oracle Corporation, 2007.

Oracle Multimedia Reference. Redwood Shores, CA: Oracle Corporation, 2007.

Oracle Database Java Developer's Guide. Redwood Shores, CA: Oracle Corporation, 2007.

Oracle Database Object Relational Developer's Guide. Redwood Shores, CA: Oracle Corporation, 2007.

Oracle Database SecureFiles and Large Objects Developer's Guide. Redwood Shores, CA: Oracle Corporation, 2007.

Oracle Database 2 Day Developer's Guide. Redwood Shores, CA: Oracle Corporation, 2007.

Oracle Database 2 Day + Java Developer's Guide. Redwood Shores, CA: Oracle Corporation, 2007.

Oracle Spatial Developer's Guide. Redwood Shores, CA: Oracle Corporation, 2003.

Oracle Spatial GeoRaster Developer's Guide. Redwood Shores, CA: Oracle Corporation, 2007.

Oracle Text Reference. Redwood Shores, CA: Oracle Corporation, 2007.

Oracle Ultra Search User's Guide. Redwood Shores, CA: Oracle Corporation, 2007.

Chapter 15: Beyond the Oracle Database

Greenwald, Rick, and Robert Stackowiak, *Oracle Application Server 10g Essentials*, Sebastopol, CA: O'Reilly Media, Inc., 2005.

Muench, Steve. *Building Oracle XML Applications*. Sebastopol, CA: O'Reilly Media, Inc., 2000.

Oracle Application Server 10g (A Technical White Paper). Redwood Shores, CA: Oracle Corporation, 2003.

Oracle Application Server 10g—Grid Computing (An Oracle White Paper). Redwood Shores, CA: Oracle Corporation, 2003.

Oracle Application Server 10g R3 New Features Overview (An Oracle White Paper). Redwood Shores, CA: Oracle Corporation, 2006.

Oracle Database Application Express User's Guide. Redwood Shores, CA: Oracle Corporation, 2007.

Oracle Database Java Developer's Guide. Redwood Shores, CA: Oracle Corporation, 2007.

Oracle Database 10g SQLJ Developer's Guide and Reference. Redwood Shores, CA: Oracle Corporation, 2003.

Oracle XML DB Developer's Guide. Redwood Shores, CA: Oracle Corporation, 2007.

Oracle 10g: Infrastructure for Grid Computing (An Oracle White Paper). Redwood Shores, CA: Oracle Corporation, 2003.

Index

We'd like to hear your suggestions for improving our indexes. Send email to *index@oreilly.com*.

datatypes *(continued)*
    SMALLINT, 85
    storage of multiple, 235
    user-defined
        objects and collections, 319
        Oracle8, 87
        VARCHAR2, 83
        XMLType, 87
DATE datatype, 85
DB_BLOCK_BUFFERS, 156
DB_BLOCK_SIZE, 37
DB_DOMAIN, 37
DB_FILE_ MULTIBLOCK_READ_
        COUNT, 168
DB_NAME, 37
DB_RECOVERY_FILE_DEST, 37
DB_RECOVERY_FILE_DEST_SIZE, 37
DBA_ views, 120
DBAs (database administrators), 122
DBMS (database management system), 3
DBMS_RLS package, 145
DBMS_STATS package, 112
DBWR (Database Writer), 52
DCE (Distributed Computing
        Environment), 28
DCM (Distributed Configuration
        Management), 344
DDL (Data Definition Language), 5
DDL_LOCK_TIMEOUT, 38
DECIMAL, 85
decision support systems (DSS), 224, 230,
        233
decision trees, 246
dedicated
    model, 73
    processes, 73
    storage subsystems
        basics, 165
        power outages, vulnerability to, 165
DEFAULT buffer pool, 50
deferred constraints, 106
deferred rollback, 261
DELETE, 141
depth of indexes, 92
dequeue, 313
DES (Data Encryption Standard), 28
development
    servers, 336
    tools, 28, 335
DHTML (thin client), 242

DICOM (Digital Imaging and
        Communications in Medicine
        version 3), 326
Digital Imaging and Communications in
        Medicine (DICOM) version 3, 326
dimension tables, 21, 229
dimensions, 229
direct path export, 288
direct path load, 240
directory structure, planning, 58
dirty reads, 189
disaster recovery, 275
    database and data redundancy, 282
    planning, 253
    preparation, 253
Discoverer, 339
    Administration Edition, 244
    End User Layer (EUL), 244
    Plus, 244
    portlet provider, 244
    viewer, 244
disk failure, recovery from, 262
disk farms, 165
disk layout, planning, 160
disk space requirements, estimating, 60
disk striping
    host-based, 164
    nonredundant, 163
    multiple spindles, 161
disk technology, 300
disks, deployment strategy, 301
dismount, databases, 69
Dispatcher process, 53
dispatchers, 74
Distributed Computing Environment
        (DCE), 28
Distributed Configuration Management
        (DCM), 344
distributed databases
    basics, 5
    configurations, 17
    data integrity, ensuring, 308
    data transfer, 310
    features, 9, 17
    history, 6
    multiple access of, 305
    queries and transactions, 18
    security, 147
    synchronization, 311
Distributed Lock Manager (DLM), 193
distributed queries, 17
distributed transactions, 17

messaging server, 315
metadata
  dictionary, 54
  management, 237
  standardization initiatives, 248
MetaLink, 138
methods, 320
Microsoft Cluster Services, 26
Microsoft Transaction Server
  distributed transactions through Oracle
      databases, 18
  Oracle Manager for, 309
Middleware (Oracle Application Server)
      Management Packs, 126
mirroring, 163
  RAID and, 263
  resynchronization, 266
mirror-pair, 39
  (see also striped disk arrays)
modules, 334
MOLAP (Multidimensional Online
      Analytical Processing) engines, 245
MOM (message-oriented middleware), 313
MOUNT state, 69
mounting, databases, 69
MTS (Multi-Threaded Server)
  basics, 73, 212
  data dictionary information, 76
  session data and, 76
MTS_MAX_SERVERS, 74
MTTR Advisor, 125
multiblock I/Os, 160
Multidimensional Online Analytical
      Processing (MOLAP) engines, 245
multidimensional query, 229
Multimedia enhancements, 325
Multi-Threaded Server (see MTS)
multiversion read consistency (MVRC), 211
mutating tables runtime errors, 108
MVRC multiversion read consistency, 190,
    211

N

naming services
  host, 65
  Oracle Names, 64
  third-party, 65
Nanda, Arup, 145
NAS (network attached storage), 136
National Language Support (NLS), 12, 83
NCHAR datatype, 83
NCLOB datatype, 84, 87

NDMP (Network Data Management
      Protocol), 136
Net Configuration Assistant, 57
Net8
  Assistant, 66
  configuration, 63
network
  configuration, 63
  network attached storage (NAS), 136
  problems, debugging, 66
  protocols, dispatchers, 74
Network Data Management Protocol
      (NDMP), 136
NLS (National Language Support), 12, 83
NLS_LANGUAGE, 38
NLS_TERRITORY, 38
NOARCHIVELOG mode
  cold backups and, 276
  defined, 46
node failure
  management and recovery, 271
  Real Application Clusters (RAC),
      management by, 271
NOLOGGING keyword, 42
nonescalating row locks, 193, 211
nonrepeatable reads, 189
Non-Uniform Memory Access (see NUMA)
normalized forms
  benefits, 103, 105
  databases, 102
  defined, 102
NOT NULL, 104
NULLs, 89
  TRUE or FALSE states, 89
  values, 90
NUMA (Non-Uniform Memory Access)
  advantages, 298
  synchronized data, 297
NUMBER datatype, 84
NVARCHAR2 datatype, 83

O

OBIEE (Oracle Business Intelligence
      Enterprise Edition Suite), 22
object identifiers (OIDs), 320
object technologies, Oracle systems, 221
object-oriented programming
  Oracle8i, since, 11
objects
  data abstraction, 319
  datatypes, 319
  development, 319

About the Authors

Rick Greenwald has been active in the world of computer software for more than two decades, including stints with Data General, Cognos, Gupta Technologies, and Oracle. He is currently a developer evangelist with *Salesforce.com*. He has published 15 books and countless articles on a variety of technical topics, and has spoken at conferences and training sessions across six continents. Rick's other books include coauthoring *Oracle in a Nutshell* (O'Reilly) and *Professional Oracle Programming* (WROX). Rick lives in Arizona with his wife and three daughters.

Robert Stackowiak has worked for more than 20 years in business intelligence and IT-related roles that have included sales and sales consulting, business development, management of software development, and systems engineering. As vice president of Business Intelligence in Oracle's Technology Business Unit, he is recognized worldwide for his work in business intelligence and data warehousing. His papers regarding business intelligence and computer and software technology have appeared in publications such as *President & CEO Magazine*, *Database Trends and Applications*, and The Data Warehousing Institute's publications. He has also coauthored the books *Oracle Application Server 10g Essentials* (O'Reilly), *Professional Oracle Programming* (WROX), and *Oracle Data Warehousing and Business Intelligence Solutions* (Wiley).

Jonathan Stern used more than 13 years of IT experience in contributing to the original edition of this book. His background included senior positions in consulting, systems architecture, and technical sales. Especially useful in his early work on this book was his in-depth experience with the Oracle database across all major open systems' hardware and operating systems, covering tuning, scaling, parallelism, Oracle Parallel Server, high availability, data warehousing, and OLTP. He authored numerous papers and presented at internal and external conferences on topics such as scaling with Oracle's dynamic parallelism and the role of reorganizing segments in an Oracle database.

Colophon

The animals on the cover of *Oracle Essentials: Oracle Database 11g* are cicadas. There are about 1,500 species of cicada. In general, cicadas are large insects with long thin wings that are perched above an inch-long abdomen. Their heads are also large and contain three eyes and a piercing and sucking mechanism with which to extrude sap from trees. Cicadas are known for their characteristic shrill buzz, which is actually the male's mating song, one of the loudest known insect noises.

Cicadas emerge from the ground in the spring or summer, molt, then shed their skin in the form of a shell. They stay near trees and plants, where they live for four to six weeks with the sole purpose of mating. The adult insects then die, and their young hatch and burrow into the ground. They attach to tree roots and feed off the sap for 4 to 17 years, after which time they emerge and continue the mating cycle. Cicadas have one of the longest life spans of any insect; the most common species is the periodical cicada, which lives underground for 13 to 17 years.

The cover image is an original 19th-century engraving from *Cuvier's Animals*. The cover font is Adobe ITC Garamond. The text font is Linotype Birka; the heading font is Adobe Myriad Condensed; and the code font is LucasFont's TheSans Mono Condensed.

CPSIA information can be obtained at www.ICGtesting.com
Printed in the USA
LVOW121615061011

249429LV00004B/3/P